NAVIGATING THE AFRICAN DIASPORA

NAVIGATING
THE
AFRICAN DIASPORA
THE ANTHROPOLOGY OF INVISIBILITY

Donald Martin Carter

University of Minnesota Press
Minneapolis
London

Published by the University of Minnesota Press
111 Third Avenue South, Suite 290
Minneapolis, MN 55401-2520
http://www.upress.umn.edu

Library of Congress Cataloging-in-Publication Data

Carter, Donald Martin.
    Navigating the African diaspora : the anthropology of invisibility/Donald Martin Carter.
        p.   cm.
    Includes bibliographical references and index.
    ISBN 978-0-8166-4777-4 (hc : alk. paper)—ISBN 978-0-8166-4778-1 (pb : alk. paper)
        1. African diaspora.   2. Photography in ethnology — Africa.   3. Ethnology — Africa.   4. Senghor, Léopold Sédar, 1906–2001 — Criticism and interpretation.   5. Senegalese — Italy — Social conditions.   6. Senegalese — Race identity — Italy.   7. Carter, Donald Martin.   I. Title.
    DT16.5.C38   2010
    305.896 — dc22   2009012485

Printed in the United States of America on acid-free paper

The University of Minnesota is an equal-opportunity educator and employer.

16 15 14 13 12 11 10   10 9 8 7 6 5 4 3 2

Contents

Preface

They perceived arts in general to be a crack in racism.

— WILLIAM A. SHACK, *HARLEM IN MONTMARTRE*

The location of my anthropological imagination began in Oakland, California, where I spent my childhood in the peculiar mix of social exclusion, racism, and normal life that the city offered. One must acknowledge one's arrivals and departures, setting in this manner the basic structure of the trope of the voyage; for me it was a particular trajectory of black working-class life in Oakland, California, from which a life in the world of the mind was as likely as a walk on the moon.

Diaspora figured in my life from its very beginnings: I am the second son of parents from Louisiana who, along with other relatives, lived in a kind of suspended South in northern California. They never spoke much about their encounters with Southern racism to their children of the North, fearing that their experiences might teach us to hate; after all these years I still find this extraordinary. Every now and then a story would emerge through an aunt or uncle, but never from my parents. It is a quintessential experience of diaspora that the experiences of one generation may seem unimaginable to another. It is the kernel of lived experience and the history of complicated identities through time that draw us back to widening circles of displacement as black people in the Western world. Every circle eventually leads to considerations of the African side of the hyphen. Navigating diaspora is an integral part of my experience, and even if I trace my family back to Louisiana and to the Native American, African, and European roots I might find there, or to a French-speaking island in the Caribbean where some of my relatives are said to have originated in another black diaspora, or again to Africa, the mystic source of all these wonderings, an element of mystery still remains, along with an uneasy cynicism that such will hold real meaning for me in the end. As James T. Campbell demonstrates in his book *Middle Passages: African American Journeys to Africa, 1787–2005*, African Americans returning to Africa, an imagined place of origin, have confronted the rich navigable waters of subjectivity in this distant homeland only to discover that little is revealed that will quell their sense of longing, while a great many questions arise that complicate the notion of belonging to this at times strange land (Campbell 2006). As a scholar I have devoted much of my life to making sense of the dislocation of others, but I am still trying to come to terms with my own location in diaspora. Like others I am navigating this experience. The nautical metaphor is not fortuitous, it is existential.

In his haunting book *Black Gold of the Sun: Searching for Home in Africa and Beyond* (2005) Ekow Eshun stands before the "Door of No Return" in Ghana, one of the many archways through which Africans pass on their way across the Atlantic Ocean, and acknowledges that this gateway had enacted a transformation of unfathomable power in one part of humanity: "I stood beside it and ran my hands along the stonework. I stepped through it as slaves had done, to the shoreline and the waves. As I did, it came to me that, in the wake of slavery, all of us black people born in the West are exiles" (Eshun 2005, 110). Indeed, this distant Door of No Return confronts each of us with our own experience as exiles in the African diaspora in different ways. Certainly the peculiar fate of the black subject in the West inaugurates an ongoing, seemingly perpetuous struggle with social and political belonging on the other side of that door for the member of the black diaspora.

During the late 1980s I was conducting exploratory research in Turin, Italy. In the heat of the summer sun one morning I set out across the historic heart of the city, across the river Po and up into the hills to meet with Italian historian Giovanni Levi. Anthropologist Vanessa Maher arranged my introduction. Giovanni Levi was best known for his work in seventeenth- and eighteenth-century microhistory, most recently the history of young people. I was about to enter my own layer of migration as Levi ushered me into the lovely house that had once belonged to his uncle, Primo Levi. We spoke of sports, the rising anti-immigrant sentiment targeting blacks and Muslims, and the resurgence of anti-Semitism

in Italy. Levi's insights on the importance of sport, anti-immigrant sentiment, and religious intolerance in this period turned out to be one of the
first acknowledgments of the early formation of what was to become a
new right-wing movement among the youth, resulting some years later
in the founding of future-premier Berlusconi's "Forza Italia" political
movement. It was a beautiful time of day and the sun filtered through
the typically long Italian windows, cascading into the room and over the
bare wood floors; all was quiet in the quarter, as the sounds that were
about to pour out of the city below had not yet begun to reveal themselves. The great warmth and openness of Levi was very winning; I was
concerned that I might be imposing, for he was so generous with his
time and so well informed on developments in the country that I might
have talked for hours. His uncle was known to be generous with students
and others who were struggling to grapple with contemporary events—
indeed, he had been a kind of exemplary activist for human rights and
tolerance, even volunteering in local schools. Primo Levi was a beacon
of light for those who did not or could not fathom the most alarming
threat to humanity lurking just below the surface. Before many other
voices related the memory of the Holocaust in Europe, Levi taught new
generations of its horrors but also (and perhaps this is the great power
of his writing) its message of hope. Only twice that day did our talk
turn briefly to Primo Levi, but the memory of the writer, scientist, and
humanist filled the room as surely as did the morning light.

In 1945 when Primo Levi returned to Turin from his internment in
Auschwitz, the full scope of Hitler's genocide and the new vocabulary
of horror it introduced to the world was not yet widely known; it would
take years before the true account was fully acknowledged. His experience speaks to us in part because every generation awakens too late
to a human tragedy that might have been avoided. For our generation
Darfur, the Congo, and certainly Rwanda ring in our ears. Immediately
after his return Levi would recount his story to anyone who would lis-
ten, beginning with those closest to him. He also found himself telling
his experiences to strangers on trains (Thompson 2002). He was struggling to make a world he had known visible to others, being true to those
who could no longer speak for themselves. While the landscape still bore
the open wounds of the war, Levi (like other exiles) became a storyteller–witness. As events would have it, his writings were among the first

accounts of the Holocaust to be widely circulated in Italy and Germany, introducing new generations to the horrors of the war years and awakening the living memory of others. Born of a generation steeped in classical literature, his account was shaped partly by the tutorials of his youth.

Contemporary poet Morri Creech in his collection *Field Knowledge* (2006) imagines Primo Levi in his home in Turin rereading the *Divine Comedy* of Dante. The poem "The Canto of Ulysses" was published in *The New Republic* some years ago, and Creech envisions Levi, book in hand in an easy chair, "nodding above the page where Ulysses/tells how his second journey ends" (Creech 2006, 22).[1] For Ulysses and for us all, life is a journey. "Drowsing, head propped above the eighth circle, he feels the present shifting like a keel": the metaphors of the "ship" on a voyage and of the Pilgrim or the author on an implied spiritual journey of the soul mark the poet's tribute as they shape a thematic in the work of Dante (21). In the tradition of nautical writing, the journey becomes a kind of metatext as the discourse of a ship was its route or itinerary and the pathway or narrative created by the writer for the reader is a route or journey of a different nature (Blackmore 2001, 29). I employ these different readings of passage in my understanding of navigating diaspora as both the individual experience and the representation of the collective experience of diaspora.

In *Navigating the African Diaspora* I explore the rich modalities of the journey in my own experiences as a scholar and in the collective experience of the African diaspora. Drawing on the work of postcolonial theorist Frantz Fanon, I interrogate the idea of visibility and invisibility, metaphors that David Theo Goldberg notes "pervade Fanon's body of work" (2000, 179).

In each chapter I take up aspects of the impact of invisibility on the lives of various categories of person, migrants, colonial soldiers, established Europeans, and newcomers. In chapter 1 I explore the meanings of invisibility for subjects caught in the power play of history. Chapter 2 discusses afrocentrism, race, and the making of an anthropological sensibility through my own experiences, training, and fieldwork. In chapter 3 I review stereotypes and other distinctions in the making of the contemporary crisis in Darfur, Sudan. I further analyze the photographic turn in the representation of Other cultures in chapter 4, where I examine the role of race in the Western photographic imaginary. I consider the play of diasporic nostalgia and political longings for the future in chapter 5 by viewing the experiences and contributions of colonial soldiers through the work of a former Senegalese president, the late Léopold Sédar Senghor and in chapters 6 and 7 by studying the late Senegalese film-maker Ousmane Sembene. Finally, the conclusion looks at our passion for exclusion in contemporary society through the experiences of people in diaspora who inhabit new and diverse subjectivities, making themselves known in creative ways against a conceptual constellation that often has no place for them (so-called Fortress Europe) or ability (or expansive cultural ideology) to consider them as equals sharing the same time and space. Throughout the book we consider an African diaspora in motion, at times driven off course only to return to it transformed, with renewed strength and vision for the journey ahead.

Acknowledgments

This project is the result of an itinerant scholar traveling the byways of academic life. The idea for this book came to me as I attempted to plow through the rapidly growing literature on diaspora and also through my exploration of the world that Senegalese migrants and others introduced me to in Turin, Italy. Anthropology is somewhat like a game of pick-up basketball: you play with those who show up and share with them the love of the game. For the anthropologist it is often the people who just show up who have the most lasting impact on one's understandings, perceptions, and research. I cannot adequately acknowledge all the people who assisted me along the way, but I will offer my thanks to some of them.

I began this manuscript while a fellow at the Stanford Humanities Center, where I was encouraged to explore the world beyond anthropology. I ventured into anthropological visions of film, poetry, and other aspects of visual culture that form the foundation of this project. I must thank a number of people for this productive push, including Mark Seltzer, Ruth Shklar Nissé, and Laurie Shrage, among my most steadfast interlocutors and instigators. I am grateful to associate director Susan E. Dunn for her kindness, encouragement, and introduction to the poetic imagination and the curious constellation of the avant-garde through her work on Mina Loy. I owe special thanks to Keith Michael Baker, who fought far beyond the call of duty for my ability to participate. I am grateful to the librarians and the archivists at the Hoover Institution at Stanford University for their kind assistance and access to the collections, and I thank the Stanford graduate students who attended my seminar on diaspora and sparked my imagination with the rich complexity of their work and experience.

Over my years at The Johns Hopkins University I have been continually educated by my students and encouraged and challenged by my colleagues. I thank many friends and colleagues for their generous comments on parts of this book; without the critical engagement of their efforts, this manuscript may never have seen the light of day. I am especially grateful to historian Sara Berry for her undying support, keen love of scholarship, and thoughtful critique and discussions of my work. Jane Guyer was a welcome interlocutor, helping me explore the nature of the postcolonial world and the entanglements of Western philosophical traditions in anthropological inquiry. Sonia Ryang I must thank for sharing her razor-sharp ethnographic sensibilities and humor. I am indebted to Michel-Rolph Trouillot for opening up for me the exploration of the black diaspora and its attendant philosophical and epistemological problems. I am grateful to Gyanendra Pandey and Deborah Reynolds for their comments and suggestions, and to Brakette Williams for helping me to recognize the curious play of violence, justice, and state ideology. I am solely responsible for any errors or misrepresentations that may remain.

I acknowledge the support and contributions of several institutions without which this book could not have been completed. Core concerns of the work emerged while I was a fellow at the Stanford Humanities Center. I began to elaborate on issues related to the study of diaspora while I was the Luce Distinguished Professor of Diaspora and Community Studies at Dickinson College, for which I thank the college and the Luce Foundation. Periods of fieldwork and writing were completed with support from The Johns Hopkins University and the Italian studies program I directed in 2004 at Villa Spellman in Florence, Italy. I'd also like to thank Hamilton College for their support in the final stages of the production process.

I thank my colleagues Shelley P. Haley, Nigel Westmaas, and Angel David Nieves of the Africana studies program at Hamilton College for the immeasurably supportive and nurturing environment they offered.

Working with the University of Minnesota Press has been a great pleasure. I thank former executive editor Carrie Mullen for her initial support and Richard W. Morrison for his many suggestions and contributions to the manuscript, as well as his continued support over the years. I would also like to acknowledge the loving attention to detail of editorial assistant Adam Brunner and freelance copyeditor Nancy Kotary; without their fine work, this ship would not have set sail.

My greatest debt belongs to my family. I acknowledge the endless care, support, and intellectual collaboration of Heather Merrill, who helped to sustain this long journey and nurture a love of theory, philosophy, and social practice. To our children, Nicolas and Eliana, my great thanks for your endurance of untold dislocations and cultural shocks over the years. During the writing of this book my mother Julia suffered a stroke that severely compromised her cognitive abilities, a fact that deeply saddens me. She and my late father Charlie taught me to see the unseen, and I am forever indebted to both of them. This book is dedicated to my family.

Since the late 1990s I have conducted periods of research in Italy, continuing with many of the Senegalese from my fieldwork at the dawn of the immigration crisis in the country. I have interviewed, argued with, and been deeply informed and influenced by a host of scholars and activists in Turin. They helped to shape my understandings of the European social and cultural world, and I am forever indebted to them.

The Anthropology of Invisibility

> No matter where on the current spectrum ... anthropologists
> locate themselves, they have to find the "out there" by entering
> the land of anthropological "dreaming," *the field.*
>
> —BERNARD COHN, *HISTORY AND ANTHROPOLOGY:*
> *THE STATE OF PLAY*

Journeys are an active engagement with the world, and are at the very least transformative and irreversible. Journeys have a sense of agency that we must keep alive through our explorations. Let me paraphrase the beginning of an old tale. It is a song of diaspora and concerns the people of the African diaspora and the twists and turns that have time and again driven people off course, transformed by the struggle to regain their way and dignity, with renewed strength and vision for the journey ahead. I invoke the spirit of the Odyssey because it is deeply rooted in the anthropological imagination—the structure of our ethnographic encounters so closely follows the notion of the journey that our discourse is marked by the journey's sequence. My work is also influenced by my location in Western Europe on the rim of the Mediterranean, the porous host to the comings and goings of people from every corner of the world. I use the idea of navigation to focus on the agency and courage of those who must find their way in the aftermath of displacement. Some journeys are never completed, while others lead to unexpected destinations and leave their trace in the experiences of the traveler. I consider the nature and meaning of contemporary black subjectivity and presence through the notion of "invisibility." The availability of invisibility often operates in tandem with ambiguous state practice or inaction, and there is a tendency to blame the individual migrant who clings to a makeshift boat and not the system of illicit labor

[handwritten margin notes: "Focus on individual agency alongside structural issues", "When was national belonging ever 'traditional'?"]

regimes, rigid immigration policies, and failed economic conditions that make such a voyage seem one of the only viable options for survival.

In contemporary Europe, immigration commands center stage as traditional notions of national and cultural belonging are challenged by the reconfiguration of notions of sovereignty, territory, and community in the making of the European Union. The notion of the coming of this postnational world raises illuminating dilemmas concerning European relations with others, especially postcolonial Africa (Carnegie 2002; Williams 1991a; Malkki 1995).[1] In the context of anxiety over the forms of belonging for members of the African diaspora, as race, gender, and historical legacy render blackness a marker of outsider status, it becomes increasingly difficult to navigate the waters of belonging.

On a very hot Turin summer evening in 2006, just minutes from the site of one the many Olympic villages (now a kind of tourist beacon) on the outskirts of the city, my friend Babacar—who has traveled to his homeland only a handful of times over the last ten years—turns to me and, after a brief outburst in Wolof to his sister and brother-in-law in the next room, shifts to Italian. "Now everyone is dancing," he says. For the better part of an hour we have been watching an endless stream of music videos on Senegalese television, an experience made possible in part by the new world of African mobility and underscored by the Senegalese diasporic spectatorship enabled by new satellite links to Europe that connect the diaspora directly with the nightly parade of television programming back home. In one of the videos, the momentary flash of a multicolored traditional fishing boat or pirogue brightens the screen and unleashes another kind of response—an unexpected (for me) sadness. Babacar's comment on dancing is a not-so-veiled reference to the lack of opportunity for young people back home "who look around themselves in their villages" and, finding no way to contribute to the lives of their families, then look out to sea. Young people increasingly comb the shores south of Dakar seeking out former fishermen that might captain a tiny wooden canoe with precious little hope of ever making European landfall. This is not just folklore of the diaspora, as earlier that year in Thiaroye, a poor suburb of Dakar that is infamous as the site of a massacre of Senegalese soldiers by French troops in 1944, one of the countries worst navel accidents occurred, taking the lives of eighty-one young people from the village attempting to reach Europe in a converted fishing boat.[2] The migration is inspired by a kind of perfect global storm. In European countries such as Italy, a quiet search has been going on for some time in an effort to continually replenish a declining and increasingly aging labor force. In addition, Italy has one of the lowest birth rates in the world. Despite official denials, Europe will be dependent on migrant labor for years to come.[3]

The dancing, at times a cross between elements of global hip-hop culture and traditional forms such as haunting contemporary rituals, signals the quiet desperation of a diasporic community that understands the hardships of displacement and economic decline. Across the satellite channels, having consolidated the direct window into Senegalese experience, more and more programs refer in one way or another to the exodus of a new generation and reflect back a dimension of its exasperation. Immigration is literally what everyone was talking about in the summer of 2006, from the local news reports to the sports commentators at popular wrestling matches—at some point all are preoccupied with the boats.

Babacar's sister calls out from the other room: "Many of them leave but where do they go—their families don't hear from them . . . their families don't hear from them." Babacar picks up the theme: "What has happened to all of these people?" he asks. "We know that they have left, but then no one has heard from them again, many, many of them and where have they gone? How can you travel to France in this?" he says, pointing the passing of a tiny multicolored pirogue. "They must be somewhere but their families never hear from them again—dead," he says at last, dropping and shaking his head, his voice now all but a whisper.

Long ago Michlet warned us of the sea's passion for erasure. The tiny pirogue in the video is a symbol of cultural pride; it is clear that it was never meant to attempt such an ambitious voyage. The waters surrounding some of the major points of arrival for foreign migrants by sea in such places as Sicily have come to be called "liquid tombs" by the local fishing people, who find the evidence of failed voyages so often in their nets that they now avoid vast tracts of these waters that are known to be frequented by the vessels of this human trafficking.

By now the conversation embraces everyone in the apartment with the weight of the human tragedy that daily touches the lives of so many. My son Nico, while keeping his sister Eliana entertained, now strains to follow the conversation across the room from where Babacar and I are sitting side by side. I catch my wife Heather's eye, acknowledging the mood change and knowing somehow that the coming moments will require our full attention so that we might reconstruct events later. Babacar now turns to Nico and draws him directly in to the discussion: A young man Nico's age, what will he do to look after his family? The old people can do nothing; he needs to help them but has nothing in his pockets, not even enough to replace the jeans that he is wearing, only a few cents a day if that. He cannot live like that and there is no work in Senegal, so he takes to the boat. There are so many of them now. . .

While my family lived in a small apartment in Turin, Babacar's children lived in a compound in Dakar and rarely saw him. When I first met him almost twenty years ago, he had already been traveling between African and Europe for more than a decade. In the intervening years he has been joined by two sisters, a brother, and countless cousins and friends that he has in a sense "sponsored." Now he hopes to return for good, a hope he has been nurturing for years. There are always others, however, who wish to come, and they rely on the kindness of people like Babacar. Worsening conditions back home have kept him here, but as he gets older he can no longer get the relatively good contract factory jobs he enjoyed when he was younger.[4] Now he must put together odd jobs, and, in his fifties, he waits for benefits and pension payments and, like so many migrants and Italians in the volatile labor market today, is caught up in litigation.[5]

Since the 1960s the population in Senegal has doubled, and a large portion of the increase is young people still dependent on their families. Despite improvements in the economy in recent years, some point to the lack of support for agriculture, slumping returns in the fisheries, rising prices, and taxation as factors contributing to the fact that so many young people are forced to leave (Riccio 2007, 47). Some of the highest rates of rural–urban migration come from the Mourid regions of the country and go quickly toward international destinations, following the well-worn path of cousins, brothers, sisters, and friends. This new movement has expanded to encompass an entire generation from diverse religious, ethnic, social class, and educational backgrounds. The slight turnaround in the Senegalese economy from 1995 to 2006 did little to stop the call of the sea. The factors causing this push and pull involve not only conditions in Senegal but the presence of a stable Senegalese diaspora in Italy and the shifting nature of European immigration practices.

In some societies, the survivors of shipwrecks were summarily executed in order to save other members of society from the potentially contagious nature of their misfortune; the incomplete journey was an ominous portent for the future. In the Canto of Ulysses in Dante's *Divine Comedy*, Ulysses calls out to his shipmates and exhorts them to "follow the path of excellence and knowledge," pushing on farther than others might dare. Modern mariners do no less in seeking a promised land heralded in their childhood textbooks, in the media, in the stories returning through the diaspora, and in the exaltation of a global economy rising up in the emergent European Union and its expanding economic realm. Robert Harrison notes that "erasure does not mean disappearance only; it means that the site of disappearance remains unmarkable. There are no gravestones on the sea. History and memory ground themselves in inscription, but this element is uninscribable. It closes over rather than keeps the place of its dead, while its unbounded grave remains humanly unmarked" (2003, 12). The disappeared become the index by which to measure what is happening in a global social order that cannot account for their loss. In Senegal the discussion of this lost generation is everywhere in popular discourse and reverberates throughout the diaspora. In some ways, to be marked by erasure, by the inability to inscribe or account for traumatic, often forced social disappearance is an integral part of the African diasporic experience.

Toward an Anthropology of Invisibility

When I conducted fieldwork in Turin, Italy, I found that rendering migrants invisible took many forms, from municipal officials refusing to register their numbers in official census records to informal policing and exclusion from public spaces. Constructed as culturally remote outsiders, the Senegalese and other migrants face social exclusion particularly during their time away from the world of work. My world of anthropological dreaming has always been complicated by this specter of invisibility. It is not the mysterious protective invisibility granted by the gods to Aeneas, cloaked in mist and descending into an ancient city. Rather it is a corrosive social erasure, insinuated into living memory, that shapes the contours of social imagination and relegates the newcomer to the margins.

As Charles V. Carnegie has pointed out, the contemporary nation-state is at once the primary enforcer of the human rights needed by citizens and others and is also the site where more ambiguous conditions deprive outsiders of these very rights in the name of sovereignty. "People are routinely displaced—turned in to nonbeings—by virtue of their beliefs, affiliations, or some socially despised but unchangeable aspect of their person" (Carnegie 2002, 3). This results in a kind of condition Carnegie calls "perpetual marginality," which operates structurally in the social order and in practice to implement various forms of exclusion (28). Because these sites and practices change through time, however, I think that such marginality is a poor signifier of the state I examine here, since it is invisibility itself which, by subjecting others to its anonymity, renders them hypervisible,[6] as if by occupying this state they mark the boundaries of the known world. The status of invisibility exists not as some transcategorical place within a discursive field accessible only to the meanderings of philosophers, but as a social and cultural space capable of dispatching entire generations, social groups, and archipelagos for disappearance.

Invisibility is not a once-and-for-all event but is rather an ongoing, often occasional or flexible employment of power, politics, and social positioning that must be configured as a kind of routine practice capable of being reinstated into the flow of everyday events. It is a set of strategic social and cultural practices and an integral part of the process of signification; it is the power to instantiate or, as in the most ominous political intrigues, "to disappear" (Coutin 2003). Indeed collectivities disappear in its wake. Invisibility is not, however, merely a matter of localized stereotyping or individual stigma but rather is a flexible phenomenon that can be generalized, normalized, and deployed in multiple contexts, allowing it to be invoked like a discursive shroud in one decade only to disappear in the next or reappear elsewhere to freeze another group of people in a zone where public discourse is afraid to visualize and acknowledge their presence.[7] This spatial and temporal dimension is critical to the deployment of invisibility.

The late Edward Said once wrote of the history of the Palestinian diaspora: "The interesting thing is that there seems to be nothing in the world which sustains the story; unless you go on telling it, it will just drop and disappear." The force of invisibility can be so powerful that it can efface the historical presence of what amounts to the symbolic "weight" of an entire people (Said 1995, 118). "Sustaining the story" is at once an act of self-creation and an effort to make oneself known, to

writing of history & normalizing certain
INTRODUCTION *aspects while 7*
erasing others

become visible, and to inhabit a socially relevant cultural and political space. The power to make the colonial soldier or the migrant worker disappear from the official narrative of the Second World War or the national economy is a peculiar and mysterious order of social magic that I wish to explore in this book. This capacity to invoke the invisibility of others must be produced and reproduced through complex cultural logics and diverse sets of strategic social practices that can change over time. As Jacquline Nassy Brown recently pointed out, "visibility itself is a moving target" and must be considered a part of the process of the normalization of the real and the taken-for-granted world (Brown 2005, 9). The mapping of invisibility therefore also claims a continuous space through time zones, Western intellectual formations, and even the frontiers of the nation-state and the protean realm of time. Indeed invisibility implies a world of the past and present that is significant yet unseen.

Foucauldian?

Mapping Invisibility

The late cultural critic and philosopher Madan Sarup (1930–1993), writing shortly before his death in 1993, noted that in the contemporary Europe of his day "it is largely black migrants who perform the function of marking the boundary" (1996, 12).[8] Indeed this process is complicated when social boundaries impact the most intimate reaches of identity. Once we consider the most recent migrations of Africans to Europe to be an integral part of the complex historical relationship between Europe and Africa, and not merely a byproduct of economic restructuring and globalization, it becomes clear that we must attend to the story of colonialism and its role in the making of contemporary Europe.[9] By broadening our historical perspective on the African–European relationship, the links between the presence of migrants today and the colonial order becomes much more clear. Italians often wonder at the presence of migrants like the Senegalese in their country, a nation with no direct colonial link to Senegal. Few are aware that Italy has for some time established a vigorous economic and commercial presence in Africa, while its growing economy and labor shortages have also encouraged many newcomers to set out for its shores. The tumultuous social conditions of economic decline, political instability, war, and curiosity have also played a part in welcoming unprecedented global population movements. ✓

The dawn of the African–European encounter occurred during the most tumultuous period of colonialism and its aftermath. I consider the colonial mobilizations of West African populations through conscription to be an inaugural moment of diaspora that significantly helped to shape the African–European relationship. During this dispersion people from all parts of French West Africa were conscripted in service of France to fight in two World Wars and participate eventually in the liberation of France during the Second World War, and in this manner the African diaspora provided a new lens through which to view contemporary problems at a remove from the present. This was a privileged relationship that carried a symbolic weight far greater than itself. Gregory Mann argues that by the time of independence "the military relationship had come to serve as a synecdoche for the African–French relationship" (2006, 205). The struggle of those drawn into one of the most comprehensive diasporic movements in era of the colonial army to become a proper colonial and postcolonial subject/citizen seems strangely analogous to some of the struggles of Senegalese workers I worked with in Italy.

During the 1990s in Italy the idea of the migrant made a dramatic transformation, encouraged by a shift in media coverage, from an innocent victim of untold misfortune, a deserving newcomer, to an undeserving or suspect worker in an off-the-books world, often associated with various forms of criminality (Coutin 1993). For black and Muslim migrants, race and intolerance amplified these negative pronouncements, particularly in light of concerns requiring increased security.[10] In one instance, a local official of the foreign office told me that the police were afraid to enter migrant residences in an area of the city where I conducted research every day, in large part out of fear that migrants conformed to the distorted vision the stereotypes had painted of them (Angel-Ajani 2006). These largely "racialized dilemmas," as France Winddance Twine has called them, complicate contemporary research and at the same time offer novel pathways of investigation (Twine 2000, 5). The police were overwhelmed by the same folk ideology that convinced others that Senegalese and Moroccan migrants were prone to violence, deeply involved with criminal networks, and hostile to outsiders.[11] These were in fact old stereotypes, some of which had been used to characterize southern Italian migrants during the 1950s, and they formed part of the local ethnosociological repertoire of local "othering." By virtue of a flurry of stereotypes that signified the general migrant experience, the migrants themselves became largely invisible.[12]

Envisioning Afro-Europe

At the dawn of the 1990s, in the context of a rising awareness of African immigration to Italy, Italian cultural critic Umberto Eco suggested that Europe was on its way to becoming Afro-Europe. The influence of newcomers was a certainty that merely had to be accepted: "We must simply prepare ourselves to live in another season of culture, Afro-Europe" (Eco 1990). This would of course require an acknowledgement of the newcomer, an acceptance of the full significance of a new context of cultural and social encounter, but the matter is far from simple, as Eco suggests with a dose of wry humor. There is, however, a veiled threat implied in this bit of humor. As political philosopher Lewis R. Gordon points out, the Western discursive treatment of blackness implies a pre-occupation with reproduction, "black reality crosses borders of quantity," meaning that there is always a concern with there being too many. In the context of Italian anxiety about belonging to Europe, the idea of an African side of the hyphen cannot assuage their fears. As Gordon notes, "in a world concerned to distance itself from blackness, any blackness is too much." In ethnosociological imagination blackness increases exponentially; "exponential blackness" then threatens to overwhelm the European side of the hyphen (Gordon 2000, 160–63).

Some relatively new terms, such as "Afro-pean" and "Afro-Metropolitan," suggest an acknowledgement of complex heritage and cultural location (Keaton 2006a, 68). The complex historical encounter between Europe and Africa has left a deep and abiding experience of social and cultural ambiguity that leads us to consider the very nature of political belonging and the cultural meanings we attempt to capture with such notions as hybridity. The peculiar circumstances of blacks in the West, in particular in Europe, and its impact on identity has been a preoccupation in the cultural production of the African diaspora for some time. The earliest short African films shot in Europe explore this theme, as do many works of literature in which the travels of African subjects come to be interrogated against the backdrop of colonialism, race, and social exclusion (Edwards 2003).[13]

Senegalese in Italy today are in many ways still coming to terms with what it means to be "African" in a European context seemingly dominated by the notion that they are outsiders not just to Europe and the local labor market but somehow to modernity itself. Negating the black modern was part of a diminishing claim to parity and vacating the "subject" status of the colonial world, and today young people associate this dilemma with their need to prove, especially to the right, that they are deserving potential members of the political community of Europe and that their connection to other people like themselves in no way threatens this sense of belonging.

Certainly the idea of "the African" or "the European" is an evolving project that is contested and recast not as a once-and-for-all time-enduring identity but as a product of the discussions, corrections, writings, lives, and thoughts of men and women "over time and across the world" (Davis 1999, 72). Surely "identities can be displaced" or recaptured, or can be experienced as "hybrid or multiple" (Sarup 1996, 1), but these identities are also subject to the discursive production of theorists, nation builders, and others who through time employ subjectivity in the service of political objectives and make various claims indexed by race, gender, and social class. While in the heart of Europe newcomers are thought to be culturally remote, sealing their position as strangers, social anomalies easily exclude and come to define a kind of social border. It is as if newcomers have to cross modernity in order to reach the shores of contemporary Europe; they are constructed as a permanent "other" (see chapter 5). I believe this strange condition has accounted for a kind of vigilant and self-reflective posture perhaps not uncommon among peoples of the African diaspora. The peculiar cultural positioning that has defined people of African descent in the West as permanent outsiders, strangers in a strange land, follows the essential logic of stigma that points to an insoluble difference that justifies permanent exclusion (Sarup 1996; Calavita and Suárez-Navaz 2003).

The classic philosophers of invisibility are those writers who struggled to express the often inchoate insinuation of domination and social exclusion set in play by the discursive strategies embedded in the traditions of philosophy, literature, and the most taken-for-granted social norms that guide everyday life. Writers who are often associated with the notion of invisibility are James Baldwin, Ralph Ellison, and Franz Fanon. The work of these scholars examines the ethnosociology of their societies, interrogating the cosmological visions encompassing social order, classification, and place. In *Shadow and Act* (1972) Ralph Ellison wrote of a similar African American mindset, the product of "our memory, sustained and constantly reinforced by events, by our watchful waiting, and by our hopeful suspension of final judgment as to the meaning of our grievances," and by the long and patient observation of a racial order. A posture, Ellison argued, that allowed people to "recognize themselves as themselves despite what others might believe them to be," such vigilance required heroic discipline (1972, 124). When we observe the subtle indignities of life visited on those relegated to the margins in which we at times also live, such heroism is hard to remember. I hope to acknowledge in this book the men and women who inhabit these "freest of spirits," who in the most adverse conditions exhibit the most sublime heroism (124–25).[14]

The many people living and working in Europe today herald the emergence of a new Europe, one that must be carefully envisioned from the classroom to the boardroom if an equitable and open exchange and transformation is to take place between those thrown together by circumstance, postcolonial conditions, and global capitalism (see Merrill 2004; Merrill and Carter 2002). The changing nature of what it means to be European may also provide an opportunity of sorts for both the African and other migrant newcomers and for the established by exploiting the ambiguity in their process and nature of European self-representation, as "not all identities are worth preserving" (Abbas 1997, 14). Europeans old and new may transform the established conventions of identity, creating and inhabiting a now potential social ontology.

The climate for migrants in Europe has become increasingly inhospitable, particularly during the period from the early 1990s to the present.[15] The evolving integration of the European Union has contributed to a great deal of anxiety over such issues as immigration with no coordinated policy and mechanisms still in their infancy for the protection of human rights. Under the direction of Silvio Berlusconi the Italian government effectively restricted entrance to those who come to the country to fill specific jobs, a kind of worker program. As the late migrant activist Jean-Marie Tshotsha put it to me one afternoon, "we are now only things to be manipulated, we have no humanity." This form of objectification drains labor of its social value as it helps to compartmentalize workers along national lines, and effectively insulates them from Italian society as they are seen as merely temporary sojourners and not potential community members.

The work of time and power may efface an event or memory in the silence of a distant archive. Such silence, as Mexican writer, poet, diplomat, and Nobel Laureate Octavio Paz (1914–1998) observed, is peopled with voices (Paz 1961).[16] Migrants live in a subterranean world that cuts them off from full social personhood, and yet their presence maintains a kind of hypervisibility as the issue of immigration has become one of the permanent features of national discourse. In fact, the issue of immigration over the past twenty years has taken on an important symbolic role, becoming an integral part of the political landscape of the European Union. Confined to the shadows of the hidden world of work, as Marx called it, the migrant experience, a lived space, seldom finds its way into popular discourse, while the idea of the migrant as a problem, outsider, and undocumented worker is caught firmly in the cross hairs of public debate.

Complex cultural experiences and boundary-transgressing notions of identity, language, and sociality are explored in new Italian fiction by authors who have for the most part crossed the border literally or figuratively in order to enter Italy. At times the momentary return to the homeland in memory or in fiction becomes an index of the dimensions of the new authors' estrangement in Europe. Authors like Maria Viarengo, Tahar Lamri, and others writing in Italian explore through autobiographical journeys and short fiction not only the rich languages and cultural world of their childhood but also the dialects and cultural differences of Italy, which appear in their work through the critical eye of an engaged cultural observer (Lamri 2006; Chandra 2001; Ganbo 2001). Viarengo describes being subjected to the racializing gaze of people of color and others: "I have learned the art of seeming," she writes. "I always seem to be whom the others want me to be. I have been Indian, Arab, Latina, Sicilian." At times her differences seem insufficiently exotic, as in her very Italian sounding name: "My name, so boringly Piedmontese, disappoints them" (Viarengo 1999, 70). In Tahar Lamri's novel *I sessanta nomi dell'amore* (*Sixty names of love*), the young Tayeb returns to his native Algeria after years of travel and study in Libya, Great Britain, Poland, and Italy, where he has lived and worked for fifteen years. Returning after an eleven year absence, Tayeb goes to see his family, explaining to an Italian friend that after all the years in Italy he had learned to drink coffee without sugar, as is the custom in much of Italy, while in his homeland the preference for sugar dominates. When he drank the bitter coffee, his mother looked at him for a moment in silence and then said, "My son has died abroad. Someone had told me but I didn't believe it." After convincing his mother that he was in fact her son by recounting memories they alone shared, Tayeb explains the fundamental truth of his mother's insight:

> My mother is a woman who neither reads nor writes and therefore is not corrupted by books, and in her ingenious humanity has said something fundamental: The stranger knows "in life" the experience of death. Moving through loves (affetti), landscapes and thoughts to be reborn in other affections (affetti), landscapes and thoughts. This is the geography of the soul, like the man spoken of in Borges that wanted to paint the world and realized in the end that he had drawn his own face. (Lamri 2006, 41)

The geography of the soul is protean. Subjectivity is not a once-and-for-all event but a recursive process of becoming through which we are often relegated to invisibility even by those closest to us. Neither home nor the elsewhere are definitive positions at rest or can be easily fixed in time and space.[17]

Navigating diaspora is particularly concerned with invisibility in three modalities: (1) that orchestrated by the state or through its functionaries; (2) that concerned with bodies and discourse associated with embodiment, sexuality, gender, race, and other classifications and the media's attention or lack of attention to these, facilitating or performing the availability of invisibility for collectives or individuals such as international migrants and others; and (3) some forms of scholarly inquiry. Invisibility is a way of making the seen disappear in plain sight; a sympathetic operation is then accomplished through the manipulation and employment of various forms of structural inequality that assist and effectively reinforce the process of invisibility, caste affiliation, gender, or class and may act to, for example, exacerbate religious intolerance. Conversely, religious affiliation may crosscut racial exclusion in one context only to complicate it in another.

An illustrative instance of the contradictory nature of invisibility being coupled with hypervisibility can be drawn from the well-known case of Cuban migration in the United States. Susana Peña in her recent work has argued that the gay presence of the largely male Mariel Cuban migrant boatlift to the United States in 1980 was subject to a disparagement campaign by the Castro government through labeling of the migrants as "ecoria, lumpenproletariat, antisociales, prostitutes, and

Ohh!

Foucault

homosexuals" (2005, 125). During this period specific manifestations of homosexuality and particularly public displays of "ostentation" became a crime in Cuba. Thus, as Peña suggests, the state by "identifying male homosexuality as a problem made it visible"; it became a visible transgression of officially sanctioned masculinity in the revolutionary state. While visible, gay Cuban men were targeted, lesbian women remained relatively invisible, suggesting in part that visibility may mask multiple and alternate discursive fields. Once the migrants arrived in the United States, their "homosexuality" was effectively silenced in the media, their invisibility reflected in personal accounts of the period. Cuban migrants fulfilled the "cold war" legacy of anticommunist policy in the United States, and any other features of the migrant subjectivity merely complicated this picture. Poised for invisibility, the body is effectively employed in the discourse of the state, the media, and the day-to-day talk of people subjected to this peculiar form of social exclusion. While the fact of the gay presence was well known, scholars were reticent to discuss its significance or speculate on its contribution to American social life, as this social fact did not conform to the discursive requirements of U.S. asylum profiles. At the same time, a portion of the gay presence from the Mariel Cuban migrants made an impact on the local cultural world of Miami—so invisibility does not always inhibit political, cultural, or other forms of social activism but in fact may enable this possibility as an unintended consequence.[18]

David Harvey views the great ambiguity surrounding the national borders and spatial relations of our times as evoking "an increasing sense of nationalism and localism," a prelude to the reconfiguration of subjectivities in national interiors and projected borderlands (1990). This sense of closure indeed resonates with the experience of those in diaspora, particularly since the Second War World, and has precipitated diverse manifestations of the idea of invisibility. Although there are a number of relevant developments deserving of attention, invisibility figures in especially important ways in works on queer and racialized immigrant subjectivities (Peña 2005; Ramírez 2005; Manalansan 2005) and African urban studies (Simone 2004), and also among feminist scholars such as Judith Rollins in *Between Women: Domestics and Their Employers* (1985) and Elizabeth Higginbotham in *Too Much to Ask: Black Women in the Era of Integration* (2001).[19]

Notions of invisibility also figure prominently in recent discussions of immigration in Europe addressing the peculiar status and nature of migrant lives in terms of both their social and cultural exclusion. In the face of new democratic deficits, millions residing in Europe have no claim to fundamental rights despite the fact that the idea of European citizenship has in some ways encouraged new claims to citizenship for those who have nationality in European Union member states; the potential impact of the newcomers' full citizenship in an increasingly diverse world is yet unknown (Guiraudon and Joppke 2001; Calavita and Suárez-Navaz 2003; Bellu 2004; Dunkerley 2002). I envision invisibility as integrally related to extended periods of "nonbelonging" to the nation-state, to a certain notion of history, to a place of residence, or to forms of second-class citizenship, while at the same time belonging to one's homeland, local, and ethnic or cultural community, creating contradictory and multiple claims on belonging and experience in the lives of those subject to the shadows (Leonard 2003, 156). Indeed visibility becomes important inasmuch as it implies a claim to a kind of truth; it is not a matter of what is seen as much as what it means to be seen or unseen. The social significance of what is seen and what is relegated to invisibility is an index of the workings of power over time and its insinuation into the taken-for-granted foundations of everyday life. What concerns us here is not optics, but rather the phenomenology of optics and the play of its politics.

There has been recent civil unrest in France in what Trica Danielle Keaton has called the "outer-cities," essentially the "high-rise public housing complexes on the periphery of urban centers," places like Clichy-Sous-Bois, where in 2005 young people protesting double-digit unemployment, social and political marginalization, and the accidental deaths of their comrades burned cars and took to the streets (Keaton 2006a, 2; Keaton 2006b).[20] I was reminded of the path-setting work of Kenneth B. Clark, educator and psychologist, his classic *Dark Ghetto:*  *Dilemmas of Social Power* (1965), in which he writes of social unrest in the African American community and points out that the situation behind the "invisible walls" of the "dark ghetto" was at times so desperate that its inhabitants "insisted on being visible and understood." He describes groups of young people taunting the police in one incident in Harlem: "He would rather die than be ignored," he wrote of one youth. Such acts were assertions of a desire for equal treatment during the 1960s (Clark 1965).[21] Many seemed perplexed that young people would take to the streets in acts of violence, overturning and burning cars as if it were a tactical decision selected over prolonged negotiations with government representatives in Paris. Young people in Harlem or in Paris in 2005 or in other parts of France communicated through their actions the same idea: "We have had enough." The youths, Clark insisted, are not taking up tactical positions; they "do not choose tactics at all" but rather "respond to the pressure of their lives and react spontaneously to incidents which trigger explosions and demonstrations." Their sponta-neity is in fact an index of their invisibility (17). The "invisible walls" of the contemporary Parisian "ghetto" are marked by locations where the Metro stops or does not, double digit unemployment among the youth, and the absence of political representation. Many in this generation of young people are seen as outsiders and are relegated to invisibility, but they are in fact citizens, having potential claim to protections guaranteed by the state, while newcomers who share a similar hypervisibility must also struggle to maintain permission to stay in Europe.

The Long March from Subject to Citizen

While the ambiguity of the present migrant position helps to mark the outer limits of the "national" experience in much of Europe today, rein-forcing various conceptions of group identity, in the past this honor was reserved for the colonial subject. During the colonial era, citizens could be defined in contradistinction to what they were not—as either "native" or indigéne—but today the undocumented workers stands outside of the confines of the national order. The contemporary migrant in Europe continues to be immersed in representational forms caught between changing historical conditions—colonialism, postcolonialism, and the myriad verities of imperialism (cultural, economic, political) that serve to delimit and justify social and cultural exclusion. This transition is most evident when people draw on discursive traditions and construc-tions of the past in order to argue their position in the present. Longtime residents of France during the 1990s, called *sans-papiers* since they held no formal residence permission and were undocumented, invoked the memory of a debt to colonial soldiers in their claim to their right to stay in France. The Tirailleurs Sénégalais, through their sacrifice to France in blood, earned the right of their grandchildren to be a part of the political community of the nation (Mann 2006).[22] Although not immigrants, the Tirailleurs Sénégalais were pioneers in the cultural encounters that took place in Europe. Many were garrisoned in French towns, creating "towns of their own making" serving as winter retreats and recovery centers, for example in Fréjus (Mann 2006, 164–72). The informal encounters with European civilians, officers, hospital attendants, and others and the extraordinary diversity of the soldiers themselves, who hailed from all over West Africa, inaugurated a unique social and cultural world in France (Figure 1). Young people invoke not only the soldiers' "blood debt" but also their complex incorporation into French cultural and political belonging. Drawing the colonial soldier once again into visibility through the notion of a blood debt to former soldiers links a new generation in an imagined political community crossing national boundaries, time, and space and demonstrates both the unpredictable nature of the practice of invisibility and its potential to sound the historical depths, shape identity, and shatter preconceived notions of belonging.

Throughout this book, I attempt to meditate on the landmark work of Frantz Fanon, whose ideas I think are critical to the exploration of the postcolonial condition. It is Fanon's concern with freedom and liberation that I take up here, his unfailing attempts to consider the possibilities of the decolonization of the mind. I see Fanon as a diaspora theorist, and his concern with identity, social positioning, power, and race are all deeply mediated by his location in diaspora.[23] Fanon's work also relates to the larger issues of the nature and significance of the African diaspora, its dimensions, and its meanings. Through Fanon, concerns about identity take on a new kind of urgency as such problematic sites of inquiry fold back on the very nature of the process of colonial domination. The colonized and colonizer fall into a battle set to shake the very foundation of such notions as race, humanity, moral economy, and subject. Fanon's insight that the process of decolonization continues long after the colonial order has ended is further enhanced by the notion that the decolonization of the mind presents the most challenging aspects of human liberation.[24] While Fanon's work has recently been written off as a kind of "third-world-ism," I think that reading Fanon against the grain of the postcolonial state in the shadow of a kind of unchecked cultural and

LE MONDE
COLONIAL ILLUSTRÉ

1ʳᵉ ANNÉE · Nᵒ 197 · NOVEMBRE 1939.
Rédacteur en chef : Stanislas REIZLER

DE DAKAR A LA LIGNE MAGINOT

Avant leur embarquement pour la France, les tirailleurs sénégalais
défilent à Dakar, devant le Gouverneur général CAYLA et le
Général de corps d'armée DUBUISSON, Commandant supérieur
des troupes de l'Afrique Occidentale Française (septembre 1939).

Figure 1. Colonial soldiers on the move. Cover of *Le Monde Colonial Illustré*,
Paris, November 1939.

economic imperialism of late capitalism may help us to consider what I
call diasporic nostalgia—a desire for an imagined world that has not yet
come into being, a desire for a liberation from the legacy of colonialism,
postcolonial states, and global conditions.

Forgotten Warriors and Other Victims of Invisibility

Through the films of Ousmane Sembene and the poetry of Léopold Sédar Senghor I explore the world of the colonial soldier, a transitional figure between colonialism proper and the postcolonial world. I see the colonial soldier as shipwrecked between these two orders and yet, because of their potential claim to fair treatment and equality with French soldiers in the colonial order and their right to agitate for more equitable sharing of power in the postcolonial world, they made a place for themselves in both worlds, however unwelcomed. The colonial soldiers recruited from French West Africa were subject to a peculiar invisibility. Although there are countless images of French, Italian, American, British, and even German soldiers of the Second World War in recreations, war films, and an almost endless lists of war-related literature, the work of these soldiers, most notably in the liberation of France (in which they figured prominently), was no where to be seen. In fact, although the Second World War military campaigns and machinery are a kind of international pastime, the figure of the colonial soldier rarely, if ever, appears as an element in the countless hours of dramatizations, filmic representations, and popular narratives. This is no accident, as the black forces that the French relied on so heavily during the war to liberate France were sent back home so that the Allies would not realize how much the French had depended on their services, and were replaced by French soldiers, many of whom had sat out the war in their villages and towns. During this period the United States insinuated its Jim Crow mentality throughout its new sphere of influence, at times coming into direct conflict with less racially segregated military traditions in France and Great Britain (Rich 1990). This so-called *blanchissement*, or whitening of the troops, created a lot of tension among the Tirailleurs, who were separated from the Frenchmen who had fought with them in Italy and North Africa (Mann 2006, 172). At times metropolitan reservists with little rapport or experience with African troops were placed in command of hardened combat units. The French, fearing a loss of prestige among their European allies, relegated the soldiers to invisibility.[25] The final staging of the liberation of France would appear much more in accord with a kind of "colonial" sensibility. Colonial troops were abandoned to await demobilization to their home villages, back pay, acknowledgement of their contribution to the liberation of France, support for those who were subjected to the camps, education for their children, pensions, honor, respect, and a future. In a most peculiar turn of events, the colonial soldiers claiming the rights accorded any French soldier were suspected of being sympathetic to communist influence, and in the end were dealt with by the iron hand of an emerging state, much like the so-called communist elements of the Resistance in metropolitan France. This potential enemy within had also to be relegated to invisibility in the triumphant narrative that would become the official story of the Liberation. British historian Richard D. E. Burton in his book *Blood in the City: Violence and Revelations in Paris 1789–1945* (2001) argues that as the allied forces were heading eastward in the wake of the collapse of the major German resistance, Eisenhower was convinced that De Gaulle would take on the liberation of Paris, a task that might delay his advance and by the burden of "provisioning an increasingly malnourished population of millions," contribute to the fear of the possibility of a "communist-dominated paragovernment" coming to power in the city.[26] The specter of a popular uprising in France began to be feared just as the possibility of anticolonial popular uprisings in West Africa began to be resolved with increasingly repressive measures. It is important to note that a particular idea of political belonging could not contain the "communist" element or as we shall see in a moment, the African soldier demanding equity—both were dispatched to invisibility through violent means, the exclusive preserve of an emerging nation-state. During the same year, 1944, De Gaulle would march into Paris in August and on the balcony of the Hôtel de Ville "proclaim not the Republic but the state, identified in the early-evening sunlight with his own massive person" (Burton 2001, 240). This insistence on exceptions, and the weeding out of unwanted political belonging, is perhaps the most troubling legacy of this now-distant era of the emerging nation-state, and is an aspect that has returned to haunt us today.

Demobilizing former prisoners of war and colonial soldiers were fired on by the French military in December 1944 just outside of Dakar in a dispute over labor conditions and back pay. The attack killed many of the unarmed soldiers, and imprisoned others thought to be associated with the protest. The soldiers, many former prisoners of war, had already been subjected to a number of indignities during their return journey, including long waits for transport ships, segregation among allied troops, and arbitrary divisions of combat units (Rich 1990). Gregory Mann has argued that this represents a breakdown of the traditional military culture that in some respects guided the relationship between Europeans and Africans over the long evolution of the Tirailleurs from their slave/soldier origins and particularly during the interwar years (Mann 2006, 171). The remains of the Vichy leadership were still in charge of military operations in West Africa and the battle-worn French fighters. Returning for fresh recruits, the newly constituted French colonial order wiped out any signs of resistance among African populations demanding improvements in work and social conditions.

For many West Africans the event marked a kind of symbolic break with the old order, as if an unwritten trust had been broken that even the most ardent supporters of the colonial order had difficulty accepting.[27] In both life and death the soldiers' experience indexed the contours of a cultural rupture between the past and an emerging and uncertain present. The soldiers represented not only the tensions between citizen and subject but also the irreconcilable nature of the honor and acknowledgement they would never receive for their service and the dishonor and disregard of the colonial order and later the African independent state for the role the colonial soldier created and the forms of power in which they could not participate. Their invisibility also helped to cut them off from the legacy of unwanted trajectories and inconvenient potentials expressed in deeply rooted tensions in the European–African relationship that at times erupted into violence.

so how is invisibility being expressed here?

The soldiers became invisible not only to the colonial regime that recruited them from their villages and mobilized them to fight in Europe but also to the postcolonial societies in which their return posed a peculiar problem. A well-disciplined group, often unable to accept the "traditional" or artificially established local governing bodies in their villages and regions and at times openly challenging the authority of these institutions and power holders, they stood alone demanding equity with the French soldiers with whom they had served, and later posed an uncertain political challenge to the postcolonial order itself (Mann 2006).

In the postcolonial order the soldiers were exemplars of a past the Independence generation wished to overcome and yet they articulated sets of demands that in the emerging state would not be attained well into the future. They were in a sense the victims of an irretrievable loss of an identity that could not be realized in their present or future. Awaiting pensions that might never arrive from France and increasingly disheartened by developments in their own countries, these men and their families lived in a world clouded by the legacy of their military service, ideas of mutual obligations, and rights to recompense for their labors (Mann 2006; Rich 1990).

The men and their families participated in the arch of a military culture that wove European and African men and women into a shared cultural world. Invisibility would bear down on the lives of the soldiers, who were, I would argue, the first proper postcolonial subjects. Their subjectivities ironically were neither reabsorbed in local contexts nor assimilated to a world of colonial desires, but in some strange and telling ways began to eclipse both.[28]

Navigating the Africa Diaspora: The Anthropology of Invisibility is an exploration of the power to establish or manifest a state of invisibility for specific categories of persons in a given space, location, time, or position. By its very nature it is exploratory and incomplete. I hope to offer new directions, insights, and provocations rather than a closed system of pronouncements. What I offer is the outline of a journey that I myself have made—nothing more and nothing less than headings and some suggestions for further navigation.

Invisibility implies a dehumanization and devaluation of personhood or a denial, as the great cultural critic James Baldwin once wrote, of a basic "human reality . . . human weight and complexity." In the United States, race has often overlapped with social invisibility to create a racial order built on "denying the overwhelmingly undeniable" dimensions of a common humanity that spun social justifications "so fantastic that they approached the pathological" (Baldwin 1985, 88).[29] Social invisibility of the type I have in mind spans beyond race, class, and gender or may incorporate these and other classifications.[30] Clearly it is possible to establish, as Michel de Certeau might say, a degree of "plurality and creativity" within and against the grain of "invisibility," but as a constraining order its sanction can only be lifted with great difficulty and may take generations at that (de Certeau 1984, 30). Working against invisibility and insisting on one's social presence is what people do all the time—Senegalese migrants create an African market on the streets in an Italian shopping district, where police detain them and sequester their wares, colonial soldiers insist on their right to equal pay, and others everyday refuse to succumb to the indignities of social exclusion, immigration restrictions, discrimination, and neglect. Subjectivity acts as a counterweight to the process through which conferring invisibility diminishes by degree the imagined nature of the very "human weight" persons already relegated to a kind of subpersonhood inhabit, making their very presence seem superfluous and unnecessary. An insistence on presence, vitality, and personal and collective narrative, however mod- ✓ est, constitutes not merely a tactical maneuver, as de Certeau might call it, but an all-out assault on marginality.

It is often when people are from the perspective of a given cultural logic designated "superfluous," imponderable as a human presence, that they become invisible. It is through such cultural root metaphors that we find interconnections of cultural and bodily notions in the production of subjectivity. In many societies, ideas surrounding the notion of social and cultural presence or weight are "embodied sensations of amplitude." As Michael Jackson emphasizes in his work *Minima Ethnographica: Intersubjectivity and the Anthropological Project* (1998), "substantiality—weight—standing—and voice" are qualities that constitute and reinforce "our sense of existence and autonomy." Other metaphors suggest a relative loss of presence—"falling, floating, drifting, being rootless, empty, ungrounded" or "reduced to an inert thing" (Jackson 1998, 13). In short, invisibility is in part a kind of master story, a cosmological origin myth of the present.

The migrants who daily attempt to overcome the myriad mechanisms of state immigration control become "superfluous" in part because their very status makes them illegitimate social persons in the national territory, a kind of "matter out of place" as Mary Douglas (1971-2007) put it (1973, 36). Of this superfluous presence even one is too many. The same thing can happen to a group of indigenous people whose history the nation may, in an act of bad faith, choose to deny or forget (Gordon 2000, 159–63). Their peoplehood, so closely associated with their "rights" to land, demands to be addressed and dealt with in a just manner and thus must be blotted from the national register.[31] This to some degree has been the fate of indigenous people in North America and elsewhere. This invisibility may operate on the basis of such categorical markers as race, gender, and to some degree class, or in terms of political and/or religious affiliations. Such operations of invisibility often, however, work across and through conventional boundaries such

how ?

as citizenship, sovereignty, colonialism, modernity, representational regimes, identity, and language.[32]

That which is visible to us actually rests on the very architecture of the unseen (Merleau-Ponty 1968). This seems to be as true of visual regimes, the constellations of dispositions toward the orchestrations of things seen in a particular place and time, as it is of the envisioning of social ontology. As Samira Kaswash points out, the modern concept of race is in fact "predicated on an epistemology of visibility" (1997, 130). Some categories of persons in the so-called modern world have encountered what philosopher Lewis R. Gordon has called an "existential limitation," a kind of wall or cultural cloak of invisibility that essentially masks their presence at specific moments and in the case of historical erasure for generations. This existential limitation may be invoked by mounting an epistemological armature, as in the case of anthropology in its confrontation with what Michel Rolph Trouillot has called the "savage slot," an effective placement of the anthropological subject on the other side of modernity from the practitioners of the art (Trouillot 1991).[33]

The availability of invisibility is not limited to symbolic modalities or actions but may have dramatic and at times catastrophic consequences for people subjected to its force, as it can cast a given subject or collective into a complete state of anonymity such that they become a kind of absence. This absence is however, as Lévi-Strauss says, "good to think," as it takes the form of a kind of resolution of the social, political, and economic aspects of the presence that must not be accounted for, the "illegal," the so-called boat people, in a racial order it might be the black as a "type," or in a colonial order the so-called native a "prodigious presence" that implies in its simplicity the idea of quantity, of standing for others of the same type, embellishing on a kind of irrepressible numeration of difference.

Crafting the Present and Its Dark Ontology

It is this dimension of what I call the anthropology of invisibility that leads us to consider the unique role of the present. In contemporary social theory a number of modes of framing the present have been at play in recent years. Of these it is perhaps the notion of globalization has been considered the most pressing feature of the present context. Globalization, however, is marked as a kind of moment of complexity and theoretical crisis in which what it means to account for the speed and dimension of the movement of capital, people, and things across the globe and the manner in which these new processes may be studied is far from clear (Taylor 2003). There seems to be no sorcerers' stone with which to cut through this crisis; perhaps we must simply sharpen our tools and take aim at a fragment on this side of the here and there. In my case I have selected ethnography, albeit a retooled version.

My concern with representation, invisibility, and identity is in part methodological and in part pragmatic. I think that we must readjust our vision of the ethnographic project of the present and consider a whole range of genres of representation from popular culture through political and academic discourse.[34] I hope to present a new vision of our ethnographic practice to encompass the exploration of the constitution of new subjects and ourselves as well as the invisibility of "others" (other people and ourselves) that is made possible through the shifting epistemological and discursive frames that at times enter our process of analysis—the terms and categories with which we conduct our work and the fragments of taken-for-granted classificatory debris in archives, photographs, narratives, popular culture, and various anthropological literatures—with which we must contend. We can see this process most clearly when we are dealing with such concepts as race rooted in the very structuring of Western philosophical discourse and practice.

Walter Benjamin long ago warned that the exultation of the "victor" inscribed in the narrative of official history comes at a great price for those who have been essentially silenced, stepped over in the "triumphal procession" to the present, a progress forever tainted by "barbarism." The "other" is rendered invisible through the ideological apparatus of analysis–history—a process that the historical materialist with whom Benjamin identifies "cannot contemplate without horror" (1968, 256). Take for example the work of G. W. F. Hegel, whose very philosophy of history begins with what is essentially an erasure of the non-Western world.[35] The problem is that we rework this body of knowledge, challenging only a limited or selected portions of its foundation, while the moment of erasure remains an integral part of the legacy and constitutive armature of the work. This does not lead me to want to pick a fight with every passing Hegelian—I am, like it or not, a product of this tradition too. We might even account Kantian moral philosophy a more perilous terrain, as the erasure of others from the Kantian moral universe of mutual respect and their copresence in the world community may be of greater and more immediate significance. The Kantian idealized world of reciprocal relations of respect did not extend to what Charles W. Mills calls "the unacknowledged dark side of Enlightenment," and this is the side of the "dark ontology" of the "others," devoid of personhood (Mills 1998, 70). Race was the magical categorical instrument through which blacks and others were relegated to a status of nonpersonhood, a journey marked by irretrievable loss. I suppose this does mean that I must someday find a way to account for the people that G. W. F. Hegel, Immanuel Kant, and the many trajectories of this work have made invisible, as I am also their direct descendant.

The Logic of Global Disappearance

The erasure of personhood may escalate into a form that renders invisible vast tracts of whole populations. A kind of logic of global disappearance can be set in motion in which the development, economic growth, and stabilization of some troubled regions is simply taken off the table altogether. The recent discussions of debt reduction between the United States and Britain underscore the fact that the failing economies of the many African nations have been in large measure unable to engage in the great global discussion. On this other side of the global coin, access to the global community becomes increasingly difficult. Anthropologist Michel-Rolph Trouillot cautioned against the unrestricted use of the notion of "globalization," noting that what he calls "globaliteralism" is in fact the "dominant ideology of our times" (2003, 48). This ideology posits the teleology of the market as "the new master narrative of Western modernity," a kind of self-promotion gone astray. The logic of "techno-capital," according to Radhakrishnan, is so deeply ingrained in the idea of globalization that the fragmentary and discontinuous sectors cast in its shadow seem to be dysfunctional family members. The idea of globalization masks utopian dimensions of a conception in which a future global real world will resolve the uneven terrain that history and inequality (economic, political, and ideological) have set in motion. The desire to "modernize" the underdeveloped world it seems has been all but jettisoned. It is better to cut all ties with sites of uneven development in order to focus only on the shining examples of modernity (Radhakrishnan 2003, 100).

In the new global vision of the world the old "developmentalist dreams" have been abandoned. Not all countries are thought to be on the same path any longer, nor do they need to be: "Some chunks of the world (notably sub-Saharan Africa) are becoming poorer every day. Even more importantly, their state of affairs is becoming irrelevant to the world economy." Trouillot also warns that "the global map has increasingly large black holes" (2003, 57). Yet these spaces are linked in the historical legacy that the talk of "globalization" has jettisoned along with politics, ethical considerations, and other ideological encumbrances (Radhakrishnan 2003, 99). The same processes that created the particular moment of global capitalist development that we attempt to name with the term globalization sent shock waves into other parts of the world. In the wake of capitalist establishment in other "chunks of the world," less fortunate state systems reeled from the retreat of foreign capital as "the global restructuring of capital also disrupted the local economies of the third world" (Basch et al. 1994, 25). This disruption sparked in part the creation of new diasporas (Van Hear 1998). Having originated in a kind of economic and cultural "black hole" marks the newcomer for invisibility; being superfluous, they fade into the background unwanted. Since they are not thought of as potential community members (the very names used to designate their presence implies they are "clandestine," "*extracomunitari*," "illegal aliens"), they fade into the workplace, the ancient workers' residential areas of the city and into the surveillance net of the authorities that monitor their stay. The coastguard is engaged to intercept the tiny crafts bringing new migrants in to the country, and the airports and other means of international transport are now home to an army of authorities hoping to stop the flow of the unfortunate—the newcomer. In the biopolitics of modernity the refugee, the exile, the newcomer, and others in diaspora have become subjects of the expanding and at times exceptional powers of the state. Hannah Arendt in *The Origins of Totalitarianism* (1976) reminds us that in the very formation of contemporary European nation-states, the management of the displaced or unwanted minority communities was of critical significance for the construction of the very contours of sovereignty, an insight taken up in the works of Giorgio Agamben.[36]

Exceptional States Orchestrating Invisibility

Long ago, Walter Benjamin in "Theses on the Philosophy of History" noted the troubling nature of the exceptional state powers, pointing out that "the tradition of the oppressed teaches us that the 'state of emergency' in which we live is not the exception but the rule" (Benjamin 1968). Invisibility is of course orchestrated in such a way that it becomes a part of a naturalized set of practices, supported by an economy of indifference.[37] Woven into the fabric of cultural traditions, it becomes a taken-for-granted grounding of the conventional ways of seeing. Agamben warns that exceptional measures and state powers have become the rule in our time as well, as the state has increasingly appropriated new ways of extending its authority, especially in times of crisis. The state of exception is characterized by the temporary suspension of conventional juridical law and the invoking of special powers through which authorities may "temporarily act as sovereign" arbiters of the fate of others during the time from the suspension of the rule of law prior to the intervention of judicial authority (Agamben 2005, 174). While special powers are accorded the state in order to fight a "war on terror" or erect "receptions centers" for asylum seekers or migrants, these temporary measures tend to curtail the extension of human rights considerations, individual freedoms, and the right to due process under the law. In such situations, Agamben argues, some subjects may "undergo a suspension of their ontological status as subjects when states of emergency are invoked," a state that I would argue in the case of invisibility may have a semipermanent duration (cited in Butler 2004, 67). Cutting off access to courts gives the accused no way to authenticate their identity or face the charges against them, leaving them in a constant state of insecurity.[38]

In his work *Homo Sacer: Sovereign Power and Bare Life*, Agamben has taken up the consideration of what he calls the "state of exception" and the changing status of subjects, citizens, and others who must face the extended reach of the state.[39] The state of exception for Agamben is realized not in the site of a prison or mental institution, as for Foucault, but rather in the *Lager* (concentration or detention camp), which becomes the critical site of the state of exception.[40] Judith Butler in *Precarious Life: The Powers of Mourning and Violence* (2004) argued that in the state of exception a kind of denuding of the subject or what she calls "de-subjectivation" takes place, a process that constitutes subjects as "humanly unrecognizable" and therefore "less than human without entitlement to rights." Subjects reduced to this state of invisibility attain an ambiguous status at once among the living and the dead: "the subject who is no subject" according to Butler is "neither fully constituted as a subject nor fully deconstituted in death" (2004, 98). Through a "governmental tactic" such subjects are "managed" to invoke the notion of Foucault's governmentality, but in a form that threatens their very status as humans. In the subject's weakened state, in which "humans are not regarded as humans," people become invisible and seem to cede even the basic outlines of a life. Subjects that are viewed as having an ambiguous relationship with the established ontology or ways of life, be they sexual, ethnic, or racial minorities, are separated from the conventional world by what Butler calls the violence of derealization. For Butler "the derealization of the 'Other' means that it is neither alive nor dead, but interminably spectral" (32–34). This indeterminate space of discourse that the spectral visage of the "other" dominates facilitates a kind of dehumanization that allows us to imagine degrees of humanity diminishing in importance the further we move from where we are to the realm of the "other."[41]

This is in part why we perhaps see this process less clearly when we consider the state. When we consider merely immigration discourse, migrant communities, and the antiforeigner reactions of the established, we render invisible the interstitial zones beyond the borders of the so-called state. In these interstitial zones it appears the state comes to manage a kind of economy of indifference, and one is struck by the fact that few contemporary states engage in large-scale humanitarian interventions. It seems to me in the wake of globalization, we cannot think of citizenship, sovereignty, and identity without first thinking through the relationship these conventions have to the "displaced," the liminal, and the invisible epistemological ruins of history among which the tiny vessels of the "boat people" must navigate. Inhabiting a dark ontology is like a shipwreck on the way to humanity. Indeed the refugee and the displaced person are critical figures in both Arendt's and Agamben's examinations of sovereignty, humanitarian policy, and international political orders because the ambiguous status of persons in diaspora "radically calls into question the fundamental categories of the nation-state" (Agamben 1998, 134).[42] How are we to think about people who are subject to a constantly changing state of impermanence and the legacy of world-ordering processes such as postcolonialism, cultural (economic, social) imperialisms, globalization, and modernity, or what I call the navigation of diaspora?

defining diaspora

I view the nature of diaspora as at least a double epistemological and ontological disjunction, an integral aspect of our times impacting both theory and practice. Ordinary people in our world have entered into the state of diaspora, a condition from which many will never extricate themselves. The legacy of displacement reverberates across human lives for generations. In the scope of a life, the many currents of identity, change, and loss brought on by living in diaspora come to be reconciled. The late Edward Said's memoir *Out of Place* (1999) concludes with the words "With so many dissonances in my life I have learned actually to prefer being not quite right and out of place." The book, Said tells us elsewhere, is a "record of a lost and forgotten world" (1999, 295, ix). Reading such a record I am confronted with the silences in social theory and areas of life and experience that are often difficult to capture, to account for and understand.[43] Those in the world of theory are forced to reconfigure paradigmatic formulations of diaspora because the world of theory, in its encounter with the real world, has taken on the qualities of the very volatile, unbounded, and ever-changing global circumstances it seeks to explain.

The search in social theory for explanatory models that define and characterize the present, a present in which notions once fixed by tradition or rooted solidly in certain taken-for-granted geopolitical configurations have been upended by both a seemingly accelerated rate of change and the very dimension and scope of such social, cultural, and economic transformations. This theoretical wondering is also marked in part by the tumultuous patterns of social, cultural, and economic dislocations of global capitalism and the complex interplay of power relations in and across nation-states that has helped to renew a preoccupation with the nature of such linkages and the consequences of these changes at various scales. The decentering of economies, people, objects, and ideas that moves across the "hypermodernity" of late capitalism, navigating vast interconnected and global systems of cultural, social, and economic relations, clears away old modes of knowledge and the sociologies that attended them. Framed by unprecedented and unimagined migrations, cultural disruptions, and social disorders, the "multi-linear quality of capitalism and modernity" take on diverse cultural forms across different social formations (Pred and Watts 1993). However the binary logic of here/there, of us/them, of Europe/the rest no longer holds, and as Michael M. J. Fischer argues, we

but when did it ever really hold, in a reality separate from a specific constructed discourse?

must turn to a "constantly comparative and difference-scanning perspective" in order to reposition our inquiries (Fischer 2003) and account for the consequent problems of people in diaspora (identity, politics, location) that no longer fit in the conventional representational regimes of the old sociologies because the positions from which sociology, anthropology, and other social sciences are possible also have changed. The scope and nature of the reactions to these changes is experienced differently in every context, not only by the people undergoing various forms of dislocation but also by the theorists that must account for it. This new world shatters the idea of territorially fixed communities and of a local knowledge capable of producing relatively stable and clear-cut identities; images of disjunction and the proliferation of identities in motion replace "essential" markers of identity and boundary. This new frame questions the very inauguration of the social science project rooted in a Western philosophic and sociological tradition. The migrant, or the diaspora community, is the figure most commonly associated with the borderlands and interstitial zones of our world, caught between at times reconfigured national spaces. The accelerated patterns of travel and the displacement of populations across the planet is one of the features that sets in motion changes in the configuration of the societies in which we live. There has been a shift from an emphasis on boundedness and territoriality to a concern with deterritorialization. This new emphasis focuses on the transitory and fragmentary nature of emergent social, political, and cultural worlds and the people that inhabit them. This shift toward politics of uncertainty and contingency requires that we craft a way of getting at emergent structures of indeterminate duration and coherence, something perhaps less like a theoretical framework and more like a method. It is in this context that we search for ways of explaining the present and are at times faced with methodological questions that challenge the manner in which we inhabit a disciplinary practice bounded by historical and at times arbitrary conceptual and epistemological boundaries. The idea of navigation helps to mediate the metaphorical distance traveled to this new state of the world.

I employ the idea of navigation to represent this new circumstance and to approach an ethnographic practice in which the anthropological object of study is in part the manner in which we as theorists and the people we work with "navigate" this new terrain. It is a preliminary, and no doubt transitional, measure, but one that attempts to honor the spirit of exploration needed to encounter the "new" in our situation, if new is what it is. I take as my starting point the "sense of exile" found in experience and theory counterpoised to this "new" world for which the incomplete journey, the shipwreck, may serve as a provisional trope. Many names mark our state of theoretical shipwreck: postmodernism, poststructuralism, deconstruction, and in the social sciences a concern with our own and other cultures, this time bounded by self-reflexivity and the politics of the self.[44]

In this work I have selected a number of cases of groups caught in the thick of journeys—some that will never be completed and others that are bound to be turned back, erased from national histories, or placed on display in a timeless world of caricature, captured in a seemingly endless archive of historical and scholarly representation. Although many of these journeys remain incomplete, neither the people involved in them nor we who acknowledge their passage can ever really return to an inaugural point of origin, as we too have become a part of the journey's logic. If we are to take these journeys seriously, acknowledging the intimacy of our obligations to these passages and at times our participation in them, we must begin to think differently about the boundaries of our theoretical and ethnographic practices.

Invisibility often operates in plain view; it is not a matter of "seeing everything" from the perspectives of totalizing theory but of understanding the capacity and power of the sanction of invisibility. States designate national territories and speak of the people in international waters just beyond their shores as lawbreakers, boatpeople that must be turned back and returned to their place of origin. States at times abandon these same people to the fates of the high seas as if no portion of responsibility for their welfare touched the state at all. Until there is an incident, for which the people in transit are often blamed, the state seems to take little notice. This rending of the people in transit into a kind of invisibility simply because they fall beyond the accepted boundaries of the state involves turning a blind eye not only to the conditions that placed the people on boats off the coastlines of the most powerful nations in the world, but also to the violence they may be subjected to in transit. The failure to take responsibility for these desperate attempts to cross the border amounts to a kind of tacit, symbolic state violence.[45] We often find out about this world from the survivors of this trafficking in human lives that crisscrosses the seas and feeds the hungry labor markets around the world. While states tighten immigration controls and political factions pander to the public through anti-immigrant rhetoric, countless lives hang in the balance. The cemeteries that crop up in seaside towns and border areas to bury unknown passengers who risked the treachery of navigation mark our complicity in the production of invisibility. The nameless passengers seem to have so little "human weight" that their lives end without our indignation, acknowledgement, or intervention. Perhaps this is a legacy of the *herrenvolk*, a Kantianism according reciprocal access to full humanity only to those who constitute the master class of personhood. The nameless, colorless inhabitants of the normative world are accorded mutual respect, a right to self-determination, a right to live freely and on equal footing in the world community, while other subpersons trek through deserts and sea lanes and hide in the backs of trailer trucks struggling to attain the most basic contours of a life and a living wage.[46]

We can no longer write ourselves out of history, representation, or theory because we are all implicated in the politics of representation. Neither can we privilege our theories of the present as just one more attempt at catching a glimpse of the moment of complexity in which we are all immersed, the photographer in the mirror. If, to follow the new metaphor, we are all inside the frame, if the new group portrait is to include not only us but in a sense the horse we rode in on, we must in some measure account for our most taken-for-granted convictions—the ground on which we stand as theorists, activists, and scholars. If these convictions are to be the theoretical and methodological tools (reflexivity, ideology, vision, distinctions, ethnography) we are to work with, we must hold this new vision of our practices up to the light. Anthropologist Kristen Hastrup in *A Passage to Anthropology: Between Experience and Theory* (1995) eloquently points to the anthropologists' situated practices in which we become both an "objectified figure" to those among whom we work and helplessly lost in "our intricate implication in the world," a place in which our experience becomes our gateway to ethnography (1995, 51).[47] This book is an attempt to do just that, employing the anthropology of invisibility and diaspora as units of analysis, but in a wide conceptual frame in which an idea of navigation helps us to get at some of the historical legacies of the experience of diaspora.

CHAPTER 1

A Nonracial Education

On Navigating Diaspora, Anti-Black Caricature,
and Anthropology

> Every mimetic text can be shown to have left something out
> of the description of its object or to have put something into
> it that is inessential to what *some* reader, with more or less
> authority, will regard as an adequate description. On analysis,
> every mimesis can be shown to be distorted and can serve,
> therefore, as an occasion for yet another description of
> the same phenomenon, one claiming to be more realistic,
> more "faithful to the facts."
>
> —HAYDEN WHITE, *TROPICS OF DISCOURSE:*
> *ESSAYS IN CULTURAL CRITICISM*

In Lieu of an Autoethnography: A Word from the Camera Shy

Autobiography lurks in the background of almost every anthropological
enterprise. This is a "social fact" one often discovers by chance. For me, it
was in the odd inherited carpet in the apartment of an African/European
anthropologist, linking him and his "people" to the imagined geography
of his lineage. Or the aside during a talk that firmly located an ethnographer in her social world through the mention of some personal detail—
a claim to a membership in some privileged order—or the colorful story
from the field when x did y, the story ending in a telling childhood
memory. It's not that anthropologists don't talk about themselves, dance
"native dances," don exotic clothing, and recount drinking stories that
mark their breakthrough or close call with the dangers of the field. They
do; it's just that this is rarely done out in the open or in public. When it
is *done*, it almost always comes as an afterthought, an accessory to status,

or a moment of discovery along the way to professional mastery—and this is for the run-of-the-mill anthropologist. Now add race, gender, and social class to the mix, and you begin to get a very complex soup in which self-making cannot be taken for granted and the politics of representation and the crafting of subjectivities are cross-cut by social classification, power, and the arbitrary inflections of history. That is to say, the notion of autoethnography still makes me nervous.

The work of "vision and division," as the late Pierre Bourdieu once called it, or the particular arrangement of perceptions and principles that inform the manner in which we structure and envision the social world, come into play for the anthropologist even before entering the "field" (Bourdieu 1998). Although the profile of the field worker has changed to some degree, there is still a veneer of "authority" and the élan that seems to hover over the emergent anthropologist. For the most part, this studied self confidence seems to mask fear rather than the decided arrogance of my generation on the way to "the field." Modernity, in part, and the ideal of a unitary cultural and economic development leveling the face of the world has resulted in the loss of the traditional anthropological object: the savage, the quintessential "other." I doubt that many would-be anthropologists sit around trading stories about the potential and dreaded diseases that await them in the field. Even the squatter and nowadays the urban poor and homeless must be treated with a modicum of dignity. Early anthropology was invested in the exploration of these other "savage"-infested worlds, only to discover out there the great unity of humankind, people in the end like "us." The exotics out there have given way to exotics that are now found on our doorsteps. The peoples who anthropologists once went to the ends of the earth to find now run the local laundromat, tend to the neighbor's children, and work in a nearby factory. Distance no longer reveals its mystery or contains it. The Bongobongo have moved in across the street, forcing a general rethinking of identity, location, and community etiquette (Trouillot 2003). This is the state of the art of anthropology today; the anthropologist is no longer the fly on the wall, but a full participant in the toss and tumble of the globe. I have always loved the description of this new state of things in the work of my friend and anthropologist Michel-Rolph Trouillot, as he captures the preoccupation of the anthropologist of the old order with the "portrait of the world" as it should appear in clearly identifiable and static "cultures" fixed in stable geographies. Trouillot says this anthropologist cannot quite figure out why people no longer wish to talk to him or her to help to orchestrate the "vision" of their experience, which he or she holds like a talisman in the mind's eye:

> His favorite model has disappeared or, when found, refuses to pose as expected. The fieldworker examines his tools and finds his camera inadequate. Most importantly, his very field of vision now seems blurred. Yet he needs to come back home with a picture. It's pouring rain out there, and the mosquitoes are starting to bite. In desperation, the baffled anthropologist burns his notes to create a moment of light, moves his face against the flame, closes his eyes and, hands grasping the camera, takes a picture of himself. (Trouillot 2003, 24)

The surgical strike of the anthropologist, facilitated by the instrument of choice, the camera, begins by attempting to capture the real world out there and ends by reflecting the workings of its own somewhat confused mind. Trouillot has recently noted that anthropology may be in search of a new object, because "a discipline whose object is the Other may in fact have no object" (27). The privileged space of enlightenment, from which all others in limited cultural worlds appeared to be in need of the light of our modernity—liberalism, advanced economies, and knowledge— is a myth that must die with the savage (Trouillot 2003). Of course, this complicates matters, as the differences between our culture and others cannot be explained merely by the contours and dissimilarities of our "cultural logic" and symbolic systems, but rather must be sought after in the legacy of principles of division and the continued workings of patterns of inequality. The visage of the anthropologist has always seemed a bit odd: the self-exiled professional expatriate, the lone fierce-eyed foreigner with unnamed and unknown modern preoccupations. But all this is getting ahead of my story. I will return to the management of the image of the anthropologist and the "other."

Marooned

As an African American male, I suppose I have had the benefit of the production of derogatory images that have in part shaped my experience (see Fanon 1967a). I am aware of the dangers of image making, but I also think that image making in anthropology needs to be investigated more closely. I wish to exercise the part of anthropology that provides a critical lens on the history of image making and the contemporary deployment of images in the world today.

When I was a graduate student at the University of Chicago, there was on the mezzanine level of Haskell Hall, where the department of anthropology was located, a massive map of the world. Pins covered arbitrary points on the world map; next to them were pictures of the students in the field. Most depicted the would-be anthropologists with their "people." When I was in the field, the office staff would send periodic inquiries about my picture, a picture I could never bring myself to send in. I could never bring myself to this very colonial mentality of representing myself and the work I conducted with Senegalese and Italians as a photo opportunity, an embodiment of the practice of the art of anthropology. Many of the photographs on the wall of infamy, and I must admit my estimation of those who sent in their pictures diminished considerably (albeit influenced in part by my graduate student angst), contained students in "native" garb, navigating rivers with their "people," shopping in local markets, or standing in front of villagers' homes. Having evidence of the exercise of "being there," happily situated among people whose "other culture," would justify the making of a monograph, a rite of passage of the professional anthropologist. I hoped the office staff would chalk up the absence of my photograph to the exigencies of international mail, or to my being camera shy. I am of course camera shy, but that has little to do with it.

On the face of it, it was just a photograph, I suppose. But as an African American, for me an entire visual regime haunted the image I might produce for that wall. Artist and art historian Michael D. Harris in *Colored Pictures: Race and Visual Representation* (2003) entreats his readers to consider the African American experience through the interrogation of contemporary and historical racially encoded images. Even the work of contemporary artists like Kara Walker cannot completely escape the legacy of black caricature and the sediment it has left in even the most mundane image making for people of African descent in the New World.[1] The weight of recursive "derogatory images" presenting the black body, and the visual repertoire these images have helped to create, effectively mediate image making in the present. This, according to Harris, places a burden on the artist, as it does on the ordinary people of an imagined black community, the inheritors of a racially encoded universe. The "we" that Harris invokes is this "community," qualified by the term "black" and divided by generation, social class, and other distinctions:

> The momentum of over 150 years of derogatory images
> and characterization flowed down on our heads with real
> consequences because white power enforced and depended on
> black racial identity. We reinvented ourselves repeatedly to resist
> and frustrate the oppressive systems and representations that
> circumscribed us collectively, acting on the belief that we either
> became co-producers or might change the worldview by our
> actions. We re-presented ourselves to counter the other form of
> representation—the substitute or stand-in—that amounted to
> misrepresentation rather than a proxy. (Harris 2003, 9)

The black body remained during this evolution a crucial site of the struggle over representation, and although the names and systems of classification that denote the black body as a visual sign or site in a racialized society have changed through time, the meanings associated with its place in racial ideology and practice remain relatively stable. That is, the social categories of perception that produced derogatory systems of representation in the past are still available for deployment. To inhabit this body, the "African/[national qualifier]/black body," as Michael D. Harris notes, "even today, at the beginning of the twenty-first century, can have dire consequences" (2003, 9). But there is the question of this "we" that stands in for a community of people housed under the term "black," a latter-day term to denote a kind of global solidarity, a translocal recognition of the linkages of the African diaspora. The meaning and nature of this connection for the people who must wear it on their skin, so to speak, is never clear, unmediated, or straightforward. What it means for my generation, for me, or for the Senegalese I meet in Italy may be completely different, mediated by location, historical accident, colonialism, various forms of belonging (caste, class, national), and experience. I will return to the issue of Afrocentric discussion later in another potential rendering of the notion of "community."

Hazel V. Carby in *Race Men* (1998) examines black masculinity refracted through meditations on the work of W. E. B. Du Bois. In a chapter entitled "The Body and Soul of Modernism," Carby explores the manner in which the actor, singer, and political activist Paul Robeson was depicted in early film and photographic work, including the work of Eugene O'Neill, photographer Nickolas Muray, and filmmaker Kenneth Macpherson. Caught in the modernist gaze of the artist, the black body became a site for the interplay of the "contradictory desires of the modern age"; at the same time, the actual brutal ceremony of lynching was being enacted in the nation at large. Yet in the world of the mind and in art, black masculinity also represented "tropes of utopian possibility" (Carby 2003, 47), affording a ritual resolution of modern problems through the elaboration of an essentially purified and primitive masculinity. The black body—the body of Robeson—was crafted into an ideal of the modernist aesthetic, portraying the Negro male body outside of time, as a site of the potentially dangerous forces, a "malleable black masculinity" fitted to the desires and needs of others (73). Black masculinity is seen through the internal tensions and violence of the self rather than through an interrogation of the forces acting upon them. Robeson came to personify this explosive and broken troubled male.

In this vision, women were absent and the rigid codes of masculinity precluded the play of egalitarianism in the domain of race. Yet the "dissecting gaze" of the black body in exhibition halls, movie theaters, and modern stages foreshadowed a displacement of the world of ordinary black subjects facing the real tensions of a racialized world. As the specter of lynching shadowed the modernist performance, so does a wider experience of racism and exclusion cast its shadow on our lives today. As Carby notes, for what she calls "postmodern times," the representation of black masculinity is a small part of a much greater set of contemporary problems:

> If the spectacle of the lynched black body haunts the modern
> age, then the slow disintegration of black bodies and souls in jail,
> urban ghettos, and beleaguered schools haunts our postmodern
> times. (Carby 1998, 2)

According to bell hooks, "stereotypes of black masculinity overdetermine" the self-fashioning of young black males today (2004, xii). The principles that guide image making are historically constituted and are therefore arbitrary in a Saussurean sense; that is, they have become a part of a conventional visual regime and its reproduction. The cycle of image creation is never unmediated by other distinctions, traditions, or the play of power relations.

Injecting race into images is of course only part of the problem; some images never come before us at all, so we are not confronted with them in the regular course of our lives. I grew up in a time when if a black political figure or celebrity appeared on the television, a host of phone calls would cycle around, alerting the unaware that "we" were on TV. The images were often framed by crisis, or mediated by parody, or so fleeting as to be easily missed. Much of this has changed, and yet blackness is almost always marked as an event, as we still have black leaders, politicians, and scholars. Rarely does the black body go unqualified in the mainstream media. For that matter, when I think of an image of the boat people that I have seen in the local papers, very few have what we might make out as families; there are no images of parents clutching their children for dear life on the edge of a makeshift craft tossed on the open sea. No, this would play to our sympathy. Instead we see would-be migrants handcuffed and humiliated, rushed into waiting police transports, or scaling fences to enter the country on the nightly news while a voiceover of a trusted news anchor talks about the loss of American jobs, the cost of human trafficking, or the decline of the American way of life.

Reflexivity begins at home. As anthropologist Kristen Hastrup points out in *A Passage to Anthropology: Between Experience and Theory* (1995), the work of reflexivity and relativity are fundamental to the practice of ethnography. "The reality of anthropology," she writes, "is constituted in a relationship of continuity between the ethnographer and the world" (49). Although many of my interests developed out of my own experiences growing up in a racialized society, I, like other anthropologists, have taken up similar issues in foreign lands. Some of the processes of exclusion and of the deployment of what I will call "invisibility" are similar to those I experienced in the United States, but the context and the nature of the rapidly changing world have put a new spin on problems such as these. In fact, the kind of anthropology I practice is related to my background; when I first began to sit down to talk with Senegalese in Italy, I found that they often knew more than I did about the details of African American politics and the careers of prominent North American figures. It was at times their desire to learn more and to understand the experience of racism in North America that animated our early encounters. Although I began working with the Senegalese through a chance encounter at a stall selling towels in the Porto Palazzo marketplace in Turin, my curiosity about Africans in Europe lead me to continue this relationship. I also did so due to the climate in Turin, beginning in 1989, as an awareness of the growing presence of migrant groups began to surface in the world of politics and as people on the street began to be courted by the first articulations of anti-immigrant rhetoric and images. In this climate, I too was a potential target and continued to be identified as "out of place" in Italian society. This peculiar positioning and its consequences are something I share and explore with the Senegalese and others.

Being, in the words of Mary Douglas, "out of place" in a land foreign to me is however always related to similar experiences at home, where I am somewhat "exotic." In my hometown of Oakland, California, I lived only a few city blocks from the city limits, which bisect a neighborhood that goes from black to all white in less than a block. The only public park within walking distance was on the other side of the city border in San Leandro. I would often take a walk in the evening down to the park, circling back around through a residential area along a main street, and I was often stopped by police, sometimes at gunpoint, who would ask what I was doing there and other similar questions. I would tell them I was a student (a safe social status) and get my identification, moving as if in slow motion. Once an officer had the presence of mind to ask if I was a law student; I laughed, and they put their guns away when I suggested they follow me home. There had been a break in somewhere in the area, they informed me, and the person they were looking for matched my description. Sometimes I wondered how they could even get the words out. Didn't these things seem absurd even to them? Most of the time, I try to forget about these things. I note the reactions of my students when I tell them about one of these incidents. I realize that for some it seems to come from another world, another order of reality.

My favorite anecdote is the story of when my cousin Russell and I were driving back to his house after making a run to Flints on East 14th in East Oakland. He had a greasy bag of barbecue in his lap as he drove and I was holding his son in my arms (this was before there were child car seats). As we entered the driveway, police cars cut off our retreat on two sides—blocked the street, tires screeching—and several officers raced toward the car with guns drawn. One threw open the car door, and my cousin looked up and said, "John, is that you?" and laughter echoed through the streets. My cousin knew the officer from the police academy. We fit "the description" and of course, no one could see the baby, the fast food, or the fact that we were not the alleged criminals in flight, just two men driving while black. Although these imaginary internal borders may fade in importance according to generation, gender, and class, young people in selected parts of the country still experience similar incidents at gunpoint. These trials, however, still rest within a privileged national context where other kinds of battles wait at the borders (international). We will turn to these in a moment.

Blackness as a Site of Possibilities .

Not long ago I picked up my daughter Eliana from her summer camp and the young woman student teacher told me that Eliana had been talking to her about how she missed her grandmother's gumbo. I miss it too. Gumbo is at the heart of family ceremony and special occasions often include the sharing of this dish. Although gumbo includes many ingredients—crab, chicken, sausage, and a host of seasonings, amongst others—it is the roux that makes a good gumbo and renders the proper consistency and flavor. When someone makes a gumbo in the family, everyone is invited to come and share the meal. It becomes is own occasion, especially now that some of us have moved elsewhere. In his film *Black Is . . . Black Ain't*, (1995) gay poet and filmmaker Marlon Riggs, who spent a lifetime charting black popular culture in American society, produced his last work while struggling with AIDS. Some scenes show Riggs in his hospital bed discussing the conclusion of the film with his collaborators. The devastating social impact of AIDS on the black community, the continuing battles surrounding identity claims, and the authenticity of the film are embodied in the film by Riggs himself lying in his hospital bed defying those who might exclude him from the world of black folk. Riggs crafted a film that takes on the many centers of exclusionary practices that separate black folk from one another, including the legacy of sexism, racial ideology, homophobia, cultural nationalism, and patriarchy. Riggs's film also takes on black institutions such as the church, political culture, and the family as sites of exclusionary discourse. In the film, Riggs elaborates and dismisses many of the myths and points of divergence in black communities, from skin color to hair texture to relations between the generations and dance. At the heart of the film is an attempt to construct an inclusive blackness, a site more open to potentiality than locked into traditions that have served only to construct divisions within the community. Riggs fixes on the trope of a gumbo, a dish named for the okra that it contains and associated with New Orleans, to illustrate the great diversity of blackness. Central scenes show Riggs in the kitchen with his grandmother making gumbo. E. Patrick Johnson in his book *Appropriating Blackness: Performance and the Politics of Authenticity* (2003) points out that the gumbo trope in Riggs's film opens a new vista for the inclusion of the manner in which blackness comes to be envisioned:

> This trope also underscores that multiplicity of blackness insofar as gumbo is associated with New Orleans, a city confounded by its mixed raced progeny and the identity politics that mixing creates. The gumbo trope is apropos because, like "blackness," gumbo is a site of possibilities. The film argues that when black Americans attempt to define what it means to be black, they delimit the possibilities of what blackness can be. At times, this process of demarcating blackness may be counterproductive to the flavor of the roux that acts as the base of the gumbo that is "blackness." (Johnson 2003, 19)

Riggs's film calls for a recognition that blackness is in North American society a kind of site of possibilities, a canvas on which various potential ways of being are projected. Beyond this, Riggs entreats us to accept not only the differences we acknowledge in the present but potential modes of diversity that may emerge in the future.

Popular representations of "folk" culture or the authenticity of "African" links to New World communities support different takes on the contemporary nature of blackness in society. The struggle is to allow a range of potential ways of representing blackness to emerge some-how, beyond the confines of the caricatures of blackness overdeter-mined by the parade of derogatory images. In the work of bell hooks, black masculinity is seen as a site that must from one generation to the next be extricated from the residue of regimes of representation of the past: "Negative stereotypes about the nature of black masculinity continue to overdetermine the identities black males are allowed to fashion for themselves" (hooks 2004, xii). The confrontation of cultural domination for Fanon was an all-or-nothing proposition. At the very core of this thought was the critique of Western civility launched by Aimé Césaire in his work *Discourse on Colonialism* (1955), which questioned the commitment to human solidarity, equality, and morality (hooks 2000). In this new twist, universal injustice is executed according to the underlying rationale of the colonial order. Anywhere was an affront to people everywhere; at one point, Fanon writes, "Every one of my silences, every one of my cowardices reveals me as a man" (1967a, 89). Following Karl Jaspers's conception of "metaphysical guilt," Fanon insists, however, that the theological justification of such solidarity is not necessary, as one need not appeal to a God in order to feel a common cause with the "other," because a common ground is integral to the very nature of being a part of humankind (1967a).

Even a cursory examination of media representations of hip-hop culture in the United States reveals a curious and ambiguous relationship to the black body, as a parade of young men and women appear as sites of pleasure, consumption, and potential violence. In some measure, as sexism has relegated women's images to an all but spectral presence and a marker of desire as a commodity, black males have increasingly underwritten the stereotype as a vector of violence in "lived experience" rhetoric and image. Cultural critic bell hooks in *We Real Cool: Black Men and Masculinity* (2004) hovers between cynicism and despair in her analysis of the state of the young black men in North America:

> Nowadays in the imperialist white-supremacist capitalist patriarch culture, most boys from poor and underprivileged classes are socialized via mass media and class-based education to believe that all that is required for their survival is the ability to do physical labor. Black boys, disproportionately numbered among the poor, have been socialized to believe that physical strength and stamina are all that really matter. That socialization is as much in place in today's world as it was during slavery. Groomed to remain permanent members of an underclass, groomed to be without choice and therefore ready to kill for the state in wars whenever needed, black males without class privilege have always been targeted for mis-education. They have been and are taught

that "thinking" is not valuable labor, that "thinking" will not help
them survive. Tragically, many black males have not resisted this
socialization. It is no accident that many brilliant-thinking black
males end up imprisoned, for even as boys, they were deemed
threatening, bad, and dangerous. (hooks 2004, 34)

Being socialized as a harbinger of violence has consequences, and
once coupled with sexism, such training provides a link to a counterfeit
of the masculine power of the dominant social order. However, hooks
cautions against this identification, as it must remain illusory, masking
the repressive order of a backward-looking masculinity. "Not to understand neocolonialism is not to live fully in the present," hooks notes;
abandoning masculinity to this subterranean and unreflective violence
may offer up another generation to the invisibility of prisons, urban
poverty, and social isolation (60).

Understanding the legacy of historical forms of cultural domination
in the present is in fact the avocation of Fanon's project, as understanding colonial domination "includes not only the interrelations of objective
historical conditions but also human attitudes toward these conditions"
(Fanon 1967a, 84). The impulse of Fanon is to examine the ideological
architecture of racism, as it crafts a separate "reality" for those who are
placed beyond the reach of official history. The stereotypes in the flight of
fantasy of a particular cultural logic are the essence of the operations of
the politics of invisibility. In the work of Fanon, those who thoughtlessly
carried out the work of the colonialist order were the worst kind of mon-
sters. Turning not only against their own interest but that of those with
whom they shared the common bond of subject hood, like the colonial
soldier, they embodied one of the most degraded and alienated position
in this social order. For Fanon, in a curious way the Senegalese soldier embodied the ultimate stereotype of the brute: a black masculinity
turned against itself and its people, glossed by natural violence and per-
versity. This same type of representation hooks locates at the heart of
"white-supremacist capitalist patriarchy" in the contemporary world:

Seen as animals, brutes, natural-born rapists, and murderers,
black men have had no real dramatic say when it comes to the
way they are represented. They have made few interventions
on the stereotype. As a consequence they are victimized by

> stereotypes. . . . Black males who refuse categorization are rare,
> for the price of visibility in the contemporary world of white
> supremacy is that the black male identity be defined in relation
> to the stereotype whether by embodying it or seeking to be other
> than it. (hooks 2004, xii)

Seeking an identity beyond the stereotypes also involves confronting the legacy of invisibility. What does it mean to "refuse categorization," as classification is something that goes on without one's consent, and such classifications are found as already-complete artifacts of one's circumstances? In order to resist, one would have to—like political activist Paul Robeson—step away from the modernist workshop in search of a more direct channel of expression, or confront the very nature of the production of black caricature in the manner of Fanon and others. It seems there is no neutral posture.

A Nonracial Education

Sometimes, situating the past is a way of imagining a possible future, or of sweeping away the dust and residue of a representation manufactured under conditions not of one's choosing through the substitution of a new or alternative vision of the present. In the African diasporic imagination, the idea of Africa has always been a rich source of such invention. When I was a graduate student at the University of Chicago, my advisor Bernard Cohn once remarked that I had had "a nonracial education," meaning in part that my interest in the Italian communist party, Gramsci, and a generation of Southern Italian workers was weighted one way or another by the fact of my being African American. At the time, I had no idea what exactly he was saying to me; I was polite, and shifted the conversation to the examination of European political affiliation. But the idea has always disturbed me. What was the notion of anthropology that made this fact matter at the level of ideas? Not that it mattered to Barney Cohn; he was only trying to warn me, as I discovered later. On more than one occasion, I faced interrogations by senior black anthropologists who wanted to know why I had studied Europe instead of Africa, when it was clear (although not to me) that the problem was to control the study of Africa. One anthropologist in particular, a luminary of African scholarship, has made it his duty to point out my lack of proper Afrocentric fervor. As I entered into the world of the mind from a working-class background, it seemed a place to have truly no boundaries; somehow I still believe it was what Fanon might have called freedom. In *Freedom Dreams: The Black Radical Imagination* (2002), Robin D. G. Kelley considers the almost obsessive preoccupation of Afrocentrists of the 1960s and 1970s with ancient African "civilizations, or kingdoms"—societies that might contain a hint of life before European presence. The search was for an Africa that could form the basis for any number of visions of a place beyond racism, social and economic isolation, and—perhaps more importantly—a space where cultural traditions and practices could be imbued with temporal depth through the "redemptive" value of an ancient world and the ancestors who once inhabited it:

> We looked back in search of a better future. We wanted to find a refuge where "black people" exercised power, possessed essential knowledge, educated the West, built monuments, slept under the stars on the banks of the Nile, and never had to worry about the police or poverty or arrogant white people questioning our intelligence. Of course, this meant conveniently ignoring slave labor, class hierarchies, and women's oppression, and it meant projecting backwards in time a twentieth-century conception of race, but to simply criticize us for myth making or essentialism misses the point of our reading. We dreamed the ancient world as a place of freedom, a picture to imagine what we desired and what was possible.... More importantly, we began to see ourselves—as earlier generations of black intellectuals had—as part of an African diaspora, an oppressed "nation" without a homeland. (Kelley 2002, 15)

Envisioning a place in the African diaspora certainly depends on the nature of our reading, meaning the state of play in a particular community at a particular point in time and shaped in whole or in part by the nature of the materials—of cultural ideology close at hand. What Kelley describes as the recognition of becoming a part of a greater "nation" without a homeland also depends on the everyday practices of ordinary people. I remember the conflicts of this same period in my working-class home, where my parents had the viewpoint that they had spent all their lives becoming Americans. One day my father said, about one of the many Afrocentric ministers traveling the country at the time: "He says he is from Africa, but that so-and-so is just from Detroit." For my father, born just after the turn of the century, the idea of "Ethiopia" still held some reverence, but anything that seemed to exploit black people through the use of the power of "Africa" was suspect in my parents' eyes. My father, who remembered talking to former slaves, felt that African Americans had a "right" to be Americans derived from the struggles of the "race" in North America. The thought of being connected with Africa was rejected not only because the primary experience (for us) of African Americans was situated in North America but also because of the feelings of entitlement this experience promised. This promise of being considered an integral part of the American context perhaps remains still unfulfilled—a kind of pragmatism that conceived of Africa only as a kind of transcendent reality. As the civil rights and black power movements dovetailed, the conversion of the image of Africa slowly began to emerge in popular culture, yet much of the popular register was occupied by "mythic" images of Africa through film, fable, and television. The few television programs that contained black actors garnered great attention: *Julia, I Spy,* and various variety shows. By the time I became involved with the Oakland ensemble theater, I found the roles for black actors were still so poor that many of those on TV used their spare time to perform, direct, and contribute to local theater companies. I found among the dancers, actors, directors, and technical folk a passion for African American theater and poetry; the theater produced a "black version" of *Richard III* for an audience often unfamiliar with such high cultural products. People yelled out from the audience, "Kill him, kill him!" during the performance, talking back to the actors onstage just as if they were talking back to the television screen. No one was ever jolted out of character; after all, it was a black production, accustomed to the unexpected in a neighborhood where the police were afraid to patrol.

Wilson Jeremiah Moses in *Afrotopia: The Roots of African American Popular History* outlined a minimal take on Afrocentrism as "a belief that the African ancestry of black peoples, regardless of where they live, is an inescapable element of their various identities—imposed both from within and from without their own communities," and has argued for the great historical and ideological diversity of this notion (Moses 1998, 6). Afrocentrism represents, according to Moses, a kind of porous tradition, one to which the early anthropology of such figures as Boas, Malinowski, and Herskovits contributed greatly. Of these anthropologists, I have always found Boas the most fascinating, as not only was his treatment of race a central preoccupation of his work, but also his activism and promotion of black and Jewish scholars offstage was a complement to his academic work. I will not take this opportunity to register my anthropological objections to each of the authors' use of African material, but note that each dealt with an exotic, elusive object, linking it to the present and its ethnographic/historical essence, and the authors are (as Moses suggests) "Afrocentrist" in a sense. For Moses, Afrocentrist writers and scholars "manipulate history and myth, poetry and art, folklore and religious tradition, regardless of authorship, in ways sympathetic to African peoples" (11). Indeed, we could continue the link in anthropological and historical writing on such topics as African ritual and religious tradition or for the African diaspora work, linking societies of slaves or former slaves in the new world with African practices and locations (Moses 1998; see also Mudimbe 1988).

When I say Afrocentrism, I am talking here about a kind of concern in part with a redemptive image of Africa that incorporated any number of ideological supports, from Eastern spiritualism to Maoist theory, and that was in my experience mostly a product of black folk culture and also infused with an emergent awareness of black cultural heritage and achievements. It was the engagement of local issues and community involvement—in part through the Panther party and other organizations—that marshaled an image of black cultural pride and resistance. For the police, it seemed that all black youth with black leather jackets were Panthers—I never owned such a jacket (but I borrowed one from my cousin). It was more than a fashion statement or the reckoning of the historical achievements of black people we had heard before; it was rather a confrontation of the police, a declaration of strength that struck a different chord. It was also the idea of a plan for black community education, programs to ensure children received breakfast and lunch at school, and empowerment. The violence of the party would lead it to implode and send its strange circle of leaders in other directions, and the legacy of an internal "Afrochauvinism" marked the real workings of the movement (Moses 1998). As a young person without such insider knowledge, I could at the time imagine other trajectories.

My other encounters with a more positive engagement with Afrocentric ideology came in my early years of college, through early Vietnam-era veterans who had entered the educational system, the political activism of the Bay Area's many college student centers, and American Friends Service Committee events. And of course, the political dimensions of a kind of Afrocentric ideology were present in the Black Panther party agenda, an organization I followed from a distance. Growing up in Oakland, the rhetoric of the Panther party about the careful eye and activities of the police first appealed to many young people, as being stopped and questioned by the police was a fairly regular part of our lives. But it was really my work in Italian literature and language that lead me to African matters. As a student in Italy in the late 1970s, I was introduced for the first time to African students, and I found they had an interest in blacks in the United States and elsewhere. Although my academic interests lead me elsewhere, into the labyrinthine world of Italian politics and literature, my notion of "Africa" and my experience of being part of a diaspora remained underdeveloped. It was not really until I began to work with Senegalese in Italy that the relationship of Africa and its diaspora again began to formally preoccupy me. I found that my students at Johns Hopkins University had rarely had the opportunity to view films directed by African directors and had only recently been exposed to African writers and poets. The same is true, I am afraid, of other locations and archipelagos. Indeed, in American popular culture and in much of the educational system, the exotic is largely filler, a background to the triumphant movement of the West. African Americans seem to have appeared in history twice: once as slaves and again as the background to the civil rights movement. I found that in order to talk about the Senegalese in Italy and the difficulties they faced, I had to first recast notions of American racial denial and ambivalence. It seemed to be easier for students to grapple with intolerance elsewhere once they had learned to use their acute concern on racial, gender, and ethnic differences—tuned to the North American context and largely dormant as a tool—for the analysis of social isolation, discrimination, and class inequity over there.

As with anything of this nature, this reevaluation was a process noted in the course of lives rather than academic years. I suppose I am inspired by the late Edward Said and hope for a more inclusive version of "our reading," one that might serve as the basis for a confrontation with selected sites of erasure. It is hard to open up to the idea of allowing "diverse and heterogeneous subjectivities" to occupy a place in an imagined "common ground," and much easier to constrain others for want of a shared cultural world to "prolong their difference and marginality," in a kind of historical elsewhere (Radhakrishnan 1996, 87).

Navigating Diaspora

The haunting 1995 work of Mary Gardner *Boat People: A Novel* charts the lives of the Vietnamese refugee community in Galveston, Texas, as the newcomers navigate their American urban experience, at times relying on the advice of African American neighbors. The memory of the sea passage is never completely forgotten. The legacy of the passage lingers in the newcomers' lives like a spirit world that shadows the present: "There were many days. I think the compass was broken. Then one morning we saw another boat. There were birds too, white ones, and they sailed above our boat like its soul" (Gardner 1995, 110). In our consideration of African diaspora, it is often difficult to find a proper compass, as we have seen. The desire to pluck from the past an empowering symbolic element that might somehow empower a vision of the present remains an illusory, though compelling, notion—to somehow harmonize our path with the purity of an exemplary voyage, as if we can find our way in the present through the passage of an ancient mariner skilled in a now-forgotten art of navigation. This idea lurks in the heart of all Afrocentrism.

The navigation of diaspora is complicated by the trope of the transport, the boat, the plane, the train, the notion of travel, and the state of displacement as the *sine qua non* of diaspora. If the navigation was what was privileged, we would have a different animal, and that is what I am suggesting here: it is the trace of the voyage and not the *process* that is often emphasized, an event that results in a kind of exile often termed "displacement." Its tales now fill the pages of our newspapers, inhabiting the corners of our cities, waiting there for a future in which we might divine its signs and learn its hidden meanings. These tales, like the valued objects of a smuggler, lay in wait for the consciousness that can unlock them. They are in the West African recordings of the reading of the Koran that blare out on Italian side streets, rivaling the strains of Jimi Hendrix favored by the local youth, or the raising of the hand to the head by a young Senegalese trader in Manhattan greeting a friend, or the "structure of feeling," which, perhaps centuries after touching down to earth, results in a contemporary expression of identity, solidarity, or creativity (Williams 1978, 132). And what of the daily forms of interchange and compassion that elicit no material forms, no objective indexical coordinates, but rather sets of relationships, longings, and familial and extrafamilial networks and rituals? Aren't these the ceremonies carefully observed by migrants in a rundown part of a foreign city, the moments of redemption we might be looking for, the making of new worlds amid the ruins of the old? How does this symbolic commerce enter our world, informing our understanding of "other cultures"?

Do diasporas exist only in the stories we tell about them and they tell us, or do they exist also in history? Certainly few—with the exception of the Haitian community—speak of themselves as being in "diaspora"; until recently that notion captured a certain vision of the modern black, a small group at best. The "telling" of the story of the diaspora, of the experience of being the "other," has become so important that the notion is at times projected backward in time, allowing other cultures that occupied a privileged discursive position in the past to lay the groundwork for an alternative modernity in the present. Indeed, although we might include early black pioneers in the sweep of diaspora, these inaugural figures of black culture—founding towns, laying brick, and forming trade unions—may not have thought of themselves as part of the black diaspora. Many assuredly did not.[2]

The critical site of intervention remains the field of representations in which counterhegemonic presentations confront this great weight of dominant cultural discourse. For Fanon, colonial language is the tool of an order that must be shattered in order for the colonized to "take cognizance of a possibility of existence" by attending to the power and "social structures" holding the system in place (Fanon 1968, 100). But the very nature of being "overdetermined" also provides the potential to shatter old ways of viewing the subject by exploiting the arbitrary nature of both subjectivity and representational regimes.

I suggest that anthropology could employ a new "dialectics of experience," engaging these emergent worlds born out of the ruins of history and perhaps finding on some new terrain a smuggled identity. That is, the search for a "cultural core," or the essence of a distant radical tradition, is a kind of politics of experience deployed at times to frame an experience or group that has been marginalized, devalued, and rendered invisible. It is here in the timeless space of history that a hint of the pan-African identity is often sought out. Yet it is perhaps in part an error to set aside a place so remote or pristine, as if it existed beyond the world, slavery, and colonialism, or to look for resistance as a redemption of a present in need of a noble tradition, a past it can claim. Of course we might say the idea of negritude, an awareness of African cultural heritage and the cultivation of positive evaluations of global black culture both ideological and aesthetic, is a kind of innovative use of the culture concept. In a paper on the relationship between the African diaspora and pan-Africanism entitled "The Meaning of Negritude: The Negro's Stake in Africa" (1964), St. Clair Drake selected the poem *Like a Strong Tree* by Claude McKay, a figure often associated with the Harlem Renaissance, in order to point to the contradictory and complex relationship between the figure of Africa, Africans, and the people of the diaspora:

> So let us live in rich imperial growth
> Touching the surface and the depth of things
> Instantly responsive unto both
> Tasting the sweets of beings and the stings
> Sensing the subtle spell of changing forms.
>
> (McKay 2008, 209)

"Claude McKay would always describe himself as the son of the Jamaican peasantry," and many of his images are drawn from the life and work of the people of the rural communities in which he grew up before leaving the island (James 2000, 11). Although there are dangers in the genealogical metaphor, there is an emphasis on the nature of an organic process here and an appreciation for the life of the people and the struggles and achievements they attend. "Tasting the sweets of beings and the stings/Sensing the subtle spell of changing forms"; and it is this process, the "dialectics of alterity," that we must explore. The poem emphasizes the process of becoming rather than the search for origins, and it is—as the poet seems to suggest—through innovation, creativity, and resilience (if not resistance) that black cultures can be discovered. The poem no doubt expresses, in part, McKay's disappointment in the failure of the leadership of black intellectuals, but he looked forward to what could be a sable and vibrant global community (Helbling 1973). McKay, in his early work, draws heavily on the ordinary lives of people in his native Jamaica; although credited with being an inspiration and font for many Négritude writers affirming the beauty of blackness, this early work contains little references to the notion of an "Africa homeland" (130).

It is an old anthropological aphorism that we see ourselves vis-à-vis the other. "To speak a language," Fanon once wrote, "is to take on a world, a culture" (1968, 38). Social exclusion is often, but not the only tool of the established. William E. Connolly suggests a tendency for both "old and new identities to fundamentalize what they are by demonizing what they are not" (1996). In many societies, the play of exclusion proceeds through "freezing or exoticizing 'alterity' and 'difference' into a mystique" (Radhakrishnan 1996, 87). Ascription of others' social status is part of the process by which the world is made intelligible and assumes a given order. In a sense, we live both in and through the systems of classification we make and those we inherit, which have become a part of our circumstance through the accident of birth in a particular time and place. However the nature and dimension of this other is not set for all time, but is arbitrary and transitive like the features of a language. In the language of identity formation, alterity has become a crucial site of self-construction. Through this very language, we come to the frontier of common ground and formulate the absolutes of otherness.[3]

Fanon wrote in *Black Skin White Masks* that "I am overdetermined from without," as the great weight of the historical construction of race imprisons the "other" in its unfolding logic (1967a, 116). The "infernal circle" of misrecognition, as Fanon calls it, and the "being" of the other must be confronted through an articulation of the self—a self unmediated by dominant discourse as body, ancestry, or race. For Fanon, "there remained only one solution: to make myself known," to provide other forms of representation, one of the steps "that might make knowing possible" (115), or, as bell hooks puts it, the play of intersubjectivity on common grounds (hooks 1992, 170).[4]

Nowhere is this interplay of the stereotype and the "lived experience" more apparent than in what I will call the historical tropics of diaspora, particularly in that intertwined play of historical trope and cultural field in the notion of the instance of passage of the sociological figures of diaspora into realms in which they are unknown or unknowable (White 1978). Detached from its historical moorings, diaspora may drift among the wreckage of an historical continuum, at times "form to background," at others, "point to field," but always a narrative form in a global economy of images of displacement and displacing agents knowing or unknown (Jameson 1971, 10). Diasporas must be understood both in relation to the particulars of lives, narratives, and identities and to the parallel depths of sociocultural backgrounds, geopolitical contexts, and the infrastructure and histories of empires. While diasporas are at times associated with the decentering of the nation-state and the antiessentialist notions of "hybridity" or sites of cultural creativity, they are also subject to some of the most repressive aspects of state intervention, and some are the survivors of racial, ethnic, or religious intolerance in national contexts in which they had few economic or political rights.[5] It is in the instances of intolerance that we are drawn to the jagged edges of "othering," as its structure crashes toward social exclusion and even acts of violence.[6]

The Problem with the Ship

There has been a great deal of discussion of diaspora that employs the trope of the voyage, of the passage from one state or place to another, such that dispossession, exile, and displacement have become the watchwords for the notion of diaspora; such terms as hybridity, transnational, border, and travel also play a part in the identification of diasporic themes (Clifford 1994, 302–6). The contemplation of diaspora that I suggest, as a residence in alterity or in the being of the other, has often been considered only as a by-product of a traumatic series of events. I never knew my boat, yet I consider myself a part of diaspora. Some would suggest that this distant trauma—the unintentional seaward movement of which I am a descendent—has left in its wake a "structure of feeling," a way of being, if you will, that has some trace of that first boat (Williams 1978).

Paul Gilroy, in *Against Race: Imagining Political Culture Beyond the Color Line* (2000), exalts the great flexibility of the diaspora concept (123). While it is a concept that allows for antiessentialist accounts of identity formation as a process, that rejects the notion of primordial identities established by nature or culture, diaspora also attenuates national belongings, making the way for alternative forms of belongings and histories of place (124–29). This is part of a critique of nationalism, of the nation-state, and of the fixed configurations of the subject that accompany this version of modernity. It is in the context of the notion of postnationalism that diaspora, frequent crossings of frontiers, nomadism, travel, homelessness, and those displaced persons stranded betwixt and between various national designations have emerged as important tropes for cultural liberation, serving as alternative sites of political and cultural locations (Gilroy 2000). In the wake of the cultural and political cultures of the black Atlantic, the voyage is viewed as a site of both trauma and creativity, forging distinctive British black "experience and meanings," as its "culture is actively made and remade" (Gilroy 1987, 154).[7]

Black Britain draws on a "plurality of black histories and politics" that contributes to the formulation of black cultures (Gilroy 1993, 46). Cultural traditions are derived from non-European elements that are in turn drawn from "the immediate history of Empire and colonization in Africa, the Caribbean, and the Indian subcontinent from where postwar settlers brought both the methods and memories of their battles for citizenship, justice and independence." In the black Atlantic world since the time of Columbus black people moved "not only as commodities but engaged in various struggles towards emancipation, autonomy, and citizenship." Yet it is here that the inclusivity underlying Gilroy's argument that invokes "a global perspective from the memories of slavery and indenture, which are the property of African diaspora" begins to fall away and we are left with more restrictive notions and diasporic formulations (16).

Gilroy misses an opportunity to interrogate the fluidity of ethnic, class, and racial classifications. In many instances, slavery and its aftermath have interacted in important ways with the legacy of indenture, not only in the Caribbean but also in the United States, where the close association of blacks and indentured Irish workers fueled early racially indexed intolerance and labor discrimination. Yet the indentured Irish— living in the same communities as their black counterparts, sharing a common agricultural background, at times marrying into the same families and being buried in the same cemeteries—also found many points of identification (Ignatiev 1995).[8]

Divergent histories index differential placement in national discourse for people of African descent or Creoles in the Indian Ocean; as Espelencia Baptiste notes, in Mauritius, the descendants of slaves are thought to have abandoned the nation in an hour of need, and the indentured workers brought in to fill the labor vacuum have inherited a privileged position in the official narrative of the nation (Baptiste 2002).

When the national story is told, the descendents of slaves in effect disappear shortly after the indentured workers—cast as saviors of the nation—arrive from various parts of India. So the role of slavery in Mauritius disappears in official discourse, much like it does in the national memory of the country that received the greatest number of New World slaves: Brazil. The meaning of slavery, indenture, or its place in a national trajectory is a part of the national narrative, achieved largely through struggle or the availability of the power to make the story stick (or not)—it is merely there for the taking. It is important that even in the casting away of the classifications of slavery and indenture, the powerless may have a role in shaping national narratives through their invisibility as a "structuring absence" (Puri 2004, 27).

Invoking the triangular trade of sugar, slaves, and capital, Gilroy suggests that a new exchange involving four geographical points is now underway, including in its network the Caribbean, the United States, Europe, and Africa. This new transfer involves the commoditization of black expressive culture, particularly music in various forms:

> Diaspora histories of racial subjectivity combine in unforeseen
> ways with the edifice of British society and create a complex
> relationship which has evolved through various stages linked
> in different ways to the pattern of capitalist development itself.
> (Gilroy 1987, 157)

Gilroy is quite right to invoke the specter of capitalism as the fundamental connective tissue of African diaspora and not the state, which is rather underdeveloped when one considers it in relation to the movement of fifty million people at the behest of capital (Mintz 1995). But what can we say about the social relations that remain outside of this "expressive culture," anterior to and perhaps constitutive of it? This daily world of the black cultures is absent. Gilroy follows a rigid linearity, despite his attempts to distance his work from classical historical discourse, returning to the point of origin (Africa) only through the meditations of the diaspora. His notion of culture also remains expressive, not generative, and is conceived of as being acted upon and not constituting the very framework of action in its own right. Yet it is in the world of practice—a world in which the music that Gilroy cites as an important component of "expressive culture"—takes on its meanings. Although painting the portrait of diaspora with a broad brush, Gilroy gives us little insight into the instances—the receiving end of diasporic living in which various traces of black cultures converge.

The imagery of the ship and the passage of black communities from "slave ship to citizenship" help to provide the architectural supports of Gilroy's notion of the black Atlantic:

> I have settled on the image of ships in motion across the spaces between Europe, America, Africa and the Caribbean as a central organizing symbol for this enterprise and as my starting point. The image of the ship—a living, micro-cultural, micro-political system in motion—is essentially important for historical and theoretical reasons that I hope will become clearer below. Ships immediately focus attention on the middle passage, on the various projects for redemptive return to an African homeland, on the circulation of ideas and activists as well as the movement of key cultural and political artifacts: tracts, books, gramophone records, and choirs. (Gilroy 1993, 4)

Blacks, however, remain the privileged other of the West, supplementing the violence and exclusion of the project of modernity, although the ship is not only a container for emergent black cultural traditions but a kind of crossroads of a broader capitalist project, one integral to the disposition, experience, and futures of the captives and others on board. It is actually the context of emergent friendship, the negotiation of different linguistic codes, cultural traditions, and collective efforts to ensure survival that enriched humanity and set in motion a new society on the ships.

Locating a transnational world on the ship, as Gilroy does, focuses our attention not only on the ship but also on the unseen social order from which the ships depart and the social world that has made this voyage possible, calling into question not only the lives of those on the ship but the possible parallel to other journeys, other ships, and the voyages real and imaginary that they bring to mind. The ship is a link not only to the shipbuilding industries and the enrichment of those who invested in the peculiar human cargo of slaves, but also the economic potential in markets and the work and sheer profit that the slaves would one day produce across the Caribbean and the United States. Contemporary appearances of migrant ships mark the hidden contours of a different kind of marginalization, as people escape from not only ethnic violence and political strife, but also weak economies, jobless urban shanty towns, and rural wastelands where desertification—a struggle over resources like water and land—has taken a toll. Other ships and other travel remain implicit in the running trope of Gilroy's black Atlantic, as Shalini Puri notes:

> Paul Gilroy's suggestive metaphor of the ship as a site of transnational identities needs to be elaborated further so that we can distinguish between the cultural hybridities and border-crossings represented by, say, slave-ships, U.S. warships, luxury cruise ships, and Haitian rafts. Only a failure to consider such issues can explain why border-crossing is so often cast as intrinsically subversive. (Puri 2004, 25)

In the end, it is the imagery of the ships that has the last word; descendants of these travelers must "chant down Babylon" and speak the unspeakable truth of their future liberation. Despite the deconstruction of racial typology and the tendency to "fix," as Fanon has noted, the "other" in the discourse of essential categorical taxonomies, the back-and-forth motion between "slave ship and citizenship," seems to leave no place in the world for alternative forms of becoming (Fanon 1967a, 116). Although the black Atlantic speaks of movement and time depth, this movement between slave ship and citizenship may be too narrowly caught in the defining terms of dominant discourse. What about the possibility of converting the meaning and nature of "citizenship" by the people who seem destined to inhabit it, or, for that matter, the nation itself?

The ship and the nation cannot act as the keys to unlock worlds of neglected history, and serves only to trap us further under the guise of its transformative powers. Slaves were not turned into transnationals though the advent of the nation-state and/or through its articulation to new territories of the globe, but rather were trans-something (trans-local, transcultural) before the nation and were never imagined in the conceptualization of citizenship.[9] The great cultural and ethnic diversity of slaves was actually negotiated before and during the Middle Passage. As Gwendolyn Midlo Hall notes, denial of the scope and dimension of "ethnic designations" of Africans merely "homogenizes them, and makes them invisible." She continues, "Africans are the only peoples who have been subjected by scholars to this level of denial" (2005, 49). The slave trade often disrupted entire regions; warfare and slave raiding associated with the trade placed many in new and alien cultural and social settings long before boarding ships for the New World. The extraordinary resilience of slaves to forge a society of sorts out of the fragments of many traditions is often undervalued (Hall 2005). Slavery represents, as Marx once suggested, a kind of total system of markets and the social relations associated with the production of this system in European port cities enriched by the trade and the outpost that became the transit centers, enabling its operation.[10]

The ship as an instrument of "international imperialism" makes at best an unfortunate metaphor for African diaspora (Mintz 1995). It is not the ship we must look to, but the shipmate, the opening of social relations among those held together in this extraordinary voyage (Mintz and Price 1992). The ship is so firmly rooted in Western discourse that it laid the groundwork in Plato for political discourse: the state was compared to the ship and the king its captain. The metaphor of navigation is implicated in notions of power, memory, and the right to the exemplary.[11] The ship however evokes nostalgia for a realm beyond captivity, and the promise of return, as in Psalm 137, which contains—as St. Clair Drake has noted—the paradigm of diaspora:

> By the rivers of Babylon,
> There we sat down,
> Yea, we wept when we remembered Zion.
> We hanged our harps upon the willows in the
>   midst thereof,
> For there they that carried us away captive
> Required of us a song:
> And they that wasted us required of us mirth,
> Saying,
> Sing us one of the songs of Zion.
> How shall we sing the Lord's songs
> In a strange land?
> If I forget thee Oh Jerusalem,
> Let my right hand forget her cunning;
> If I do not remember thee,
> Let my tongue cleave to the roof of my mouth.[12]

The black cultures that Gilroy speaks of may be a collectivity in the making of a part of potential "communities," emergent components of the interchanges of the "routes and roots of diasporas" (Gilroy 1993, 19–20). We might begin an analysis of continuity in the [dis]continuity of such communities, rather than assuming that their movement in space and time alone mystically creates a new world.

Is Paul Gilroy exploring a kind of Afrocentricism—an antiessentialist site of creative expression in motion? Fanon once wrote, "I was haunted by a galaxy of erosive stereotypes"; this haunting and diffuse legacy of rule and the diverse manner in which the notion of race has been and is presently configured through and in spite of such conceptions as nation, gender, and class may chart our coming travels (Fanon 1967a, 129). Some of our transnational listings of race, along with other features of an emergent globalization, have lead us to view race as a single piece, disregarding its transformations in various historical and social formations.[13] Perhaps, like the gumbo trope employed by Marlon Riggs, black cultures can survive without being reduced to a single form of artistic expression, political affiliation, or social concern.[14]

New African Diasporas: Black Culture in the Plural

The New African diaspora creates complex transnational links between Africa and the diaspora, and follows interests in a global black community inspired in part by post-Independence rhetoric in Africa and a post–civil rights expansion of international concerns in North America and elsewhere.[15] In Turin, Italy, Senegalese avidly followed political developments in the African American community in the United States. Senegalese in diaspora in New York and Los Angeles interpret and communicate the nature and meaning of the changing social and political climate in these cities, drawn ever closer to Turin and Dakar.

In the heat of a summer afternoon in 1995 I rode across the web of Turin streets with Dominique, the radio blasting out a speech by Félix Houphouët-Boigny, the now-deceased French-speaking president of the Ivory Coast, to a reggae rhythm. Houphouët-Boigny was discussing the potential of the formulation of French West Africa under a single president, an office for which some suggested he should run. It wasn't out of self-interest that he had suggested the idea of appointing himself to the office, Dominique told me; it was rather for the love of West Africa.

There is a kind of pan-Africanism that speaks to young Senegalese like Dominique; the actions of such figures as Houphouët-Boigny don't matter as much as it does that they were premier black figures capable of rivaling any European—in short, that they were heroic figures. Such discussions do not wait for the pronouncements of intellectuals or the charting out of the historic interchanges between crucial figures, but escape this small circle to circulate freely in the common sense of an emergent diaspora. "My blackness was there," Fanon once wrote, "dark and unarguable" (1967a, 117). This is the daily context of Senegalese living in Italy and other European countries today; they must confront the "othering" of cities, quarters, and back streets in which people are unaccustomed to their presence. While some newcomers remain relatively unnoticed until betrayed by an accent or particular style of clothing, the Senegalese remain at all times hypervisible as outsiders, making them easy targets for anti-immigrant violence, intolerance, and social exclusion.

The states here and in Senegal, the Ivory Coast, and elsewhere are the counterpoints of this "Europe," as the daily interplay of Senegalese and Italians becomes the daily topic of connection to diverse black cultures forming their own relationship to Italian society. There is in fact a sense of distinction drilled into newcomers through the media, job sites, and national legislation. Alterity, read in appearances and concretized by common sense, lays the groundwork of diasporic practice, which entails the exploration of forms of being other, of being "overdetermined from without" (Fanon 1968, 116). Yet I would hesitate to include Dominique in Gilroy's formulation of diaspora. The sense of the political here is derived from an assertion of "othering," in contradistinction to a Europe that Gilroy has barely considered; yet that is the stock and trade of daily conversation in Senegalese diaspora.

In the houses of these migrants, former university students, former cultivators, welders, bricklayers, travel agents, and union organizers gather from all quarters to discuss the fate of their home societies and the nature of the work contexts in Europe. They approach the same trade union officials to be informed on the particulars of Italian labor law and entreat one another to carry gifts back to their relatives at home or elsewhere in Europe, should someone decide to travel (Merrill and Carter 2003). In all of this, we meet several perhaps contradictory readings of diaspora, a concept that may be historically situated in the Harlem renaissance, Gilroy's black Atlantic, and the diaspora young men and women in Italy or elsewhere, but that changes its meanings with each context. The wake of the first slave ship may be felt centuries later, but the manner in which this may be true and its meanings are open to exploration.[16]

Dominique and I talked about how African driving licenses were no longer accepted in Italy as we listened to Houphouët-Boigny speak about the cultural unity of French West Africa to a reggae beat and conversed in Italian across the diaspora. The interplay of black cultures in Paris and Turin and New York and Los Angeles, who at times were living on the margins of the law as undocumented workers, today has a texture not always shared by relatively privileged communities of intellectuals or globe-trotting musicians, producers, and business persons (MacGaffey and Bazenguisssa-Ganga 2000). Senegalese and other migrants constitute key elements in the building of European national myths of identity, representing the exemplary outsider and newcomer, and are subject to the symbolic violence implicit in the selective "forgetting" of European colonialism.

A new set of issues is starting to dominate domestic discourse in European countries, bringing a peculiar advantage to exclusionary rhetoric and anti-immigrant policy and a rising power to political parties that champion such issues and are rapidly becoming a permanent feature of contemporary life (Ross 1995). These relations depart from a strict linearity and don't stop and start merely in the United States, Europe, or Africa, but rather take detours, at times ending up mapping out a new cartography of diaspora making and the conditions under which this formation takes place.

This process of diaspora formation does not end because some government no longer tolerates the presence of "outsiders" on national soil. Although we must recognize that "economic downturns and local fascism are powerful dampeners in their effects on such movement" (Mintz 1995, 20), this movement may at times continue despite immigration policies, local anti-immigrant sentiment, and hostile communities of reception. Mintz has cautioned against treating diaspora as something "new," that is, as a new form of global encounter.[17] During the nineteenth century, some hundred million persons set out across the oceans "mostly to colonies or erstwhile colonies," often to participate in emergent labor and colonial regimes (20).[18]

The unexpected encounter of the traveler or migrant in the backmost of back streets of Rome, of course, is not the way we think of meeting up with the conception of diaspora. The images of the world that have plagued the media have given short shrift to the notion of people moving from place to place, often forced to leave behind everything familiar to them in search of a world that may replace the one they have known. Darting across our television screen and over the highways of newsprint, we have witnessed their passage into the fourth columns and newspeak of our times; they are the refugees, the migrants, the immigrants, the asylum seekers, and the displaced persons. In the logic of the a new world of post-everything,—post-Soviet, post-Fordist, postmodern, postindustrial—the event has become paramount, and the processes by which people make sense of their lives in such a world have often taken a less-well-defined pathway to our attentions.

Reading world geography through disastrous events is like painting world history by the numbers; relief programs and humanitarian aid campaigns quickly come to color the globe, mapping a pathological geography like a contemporary dependency theory. Conflating an image of Africa into a media-friendly human-interest event helps the continental colors fade in the minds of viewers, turning it into a place where famine is visible, or a seemingly random and endemic violent coup d'état and little else.

Diaspora has come to be seen in folk ideology as a move from situational trauma to exodus, from the catastrophic event to its aftermath, leading us to imagine it as a form of negation, as if it signified the systematic rehabilitation of a temporary or forced stage of displacement. In popular imagination, the classical figure of diaspora has come to be conflated then with the so-called boat people. Italian and other European officials often justified their expulsion of unwanted immigrants by referring to similar measures taken by Britain or the United States, under which "boat people" meant global exclusionary policies toward migrants.

The Senegalese were not really boat people, but mostly airplane and sometimes train people; others even more or less walked across the border. Most had taken a plane from Dakar, some had taken a train from other European countries, some had driven, and others had even allegedly walked. Some had taken a boat from the Italian islands to the mainland, but none remarked on the voyage as significant. Even Italian officials had the notion of the boat in their minds when facing the immigration question; a former minister of justice suggested using a flotilla of the Italian navy to stem the flow of illegal immigration into the country. This notion was dismissed by former prime minister Giulio Andreotti, who argued that the military had no policing function (Carter 1997). The new immigration "state of emergency" has once again revived such notions, empowering local officials to become the new gatekeepers of Italy. Today, the winds have changed, and the use of force to stop the flow of migrants is a welcome, perhaps comforting, thought for many Italians experiencing a kind of humanitarian fatigue.[19]

The idea that migrants live in "other cultures" so different from those of the rest of us becomes the primary reason for not incorporating them into society. Debates over the nature of human rights, the structure of hospitality and citizenship, and the delineation of common policies regulating asylum and immigration are truncated by an outdated notion of people in transition as having no justifiable reason to seek access to "our" territory. As Seyla Benhabib points out, the very "right to have rights" exercised by states must acknowledge the contradictory and countervailing claims to human rights of those who have neither national nor natural rights in the nation-state:

> Defining the identity of the sovereign nation is itself a process
> of fluid, open, and contentious public debate: the line separating
> "we" and "you," "us" and "them," more often than not rests on
> unexamined prejudices, ancient battles, historical injustices, and
> sheer administrative fiat. The beginnings of every modern nation-
> state carry the traces of some violence and injustice.... Yet modern
> liberal democracies are self-limiting collectivities that at one and
> the same time constitute the nation as sovereign while proclaiming
> that sovereignty derives its legitimacy from the nation's adherence
> to fundamental human rights principles. (Benhabib 2002, 177)

Indeed, making the boundary seems to require the revitalization and marking of cultural territory; boundaries are increasingly conflated with national borders. The boundary between refugees, asylum seekers, foreigners, aliens, and other terms we employ to describe those who fall on the other side of "we the people" is not only arbitrary, but also holds a key to the way belonging is organized, negotiated, and navigated within these confines. A stranger in possession of the right to universal and fundamental rights might cross over this divide and become more like the rest of us, no longer uprooted but at home in the ideal juridical world on which all states are said to rest.[20]

In the morning press, the perils of transportation confront us with the searching of the hulls of ships in California or Spain, the sounding out of the contexts of a Ryder truck or a tractor-trailer. The worst immigrant tragedy in the United States occurred not in an attempt to cross the U.S. border but to navigate the terrain from Harlingen, Texas, to Houston, Texas. Although it is unclear how many people were actually inside the truck in Victoria, Texas, in May 2003, in the end 19 people that had been locked in the back of the trailer for the ride between two American cities lost their lives. In his book on the tragedy, *Dying to Cross: The Worst Immigrant Tragedy in American History* (2005), Jorge Ramos notes that increased attention to border crossing has forced people coming into the United States from Mexico into more risky situations, and that after crossing they must avoid capture by immigration officials, human smugglers, and other criminal networks:

> In the past, people could and often did enter the United States
> near the border towns, but now they were finding themselves
> forced to travel through white-hot deserts, rugged mountains,
> and a rapidly rushing river. Once inside the U.S., they would
> often have to travel in sealed truck trailers, railway cars that
> locked form the outside, and via other exceedingly unsound
> transportation methods just to get away from the border. That
> was why so many were dying. (Ramos 2005, 149)[21]

The idea that we can ignore the human rights violations at our borders is a contemporary myth; in the name of protection of our borders, we are complicit in what amounts to gross negligence at best and veiled violence against human striving at worst. We don't think of ourselves as the accomplices of the smugglers, but if we merely build better fences without looking at human rights violations along the border, comprehensive incorporation of immigrants into daily life, and proper long-term residence programs, we may contribute to the human traffic and its facilitators.

We may never really know what draws people into the dance of borders and at times abandons them there. Unlike the coverage of the local news channels on the Cuban diaspora or the Haitian diaspora during the early 1990s, in North America diasporas do not end; they do not lend themselves to easy closure, at least not exactly, but instead fade into the invisibility of routine national forgetting, of border patrols, special courts, and detention complexes hidden from our view.

I wish to challenge the notion that diasporas are primarily or only about the movement of people through territory or space and time. Diaspora seems to be as much epistemological adventures into conceptual space as it is actual marches through "real" spatial coordinates, territories, or regions. One's own diaspora creates problems that cannot be resolved through mere relocation. Diasporas are not always good to think (Lévi-Strauss 1963, 89). Many diasporas, we must remember, are the product of an incongruity with the "imagined community" of a certain domain, and the people in diaspora are no longer free to be imagined among "them" (the dominate culture) (Radhakrishnan 1996; Hall 1994). The routes and roots of diaspora are often about selected imaginings of which movement is product and not predicate.

Although Italian host society, for instance, is ready to hear tales of the Third World migrant exile, there is little tolerance for stories of the experience of racism, violence, or social exclusion—these do not nice acceptable stories make, and therefore do not enter into a realm of acknowledged discourse. "It is not the voice the commands the story but the ear," as Italo Calvino once wrote; no matter how eloquent the resistance of migrants in Italy or elsewhere, there is still the issue of power differentiated by the ability not only to be heard but to act effectively within the same world (Calvino 1974; Jordan 1992).[22]

Speaking of his choice to remain in Germany, German cultural critic Ralph Giordano invoked a sense of community and belonging now contested and at times denied:

> For my sense of belonging naturally comes under heavy
> attack from that smoldering racist faction, which is spreading
> over united Germany and is far from being stamped out. It is
> dampened by that notorious, Nazi-inspired misanthropy which
> lurks behind the guise of xenophobia, which has cost dozens of
> lives and hundreds, and I mean hundreds, of casualties. But even
> though I myself am seriously threatened by the anti-democratic
> right wing, even though I am shattered by the passive stance

taken by the government power monopoly towards the danger
from the right and am aware of a dismaying lack of courage
among citizens to stand up for the victims, I still do to believe
that the "ugly Germans" will score another triumph in history.
(Cited in Stern 1995, 47)

Giordano poses a sense of belonging complementary to an alterity
that has come to have a place in the new Germany, in spite of the "smoldering racist faction," which threatens "diversity and democratic pluralism," as Connolly calls it (2002). The challenge of imaging a community,
of being part of the resident "other," will be part of the day-to-day experience of living in diaspora as long as the ideological legacy of modernism and its essentialized categories and stereotypes haunt the texture of
everyday life; as Fanon writes, "I was haunted by a galaxy of erosive stereotypes," and we must seek to liberate some small livable space (Fanon
1967a, 129). This knowledge and experience is perhaps the rocking
of the ships, the experiences of the boat people, the rocking between
the overdetermined discourse of "othering," and the being in alterity
unfolding in everyday practices. By speaking out in this manner, Giordano loses the right to speak as an exemplary German, and gains the
right to be German; among other things, his statements call into question the very registers of German identity. This quality of being German
is now complicated by relations of power, memory, and the emergent
order of the present—a new position from which a way of speaking may
transport what it means to be German in new directions. The change
is slow-going, perhaps; yet this is the movement that may allow us to
accept alternative or perhaps even "new modalities of otherness" (Sarup
1994, 99). Giordano notes that it is the day-to-day "community of fed-
erated Germans, men, women, young people" that are the center of his
sense of belonging—in this day-to-day emergent reality, hope may find
its voice (Stern 1995, 46–47).

CHAPTER 2

Remembering Khartoum and Other Tales of Displacement

> Our view of the passage of time influences the value we attach
> to past events far more than is the case for the Dinka, whose
> points of reference are not years counted serially, but the events
> themselves. In the example of the man who called his child
> "Khartoum," it is Khartoum which is regarded as an agent, the
> subject which acts, and not as with us the remembering mind
> which recalls a place. The man is the object acted upon.
>
> —GODFREY LIENHARDT, *DIVINITY AND EXPERIENCE:*
> *THE RELIGION OF THE DINKA*

If we were to configure the architecture of contemporary anthropology, the resulting structure might reveal the explorations of experience, material culture, and space and time to be essential features of its fragile identity. One of the pioneering figures of this world was no doubt Godfrey Lienhardt, who mapped the meanings of Dinka cosmology in his classic *Divinity and Experience* (1961). In the heart of the work, Lienhardt considers memory, experience, and the significance of naming a child "Khartoum"—the son of a man once imprisoned in the city. Located at the confluence of the White and Blue Niles, the two tributaries of the Nile River, the capital city of Khartoum has long been associated with events that mark it as an international crossroads: hostage crises, diplomatic assassinations, and the rising and falling of refugee slums on its outskirts accommodating both the displaced from neighboring nation-states Chad, Eritrea, and Uganda and its own citizens fleeing war-torn regions in the south and west. Remembering Khartoum does not just entail the acknowledgement of the enduring traces of place on both a present and future life. It also constitutes an "act of exorcism," ensuring against potential harm of any kind. For the many people of southern Sudan, Khartoum has symbolized not only a seat of the national political power but also a site of ethnic discrimination, and religious and cultural intolerance. Indeed, as the legacy of residence in a place may have lasting significance across the generations, this type of experience can be integral to diasporas. In fact, some diasporic experiences are bounded by exclusionary activities of states, militias, and others in the homeland only to be met with intolerance and racism in the adopted lands that act as safe havens to those escaping violence elsewhere (Pred 2000).

Lienhardt introduced a generation of anthropologists to the complexity of experience and the embodiment of aspects of the profane as well as the unseen world in everyday life. As we consider the nature of New African Diasporas, we must perhaps acknowledge the capriciousness of the work of historicity and the precarious state of those at times figured by diasporas through the disfigurement of their dispersal and the provisional status of all cultural identity. I think it is this kind of presence and contingency that we attempt to capture with such words as *diaspora, dwelling, travelling,* and *exile,* the lineaments of profound change expanding outward like the spokes of a wheel in the real time of daily practice and future lives. We make the vehicle of displacement the trope that stands in for the experience of diaspora or what we might even call the culture of diaspora. Cultural innovation is an integral part of any journey, as it is often what people do in moments of transition that marks their arrival in a new world. As in Dinka, remembering Khartoum, we tend to focus on an event (often departure) and the prolonged state of arrival and displacement of the migrant, the refugee, or the exile. I would like to suggest that diaspora is not merely a form of transportation—a way of going from here to there—but rather a way of *being* here or there and all the points in between.[1] What I have in mind is what Clifford has referred to as "dwelling in travel" (Clifford 1997). Diaspora is a kind of passage, but a passage that encompasses the possibility of never arriving, of drifting endlessly betwixt and between the new world's boundaries. Rather than seeking "assimilation" as a goal, diaspora is a way of being "other" among the established, of keeping alive the drama of the voyage of "otherness" in worlds that seek sameness and homogeneity. At times, the ambiguity of the voyage is imposed (refugee, displaced person, rebel, immigrant), and at others, it is embraced as a marker of identity.

There is "an art of being in between," according to Michel de Certeau, and this art accords "a degree of plurality and creativity" for those living in such spaces (1984, 30). As I see it, the power of remembering Khartoum is an acknowledgment of entering a new state of being, of the act of the transformative in the mundane world. Perhaps we might say that it is the act of embracing the ambiguities of becoming and belonging. The trauma and trace of loss may not always be the defining aspects of a diasporic identity, but this plurality and creativity, I would argue, remain a constant. What Clifford calls "collective histories of displacement and violent loss" (1997, 250) are not the only possible articulations of identity, but rather one of myriad possible positions that may be occupied. Diasporic cultural forms may have a future in spite of "homecomings" real or imagined, as these forms—like the "act of exorcism" of naming the Dinka child—take on a kind of autonomy from the inaugural event that gave them life. It is in these futures, in the daily living of diaspora, that we must come to explore the changing world or worlds of New African Diasporas.

There are a number of ideas that attempt to draw together New African Diasporas by looking backward to an ideal African homeland and to sets of Afrocentric values that stream from this common origin (Palmer 1998). Yet this African homeland often occupies the realm of an ideal and seemingly timeless reality that imagining Africa in historically specific moments may disrupt. Beneath the pan-African imagined global networks, however, run fluid discursive structures that blur conventional and taken-for-granted classificatory practices with emergent nodes of cultural identity that we have yet to imagine. Explorations of pan-African diasporic consciousness must therefore be disambiguated from the essential markings of race, place, and temporal anchoring (see Ifekwunigwe 1999). There is no transhistorical box large enough to contain such disparate and heterogeneous processes; rather, linkages must be accounted for with greater care and specificity. As Ifekwunigwe points out, the "historical and contemporary narratives of continental Africa and its diaspora(s) . . . have always been intertwined" (2003, 66–67), such that the interplay of racial, gender, and class ideologies with the discursive features of divergent nation-state(s) forms the historically specific surfaces that are an integral part of lives in diaspora. It is to these voices that we must increasingly turn in order to understand the "paradox of belonging." These forms of belonging—cutting across diverse ethnic, cultural, racial, and gendered boundaries—reveal lived experiences that do not succumb to classical binary markers like black/white or the many national identifiers from which diaspora identity comes to be excluded. There is a danger of viewing these social forms merely in relation to a local racial currency and ideal of origin, thereby reducing the scope and dimension of New African Diasporas.

Networks that constitute and sustain diasporas vary from one place to another (see Riccio 2003; Koser 2003). Popular music introduces young Congolese to Parisian life long before they board the "plane to see the city for themselves." As Désiré Kazadi Wa Kabwe and Aurelia Segatti point out, the very geography of European capitals like "Paris and Brussels, is often integrated into popular songs, so that the names of Parisian quarters such as 'Quarter Latin,' 'Mairie de Montreuil,' or 'Château Rouge' are as familiar to Congolese youth as they are to Parisians" (Wa Kabwe and Segatti 2003, 128). Indeed, the connections between the local "imagined worlds" of young people, although grounded in place, resonate with the "lived experience" of a generation of global proportions (Weiss 2002). The links between a homeland and the places and people in diaspora is only a cell phone call, a song, an email, or a cable away. These connections are constantly updated by the arrival of newcomers, the back-and-forth junkets of traders, and the turnstile lifestyle of members of the transnational communities in diverse locations that dart between various national spaces carrying on the work of religious organizations, business concerns or visiting friends and family (MacGaffey and Bazenguissa-Ganga 2000). People often send letters or cassettes that are hand-delivered from one part of the world to the diaspora in another.[2] No region or place cries out to be identified definitively with one group or another. West African groups who carry different passports may claim solidarity on the basis of a common religious affiliation, ethnicity, regional origin, or occupation.

Being African in Europe often entails being subjected to the homogenizing gaze of a dominant society, one that tends to lump groups together into quasiracial classifications (migrants, blacks, Arabs, Vu Comprá). Yet groups sharing a common colonial language may subvert such identifications by claiming allegiance through a local African language diminishing the European tie. Old classificatory systems of African populations such as Francophone and Anglophone, as David Styan points out, do not resonate with a contemporary world in which other languages may come first (Styan 2003). Nor do such designations account for national, regional, and religious affiliation that may influence language use in various contexts. Senegalese from rural areas, primarily ethnic Wolof, often insist on speaking an "African language" and take great pride in the purity of their Wolof, while their counterparts—educated youth from urban centers—feel more at home with French (Carter 1997). Furthermore, ethnic Wolof will often identify as Senegalese rather than claim the national identities that their passports afford them, in effect blurring the boundaries of nation, ethnicity, and language by invoking the solidarity implicit in diaspora. Senegalese in Italy often speak Italian when the topic of work comes up, slipping completely into Wolof when watching a video from home, and to a mix of Wolof and French when speaking to a relative in France or Senegal. While it is an encompassing national language in Senegal, in diaspora Wolof can act as a marker of ethnicity or of the non-European.

If, as Rey Chow suggests, modernity is characterized by pressing demands for clarity and demarcation of boundaries, then our time may be indexed by a kind of "boundary dissolving." Yet this "dissolving" seems a contradictory dynamic that often moves against the grain of the local while engendering a greater heterogeneity in the global. Yet favoring dissolution (if that is what is happening) is not the same for all. It may come to be experienced differently in other cultures. "Modernism is for these other cultures," writes Chow, "always a displaced phenomenon, the sign of an alien imprint on indigenous traditions" (1993, 56). Yet the line between the West and the rest is increasingly unreliable, because—in practice and for the quotidian routine regimes of most lives—no such distinctions exist.

African diasporas emerge not only in sites where relationships have been established through colonial ties, but also in new contexts, often following the circuitous pathways of nongovernmental organizations (NGOs), religious organizations, political affiliations, transnational refugee networks, and familial reunification. It is the diaspora, according to Paul Gilroy, that sets up an "alternative to the stern discipline of primordial kinship and rooted belonging," and sets free such determinations of identity which, linked to territory, produce a taken-for-granted chain leading from place to consciousness (2000, 123). Diaspora is often seen as a kind of moving point of virtual creativity, one that, through its movement in time and space, becomes insulated from its surroundings. It source of creativity is imagined in part to be its embodiment of the arbitrary; like the master of the crossroads, diasporas attain an almost mystical relationship with change, transformation, and a notion of integrity in contemporary theory.

Shortly after I arrived in Rome, en route to Turin for my fieldwork, I went to the St. Egidio Center in Trastevere, which serves as a way station for people who like many newcomers are down on their luck, homeless, or in transition. I was directed to go and check out the center by a friend of a friend before I even had time to unpack my bags or recover from the journey. After my long absence from Rome, I looked forward to wandering through the twisting streets of Trastevere, hugging close to the walls to avoid the intermittent motorists and scooters. In recent years, the Roman heart of Trastevere had become a home to travelers, migrants, and refugees from many parts of the globe—more a kind of turnstile than a quarter, especially for those longing to go elsewhere, a rest stop for those wishing to move on to somewhere else, such as New York, Montreal, or London, and a refuge for those not wanted anywhere.

Wandering the streets of Trastevere, my guide (the center's director) pointed out the changes that over the years had transformed the sleepy quarter: the well-appointed cars, the new shops, and the not so newly acquired taste for the good life of the consumer world. Becoming a world economic power had been beyond the dreams of most Italians a short time ago; now they were living in an undreamed-of reality. As we walked into the hall where volunteers were serving dinner, he pointed out that many Nuer and Dinka were frequent visitors to the center's meal and language programs. Standing by the wall and waiting for the dining room to fill up were two young men, one Nuer and the other Dinka, who joked with the director about the fact that they were all still there (in the center and even in Italy).[3] I knew then that this was not going to be an easy field experience, that the world of the anthropological imagination was meeting, full scale, the world of a changing global, often volatile, and certainly unexpected reality. Notions of divinity and power cast by the generation of Godfrey Lienhardt and Evans-Pritchard were impossible to reconcile with the waiting room of a lay Catholic Trastevere center, a place accustomed to serving the homeless and less fortunate of Rome.[4]

The Nuer and Dinka are agropastoralist, Nilotic cultural and linguistic groups who subsist on a mixed economy of animal husbandry and cultivation and have been a standard feature of virtually every basic anthropological text. Many anthropologists have spent much of their academic lives reexamining and often recapitulating the wisdom imparted by founding figures like Lienhardt and Evans-Pritchard in classrooms, professional journals, and documentary films (Holtzman 2000). Jon Holtzman suggests that the Nuer may be the most important case study in the history of anthropology; they are certainly one of the most well known. In this manner, already prefigured in a collective encounter with "other cultures," it is perhaps not so surprising that the Nuer and the closely related Dinka are now an integral part of a New African Diaspora. The Sudan, Africa's largest nation by the late 1980s, was the site of a protracted civil conflict. Residents of southern Sudan were bombed by the government because of the concentration of rebel activity in the region.[5] The Nuer and other southerners saw their homelands become a battlefield, their fields burned, their herds looted to feed the rebel forces, and many of their number jailed by the government in Khartoum as suspected rebels or rebel sympathizers (Holtzman 2000).[6] The romantic vision of the remote pastoral Nilotic people, represented on the cover of E. Evans-Pritchard's *The Nuer* (1940) with a photograph showing Nuer harpoon fishing from a canoe on the Sobat River, was perhaps being shattered forever and replaced by the visage of refugee camps and a world in motion, hemorrhaging slowly to neighboring countries.[7] The photograph depicts in the foreground young Nuer on the waterways in a small craft, one intent on harpooning his prey, and behind them a vast expanse fading into the horizon line. Fishing is part of the delicate balance of a mixed economy in which there is still little room for error, and fish form an indispensable article of food in a diet that influences the group's seasonal movements in harmony with the natural world. This world—bounded only by the local ecology and the marking of time by shifting subsistence agriculture, herding, and fishing—comes full circle with the entrance of southerners into the world of the refugee and the subsequent loss of livelihood, land, and cattle.[8] Even the tranquil waters of the river would become a contested resource in a contemporary war zone. Evans-Pritchard envisioned the world of the Nuer as in a delicate "equilibrium" with nature: "Man holds his own in the struggle but does not advance" (1940, 92). Yet even in this semimythic world of the Nuer, in the distant beginnings of anthropological wanderings, this notion of bounded cultural realms was already beginning to break apart. Even now, years later, standing back from the "anthropologist tent" a bit might require admitting that the Nuer and others did not live in cultural isolation in reality as much as they did in the ethnographer's theory.

Today Nuer and Dinka in diaspora face many of the problems of transition and cultural dislocations that other groups confront, including the Eritrean and Somali communities: a diasporic experience bounded if at all by a kind of new global ecology at times beyond the reaches of the "cultural account." We now find people who maintain what anthropologists once referred to as "simple" lifestyles caught in the center of the most complex ethnic and political conflicts in a world in which organizations like NGOs and the international community figure prominently. The Nuer and the Dinka are just as much part of the New African Diasporas as are the Senegalese, Eritreans, and Somalis with whom I would later work in Turin. For all of them, the transition from refugee camps to centers in Italy or their final destination in the United States or elsewhere is difficult. Some have lived for times in refugee camps in a number of countries, many have walked for hundreds of miles in order to reach these camps, often facing the resentment of local populations fed up with the flow of outsiders and insensitive to their pasts. Traveling without documents, the migrants—not having attained the official status of the "refugee"—may face periods of questioning, detention, and even imprisonment by local authorities. The loss of immediate families, friends, and relatives further complicates this passage from homeland to diaspora. Others have struggled to remain on the frontier of the visible, to be acknowledged by a world community that might ensure their survival for another day, another planting season, or until the fighting stops and they can return home. At times, international organizations like the United Nations and countless NGOs that work in providing humanitarian assistance to the less fortunate of the world fight to keep ethnic groups and entire populations from falling into invisibility and fading from the immediate concern of a world that might save them.

Diasporas in the Making: The State Orchestration of Invisibility

On an altogether too hot summer afternoon, I climbed the hill just across the Po River in Turin, Italy, and made my way up the "Turin geometry" of winding streets to meet with historian Giovanni Levi. We sat in large airy room in a house Giovanni had inherited from his uncle, Primo Levi (1919–1987), and talked about my proposed research, the complex relationship between sports and politics in Italy, and rising anti-Semitism in throughout the country; he cited information collected by his brother, who was a journalist, and the growing number of migrants coming into Italy at that time (the mid-1980s). Turin, like other important Italian cities, was home to a vibrant Jewish community before the Second World War; the city's senior residents are still able to grasp this world in memory and recount its splendor. But these same streets, like many throughout Europe, also hold the memory of the countless journeys of people passed through their local quarters, train stations familiar to them and on to distant death camps. The late Primo Levi was a survivor of Auschwitz. In his mid-twenties, this trained chemist became a member of the antifascist resistance and was arrested in Turin and deported to the camps in 1944. He grew up in Turin in a family of nonreligious Sephardic Jews of Spanish ancestry. His fiction, poetry, and memoirs document an indomitable sense of wonder, a passion for life, and a deep faith in humanity. His account of life in the camps, *Survival in Auschwitz* (1958), is a stark account of the reality of genocide but also a warning, "a sinister alarm signal" to future generations. The book became a classic in Italy and was one of the first accounts to be widely read in Germany. In the preface to the book he warns "many people—many nations" against holding the conviction that "every stranger is an enemy," which is the prelude to genocide:

> For the most part this conviction lies deep down like some latent
> infection; it betrays itself only in random, disconnected acts,
> and does not lie at the base of a system of reason. But when this
> does come about, when the unspoken dogma becomes the major
> premise in a syllogism, then, at the end of the chain, there is the
> Larger. Here is the product of a conception of the world carried
> rigorously to its logical conclusion; so long as the conception
> subsists, the conclusion remains to threaten us. (Levi 1996, 9)

The story of the death camps is also a story of state-sponsored genocide—the exercise of the ultimate form of invisibility, the death of innocent subjects. The elimination of the "internal enemy" is a hallmark of statecraft; from the calming of the "dangerous masses" to clearing away the indigent from urban sites, the ideological war against the imagined threat is conducted in the name of a common future, peace, and security and the illusive state of national unity. The orchestration of genocide has become one of the many tools of state and a technique in nation-building practice, hidden under the cloak of sovereignty. But like other, more familiar state practices, it is nothing new.[9]

I am now compelled to say a word about genocide. The lack of transparency in the employment of the term is underscored in the very title of Gérard Prunier's recent discussion of the crisis in Sudan, *Darfur: The Ambiguous Genocide* (2005), a sad commentary on the nature of international equivocation. The international community—shuttling between "ethnic cleansing" and "genocide" for a name to characterize the conflict in Darfur—have stopped far short of military intervention, perhaps one of the only things that might definitively check the war. The fact that the conflict has moved from "massive murder campaign to radon harassment" in rapid episodic bursts does not help matters, as both the government and the opposition can claim peace while conducting hostilities (Prunier 2005, 136). While the quagmire of Iraq has in large part overwhelmed military forces in the United States, Europe has preferred to send money for the western Sudan crisis, and the United Nation is immobilized without the backing of member states. Much of the humanitarian support has been inhibited and slowed down by the government of Sudan, augmenting the death toll from fighting on the ground through a war of attrition as food shortages, health conditions, and exposure complete the destruction of human life. The sad truth is that as Prunier points out, in a war zone "the horror experienced by the targeted group remains the same, no matter which word we use" (156). It is difficult to talk about contemporary diaspora or migration without mentioning genocide, the attempt to expunge from the world entire groups of people based on arbitrary and imagined notions of purity formulated around conceptions of class, race, ethnicity, region or location, religious affiliation, and other distinctions. There is, however, a problem with the use of genocide as a threshold for intervention; the sociological netting of conceptions such as genocide may be altogether too large to capture the nature and complexity of the economy of violence of the contemporary world. If we wait for some constellation of events to fit the grand proportions of genocide or the Holocaust, we may miss the amassing of quotidian atrocities that accumulate as if in slow motion. By the time these events are recognizably reaching the epic proportions of other known human tragedies, it will be too late to stop them. We have only to look at survivor accounts like that of Primo Levi's to remember the important fact that even in the aftermath of the liberation of the death camps, it took several years before the nature and scope of this tragedy was widely known. For such human suffering to merely fall through the classificatory net of social science would be a travesty. Although such configurations of violence occur over time, the scale and dimension of the process can and must be accessed rapidly monitored and stopped.

Genocide stands at the crossroads of grand narratives of identity, culture, and society and of attempts to create one people out of many by eradicating unwanted populations. It is the most tragic consequence of seeing the world as divided into cultural isolates, discrete unities of human society easily separated from one another. It is the result of misguided attempts to embrace a utopian ideal of "purity," a vision seemingly so simple that it leaves a world littered with uninhabitable terrains of incalculable loss. For survivors like war veterans, finding the context in which to talk about the trauma, the camps, and their memories of complete lives before the event is difficult, and is often reserved for others who understand the experience in the quiet of safe spaces far from the heart of the conflicts. There is no way to theorize about genocide—it is the product of absolutist thinking applied to the same ideas that otherwise result in stable unities (nation, ethnicity, race, region, religion). That is, this is a case of distinctions gone astray. States, groups fighting for control of them, and their allies are often at the heart of genocide. The chilling massacres in Rwanda in April 1994 were facilitated in part by the use of identity cards that confirmed the ethnicity of the bearer as Tutsi; when identified, Tutsis were summarily executed on the spot, and persons found without their cards were thought to be attempting to pass for Hutu (Longman 2001).[10] When not guided by identity documents, lists of the political opposition served to direct attacks. In a sad negation of an old myth of colonial legacy—the idea that Tutsi and Hutu might be distinguished from one another on sight—identity documents provided proof of identity. The nature of ethnic cleansing was already associated in the world community with the violence in Bosnia-Herzegovina,

Croatia, and later Kosovo, in the wake of the creation of new states; the reconfiguration of the former Yugoslavia produced new diasporas in the 1990s throughout the world. These conflicts demonstrate the great capacity of societies everywhere to draw on distant religious affiliation, emergent nationalism, or ethnic caricature in order to construct the rationale for the displacement of selected groups. Often it takes some time to fully acknowledge the scope of such tragedies; fear, the shattering of witnesses, or the absence of survivors often mean that we are limited to the strategic forensic account to reconstruct a trace of these lives cancelled out by crimes against humanity. The land mines, unused military equipment, and general devastation of a village, city, or region are not just reminders of the past; they also constitute potential dangers to those left behind. The experience of survivors warehoused for years in refugee camps where rebel groups try to recruit them for the conflict from which they seek refuge, shuttled to housing developments in a host of international cities, attempting to pick up life in settlements in plain view of where such crimes took place is unimaginable and yet all too common. I will consider in the following discussion what many consider genocide in Sudan, one of the most recent tales of displacement.[11] I will use the term "genocide," on which not all agree, though most would acknowledge that massive atrocities were perpetrated and some, as the United Nations commission of inquiry reported, no doubt constituted large-scale war crimes in the region (UNICOD 2005, Section V 58–159).[12]

The boundary dissolving in this new world of the present confronted by the anthropologist not only recasts subjectivity but dramatically reconfigures the context of a "classical" anthropological moment. While once the anthropological portrait of life in the field crops out any hint of the intervention of the colonial state or the infiltration of the market economy, a new figure now clouds the lens of the ethnographic camera. The notion of the "peoples of Africa" and the isolated cultures that formed the patchwork of the continent may be replaced by an Africa in motion or Africa as Diaspora, as today we are fascinated with hybridity, global migrations, and the rising population of African urban constellations. In the investigation of the present, however, the visage of European modernity continues to blurs the picture. Eurocentric imagery and the assumptions informed by it not only accompanied the cartoons, stills, and histories of Africa during the colonial period, but also still haunt neocolonial and postcolonial rhetorical discourse and image making. The contrasts between other cultures and their way of life and the West, between savagery and civilization, were on display on cigarette boxes, soap containers, and even worked into the patterns of clothing, making passive consumption almost an act of "imperialism" (Pieterse 1998). But the visions of a continent lagging behind an idealized West in the domains of governance, the economy, and society still plague contemporary representations of Africa.

Characteristic of the new "fragmented globality," an uneven global world, in which power differentials between nations are pronounced, is the consideration of the postcolonial state and the manner in which its "internal dissolution" has created within its borders zones ravaged by warfare, ethnic violence, and the proliferation of criminal cartels (Trouillot 2003; Mbembe 2001). This state of affairs takes place as the postcolonial state disintegrates to such an extent that the notion of "common good" is overturned, as the state becomes the site of a kind of mediation of private interests employing the mask—the mere shell—of a state designed to enrich only individual and groups that deploy systems of exploitation and domination. Some theorists make an assumption similar to the early anthropologist that I find both fascinating and troubling: that the African state is the complete opposite of an idealized European state, the latter of which is one that functions like clockwork, governed by a sacred "social contact" between the governed and the state concerned to uphold the "common good" of its citizens. This is no doubt an ideal of the European state; there are many ways in which such states do not live up to such a purified ideal. I am concerned that this new transparency of contemporary "Africa, a world in chaos," a crossroads of violence and private capitalistic adventurers like the old slideshow of the "stateless societies" of an old anthropology, may be projecting a new version of a theoretical construct that may never do justice to a complex African reality on the ground. Indeed, this view recapitulates traces of Western views of Africa startlingly similar to those that began perhaps with Hegel, resting on the contrast between the ordered European society and the chaotic African world, threatened by an economy of violence similar to the essence of the old rhetorical contrast between savagery and civilization, a "savage slot" (see Trouillot 2003, 25–28; Pieterse 1998, 91). So-called stateless societies are balanced by the device of the feud, a ritualized and local tear in the social fabric, an incident that required the execution of seldom-used structural principles in order to accomplish resolution through calling on higher orders of organization, allegiance, and diplomacy. But the feud itself, precipitated by the death of a kinsman or in more organized forms of warfare, was the foundation of a social order, loosely organized around a economy of violence and its occasional resolution, not unlike the postcolonial African state (although for different reasons). Beyond the frame in classical anthropological texts was the ultimate arbiter of all conflicts within its domain, the colonial order. Today the ultimate site of intervention is not the African state but rather the overarching domain of a global order that is not a unified formation but rather is rife with contradictory interests, power struggles, and long-term geopolitical agendas.

Using the example of the crisis in western Sudan, I will argue that the historical reality is much more complex and contradictory than some models of economy, democratic transition, and the disintegration of the postcolonial condition might suggest. The Sudanese state cannot be separated from the interlinking system of powerful states that shadow its every move. The weapons in the Sudanese arsenal—originating in the former Soviet Union and the United States, at times through third parties— are a testament to the shifting nature of allegiances, political intrigues, and external pressures that affect nation-states like Sudan. Furthermore, the African postcolonial state is more often in the so-called global age a crossroads, an operating theatre for more powerful states, NGOs, and other international organizations; we might say that what these nation-states fail to control—economic sectors, humanitarian crisis, and local rebellions—opens the door to the work of the global community and its intervention within the territorial borders of weak states. Such forms of intervention have an impact not only on the target states, but on entire regions, as refugee camps are set up in neighboring states that also become the site of rebel headquarters, and are a virtual gateway to the international community. The geographical imaginary of Africa zigzags across countless ethnic, racial, and cultural faultless unities that defy national closure. In such conditions, we are reminded that the nation is an achieved state, and can never be taken for granted, as other more compelling forms of belonging (religious, ethnic, political, protonationalist) are only a heartbeat away. It is not uncommon for refugee groups to be recruited as combatants in the ongoing civil conflicts of their new host country, further marginalizing their tenuous status on foreign soil and complicating the conditions of their return.

With the proliferation of internal "troubles," to borrow the Irish term for protracted civil unrest, it is no wonder that the vast majority of displaced persons today are virtual refugees within their own countries; having never crossed the international border, they are not officially "refugees," but their numbers are growing every year. Some fifty million now far outnumber the refugees that have crossed the frontier (thirteen to fifteen million). These internal zones, ever more common in the world today, are prime sites for diaspora making, as return to war-torn areas becomes impossible for many; for these people, relocation and integration into new countries is the only option. Indeed, these virtual "international zones" eclipse the nation-state, for varying periods of time usurping sovereignty and establishing areas of "limited sovereignty," which is in fact an indeterminate loss of sovereignty altogether. Yet it is at these very junctures that the state may call on its arsenal of diplomacy, the strategic deployment of sovereignty, and the use of force to tip the balance to its advantage. For all this fluidity and movement, the Khartoum may impose its will, appropriate food or other materials, block humanitarian missions, execute foreign nationals suspected of helping the rebels, and arm militias, because it is a state struggling to control its territories.

In this story, Khartoum remains a formidable figure from which one needs protection, a protection no longer sought in the realm of Dinka spiritualism but through the force of arms. Khartoum is at once a crucial site in the making of new diaspora and the administrative heart of new forms of state domination that are supplanting local traditional administrative and judicial powers. Khartoum seeks to eradiate the final vestiges of power left in place by the former colonial order, to displace local populations who might make claims (land rights, power sharing) that do not conform to the projected national order, to gain definitive control over the country's important natural resource, and to establish groups loyal to the government as its surrogates throughout the country. It is posed between Islamist ideologies that inform national political parties claiming the right to craft a state resonant with Islamic principles and secular models of the state imagined as a refuge for the many non-Muslim and Muslim minorities alike. This is all classical statecraft reminiscent of the colonial power pacification, of groups thought to be a threat to central authority and the careful management of ethnic conflict.[13]

The often volatile nature of the postcolonial African state sets the stage for the play of invisibility, but in the case of the Sudan, ethnic, racial, and regional tensions date back to colonial and even precolonial times. However none of the conflicts in this corner of contemporary Africa are primordial, since all follow specific historical trajectories crafted in local contexts over particular resources (oil, land, and water), political advantage, and the right to shape the future of the nation-state. In fact, the notion that there are discrete groups being referred to by such names as Nuba, Nuer, and Dinka may at times be misleading, as these groups can be found on every side of a conflict. The politically dominant North—with its heart in Khartoum, the national capital, and deeply rooted in the Arabization and Islamization of culture and society—has stood in sharp contrast to the resistance of the South, where people of African religious and cultural practices live in a radically different world (Deng 1995). Conflict in the western regions of the country has revealed new tensions between Muslims, divided by a diffuse pan-Arab identity of nomadic groups and the African heritage of agriculturalist, yet the conflict seems to be more of an orchestration of belonging, put into play by the state in order to stop a recent uprising by rebel forces. Rebel forces have taken up arms to fight against the long history of economic and political marginalization in the western region. Indeed, through the North–South conflict, rebel organizations have begun to articulate a comprehensive reintegration of the entire country unconfined to the South in an attempt to address widespread inequalities and complete a process left unfinished after independence.

In ever-widening circles of crisis, the Sudanese state has involved the world community in its internal troubles directly or indirectly through the United Nations, international NGOs, Europe, and the United States, not unlike other hotspots in which the state is compromised through identification with one ethnic or political group. This involvement has been so pervasive in some cases that it is difficult to disambiguate the postcolonial African state operating in crisis mode from the domains of intervention, increasingly occupied by international actors in the form of NGOs, banking concerns, and more powerful states (not all former colonial powers). In addition to this, the regional conflict between Chad, Libya, and Sudan clouds events in western Sudan. Darfur, as we shall see in a moment, is the crossroads for conflicts between expansionist nation-states and political and ethnic factions within and between them. Some theorists believe this kind of crisis to be indicative of a trend, particularly in postcolonial states struggling with the legacy of colonialism. In his recent book *On the Postcolony* (2001) Achille Mbembe, no doubt one of the leading theorists of postcolonial studies working today, offers a portrait of African society caught between the legacy of colonialism and the emergence of contemporary African society. I would like to consider Mbembe's notion of what he calls "private indirect government," a condition in which the postcolonial state is driven by private interests to such a degree that it no longer acts as the custodian of its citizen's peace and security. The state rather engages in a kind of state of total war, converting internal territories to zones of private enrichment that become a crossroads for illicit trafficking and trade. The creation of "internal borders" and the operation of "identity closure"—essentially reifying ethnic, religious, and/or racial markers between groups—results in a kind of struggle to consolidate new ethnic "homelands" in countries like the Sudan. Unfortunately, this state of affairs describes the contours of the Sudanese state. I would suggest that this profile is a potential of all states and not a unique property of the postcolonial condition. Giorgio Agamben has suggested that the play of biopolitical borders between life and death, inside and outside, and the interplay of identity between us and them is indicative of the transformation of sovereign power in the contemporary world in which life and politics become indistinguishable (Agamben 1998). But it also has the markings of a global system of power relations in the post–Cold War world, particularly marked after terrorist events in the United States and Europe in which the new interest of the world community includes preemptive unilateral military actions unprecedented in recent history. Although we usually think of these conditions as defining states in transition or the breakup of states, as in the Bosnian or Serbian examples, we might consider the postcolonial state in light of these broader circumstances, that is, as undergoing just such a transition. The transition is marked by the new state of the world, in which greater care is exercised to rein in "rogue nations" with incentives of investment, arms sales, and technical knowledge. Though the administrative and coercive arms of the state have defined a certain style of governance, the development of the nation has been sacrificed in Sudan. In a sense, the period after colonialism has served to make the state and its institutions, but has never succeeded in making the Sudanese people. It's not just that in Sudan there are the Nuba, Nuer, Dinka, Fur, Masalit, and other groups; it's that no shared vision of a nation that might encompass them all has emerged—certainly not one that might include all of its diverse populations in a power-sharing arrangement. What the society might look like after the central control of Khartoum has ended is hard to imagine; any form it takes will have to accommodate the many religious, cultural, and social differences of the country. At present, the ruling elite is hunkered down in Khartoum, as whole regions of the country are engulfed in open warfare—not a very promising condition for the making of the nation.

The African postcolonial state that Mbembe outlines reveals a kind of counterpoint to what often in his work remains latent, a highly idealized version of the European state tradition. Mbembe distills the European state down to its juridical ideology and often invokes a state in the distant past, during the process of European state formation, against the fully formed African postcolonial condition. Of course, the stories that states tell in order to mask often violent and nightmarish origins cannot be confused with the visions that crystallize as state ideology justifying present conditions. Let me say that the distillate of a generic European state in the work of Mbembe acts as a foil for the flesh-and-blood African reality and postcolonial condition seems to beg the question of the nature of state discourse in general, as this must be considered not simply as an abstraction, but through the "concrete" conditions of the state in a particular time and place. Any consideration of the state in its postcolonial form must include the legacy of the colonial order and the institutions it has imparted to the present. I will leave these objections for another moment and restrict my discussion to the form of government marked by a peculiar economy of violence that Mbembe delineates in his work. I would like to consider, however, some of the developments that Mbembe highlights in his discussion of the contemporary African postcolonial state.

For Mbembe, the contours of an economy of violence develop in African societies centered on the authoritarian and centralized postcolonial state that is overwhelmed by the outbreak of internal dissent and the disintegration, as if in slow motion, of the its economy. Mbembe describes a kind of implosion of the postcolonial African state that precipitated a state that has adapted itself to the exigencies of scarcity, economic downturns, and the imposition of austerity measures by international monetary agencies—the pressures, in short, of the global economy: a growing debt structure and the rising costs of maintaining a centralized state and its bureaucracy. The boundaries of the state are being reconfigured increasingly by illicit trade networks, the local personnel needed to maintain them, and the international links and outlets of this new trafficking. The official frontiers are overwritten by these invisible boundaries as "the real map of the continent is in the process of being reshaped" (Mbembe 2001, 86–87). Cut off from much of the country in the capital, state functionaries seek a new basis of power, a new technology of coercion and control.

This new world is characterized by the increasing privatization of the monopoly of coercion once held by the state. The loss of this monopoly means that this privilege is dispersed throughout the society and deployed by those capable of managing force in the service of private enrichment. The bond between the governed and the state has been broken; no longer do modes of taxation imply a reciprocal interplay of rights, transfers, and obligations and provide the basis for the foundation of postcolonial citizenship (Mbembe 2001, 84). Rather, new forms of "subjecting and controlling people" come into being, operating through the shell of the former state by a host of local and international agents having the clear advantage of the availability of the use of force:

> Having command over individuals thus becomes inseparable from
> use of their property and administration of their death. In such
> circumstances, taxation is transformed into an extended category
> for which no consent is required and no demand tied to any
> precise idea of public utility or common good. . . . In other words,
> there is no longer difference between taxation and exaction.
> To territorialize domination, there is no hesitation in resorting
> either to the support of foreign mercenaries or to the formation of
> parallel forces, militias, and action groups, form refugees, or from
> the common people in general. (Mbembe 2001, 85)

A shadow economy emerges from fragments of the military, government functionaries, police, customs agents, and others who attempt to gain control of the flow of illicit funds through drug trafficking, arms trades, and other activities. Others gain access to this world only through cheap labor in the new complex or through a system of patronage, leaving vast segments of the population with no form of access to the new order. The profusion of private networks, secret contacts, and privileged sectors of the economy of "local businessmen, 'technocrats,' and warlords" in the African state is then coordinated with developed international networks, constituting a mode of economic relations quickly "swept underground" masking the "indiscriminate violence and high-level corruption" on which the whole system rests (Mbembe 2001, 86). The power of this new state of affairs is felt most forcefully within a given state as whole areas of national territories are given over to the operation of these emergent cartels, ethnic groups, and criminal networks. In the end, according to Mbembe, an emergent form of violence takes hold and engulfs the state. Typically, this "specific form of violence" manifests itself as "warfare" (87).[14]

This generic outline of the postcolonial state resembles in many ways Africa's largest state—Sudan. Since the 1970s, the struggle over land, water, and oil has transformed the country into a virtual war zone. With Agamben's cautionary tale of the state appropriating greater powers through exceptional measures that become the rule, we must note that Sudan has been under a continuous state of emergency since 1999. In 2004, the government announced the renewal of the state of emergency for an additional year.[15] The interplay between international organizations, NGOs, the Sudanese government, and multiple regional conflicts—at times involving neighboring states—has gone on throughout much of the country's independence. The proliferation of ethnic militias and the attempt of the state to displace traditional local administrations have resulted in a battle over control of a number of regions and an overall militarization of Sudanese society. But many of these features of the postcolonial state, including the structure of its particular orchestration of violence, date back to the colonial period; no account of the contemporary conflict would be complete without being situated within the broader framework of this and other colonial legacies. Warfare is not, as Mbembe suggests, something new; it is, in fact, something old and familiar.

Darfur: Sliding from View

In the masterful work of writer Juan Rulfo *The Burning Plain and Other Stories* (1971), the image of the parched and dry Mexican plain at times overwhelms and dwarfs his characters, who at times seem to merge with the harsh physical environment, finding in their daily existence the simplicity of a bit of dignity in their almost rhetorical resistance. A haunting stillness is captured in the collection of stories; particularly in one tale, entitled "They Gave Us the Land," in which a meandering narrative of resignation unfolds: "So they've given us this land. And in this sizzling frying pan they want us to plant some kind of seed to see if something will take root and come up. But nothing will come up here . . . this hard white earth, where nothing moves and where you walk as if losing ground" (Rulfo 1971). They have struggled and won a plain that seems all but uninhabitable, in the aftermath of the revolution. This is a bit like the Dinka saying, "I named my child Khartoum," acknowledging the difficulty and pain associated with a life of marginal employment and discrimination in the capital. The delicate balance of the human and cultural ecology of the Sudan has become much more perilous than that suggested by Evans-Pritchard; the dangers, however, originate in the battle over resources between human actors, rather than as a struggle with the natural world. In recent years, conflicts in Sudan have taken on the character of a "resource war" in which people, natural resources, and minerals become the prizes in a struggle to control potential markets for oil, water, land, and precious metals. Although Sudan is now entering the "select club of international oil producers," the neglect of the provinces—a legacy of the condominium period—has changed little since independence (Prunier 2005).

What the United Nations has called the world's worst humanitarian emergency has taken shape in Darfur in western Sudan since 2003. Republican U.S. Senator Sam Brownback of Kansas, returning from a fact-finding mission in the region, called for more "high-profile visits," in his words, "to keep the dying in Darfur from 'sliding out of view'" (Kramer 2004). After twenty-one years of civil war in the south, the Sudanese government in Khartoum signed a peace agreement on May 26, 2004, ending conflict—albeit in a shaky peace. Peace has to often come to mean "merely an interim truce between civil wars," in the Sudan (D. Johnson 2003, xix). The North–South conflict began to bleed into other regions, particularly during the second major phase of the civil wars that began in the 1980s. One of these spillover sites is Darfur, in the western region of Sudan; victims of ethnic cleansing in a conflict ethnically coded as between "African farmers" and "Arab pastoralists" will remain for an indeterminate period of time in limbo, as the displaced villagers are identified through a diplomatic euphemism that does little to mask their vulnerability.[16] Villagers are huddled by the international community into the container category of internally displaced persons (IDPs).[17] Many of the features of the conflict are patterned on the war in the South, including the "targeting of local leaders and the forced dislocation of populations" (131).[18] The brutality of the statistic reveal that tens of thousands of people have died in the course of the conflict, over 2.6 million people, at this writing, are "suffering" because of it, and 1.9 million have been displaced from their homes within the Sudanese territory (Annan 2005).[19]

The idea of sovereignty in theory and sovereignty on the ground in practice are often words apart. Sovereignty holds to no privileged geography where the climate or people are more favorable to its realization, nor clearly is it ever and always the same, but rather—as we have seen in Iraq, where the United States employed the notion of "limited sovereignty"—it may come to be attenuated, transformed, and curtailed by the operation of greater orders of power. The vision of a unified and peaceful Sudan lies on the distant horizon for many today. This dream has had many champions along the way, and John Garang, a leader baptized in the fire of civil war for over twenty years, was recently lost in a helicopter crash as the former rebel leader made his way from Uganda to the South of Sudan. The peace accord ending the conflict in the South of Sudan resulted in John Garang being sworn in as vice president of the national government and president of the South only a few weeks before his untimely death in August 2005. The peace agreement called for a new constitution—a transitional period under a government of national unity—and postponed the question of the division of the North and South to a referendum, in five years' time, through which the people of the South might decide their own fate. Garang pressed consistently for a unified Sudan, rather than simple autonomy for the South. His background represents in many ways the great complexity of the people involved in the conflict: a southern Dinka, educated in the United States, where he earned a doctorate in economics and even received military training. Sent to quell a disturbance among southern troops by the Sudanese government, he would become a rebel leader commanding the Sudan People's Liberation Army, only to return some twenty-two years later at the conclusion of one of Africa's most bloody civil wars to assume a post in the national government. Through the years, warfare spared no faction, rebel, government or other, the accusation of human rights violations or the exploitation of the civilian population. It was Garang's vision that distinguished his leadership; however, even his initial radio addresses to the people of Sudan at the beginning of the civil war framed the problems of the South in the context of a unified Sudanese nation and not in terms of secession. But the issues affecting the entire country—power sharing, wealth sharing, and development (local and regional)—have not changed a great deal over the last twenty years and remain as yet unresolved on the ground. Darfur and its disposition remained, despite many objections, largely outside of the agreement. Fearing a breakdown of negotiations in the South, developments in Darfur escalated out of hand, from low-intensity conflicts between settled populations and herding peoples into a full-blown large-scale humanitarian crisis. Garang's death underscores a deep sense of insecurity about the direction of the new unity government and its future. His presence in the government might have assured continued attention to developments in the West, his death has made any real resolution of the crisis doubtful.

The state of the crisis in Darfur at the time of this writing is not encouraging; there has been an increase in attacks on internally displaced people in some parts of the region; sexual violence, particularly through rapes and attacks on young women under the age of eighteen, who now constitute about one-third of all victims, seems to be on the rise, and humanitarian workers, African Union Mission in the Sudan (AMIS) soldiers, and other personnel have been attacked, resulting in a number of deaths. Many displaced persons who had returned to their home areas are being forced back into camps in which security increasingly cannot be assured. Both external security monitors and humanitarian workers have come under fire. Because of the deterioration of the security situation, the "culture of impunity" that protects the perpetrators of human rights violations persists, according to Sima Samar, the United Nations Special Rapporteur on Human Rights to the Sudan (Reuters 2005). In addition, the Official Armed Forces of the Sudan have participated in "coordinated offensive operations" with tribal militias on a number of occasions, as confirmed by AMIS officials. The support and coordination of the proxy militias is deeply insinuated in the structure of the Sudanese state. Banditry and hijacking on the main roads leading to the South forced humanitarian aide agencies to declare regions temporarily off-limits until authorized military escorts might be arranged, delaying badly needed food relief and other supplies to the region. Although many children have been demobilized as combatants, the abduction of children used for military service continues. One of the Secretary General's monthly reports on Darfur to the Security Council of the United Nations stated:

> The recent brutal wave of violence makes real improvements
> to the humanitarian situation impossible and has forced many
> returnees back to the camps they had left just weeks before. This
> tragic reversal of fortunes must not stand. (United Nations 2005)

Despite the relatively late start to the resolution of the Darfur crisis— which I will address shortly—ample attention has now been given to the contours of a peace. Both the Sudanese government and the Sudanese Liberation Movement/Army have made commitments in the Ceasefire Agreement of April 2004, the Humanitarian and Security Protocols of November 2004, and the Declaration of Principles for the Resolution of the Sudanese Conflict of July 2005; ongoing talks are also being conducted. But both parties seem to be presently engaged in a clear disregard for the commitments outlined in these protocols and agreements. All parties have continued hostilities while conducting negotiations, presenting a unified front at talks and fragmenting on the ground. In fact, the plight of civilians continues; in the discussion that follows, I shall outline the crisis briefly and consider its implications for the constellation of the Sudanese state.

Darfur is Sudan's largest region, defining a western border with Libya, Chad, and the Central African Republic. The region incorporated into the North only after 1916; post-Independence, Sudan has remained largely underdeveloped, with many linked to the outside world through infrequent truck routes and itinerant traders. Nomadic peoples still visualize the lands as a patchwork of intermittent agricultural spaces and grazing lands through which tradition affords passage along invisible herding routes. Since 1999, Darfur has been divided into three states—North, South, and West—where the majority of its population live in "small

villages and hamlets often composed of only a few hundred families"
(UNICOD 2005). About two million people have been displaced, refugee
camps dart the Chadian side of the border, and an estimated 2.6 million
have been in some way affected by the crisis since February 2003. Some
fear that these camps may become permanent, as the "scorched-earth
policy" in the region has left large tracts of land that now reveal little sign
of human habitation, save the occasional outcropping of burned and abandoned villages. The camps are mostly improvised settlements; in those in
Darfur, where most of the displaced are literally trapped under government control, the residents face the constant fear of continued attacks.
In Darfur, so-called Arab pastoralists and African farmers (Fur, Masalit,
and Zaghawa) have experienced the not-uncommon conflicts between
nomadic and settled groups for years, over such things as cattle raiding, grazing, and water rights.[20] The conflict "escalated in February 2003,
when two rebel groups, the Sudan Liberation Army/Movement (SLA/M)
and the Justice and Equality Movement (JEM), drawn from members
of the Fur, Masalit, and Zaghawa ethnic groups, demanded an end to
chronic economic marginalization and sought power sharing within
the . . . Sudanese state" (Flint, Rone, and Lefkow 2004, 1).[21] So-called
Arab pastoralists have in recent years increasingly encountered difficulty
surviving periods of prolonged drought and the ongoing desertification
of the area. The rifts between local groups (tribes), according to a recent
United Nations Commission report, and "political polarization around
the rebel opposition to the central authorities has extended itself to issues
of identity," culminating in a justification for escalating conflicts between
traditional adversaries into a full-scale armed conflict (UNICOD 2005,
130). The nomadic groups were organized, trained, and armed by the
government into militias called the Janjaweed, in part as a "tactic of
war" in a counterinsurgency campaign.[22] In an effort to neutralize the
rebel groups and the emerging threat of a politically organized population in the area the government with its partners, the Janjaweed pur-
sued a campaign of ethnic cleansing and relocation targeting the civilian
population of Darfur (Flint, Rone, and Lefkow 2004).[23] Despite international pressure, the Janjaweed have not been "disarmed or neutralized"
and continue to pose a threat to the former inhabitants of the region.
At this point, Khartoum may be unable to stop the growth of the proxy
militias, as the government is not the only source of their support. The

campaign of the Janjaweed has been, according to Human Rights Watch, coordinated with government forces—the Janjaweed even wear uniforms indistinguishable from that of the Sudanese army. Jemera Rone, Sudan researcher for Human Rights Watch's Africa Division, has repeatedly cautioned the United Nations Security Council to deal harshly and swiftly with the Janjaweed because "the Janjaweed are not an independent body, but a tool created by the Sudanese government. The Security Council must place the responsibility for the crimes against humanity squarely with the Sudanese government" (Flint, Rone, and Lefkow 2004). Although the Security Council has expressed its "deep concern" and called for the disarming of the Janjaweed, it has stopped short of placing strict sanctions on the government itself (see UNICOD 2005).

The classical ethnography of the Nuer and Dinka is so firmly fixed in the heart of an anthropological past that it is difficult to place these notions of people and their cultures in motion. Even the Nuer and the Dinka were once thought to be organized in various "tribes, sections, and clans"; the term "tribe," widely used in contemporary Sudan, was inherited in part from the colonial period, taking shape from the period's anthropological gloss, and is now widely used in Sudan in reference to a political unit, its principles varying from group to group.[24] Because tribes are fluid and ever-changing entities, sections may even over time act as "autonomous political groups" (D. Johnson 2003, xvii). Once the notion of Nuer and Dinka are considered in terms of the contemporary Sudanese conflicts, political and regional developments become key.

The term "Janjaweed" is like an old anthropological gloss for a more complex social reality and is an invitation into the great ethnic, racial, and political complexity of Sudan. The so-called tribal militias are not a contemporary inventions, but date back to the colonial period when such groups were used to harass the civilian population, much like they are today through "pacification patrols" and raids (D. Johnson 2003, 83). In the mid-1980s, so-called tribal militias became a significant factor in the efforts of Khartoum to combat the Sudan People's Liberation Army (SPLA) in the South and elsewhere. Although the policy to incorporate the militias as a kind of paramilitary alongside the army was initially contested by some senior officers from the late 1980s, the line between the militias and the army or regular forces has continued to blur.[25] Khartoum recently has claimed that it is difficult to find the former Janjaweed, as the term is an amalgam of Arabic words meaning "devil" or, roughly, "a devil on horseback with a gun" that denotes the marauding subject in the act of going out to loot and burn, so it is not clear who this might refer to: members of tribal militias, elements of the popular defense forces, or even disorganized and intermittent raiding. Because Janjaweed do not wish to identify themselves, for fear of prosecution for human rights violations, they fade back into their former lives, "policemen or pastoralists by day, Janjaweed by night." Some even concede that a portion of the regular army contains Janjaweed, and it seems that if they are not caught in the act of "raiding," they simply fade into the woodwork (Lacey 2004). In fact, many of the Janjaweed may be members of local police, popular defense forces, or the army, which allows them to act with impunity and return to their regular daily activities in the aftermath of attacks. One wonders how the government of Sudan and its allies—in many cases, foreign governments—during the 1980s identified and armed so many of these hard-to-identify fighters.[26] What has made the militias so powerful has been the combination of government issued ordnance and the license to operate with impunity, the relatively well-organized fighting units, and their ability to disband and reappear at as if at will. Douglas H. Johnson credits the use of militias and the preference of various factions in Khartoum that employ them in strategic political, economic, and military campaigns. The militias are, in short, a dimension of governmental politics used by Khartoum as well as extra-governmental groups. Such nonstate players have become increasingly common in combat zones over the last decade; often part-time combatants—"farmer by day, fighter by night"—the fighters have made security even in refugee camps problematic, as they fade into the local population, drawing even areas thought to be refuges into the conflict. Their ability to hide from view blurs the lines of conflict, lending a military character to such civilian locations as camps, markets, and transitional regions. Separating civilians from combatants is no simple matter, and the presence of the fighters among civilian populations contributes to the sexual assault and exploitation of women in camps and elsewhere and the general militarization of neutral zones. Once identification is in fact made, disarmament, demobilization, and internment or transfer of the combatants becomes a serious problem. A lack of monitoring, policing, and patrol personnel remains a problem for these spontaneous camps.

Darfur—a region of some six million people shaped by independent sultanates that predate the Truco-Egyptian conquest of the 1870s—was finally incorporated into the Sudan of the Anglo-Egyptian condomnium (1898–1956) in 1916 (D. Johnson 2003; Flint and de Waal 2005; see also Flint and de Waal 2008).[27] Much of the institutional structure of the sultanates was retained under the Native Administration, an indigenous administration that acted as mediators of the conflicts that arose between the sedentary agriculturalist populations such as the Fur and the semi-nomadic pastoralists like the Baqqara and other groups. The abolition of the Native Administration in the 1970s wiped away the entire structure of traditional patterns of conflict resolution mediated through local community leaders. Fur officials of the regional government found themselves increasingly pressed between the claims of local communities and political dynamics in Khartoum and attempts on the ground of immigrant groups to carve out "home territories" (D. Johnson 2003, 140). This merely helped to polarize the pastoralist/agriculturalist conflict. Further changes in the governance of the region after administrative reorganization programs under the government of President Omar El Bashir brought about more direct state control of the area. The state's attempt to impose greater authority in the region coincided with a period of prolonged drought of the 1970s and 1980s. While agricultural areas were expanding, converting more land to agriculture in response in part to an increasing demand of internal markets, large groups of pastoralists from the North began to resettle in the farming belt. Many of the pastoralists, having lost their livestock, turned temporary stays in the region into permanent relocation. During the the mid-1980's, Darfur became a crossroads for the civil unrest in neighboring Chad; arms and resources flowed freely across the borders as populations such as the non-Arab Zaghawa and many Arab groups had done for centuries. The arming of so-called Arab militias stems largely from this period (see D. Johnson 2003). While elements in Chad incorporated non-Arab ethnic militias from the area, after the outbreak of the Chad–Libyan war (1986–1987), Libya—with the permission of the Sudanese government—moved troops through Darfur and began to arm and fund Arab groups in the region. Some scholars view the period as a de facto annexation of the area by Libya. The region became a staging area for Libyan designs to create a corridor linking its national territory with portions of Sudan and Chad; thus, "Libya kept operating on the ground as if Darfur were already Libyan territory" according to Prunier (2005, 70). With Libyan "oil, weapons and money" flowing into Sudan through the West, Darfur has been deeply rooted in the "Chadian–Libyan–Sudanese triangular conundrum"; this is not a new development and has not been since the 1980s, in spite of the most recent attention to the border crossings of the conflict (Prunier 2005, 66; Polgreen 2006). The ideology of "Arab supremacy" also stems from this period, coming not from Khartoum but through various associations inspired by Libyan influence. The militarization of Darfur continued, with the Arab groups influenced increasingly by a rising pan-Arab ideology, as the spillover of war in Chad effectively polarized Arabs and blacks "with the Sudanese Islamist parties now equating Islam with Arabism" (Johnson 2003, 140). Sudanese conceptions of race, region, and religion identifications are highly volatile and given to shifting meaning in different historical situations. Darfur, although predominately Muslim, differs between divergent religious factions, and international pan-Arab ideology was deployed to "over-code" distinctions. The organization of the Janjaweed represents an advanced process of militarization (from the 1980s to the present), the spread of a "racially coded ideology," and the polarization of non-Arab and Arab cultural traditions.[28] It is, however, important to keep in mind that the conflict is political and not racial or cultural.

Khartoum has come to symbolize the accumulation of wealth through oil revenues and the consolidation of centralized administrative powers; the rest of the country is marginalized, resource-poor, and far from the site of decision making. Khartoum, like an island of centralized power, "has evolved into a kind of separate country," with its political culture in part articulated through vote-rich sections of the country, like Darfur (Prunier 2005, 77). After 1989, the government abolished much of the structure of local decision making when it swept away many of the customary councils that traditionally settled area disputes. The scorched-earth policy of the government is a way of providing a corridor of security in the regions by replacing dissidents with claims to local land, water, and oil rights with loyal supporters of the regime who owe everything to the government. It seems more a matter of political and cultural fragmentation than resettlement on a grand scale, as many of the groups in the proxy militias are nomadic, although prolonged drought has certainly threatened the livelihoods of many herders.

As in the unfolding of any series of atrocities, for the victims the events will occur and recur in a never-ending present burned into the memory like a scar. The attacks begin early in the morning when the drone of Russian-made Antonov aircraft can be heard overhead just before the bombing starts. The Antonovs are followed by the helicopter gunships that on occasion bring supplies, according to eyewitnesses, for the Janjaweed.[29] The Janjaweed begin their attack with automatic weapons fire, stopping from time to time to talk on satellite phones, and destroying everything they do not plunder.[30] The Janjaweed walk through the local markets with guns slung over their shoulders—neither the police nor the military check their activities—as they confidently announce to some villagers that they, not the local authorities, are in charge now. The Janjaweed use rape as a weapon; women who leave the camps to collect firewood or straw fear being raped and so prefer going outside in groups. Men outside the camps are at times summarily executed by the militia fighters; only inside the camps do they feel a modicum of peace.[31]

Driven from their villages and homes, crops destroyed, the farmers have no opportunity to plant, so next year there will be no crops as well. Their displacement will be long-term, as the Janjaweed steal cattle and destroy even cooking pots in many of the villages they raid. In the aftermath of the conflict, the militarization of the area stands in stark contrast to the complete absence of any of the necessities that might support human life. Food stores are systematically destroyed in village after village; as journalist Julie Flint notes in her visits to the area in March and April 2004, "Food buried in pits in advance of the attacks remains in most cases uncollected, as the risk of retrieving it became too great" (2004, 2). Everything that made life possible had been obliterated. In addition to the indiscriminate killings of civilians, women of all ages were raped and mosques desecrated, as according to eyewitnesses government soldiers looked on. During the night, villages would hurriedly bury the dead before abandoning their villages. Women and children on route to Chad or other relatively safe sites had to avoid the Janjaweed checkpoints.

Violence continues in the region, as the camps for those displaced grow daily despite the lack of basic services, the threat of disease, and the slow pace of humanitarian aid to the region. Although humanitarian organizations stand ready to act and by mid-summer 2004 are hoping to provide aid to some eight hundred thousand persons, the lack of logistical hardware (airplanes, helicopters, and trucks) thwarts the progress of the agencies. Monitors of the African Union suffer from a similar problem: faced with the task of attempting to survey an area the size of France, they sit in hotels in the capital, waiting for proper transportation.[32] Even when personnel are in place for monitoring groups and humanitarian agencies, they lack the ability to fully deploy relief campaigns. United Nations and other aid groups hope to provide aid for two million people in camps in Chad and Darfur by October 2004, but this would be under ideal conditions, in the absence of interference of militias or government officials. When the Secretary General of the United Nations tours the region, he carries a simple message—"the violence must stop"—to refugees who meet him in the camps with such slogans as "voluntary return and security" and "peace, not war." In Chad alone, some two hundred thousand people have taken refuge from the systematic violence in their homeland. United Nations Emergency Relief Coordinator Jan Egeland tells reporters, in a sad comment on the deteriorating situation in Darfur on July 1, 2004, "The only thing in abundance in Darfur is weapons." Indeed "the Kalashnikov rifle transformed the moral order of Darfur" (Flint and de Waal 2005, 48). The weapon, capable of slaughtering an entire platoon, truckload of passengers, or family,

> made the scale of fatalities escalate beyond bounds of a moral
> economy considering the collective responsibility of single
> acts of violence of a feud. The gun violence facilitated by the
> Kalashnikov seemed indiscriminate, authorless and impossible
> to account for in a moral order where social relations took place
> primarily between people known to one another and groups
> that shared culture, geography and religion. It is easier to get a
> Kalashnikov than a loaf of bread. (Reuters 2004a)

In a place where, prior to the 1980s, such weapons were a rarity, a local expression now sums up the situation in the slogan "Without a Kalashnikov, you're nothing." Despite the ceasefire, reports continue of massacres, rape, and torture coordinated with government forces (Reuters 2004b), and in early July 2004, rebels initially refuse to meet with the government due to claims that air attacks and bombings continued in the region. After confirmations in early July 2004 that villages in northern Darfur continue to be bombed and that trucks belonging to humanitarian organizations operating in the region are being looted, much internal wrangling within the United Nations Security Council finally produces Resolution 1556 on Darfur.[33]

The details of the individual testimony are heartbreaking, but all too familiar; the arid terrain of Darfur, stretching some 200,000 square km (125,000 square miles), or about the size of France, into the western regions of Sudan will doubtless not be the last site of such a conflict. The anticipated costs of humanitarian aid for 2005 totaled well over $1.5 billion a year and, with incursions into Chad and the dislocation of people from camps in renewed cross-border fighting, the cost and consequences of the conflict will no doubt continue to escalate. Observers have cautioned against any placing any great faith in the agreements of the government, which has recently renewed its offensive in Darfur. "The Sudan government has decades of experience in impeding humanitarian operations" and will waste no time continuing to harass humanitarian efforts until monitoring agencies have recourse to some form of enforcement, through sanctions or an international military intervention (Flint and de Waal 2005, 119).

The vast majority of the displaced are still in Darfur in camps that are virtual prisons, with little hope of leaving them in the foreseeable future. Trucks loaded with food for the camps take three weeks to drive across the country from Port Sudan on the Red Sea to Darfur. All-terrain trucks capable of making the trip during the rainy season are in short supply, and the airdrops in July 2004 had only begun to offload needed supplies. Even in normal years in the region, tens of thousands die from preventable ailments such as diarrhea, dehydration, malnutrition, malaria, and others; today in the camps, the lack of food, water, and proper shelter will cause the death toll to rise, particularly among children and the elderly. Although I speak here about estimates from 1994, the problem of the assessments of death tolls remains the same, although now an acceptance of a number around three hundred thousand is not controversial. Some estimate a toll even as high as four hundred thousand. The unfortunate game is the same—changing only the floor and the ceiling of a tragedy, the numbers enter into a politics of international shame. That 350,000 to 1 million people might die by the end of 2004 simply because the humanitarian response was blocked through a war of attrition and because intervention from the world community to stop the

death toll came too late or not at all was a sad commentary on the state
of the global community, and such a sad calculus may rise even more if
the region slides further from the attention of the world. African Union
monitors now number some seven thousand but still fall far short of the
force required to properly patrol the area; an expansion of force using
United Nations soldiers would work only with the unified support of the
world community. This force requires a great deal of time to amass and
equip properly, while every moment that security remains fragile costs
lives on the ground. Even though the United Nations Security Council
has authorized the use of their soldiers, the "blue hats," the government
of Sudan impedes the deployment of these troops.[34] Humanitarian aid
workers continue to be targets of attacks; during the summer of 2006
twelve lost their lives and nearly three million people are now dependent
on international food aid, shelter, and medical treatment. Hundreds of
thousands of people have been cut off from food aid due to an escalation
of hostilities, in spite of the so-called truce. In an address to the Security
Council on September 11, 2006, Secretary General Kofi Annan raised
once again the specter of genocide:

> Can the international community, having not done enough for
> the people of Rwanda in their time of need, just watch as this
> tragedy deepens? Having finally agreed just one year ago that
> there is a responsibility to protect, can we contemplate failing
> yet another test? Lessons are either learned or not: principles are
> either upheld or scorned. This is no time for the middle ground
> of half measures or further debate. This latest fighting shows
> utter disregard for the Darfur Peace Agreement.[35]

The unraveling of the peace agreement is only part of a very sad
truth—that in the contemporary era, we cannot name one occasion in
which the international community has intervened on the part of those
caught up in such a humanitarian crisis.[36] The hybrid United Nations–
African Union peacekeeping force is taking shape at a snail's pace, but
can be no substitute for real peace.

Beyond the confines of the camps, the Janjaweed operate with impunity.[37] The ethnic differences between the so-called African farmers and
Arab pastoralists have been exaggerated since the 1980s among groups
that have intermarried for centuries. Religion has nothing to do with the

does it also have nothing to do with peacemaking?

conflict, as both sides share the same faith, yet in Darfur mosques and schools alike are reduced to ashes.[38] As Mbembe notes, the permeability of borders in contemporary African postcolonial situations rests in part on the exploitation of "ethnic" and regional antagonisms, drawing whole populations into an effective redrafting of internal and international borders. The passion of belonging provides the modalities through which this territorial reconfiguration takes place: "The feeling of belonging of forged and identities [are] reinvented increasingly through the medium of disputes over what belongs to whom and through manipulation of indigenousness and ancestral descent" (Mbembe 2001, 86). Entire regions like Darfur are left filled with chilling memories that may never abate, smoldering ashes, bomb fragments, and the hope of return from which diasporas are born.

CHAPTER 3

The Inexhaustible Sense of Exile

Other Cultures in the Photographic Imaginary

> To travel is to see—travel is essentially a way of seeing, a mode
> of seeing; it is grounded in the eye, in our visual capacity. The
> traveler is Argus-eyed; there are no blind travelers or explorers
> in either physical or imaginary voyages.
>
> —BERNARD MCGRANE, *BEYOND ANTHROPOLOGY:*
> *SOCIETY AND THE OTHER*

The Culture of Theory

The Famished Road, a novel by Ben Okri, opens with the meditations
of a spirit child contemplating whether to continue life in the mundane
world or surrender and returning to the ethereal realm. In a phrase
that speaks to the underlying tension within diasporic experience, Okri
writes, "To be born is to come into the world weighed down with strange
gifts of the soul, with enigmas and an inextinguishable sense of exile"
(1992, 5). This sense of exile—often cast as a trope of travel, an opposition between home and elsewhere—remains at the heart of attempts to
configure diaspora in the culture of theory. The intangibles of longings
and unattainable places and times haunts the waking days of those in
diaspora and in theory. Diasporic social practice is at once inflected with
new possessions drawn from a world in motion, and imbued with an
uncommon sense of loss gained from peculiar and multiple locations in
the transparency of such notions as national, global, local, and implied
in the idea of community. While those in diaspora are not betwixt and
between the spirit world and the everyday as is the spirit child of the
novel, they must contend with an "inextinguishable sense of exile," if
only among the theorist who attempts to shadow their transnational

movements. The late Madan Sarup suggested that the foreigner is read "psychologically" by others; like a kind of symptom "s/he signifies the difficulty we have living as an other and with others" (Sarup 1996). The newcomer often becomes the symptom/sign of the changing nature of a social formation one contested by the established. The image of the migrant then can come to signify social disorder, urban decline, and the ending of "our way of life." Part of the urgency of seeing images of the newcomer comes from the effort to confirm the ultimate difference of other cultures, other ways of life.

In *Towards the African Revolution*, Frantz Fanon notes that, "It is a common saying that racism is a plague of humanity. But we cannot content ourselves with such a phrase. We must tirelessly look for the repercussion of racism at all levels of sociability" (1967b, 36). For Fanon, the idea of racism deeply insinuated itself into the very fabric of the contemporary world; discovering its traces and exploring its "repercussions" in daily life is thus a fundamental duty for those wishing to change society. The anthropological imagination has inherited, no doubt created, a conceptual landscape employed by some to promote the ideological foundation of boundaries separating social groups or connect them through a set of arbitrary characteristics drawn from the endless stream of human variation (Cohen 2000).

In Turin, Italy, a young migrant once turned to me at a public "Senegalese dinner" and, drawing my attention to an Italian researcher, camera in hand, demanded "Where are those photographs going to go; who are they for?" Migrants face the inexhaustible weight of "immigrant caricature" as their photographs become a critical feature of a national discourse on immigration.

Immigrant caricature employs techniques that enhance the outsider status of the migrant and takes varying forms, like the slight exaggeration of the presence in official statistics. Coupled with Italy having one of the lowest birth rates in Europe, the idea that the migrant population may come to overwhelm Italians has been the cause of a great deal of concern and anxiety. Other methods include the targeting of migrant bodies as sites of medical intervention or neglect, and the use of cartoons, photographs, and media that underscore the absurdity of including migrants in the national collectivity. Popular myths are populated by the idea of the immigrant/symptom. The images of immigrants cut to the very heart of our imaginative worlds—of our present, in part because they transport us beyond the commonplace. The taken-for-granted backdrop of peoples and places and the myriad props that once supported visualizing them have been transformed as context rushes in to disrupt the photo studio.

The Photographic Imaginary

Victor Burgin cautions us in *Thinking Photography* that "To look at a photograph beyond a certain period of time is to court a frustration; the image which on first looking gave pleasure has by degrees become a veil behind which we now desire to see" (1982, 152). The most basic tensions are set in motion for those living in multiple sites by the mundane, acts of everyday living, flights of memory, a neglected medical condition, a haunting communication from home, or the turned-up corners of an old photograph. Guarding against nostalgia only goes so far, as the appearance of an unexpected friend from home, a gift from relatives, or the request of money for a family emergency may be the trigger of a world of memory. As Eduardo Cadava reminds us, we must be attuned to the hidden history implicit in the photograph: "Forgetting is inscribed within every photograph, there is history—the history of photography as well as the history inaugurated by the photograph" (1995, 227). But photographs hold in the lives of many of the Senegalese migrants a place of importance—images of migrant familial contexts, religious leaders, and even home villages and cities provide tokens of identity and comfort.

What may appear as a form of abandonment of a place or to those who live lives of the established, here and there, may seem otherwise to people in motion. Living in diaspora also means a perpetual longing for and at times rejection of the lives of those left behind. And the newcomer remains a stranger in a new environment, one in which he or she is destined to explore the modes of being that define the other in myth, humor, and image. From a location in diaspora, we must guard against nostalgia in one moment, while embracing memories of "home" in the next. Of course, some of this play of memory operates in the lives of each and every one of us—its lasting trace, I would argue, is however deeply framed in diaspora, becoming a critical part of our experience, identity, and memory.

Standing as if between these worlds, the migrant marks a terrain of potentialities. The misty outlines of a future lend urgency to the presence of the outsider. What they may become will in a sense determine the contours of an emergent social world. The appearance of the immigrant—the stranger in our visual regime—signals a period of crisis in which we must understand who and what we are in relation to who and what we are not. Although seemingly oblivious to the camera, many of the migrants that appear in Italian newspapers are not caught completely unawares, and at times maintain a kind of defiant posture toward the process of being photographed.[1]

During my fieldwork in Italy, the aggressive methods of the photographers and journalist became so pronounced and problematic for many migrant groups that a kind of moratorium on filming and photography in the residences was in effect put into place.[2] The Senegalese and Moroccans hoped to ban journalists from access to their residences altogether; meetings or interviews were to be arranged on some neutral ground. For a time, the ban held. A preference developed for the use of archive photographs and the representation of migrants washing windows, selling goods on the street, or holding small public gatherings. Few official sources presented migrants as working members of an emergent society; rather, their presence was viewed as a kind of social crisis.

Some members of the press literally pushed their way into migrant dwellings, cameras flashing and film crews in full operation; these images were meant to show how migrants "really" lived. The wholly "alien" world of the migrants filtered in through still shots that hovered over the standard contents of the daily newspapers or footage on the nightly news, accompanied by talk of the "immigration problem" or documentary coverage of an eviction of migrants. The hunger for images of the migrants stands in sharp contrast to the migrants themselves, who often just want to be left alone. Further, they wished to represent themselves and not be represented by others. "We don't want anyone to see us living like this," a young Senegalese migrant once told me, as others nodded in agreement.[3]

A shift from the more traditional openness of Italian political culture to what I call the "politics of closure" dominated the 1990s and beyond; it has a great deal to do with the emergence of a new configuration of folk models and popular figures that now populate Italian culture, society, and the media. In this new complex, the immigrant—increasingly drawn into the world of work and social life in Italy—is seen as an illegitimate presence. Commonsense models of Italian society relegate the immigrant to the realm of invisibility. The important and public social fields of ritual and symbolic orders of Italian society must remain free of any trace of the life of the migrant. An incident in a small Sicilian town illustrates this point, as parishioners explained their desire not to have a black priest officiate at a local wedding because he would "ruin the pictures": a visual frontier, a definitive shield against the outside world. The immigrant becomes a ritual object or objectification that evokes the boundaries between the everyday world of Italians and others. In this liminal world, the immigrant is increasingly the very embodiment of the outsider.[4]

In Italy, the scandal-worn political parties of the left and center have taken a beating, as rising right-wing factions increasingly deploy images of immigration to promote fears of the eventual heterogeneity of Italian society. There is a way in which we may view the current immigration process as empowering the right in many contexts, as the "immigration crisis" has allowed many to rethink the right's adoption of the language of action, authority, and decisiveness from the register of right-wing populist parties. Perhaps no other political discussion has been so accommodating as to allow right-wing positions relatively free reign in public discourse. Promoting fear of the newcomers while carving out a respectable place among parliamentary factions, the right has established a new beachhead and claim to political centrality.

I would argue that the visual play of images of the immigrant in public discourse has contributed to an increasing anxiety and concern about the presence of migrants in Italy. Unlike political discussions proper, where the range of what can be said is fairly limited in public popular discourse, in the realm of images we may entertain the unimaginable, suggest the desirable, and entreat the viewer to the most violent fringes of actions seemingly free of consequence. The asymmetrical relationship between the migrant and Italian ensures reinforced by the manner in which the outsider comes to be represented in public discourse. It is clear that representation of immigrants in public discourse merely signals and reinforces a social and classificatory erasure of the migrant from a new (host) cultural order. What Tony Bennett has called "the ambition towards specular dominance over a totality" comes to be employed here without restraint, and perhaps more importantly, it is in the realm of the visual that this desire comes to manifest itself (Bennett 1994). The culture of closure announces its arrival just as the social formation dawns a new age, marked by the melting of borders and the wedding of economic fortunes that converge in the idea of Europe. The correlative of this new social formation seems to be the immigrant, constituting what anthropologist Mary Douglas has called a kind of "matter out of place" and destined to occupy the hidden world of work and leisure and to stand in the new world on just the other side of inclusion (Douglas 1973). This play of images is only possible through the use and manipulation of a repertoire image making and black/immigrant caricature.

Our world is permeated by images. We encounter pictures of one kind or another every day in newspapers, family snapshots, magazines, textbooks, and waiting rooms; in short, in every corner of our lives. Many of these images are shaped by the popular slogans and fashions of the day; moreover, ours is a traffic in stereotypes, condensed understandings drawn from film clips, surgical strikes of journalists and instant replays of let's-see-it-again sensationalism that seems to distort our sense of time. It is the ability of such visions to fade into our taken-for-granted processes of "looking" that often affords our peculiar inattention to what we see and in many cases what we no longer see. Because "photographic representations lose themselves in the ordinary world they help to construct," such information becomes a naturalized feature of our experience (Burgin 1988, 142). Susan Sontag, in her discussion of the heroism of photography, suggests two distinctive orbits or imperatives of the frozen image in a struggle one with the other throughout the history of photography. One set of practitioners searches for the beautiful; another finds themselves the servant of an alternate orbit that appears to hold the highest value of the visible, as it is accorded with the ability to represent the mysterious visage of the true—of a reality out there. But it is not enough to be convinced of this mirroring of the world that in the end may pale before the magic of the shutter. According to Sontag, "It is reality which is scrutinized, and evaluated, for its fidelity to photographs" (1990, 87). The visual encapsulation of a world constructed through images and captured in an ideal archive of diverse orders, disciplines, and collectivities is no doubt a kind of contemporary commonplace. The images themselves do not readily lend their light to knowledge, but resist disclosure in what Elizabeth Edwards calls "a dangerous ambivalence"; as traces of the world's motion, they are mute, porous to meanings and ambiguous to the core. Images command their own realm, it seems—a dimension beyond our control.[5]

Although we link the photograph to the death of an instant, its connection to this or that "piece of the world" and the window on reality that it affords us holds the hint of—or, we might say, the promise of—a fictional world, a world of the exotic, a realm beyond time, at least— and this is what is important—on the periphery of our cultural shores and our particular arch of time. The photograph is a kind of marker of modernity, a dividing line in the representation a truth embedded in the very textures of the world or worlds that we inhabit.

Turin's Ancient Heart

To speak of Turin and its ancient nucleus revolving around the so-called historic center is to speak largely about a kind of imagined essence of the city. After hosting the 2006 winter Olympic games, the city received renewed attention and was situated as an important symbolic city in the nation, counted among the most well-known European cities. The idea of the historic center is deeply rooted in the historical memory of Turin and in its role as symbolic or inaugural city of the nation. Turin has been so long separated from the actual workings of government—long ago lost to Florence and then Rome as the practical capital cities of the country—that it has taken on an even more central symbolic role in the constellation of Italian places. Like Florence, it is associated with the prehistory of the nation and gave rise to the idea of the nation in the work of Italian historian Federico Chabod (1901–1960). Chabod cultivated an idea of Europe set to eclipse the troublesome notions of both nationalism and universalism, under which Europe might become a fulcrum of morality and culture, essentially becoming an ethical category in the thought of Chabod (Dainotto 2000).[6] The "nation," on the other hand, was the repository of "the sense of individuality of a people, of respect for its own traditions, and a cult of its peculiarity" (cited in Dianotto 2000b, 22). The city inhabits the strange and ambivalent qualities of a society teetering between peculiar localisms and more inclusive elements, unsuited to being a capital, in part due to the Savoyard preference for French as the language of the court and the lingering support of European court society and little interest in a nation (Italy) seemingly devoid of cultural riches. Preoccupied with the practical rather than the expansive humanitarian culture of the Tuscan capital, Turin supplies the rationality of governmental operations, documentary protocols, and beloved seat of Savoyard power and identity.

The idea of Turin associated with this Savoyard legacy and its inaugural state institutions infuses the city with a sense of being a special place in the heart of the nation, integral to the cult of its peculiarity. Very early on, this penchant for localism and an intense concern with modernism in the intellectual life of the city destined it to become one of the country's industrial powers, developed through the university of Turin in the faculties of history, political science, and philosophy. Historical studies of the Savoy state prefigure contemporary concerns with power, statecraft, and military history.[7]

The symbolic nature of Turin is overdetermined by the history of the Savoy, the historic developments and conflicts between labor and capital, and the emerging intellectual and cultural life of an increasingly industrial city; it became a place to watch. This is one of the reasons that conflict between newcomers and Italians in the city quickly gained the attention of the entire nation; quarters like San Salvario and Porto Palazzo are well-known sites in a national ideological debate over immigration. Indeed, the streets of its historic center—cascading out as far as Corso Guilio Cesare and San Dalmazzo or Corso Vercelli reverberate with stories of immigrants to the city, including the internal Italian workers of the past who crowded into dormitories along these streets and others, and the present day migrants form Senegal, Morocco, and Tunisia. As anthropologist Filippo Osella of the University of Sussex, recalling his childhood memories of the city, recently pointed out to me, the great rail lines and industrial zones of Turin literally ran through the very heart, connecting the working world to a tiny island of dormitory quarters. Indeed, as Osella suggested to me, there is something about the expectations of modernity of a great industrial power that remains somehow unfulfilled—almost palpable—in the city; dreams of what it might become and dreams of newcomers who envision their own futures in its imaginary futures are intertwined amid the ultramodern retrofitted buildings, the ancient cemeteries of factories, and desires emerging or yet unformed for all who reside (for whatever duration) under its spell.

Turin is perhaps best know for its enchanting historic center, with its arcaded promenades that crisscross the city for kilometers, revealing every now and again lovely baroque cafés, antique shopfronts, and hidden quarters. It is here that the presence of the newcomer is most suspect. This world rises from the neoclassical elements and baroque façades and arcades of the historic center, situated on the skeleton of the old Roman settlement of Julia Augusta Taurinorum. Its architectural garment was crafted during the Italian baroque and late baroque by such masters as Carlo di Castellamonte (1560–1641), Amedeo di Castellamonte (1610–1683), Guarino Guarini (1624–1683), Filippo Juvarra (1678–1736), Ascanio Vittozzi (1539–1615), and Benedetto Alfieri (1700–1767), who not only expanded the urban reach of what was once an old Roman settlement but gave the city its characteristic visage. At its center, Piazza Castello, the historic *zona di commando* (command zone), the center of the political life of the Savoyard domain prominently on display during the 2006 Olympics, with the Palazzo Madama incorporating the Roman Porta Pretoria in its façade, realized under the direction of Filippo Juvarra (1718–1721). Intersected by Via Roma, Via Po, and Via Pietro Mica, the quadrangle contains the essential baroque works of the city, including Palazzo Reale (the royal palace). And just beyond this are perhaps the two finest examples of baroque architecture: the church of San Lorenzo and the nearby ethereal Sindone Chapel, "Sacra Sidone," both by architect, Theatine priest, mathematician, and writer Guarino Guarini. The Sindone Chapel was designed to house and display the shroud of Turin, thought by some to be the holy shroud in which the body of Jesus Christ was wrapped when taken down from the cross.[8]

I rarely carried a camera with me, and for the most part appear in more photographs than I shot. It did not occur to me that the group shot I stood for would be sitting in some photo album in Senegal, circulating among close relatives and friends. There are still few photographs taken by Senegalese in sites around the town; private venues—a ceremony, a marriage, a baptism, or local performances of Senegalese dance or drumming—are more common sites in which photographic events might occur. Much of the social space in the historic center of Turin is seen as hostile and inhospitable terrain; some pockets now where migrant shops have sprung up following a deregulation of small business in 1996 seem more welcoming. Outside of this small circle, in

Porto Palazzo and San Salvario, exclusionary yet invisible walls hem the newcomers into an unbreakable circle (Merrill 2006). The appearance of the migrant has signaled a kind of change in the local landscape and political community, often seen by locals as part of the cause of urban decline, rising criminality, and social disorder. As Heather Merrill points out in her book *An Alliance of Women: Immigration and the Politics of Race*, the presence of the migrant provides a kind of metaphoric marker of social and economic changes:

> The emergence of a highly visible degree of ethnic diversity,
> as well as the effects of wider economic restructuring on the
> neighborhood, seems to have triggered a defense of territory
> among some members of the local population, or a "turf war."
> For some, cultural difference signals collapse of the known
> world. Among many, there is an impulse to blamed someone
> (the stranieri)—some entity that is identifiable, that one can
> point to with a modicum of certainty. (Merrill 2006, 91)

During the 1950s, the southern Italian workers that came to occupy buildings on this side of the city were thought to be a disruption and source of social decline. Contemporary African migrants are seen in much the same way, yet they lack citizenship, making their lives more precarious than their predecessors. They exercise rather what James Holston has called an "insurgent" citizenship and urbanism shaped by their everyday practice and living in the city (1999, 171). In the great Piazza della Republica on Sundays, an African market fills the streets; friends greet each other in the abandoned stalls that Italians have left for the holiday. Small stands make makeshift stalls on which bread, tea, and other items maybe placed on display. The atmosphere is relaxed and convivial, as people stop to chat and take in the surroundings. The regular police patrols stand down on such occasions and the streets are left to the crowd. The streets are transformed into a park—an open African market and place of gathering. And none of this would have be possible ten years ago, when many Senegalese feared to walk alone in many parts of the city. They once made appearances in this piazza primarily to shop or take part in the market of day laborers, who cued up before dawn at the halfway point of the arch that defines the piazza.

Located just beyond the open market of Porto Palazzo, the Corso Vercelli house—where many of the Senegalese I worked with lived— had a certain reputation in the city; it was the symbol of migrant over-crowding and the seeming uncontrollable influx of foreign persons that appeared as if by magic in the working-class sectors of the city and occu-pied garrets that once reserved as storehouses. The Vercelli house became a kind of idealization of the "immigrant residence a focal point of a kind of 'regime of idealizing images' that placed the migrants within local dis-course" (Watney 1999, 145).[9] The story was actually one merely trans-formed for the contemporary immigration crisis; its vintage was from the years of internal Italian migration, when workers swept up from the South and other regions of Italy to take up the industrial jobs open-ing up in the heart of the new industries in Turin. The story was always directed toward a handful of locations, of which the Vercelli house was a leading example. The same justifications were given in the 1950s, when southern Italian migrants sought residence in this area of Turin. For the Italian migrants of another era, the residence becomes a kind of index of outsider status.[10] Some of the retired residents of the area looking at the newcomers often recognized trace of their own now distant working lives. In fact, many of the streets and residences in the zone constituted working-class housing that in some cases dates back to the 1840s, form-ing an identifiable series of sites in memory, local knowledge, and con-temporary ideological discussions that form a kind of archive.[11]

Representational Regimes

Photography has from its very inception been associated with the real-istic rendering of the appearance of objects (Slater 1995, 220). The mod-ernization of vision at the dawn of this visual art was understood to embody the privileged and scientific power of an unmediated apprehen-sion of the observable world. The linkage of the visual product of the lens of the camera and the "scientific valorization" (McQuire 1998, 32) of an objectifying eye brings together a moment in the development of West-ern knowledge in which mechanization, notions of fidelity to the real, and an emergent ideology of positivism captured the imagination. The fledgling arts forms held out a promise of utopia, of the power of knowl-edge in an age to inaugurate cultural modernism in a moment when "photography (and later cinematography) became new repositories for the old dream of the universal language" (Harvey 1990, 308).

Representational regimes gradually acquired a kind of hierarchy; as photography was compared to other modes of representation, such as painting, each constellation of visual practices was evaluated according to the fidelity of its images and the distinctive distancing of the problematic of an imagined "objectivity," all designed to articulate a kind of essential expression of the human subject. The orchestration of various representational realisms through an intense fidelity to the world of appearance, resulting in the diminution of the "subjective," or subject position, was to occupy a privileged place in the order of scientific knowledge (Slater 1995; McQuire 1998): the triumph of the impersonal and the exaltation of the technique of vanishing context, that is, the removal by means of the technical or mechanical manipulation of the process. All of the problematic aspects of context assured photographic utopia: a vision of the nature of knowledge, a purified knowing, disambiguated from the fallible human subject (McQuire 1998, 35). "As subjectivity was increasingly identified as a dangerous and polluting attribute, the pursuit of mechanical objectivity assumed the status of a moral quest" (34).

Photography held out the aura of transparency, a claim to objectivity, derived from the perceived "evidential force" of the photograph, a representation accorded "parity with direct perception" (McQuire 1998, 29). Immediately measured against other technologies of representation, photography was thought by some detractors to degrade the artist with its replicability and fidelity to the appearance of the object; others saw a transhistorical certainty in its technique and a promise of producing a mysterious gateway to the natural world, a privileged "optical connection to the universe," as in the optimism of a positive scientific vision (Benjamin, cited in McQuire 1998, 29). The camera ushered in for nineteenth-century consciousness, according to Scott McQuire, "a new language of truth," not merely a new way of imaging society (31). Nevertheless, this device that seemed to provide access to an unmediated world also introduced an instability in the relationship between the seen and the observer; it transmitted information and brought to light the previously unnoticed, along with an uncommon play of temporality, identity, and form. A certain democracy of the image contained in easily transportable and reproduced units helped the "everyday realities of the visible world" to "suddenly became important" in new ways (Freund 1980, 72). The presentation of this new vantage point is juxtaposed against the inchoate and anguished realms of visibility that lie on the boundaries of rationality and perhaps even corporeality (Mohanram 1999, 27).

Looking Through the Lens of Walter Benjamin

The new technology of perception provided for the imagination ways of seeing unknown to conventional visual culture. Photography with split-second timing and pictorial enhancement revealed the existence of a kind of "optical unconscious," as Walter Benjamin called it: a realm he compared to the "instinctual unconscious," brought to light by psychoanalysis (1979, 243). The camera facilitated the possession of a new visual frontier; its work was not merely on the surface of things, but promised to delve more deeply into the very nature of the world. While painting crafted figures whose significance would fade with the passing of the community of viewers, the person depicted held out some semblance of significance, remaining merely "a testimony to the art of the painter" (243). Photography could uncover the minutiae of the world, and through it, the magic in the image, a hint of its vibrancy, and a gateway to a lived world.[12]

For Benjamin, "there is another nature that speaks to the camera than to the eye," through the "optical unconscious," the instantaneous, fleeting moment revealed by the act of the lens, providing a kind of incision in time (1979, 243). The indeterminacy of the event is vivified through the photograph. Photographs liberate the present as they uncover a moment other than our own—one integral to anthropological interest in the subject as personal narrative, the social type of a social milieu, representative of the singularly unquantifiable inflection on a time (a kind of zeitgeist) and the mundane routines of everyday life—as if the secret of time could be revealed in the magic of capturing the visible.

For Benjamin, "history can be grasped only in its disappearance," as Eduardo Cadava nicely puts it (Cadava 1997, 104). Anticipation of finding the contingencies of the day-to-day draws us beyond the surfaces of the picture, toward the promise of the historical, the allure of meanings distanced through time, locked in a glance, a posture, an odd relationship with the operator of the camera, or a complete disregard of the machine and its accomplice: these and other concerns animate our relationship with images. The magic of this process Benjamin saw in the early photographers' apparent ability to conjure up the hidden mysteries of "the reproduction of nature's details unseen by the eye" prior to the intervention of the photography (Price 1994, 43):

> Photography reveals . . . the physiognomic aspects of visual
> worlds which dwell in the smallest things, meaningful yet covert
> enough to find a hiding place in waking dreams, but which,
> enlarged and capable of formation, make the difference between
> technology and magic visible as a thoroughly historical variable.
> (Benjamin 1979, 244)

For Benjamin, people seemed to encounter this early visual space provided by photography with a kind of innocence. Benjamin notes that "the human countenance had a silence about it in which the gaze rested," a silence inextricably bound to the novelty of the art and the lack of familiarity with its technique (1979, 244). The realm of the obligatory in the photographic—an idea of what *must* be pictured—had not yet been defined; rather, subject, art, and the professional and amateur photographer created from moment to moment the contours of a new visual culture.

However, Benjamin's characterization of the early photographers seems to have less to do with the history of photography than with the setting up of a decisive role in the reading of the history of the industrial world. Presenting the photograph with no prehistory allows Benjamin to contemplate the perfect incorporation of the new technology with the rise of capitalist society and the authoritarian forms it made possible. Linking the new technology with the market, Benjamin makes of photography a symptom of the capitalist mode of production, of scale, of speed, and of the astonishing reproducibility of typifications of an original object.[13] It helps to tell the tale of a peculiar shock of modernity.

The photograph is part of a history of the decline of tradition; its transparency sounds the death knell of the intimacy of storytelling and of a preindustrial way of life in which collective memory served to strengthen the ties of community. The dehumanization of the object in the instantaneous flash of the camera captures images outside of the narrative space of human society, in a domain that the consciousness cannot travel, and as such, details escape its grasp in the flow of time. So often the photograph is associated with distraction or a peculiar inattention; though the painting stands as the symbol of absorption for Benjamin, the photograph marks the boundaries of the incision, as if in consciousness. It is here that Benjamin attempts to restore the image to human society and language as he "invents a story—instantaneous, compressed, elusive, incomplete—in order to claim reality and a place in the world" for the image (Price 1994, 41).

Although Benjamin sought to restore a claim to a kind of authenticity, the surface of the text often remains refractory and silent. As the photographic process has come to be considered emblematic of modernity, an unquestionable site of copies of the real world, our attention has turned to the social world made possible in part by its use. We are now most familiar with the photographic image as an article of mass consumer society and global culture, although this function of the image as personal testimony to an intimate set of associations and relationships or as public mnemonic retracing or remembering a discontinuous past is fairly recent (McQuire 1998).

Dreams of Other Cultures and the Remaking of Black Visual Histories

The World's Fair complex was designed to bring the public face to face with the most mundane, utopian, and social achievements associated with cultural modernism and the idea of Western culture. It was inaugurated in the age of high capitalism and imperialism, and the very nature of the expositions was permeated with diasporic rhythms. Lasting no more than six months, the complex dislocated people from the world over, at times disassembling entire villages, only to establish them again in the ephemeral space of the exhibit (Figure 2). The vision of a global human history, however, had to be constructed from fragments and artifacts and was peopled by those for whom the idea of representing a racial type held no meaning. Although one might think that the portable studios erected on the spot by some of the photographers could reproduce only the most alienated and decontextualized images, the work of Eric Breitbart in *A World on Display: Photographs from the St. Louis World's Fair 1904* (1997) suggests that at least some producers of pictures revealed a startling integrity of the subject. For Breitbart, part of the work of recovering the St. Louis World's Fair was an attempt to restore names

Dans ce numéro:

LES AILES FRANÇAISES

AUX COLONIES

LE MONDE COLONIAL

Figure 2. Africa in the Western photographic imaginary. Cover of *Le Monde Colonial Illustré*, Paris, February 1939.

and clarify the collective identity of the people who were commissioned to represent specific social types, perform dances, and reenact local life as authentic "native" peoples.

The dreamscapes of the exhibition mapped out not only the "utopian world of the future" but also the full-scale possession of a world of the present, one that included human and material resources that could be placed on display and consumed and one that delineated the contours of an empire otherwise unknown to metropolitan audiences. The cycle of World's Fairs coincided with the expansion of the public museums and with the advance of amateur and professional collecting. Moreover, the fairs promulgated a vision of modernity, allowing the placement of a region, city, or society into a conceptual scheme indexed by the idea of the progress. Such a schema of relative points of arrival along this developmental journey, read in the international exhibit and its environs in this era of rapid colonial expansion, helped to render this New World visible and to people it.

The anthropological imagination was drawn into the great world of spectacle through anthropological and documentary concerns and the growing sense that "native" peoples inhabited a vanishing world whose trace would have to be preserved for posterity. Salvaging portions of a dying world in an era of cultural modernism reflected a self-image of a modernity that placed a primacy on the nostalgic logic of "preservation," a correlate of the idea of progress and an idea suggesting that social and cultural unfolded in evolutionary stages, effacing the small communities of an imagined past for the fast-paced, high modern world of an envisioned future. This future would be dominated by the more impersonal social and cultural inflections of a new form of capitalism, posing a threat to notions of identity that did not seek confirmations in more expansive iterations of self, that is, in the realm of empire, of the universal, and of the transcendent domain of desire.

Employing stereotypes drawn from the raw materials of ideas about ethnic, racial, or gender classifications "is a prototypical realm for . . . drawing boundaries," used to define social collectivities (Cohen 2000, 28). Such bounding devices serve to impose "a false conceptual order on a field of much more diverse cultural variation" (28). When that field of cultural variation is set in motion and subject to notions of "the way things have always been" or of "the ways things should be," a normative force tends to ossify into a taken-for-granted tradition. When this tradition is further reinforced by an endless repetition of ideological, educative, and social elaborations, this "false conceptual order" becomes the bedrock of systems of belief and classification a kind of all-encompassing contemporary cosmology. As many authors have suggested, a constellation comprising race, nation, and gender in the late nineteenth century provided an important way to envision society while justifying utopian visions of empire and racial rule. A full-blown and global outgrowth of such justifications culminated in the following century when "racial rule denied the existence of commonalities among colonizers and colonized, Europeans and non-Europeans, whites and 'others'" (Winant 2001, 12). This world—filtered through the colonial regime—Fanon would characterize as hopelessly divided: "The colonial world is a Manichean world," a world in which native society was in every way the mirror opposite of the masters of the colonial order, engaged in a terrestrial battle between the material and spiritual realms of existence (1967b, 41). Indeed, in the United States, "a peculiarly American version of white supremacy, twinned with Herrenvolk democracy, consigned all black people to the shadowy margins of national life where their invisibility would long remain indispensable to the identity of white people" (Lewis 2003, 48).

The fair complex had the ability to transform consumerism and leisure into a visual feast, a representational regime with an implicit classificatory system separating and defining aspects of race, gender, and social class. One of the critical elements of this visual regime was the ethnological village. The World's Columbia Exposition in Chicago in 1893 provided the opportunity to demonstrate American homogeneity and resilience in the wake of the bitter divisions and social pressures amassing from new immigration, rapid urbanization, and fast-paced industrialization. It also was the first American International fair to include an ethnological village "sanctioned by a prominent anthropologist," a practice that would continue through the First World War. The idealized "mobilized gaze" of the fairgoer was however both gendered and restricted by notions of race, ideas about human evolution, and social class. Making the social limitations imposed by race a critical aspect of the exhibition for both black and white fairgoers, the contradiction of the "modernist looking from the racial margins," and the ideal location of the mainstream viewer mark the exhibition as an important visual manifestation of an emergent American social and racial order (Stewart 2005, 120).

At times, the ethnological exhibits were complimented by formal summer offerings of university classes, lectures, and other displays (Rydell 1993, 21). The living ethnological demonstrations—including representations of Native American, African American, and Asian Americans—reinforced notions of white supremacy and underscored ideas of American imperial practice abroad. Darwinian theories concerning racial development were counterposed with utopian visions of progress of the nation and industry (235). The display of "primitive" people served, according to Robert W. Rydell, "to anthropologically validate" and legitimize racial exploitation and hierarchies at home, while supporting the idea of the building and maintaining of an empire abroad (1999). Indeed as Jacqueline Najuma Stewart has noted, "people of color were imagined more as spectacles than spectators by the Exhibition organizers" (2005, 120). White supremacy provided whites with a "sense of shared national purpose" in the face of divisive class and ethnic social pressures, coupled with the "utopian agency" allowing for the domination of subject peoples overseas (Rydell 1999, 236). Moreover, contributions to the fair organized or conceived by African Americans were simply rejected by the fair organizers, who restricted participation on any level other than token representation of those selling products and or signing on as hired hands and living exhibition actors on the midway.

Disapproval of black caricature and exclusion at the Chicago Columbia Exposition was expressed through two powerful voices, when journalist and antilynching activists Ida B. Wells-Barnett and Frederick Douglass published a pamphlet entitled "The Reason Why the Colored American Is Not in the World's Columbian Exposition" in 1893, elaborating on the struggles of black Americans living in both the North and South and the progress they had made since the end of slavery. Hoping to publish their objections in a number of foreign languages, the authors were eventually forced to scale back the ambitious pamphlet due to lack of funding. The final product reached a small audience at the time; the pamphlet has been recently recovered largely through the efforts of historian Robert W. Rydell (1999).

As Rydell notes, the racism and exclusion of the fair by rejecting the exhibitions of African Americans hoping to represent the achievement of their community since slavery "mirrored, framed and reinforced the larger horrors confronting blacks throughout the United States where white supremacy meant segregation, second-class citizenship, and sometimes lynching" (1999, xli). Rendering blacks invisible in the public domain was a critical part of the development of a kind of social order and visual regime that served to level differences between whites while promoting ideas of racial and political superiority accommodating utopian visions of empire (see Rydell and Kroes 2005). David Levering Lewis explores the manner of African American exclusion:

> The ironic tragedy of the American racial situation, however, was that too many whites insisted on believing that they could rise only if blacks declined, that the former's civic and cultural respectability depended on the latter's invisibility in or extrusion from the public sphere. (Lewis 2003, 41)

Proper respect and acknowledgement of the contribution of blacks and the progress made since the end of slavery was what Wells-Barnett and Douglas certainly awaited in the participation of blacks themselves in representations of the black subject. As if the ethnological exhibitions were not enough, the fair inaugurated such black caricatures as Aunt Jemima, an iconic figure portrayed by Nancy Green, a fifty-seven-year-old former slave who became a living advertisement for the self-rising pancake mix of the R. T. Davis Milling Company. Such stereotypes were to become a fundamental part of the mass marketing of a great range of products in American consumer society. The continued derogatory representation of African Americans in this manner held the promise of blacks remaining in a subordinate social position in a changing American society, an idea repeated though the exhibitions and product promotions, and the refusal of the organizers to allow for the self-fashioning of the black subject among the palatial exposition pavilions.

Perhaps the first significant and self-conscious representation of African Americans in an international exhibition took place in France. The spirit of the Paris display, deeply rooted in the vindicationist tradition and composed in accordance with historical and comparative methodology, set it squarely within the anthropological tradition (Harrison and Harrison 1999, 12). As Faye V. Harrison has argued, W. E. B. Du Bois must be placed within the lineage of black anthropological practitioners, and indeed, the intervention in Paris is a unique example of an engagement in European and American public culture at a venue designed for the consumption of a mass audience (Harrison 1992). Shawn Michelle Smith has also suggested that Du Bois is an "early visual theorist of race and racism," who both employed visual images in his analysis of racial ideology and "conceptualized the racial dynamics of the Jim Crow color line as visual culture" (2004, 26). Smith points to the heavy reliance on the visual in what become key concepts in the work of Du Bois, such as the symbolic violence of the recognition of a racialized subjectivity in double consciousness, the veil, and second sight—the veil, as a product of the psychic slitting across the color line, is seen to "shroud African Americans in invisibility by making misrepresentation of blackness overwhelmingly visible" (40). The veil is at times associated with a screen upon which images are projected, which fixes the distorted images of a divided society, while second sight provides the victims of racial apartheid a new vision of society. As Smith suggests, Du Bois's notion of second sight "enables the racialized subject to see what (white) others are blinded to by their visions, namely the psychic projections that enable white viewers to maintain a sutured self-image of ideal wholeness" (42). Certainly the exhibit manifested a kind of philosophical anthropology, featuring cultural, visual, and sociological dimensions of black experience.

For the Paris Exposition of 1900, Du Bois organized the Exhibit of American Negroes in Paris, including hundreds of photographs drawn from the work of black photographers working to create documents specifically for the Paris display (Figure 3). The 1900 exposition was

Figure 3. Paris on display. Cover of *Le Monde Colonial Illustré*, Paris, August 1937.

generally an important corrective event for the good American, as the United States had presented uninspiring pavilions in past European fairs. Although the American Negroes exhibit received the distinguished grand prize, along with 15 other awards from the French, in the official American record of the fair written by Commissioner General for the United States Ferdinand Peck, the exhibit was barely mentioned and only as "scholarly and intelligent representatives of race work" (Lewis 2003, 48). In fact, save for the work of photographer Thomas Askew, uncovered in part through the work of Shawn Michelle Smith in her work *Photography on the Color Line: W. E. B. Du Bois, Race, and Visual Culture*, we know little of the portraitists and subjects of the exhibition (Smith 2004, 76). Although most Americans were neither enlightened nor informed about the exhibit and its celebration of the achievements of African Americans since emancipation, as political culture and news media relegated the event to invisibility, the display demonstrates acutely what I would call an emergent politics of invisibility.

Du Bois's collaborator and friend on the Paris 1900 Exposition American Negro Exhibit section, Thomas Junius Calloway, succeeded in depicting (in Du Bois's phrase) a world "a small nation of people": a black community, seen largely at the time solely through the lens of stereotype and caricature, relegating blacks to an impoverished, backward cultural wasteland in which they languished as if destined to a life of forgetfulness, indolence, and ignorance (Lewis 2003, 41). The use of photographs at the exhibition made a world only cloudily imagined visible to an international community. Inasmuch as photography is in the creation and composition of the photographer in the delicacy of a relationship with a subject, black photographers during the 1890s began to counter pervasive stereotypes of African Americans through the use of their cameras and the increasingly popular modality of self-presentation: the portrait.

Historian of photography and imaging Deborah Willis has argued that black photographers during the 1890s began to record a new image of blackness through the range and scope of their work, influenced by both documentary photography and portraiture, demonstrating through their photographs that black Americans were as multifaceted as anyone else and crafting an image of the black self in photographs coveted in black middle class and working class homes. Not only in fighting against negative images of blacks, photographs played "an important role in making the black experience visible" (Willis 2003, 51). The photograph in turn helped to craft a new social subject, the "New Negro," heralded by Booker T. Washington's speech at the 1895 Atlanta Exposition. In the hands of these photographers, however, a more democratic visualization of the "New Negro" appeared to be taking place, one including blacks of diverse social class, skin colors, and cultural education:

> Photography played a role in shaping people's ideas about identity and sense of self; it informed African American social consciousness and motivated black people by offering an "other" view of the black subject. In a sense, photography was used as what I call "subversive resistance." (Willis 2003, 55)

This visualization provided a kind of "corrective visual history" and "self-recovery" of black subjectivity (Willis 2003, 77). The broad social participation in the self-conscious representation of blackness, although largely privately purchased from black photographic studios and other locations offering photographic services, marks a significant resilience of the black subject in the face of social invisibility. These true-to-life images were a counter-discursive force in black life. As bell hooks notes, "When the psychohistory of a people is marked by loss . . . documentation may become an obsession" (hooks, cited in Willis 1994, 48). The presentation of such photographs in the context of the exposition served, according to Willis, as "a body of images of a vibrant family life and a growing middle class, transform the subjugated black imagery, and force all Americans to reexamine history as they learned it" (2003, 78). This process of the visualization and crafting of the self through the photograph remains even today a powerful weapon against the practice of invisibility, manifesting itself in the simple group portrait or family photo album. As Shawn Michelle Smith argues, Du Bois's work in the Paris Exhibition helped to reclaim "the African American image, wrenching it from the confines of the scientist's racist archive, from those institutional sites that would define African Americans as inferior, bound to the lowest rung of an evolutionary ladder"; the show "took images of African Americans out from under the presumed mastery of an 'objective' white supremacist gaze," delivering them back to both a reclaimed African American community and the world (Smith 2004, 76).

At the same time, the images in their response to black caricatures, as Smith has argued, tended to reinforce a notion of African American patriarchy, anchoring women at home and family through the prism of Victorian respectability (112).

If we were to imagine, as Robert W. Rydell suggests, the cultural experience "carrying a national audience across a threshold," toward an unprecedented merging of consumerism and leisure then we must see this movement as coming to culminate in "a new national identity" (Rydell and Kroes 2005, 78). African Americans moved by these same forces were however faced with the fact of blackness, of their location within a racial order imposing invisibility on the basis of race. A fascinating picture of this world and the implicit contradiction in envisioning separate worlds, divided along racial lines and informed by hierarchies and systems of classification based on imagined stages of evolution,[14] begins to emerge when we consider the great creativity and opportunity for self-fashioning presented through the situated black urban modernity available in the wake of the great migrations to the North.

In her book *Migrating to the Movies: Cinema and Black Urban Modernity* (2005) Jacqueline Najuma Stewart presents a compelling portrait of an emergent migrant community in Chicago in the wake of the great migrations from the American South. The novelty of the urban setting framed by the articulation of racial ideology filtering through mass cultural forms and the search for the safety of a home community shaped a unique context in which black spectatorship was forged. Many of the forms of mass culture and entertainment anticipated no place for the black masses migrating to the North, and yet like their fellow Americans, blacks increasingly joined in the growing consumer society. Such forms of mass entertainment as dime novels, vaudeville shows, circuses, and Wild West shows, along with the transformation of the so-called pleasure garden into a permanent attraction open to the working class as an amusement park, served to merge consumerism and leisure while remaining bastions of racial segregation and exclusion. Stewart explores the manner in which African Americans began to create within the confines of this world a place for themselves and a way of making sense of medium constructed assured of their invisibility, although it is clear that "while racism continued to shape Black public life, Black migrants could learn to navigate discrimination in the city (identify which theaters to attend, which stores to patronize)," creating the safety of a livable world and a community responding to the demands of their new urban reality (Stewart 2005, 151). And yet blacks attending the fair and cinema began to craft these spectacles to reflect their own sense of an emerging urban identity. The recasting of the "mobilized gaze," imagined by Walter Benjamin for the nineteenth-century self-possessed figure strolling through the streets of Paris, may hold some clue to transforming the gaze into a highly flexible form of social critique and empowerment:

> Black subjectivity is forged in a social context of its own making,
> as Blacks appropriate the meanings of the cinema, urban life
> and work and interrogating the new media through the lens of
> their own experience. Viewing the fair or urban life from this
> emergent Black perspective reinvents the gaze of the flâneur for
> the Black working-class modes of modern looking, both creative
> and at times involuntarily imposed by social conditions of the
> broader society. (Stewart 2005, 106)

Through the everyday practice and re-creation of black subjectivity in visual and cultural practices, its interpretation and appropriation became an integral part of urban life in the North. The emergence of black spectatorship and the importance of the making of a black urban modernity provided the social context in which new ways of looking were infused with vibrant and unanticipated new ways of living. The establishments of neighborhoods, leisure institutions, and the rudiments of social and political representation had an impact on the manner in which black spectators framed and interpreted images on the silver screen.

While venues like the fair and the cinema continued to treat African Americans as if they were invisible—in effect, "marginalizing Black spectators from the realm of cinematic 'universality'" and distancing them from the imagined ideal (white male) fairgoer, a transformation and redirecting of this imagined gaze was taking place (Stewart 2005, 110). African Americans inventing a self-fashioning and a new way of looking sought what Stewart calls "reconstructive spectatorship" (94): a "liberal and symbolic space in which to rebuild their individual and collective identities in a modern, urban environment," both empowering and revitalizing a community forced into invisibility (17). While the fair, the cinema, and other mass cultural leisure forms foreclosed prematurely on the creative contributions of black urban modernity, African Americans continued to refine and elaborate a new identity:

> The carnivalesque ethnic displays on the Midway and the utopian future imagined by the White City functioned together to deny the progress of nonwhites, as well as their contributions to American modernity. We can imagine that the thousands of African Americans who visited the fair practiced a type of flânerie that foreshadowed the range of reconstructive practices that characterized Black spectatorship in moving picture theaters; that is, a mode of looking with complicit and resistant possibilities shaped by the exposition's racial (and racist) politics of organization, display, and public circulation. (Stewart 2005, 120).

Such a form of resistance through practice is emerging for the migrants with whom I have been working in Europe, but as noncitizens, their resources have been somewhat restricted until recently. As migrants gain greater control over the spaces in which they live and demand more from the Italian social and consumer world, their identity and presence will no doubt fall from the shadows and invisibility. We return to this in a moment.

The anthropological imaginary was increasingly peopled through the expansion of empire, through travelers' and explorers' tales, and by the interest of the public in exotic locales. A derivative of new technology of photo reproduction, used to publish the popular *musée de poche* (pocket museums) and other facsimiles of great works of art; the postcard became an immediate success at the turn of the century. The origin of the postcard "can be traced directly to Europe and the efforts by European merchants to promote products" (Rydell and Kroes 2005, 83). The photographic postcard was soon within reach of the general public throughout Europe; well over one hundred million were printed in France alone in 1910, an industry that now accounts for billions of annual sales (Freund 1980, 99–100). Early postcard images such as the great exhibitions were embedded in an ideology of progress and a desire for the possession of the exotic (Figure 4). Postcards really caught on as a popular form when they began to be used to convey both "images and written messages from fairgoers to the folks back home"

Figure 4. Cameroon. Cover of *Le Monde Colonial Illustré*, Paris, May 1926.

(Rydell and Kroes 2005, 83).[15] Early European production of images of Africa focused largely on the postcard, providing exotic and often erotic visions of this other world.[16]

The exhibitions at these public events were also photographed for popular postcards, some of which sold as many as a quarter of a million copies in the Edwardian period (Street 1992, 122). The companies orchestrating the fairs not only commissioned photographers to record the event through the creation of a kind of official archive, they also charged a fee enabling them to take photographs at specific exhibits (Breitbart 1997, 44). Newspapers reproduced photographs detailing the nature of the exhibitions, and other forms of the distribution of images were carefully regulated and confined to booklets, brochures, and postcards. The presence of the portable cameras of the amateur could not be so easily regulated; the popular handheld camera and their enthusiasts were left to go about their image making without the restrictions of the professionals.[17]

The anthropological village and its images of real life, coupled with commercial sponsorship of ritual enactment, became a standard feature of the fair process (Figure 5). These human exhibits served not only as domestication of the idea of ethnocolonial power, but also as

Figure 5. Malagasy women in Western dress. Cover of *Le Monde Colonial Illustré*, Paris, August 1931.

the definition and organization of spatial and symbolic domains that inscribed in the simultaneity of the other an new interplay of distance, time, and culture through means of the display.[18]

By the 1870s, even the United States was developing what Curtis M. Hinsley has called "an ecumenical cosmopolitanism" through the peculiar notion of the universal principles of human development from "savagery and barbarism to enlightenment" (Hinsley 1996, 120) and claims of a kind of "humanity" thought to be universal (Breitbart 1997, 48). International exhibitions inaugurated by London's Crystal Palace in 1851 continued across the great cities of Europe and also took on local forms throughout the United States. Mounting an exhibition was a way of establishing a symbolic linkage to the heart of advanced technological and cultural achievements. The Columbia Exposition in Chicago in 1893 and the Louisiana Purchase Exposition—a more local version of this pattern—ushered in a form of "imperial display" that naturalized the contours of a known world through the legitimating discourse of scientific classification.[19]

The creation of an archive is not arbitrary. Both image making and image makers change in the course of time. One of the most memorable gifts I received as a child was a camera. One of the only mechanisms through which the image of people of color was seen in those days was in the grain and flash of the black-and-white family photo album. The power of an image is never lost on the child who learns to craft the rest of the world as the backdrop of a very local understanding of images. Not only does class index photographic practice; it is also raced and gendered in peculiar ways. Although it is an art accessible to everyone, photographic practice remains constrained by diverse and multiple forms of cultural logic and tempered by the interplay of competing tastes; what is "photographable" is in no way universal, according to the late Pierre Bourdieu (Bourdieu et al. 1990).

The "photographable" is, in short, a social product with a history. In the African American community in which I grew up, public images of blacks were so few that the appearance of a magazine article or the appearance of a political figure in a local newspaper was marked by a flurry of phone calls and word-of-mouth notices. Each "positive" utterance of or about black people was considered another blow against the overwhelming weight of black caricature. Shaping the photographic event is a desire to see the world inhabited by the loved ones and others engaged in the most mundane activities. Yet power changes everything, as a visually indexed ideology presents the hidden frontiers of identity, constraining at once what is seen and what must not be envisaged. The camera in black life hooks argues became a "political tool" and a way to "resist misrepresentation" through the production of alternative images. The effort to capture a visual world essentially denied in dominant culture imparted a primacy on image making and interpretation. The documentation of black life, as bell hooks suggests, employed the shield of photography in order to counter a discourse predicated on the "negative" image of dominant culture:

> The sites of contestation were not out there, in the mainstream
> world of whites, of power, but were rather within segregated
> black life. Since no "white" galleries displayed images of
> black people created by black folks, spaces had to be made
> within diverse black communities. Across class, black folks
> struggled with issues of representation. Significantly, issues of
> representation were linked to the issue of documentation, hence
> the importance of photography. The camera was the central
> instrument by which blacks could disprove representations of us
> created by white folks. The degrading images of blackness that
> emerged from racist white imaginations and circulated widely
> in the dominant culture (on salt shakers, cookie jars, pancake
> boxes) could be countered by "true-to-life" images. (Willis 1994,
> 48–49).

This visual representation cultivated through the gaze of the "other" transforms the process of making and interpreting images into more than a pastime. Image making and the reading of images of and about blacks and others caught in the headlights of exclusive dominant representational traditions, or what John Tagg has called the "the burden of the surveilled," the refinement of a form of power and control of the social body inaugurated by the early uses of the photograph (1993). The series of preconditions for viewing and "making images" are then a process structuring the very taken-for-granted normalcy of the everyday use of photography, and its exploration. Beyond this is a hidden pretext in which gender, race, and social class prefigure our seeing of the world. Photographs are not merely "read" or filed away in a social category of "use value"; photography becomes a medium through which a social and cultural world is envisioned, reacted to, and set into an intersubjective realm of give and take across generations.[20]

Making Visible Worlds

In *Photography and Society*, Giséle Freund explored a world in which images have become a taken-for-granted reality of contemporary life. "Photography is now so much a part of our daily lives," she laments, "that our familiarity causes us to overlook it" (1980). Fading from seen to unseen, the visible is crafted like other contemporary fictions. Falling below the level of discourse, we rarely consider the great power and influence of the subtle ways our seeing the world is shaped. We learn to rely on certain images and to suspect others. Yet as anthropologist Arjun Appadurai reminds us, "imagination in the postelectronic world plays a newly significant role," as the work of the imagination is the stuff of popular culture (Appadurai 1996, 5). The encounter with images, and I extend the discussion throughout this discussion to forms of visual matter other than photography, can be devastating or exhilarating, depending on what side of the gaze one finds oneself.

African Photography

The great Western photographic archive of Africa has unfolded through nature photography; colonial-era postcards, ethnographic documentation of colonial enterprise, and the many peoples set off in pseudoscientific cultural, racial, and ethnic types bound up in supremacist notions and dreams of global rule. Images that did not help to compile a scientific record of sorts easily contributed to the world of fantasy of an exotic elsewhere. In their exploration of colonial imagination, Okwui Enwezor and Octavio Zaya remind us that both in film and literature, "Africa has been made completely invisible, obscured and masked, screened from our consciousness, and elided from the world's memory banks" (1996, 17). There is of course another photographic history of Africa, from the early 1860s: African photographers were active in the colonial world and some African studios were established shortly after this period (Enwezor and Zaya 1996). Most recently, the legacy of the studio work produced in many of the African studios established during the 1940s—many working through postcolonial times—has captured the attention of many Western viewers. African photographers creating images of African subjects for home consumption or to exchange as gifts for distant relatives and friends gives us an opportunity to consider cultural politics of representation in colonial and postcolonial setting from a different optic—not unlike James Van Der Zee (1886–1983), the African American photographer of Harlem, New York. African photographers initially catered to a local elite documenting Victorian–Edwardian era–inspired notions of respectability and social prestige. Van Der Zee's record of the emergent black middle class and others of Harlem was in 1969 included in an exhibition at the Metropolitan Museum of Art, drawing his work back into public attention, now as a form of art—much like the African photographers of his era in the 1990s. Prominent shows in Paris and New York showcasing African photographers like Seydou Keita (1921–2001) and Malick Sidibé (1935–) of Mali, and the Senegalese Mama Casset (1908–1992) and Salla Casset (1910–1974), all commercial photographers of pre-liberation times who documented a vivid social and cultural world in emerging urban centers and the complex transformation of people coming to terms with a world in flux. The portraits of these photographers are "claiming a specific presence in representation," balanced between "glamorizing the sitters" and revealing the shaping direction of their producers; their work gives us insight into the making of new ways of seeing and being in African societies of this period (Enwezor and Zaya 1996). Indeed, through the careful orchestration of props, radios, bikes, flowers, and other items, the presentation of cultural makers of identity and signs of ethnic affiliation charter the emergence of their worlds from village life to racing urban centers, from ethnic homeland to the social and political capital of a new world.

Collaborations between photographers like Seydou Keita and Malick Sidibé of Bamako, Mali are exemplary in many ways and allow us to understand the complex and dynamic changes taking place in African societies in preliberation and the immediate postcolonial era. During the 1940s, Bamako emerged as an important French colonial center; the rail links to Dakar brought it that much closer to Paris. As a more cosmopolitan world pulsed through its markets and meeting centers, people began to reflect these changes in their everyday lives and to hope to document the changes through their access to photography. Manthia Diawara has suggested that Seydou Keita, taking most of his portraits in the courtyard of his home and not a great distance from the train station and the great marketplace of the city, used the location that provided a kind of crossroads of the social transformation in society. "Keita's Bamako," Diawara argues, is "Bamako at the birth of modernity in West Africa," and in his portraits "aspects of the moment, its mythology and attendant psychology" seep into the process of image making (1998b). Migration from villages all over the country populated the city. This process for important colonial centers was repeated all over French West Africa and such cities became the site of the symbolic transformation of a social order, urbanity, the makings of identity of the world to come; local iconography and a mixture of tokens of ethnic affiliation combined to form the elemental ground work of fashioning contemporary African identity (see Figure 6). To tell the truth of this process, we must

Figure 6. Celebrating French West Africa. Cover of *Le Monde Colonial Illustré*, Paris, December 1933.

acknowledge a kind of emergent form of black spectatorship in which we must "account for the gaze of the black subject," and in this back and forth between the studio effect, the sitters, and the photographer we must say that Keita "participated in the shaping of a new image of the city" (Fristenberg 2001; Diawara 1998b). Diawara suggests that this process, the search for beauty, and the construction of new persons in a new urban world all came together in front of the lens of Keita—"His camera made them Bamakois"—altering the traditional scoptic relationship between colonizer and colonized (Diawara 1998b; Fristenberg 2001).

What James W. Fernandez once called an "argumentation of images" began to take shape with the first studio as Africans crafted images in a style that diverged from that of the colonial present and was to move even further away in postcolonial times (Fernandez 1986). I cannot chart the full range of this process, which is beyond the scope of our concerns here, but wish to point out that the images were created for an African audience guided by an African sensibility. In the context of rapid social transformation, people representing themselves by taking pictures might end up sending that picture to a distant relative or using one to honor a revered departed member of the family. Through these images we begin to see the emergence of a postcolonial subject not caught between tradition and modernity, but rather balancing aspects of the past and present, like so many props of the studio tradition. Lauri Fristenberg argues that the work of African photographers provided tactical armature used in "countering colonial typologies of African identities by reimagining the self in the studio setting during the drawn-out processes of decolonization" (2001, 175). Indeed, such a counterdiscourse was taking place through the studio work of major American cities at the dawn of modernity.

Deborah Willis, curator of exhibitions at the National African American Museum Project of the Smithsonian Institute, reveals in *Picturing Us: African American Identity in Photography* (1994) a startling encounter with the work of Harlem photographer Van Der Zee, whose work became part the Metropolitan Museum of Art "Harlem on My Mind" exhibit. The controversial exhibit was boycotted by many African and Jewish American groups, and was what Willis calls her introduction to a "formal education" in the world of the photography. "At twenty-one," Willis reflects, "never having seen images of black people exhibited in a major museum, outside of a national history museum, I felt great pride in the presentation" (1994, 7–8). This pride was tempered by the various protesters' complaints, including the lack of black artists on the curatorial board and a statement in the show's catalog that seemed to suggest tensions between blacks and Jews in the making of Harlem. The absence of Van Der Zee in any of the books on the history of photography led Willis to question the silences in the official version of this story, and the images recalled a world—however idealized—of the period of the Harlem Renaissance. Although the Harlem Renaissance has been to some extent frozen in time as the specific moment of black creativity and strength, the period has become a symbol of internal diversity, balanced with the economic and cultural achievements of the African American community, through the assertion of a clear and combative identity and its relationship to a black elite and intellectual group. In her closing remarks on Van Der Zee, Willis asks, "Where were the newly arrived migrants form the Deep South? Were they invisible to Van Der Zee?" (9). The celebration of black achievement may have demanded the silencing of these new migrants, who did not readily embrace the values of middle-class respectability.

I therefore have no problem imaging a visual regime that holds no trace of a selected ethnic and or racially designated group; I have seen exactly this in much of my life, as African Americans have been excluded from much of popular culture as actors in their own right. The chain of stereotypes that has cast African Americans in the helper role to main characters and comic relief to others is well known. Only recently has black independent American cinema developed the capability of challenging such representations, and indeed much of this production still maintains a gender bias celebrating the beleaguered African American male, at times at the expense of solid and complex roles for women. To encounter the very Italian world of popular culture—tempered by the massive presence of American television shows and films—is to become aware of a certain kind of cultural dissonance at play within the Italian sphere and beyond it. Italian images are dwarfed by the dubbed American offerings of television stations, and many of the newcomers to Italy are represented—if they are represented at all—in news clips on the national news stations. Italians do not for the most part see migrants as part of their society. There is little evidence of their presence in popular culture. Migrants rather construct a visual world of their own making, celebrating a way of viewing themselves in the new surroundings that affords a glimpse of home from time to time.

There has been in the past ten years or so in Italy a dramatic shift in the making of the visible world surrounding Senegalese migrants, revealing an unimaginable rich world of images drawn not only from Senegal but also from the lives of migrants in diaspora. The television and other visual centers are dominated by Italian programming and an endless series of international advertisements. When Senegalese workers come together on the weekends, a very intricate system of videotapes is substituted for Italian television, showing various themes important to the viewing audience in diaspora. Some of tapes contain wrestling—a very popular sport practiced all over West Africa—yet the Senegalese version is particular. The contestants are national figures with large followings and the camera almost always shows them preparing for a contest by employing a personal ritual of purification and protection. Then there are romantic soap opera serials that are set in cities like Dakar, giving migrants a longed-for view of home. "We just like to see something from home," they often say. But it's not just a passive viewing, as people react and interact with the events. One Sunday afternoon when a wrestling video was on, viewers pointed out the various amulets worn by the wrestlers, explaining the powers attributed to each and noting the diverse ceremonies associated with the national prestige of the sport and the many powerful political and religious officials in the stands. As a dance sequence came up, people joked and talked about learning dances back home, and about the children in the diaspora who can perform similar movements, and about the events held in diaspora at which Senegalese drumming or dancing are preformed.

Other forms include videos made in Italy. Particular attention is given to ceremonies that take place for the first time in diaspora, such as the preparation and consumption of meals celebrating the birth of a child or a religious holiday. The viewing of such documents is so widespread that some migrants make a living preparing and importing tapes; tapes are also made to order, and a selection may be listed and culled from the many tapes in the possession of those responsible for tape distribution. Some include recordings of programs on national television in Senegal, or events that include Italians, such as musical concerts that feature local Senegalese musicians who accompany Italian theatrical performances or play on their own account. One of the Senegalese who makes his living primarily as a tailor for the Senegalese community also teaches traditional drumming to young Italians and stages concerts in local town squares; such events are not only filmed by the Senegalese but also supply footage for local television stations as well. The films' viewing context is social: a constant conversation is launched at the screen and addressed to the viewers as the meals are prepared, or afterward as tea is served. While some sit laughing about the wrestler that seems much too old for the sport, others call Senegal to speak with their families on cell phones, and another sits glued to the Senegalese radio news—no doubt just barely audible on the satellite radio. Creating a world of visions and sounds that envisions the larger community of Senegalese, the migrants for a time block out the host society that holds no image of them, or rather that trades images of migrants as so many tokens in a political battle over their presence in the country.[21]

CHAPTER 4

Crossing Modernity

The Journey from Imperial to Diasporic Nostalgia

Presenting Cultures

"In presenting culture as a subject for analysis and critique," anthropologist Renato Rosaldo once wrote, "the ethnographic perspective develops an interplay between making the familiar strange and the strange familiar" (1989, 39). Presenting culture—whatever we might imagine these days the concept of culture to be—it seems to me is no longer an activity restricted solely to the ethnographer. It has in fact become the peculiar preserve of the fiction writer, the filmmaker, and, increasingly, photographers or image makers of various sorts. Making the taken-for-granted aspects of our lives seem less than the working of grounded "universal truths"—that is, rendering "normalcy" strange by shaking it loose from its moorings—is at times a part of the state of play of the unexpected: an event or incident that cannot be accorded a place in the way we see things in the normal course of our lives. What Rosaldo in *Culture and Truth: The Remaking of Social Analysis* (1989) calls "home cultures," like those established anywhere, hunker down in their "common sense" and ride out all storms of change, while "alien cultures" seem so exotic and so distant that they cast an impenetrable "mentality." We may fail as outsiders to see the human contours of such seemingly different lives. In the process of presenting these lives and describing the texture of lives at a distance, we share a local knowledge of the world of "our own homes" with, let's face it, an audience composed in part of the very people we claim to study. Such social descriptions, Rosaldo claims, on the one hand need to undergo a process of familiarization and defamiliarization; on the other, the compression and decompression of points of view:

> Home cultures can appear so normal to their members that their
> common sense seems to be based in universal human nature.

> Social descriptions by, of, and for members of a particular
> culture require a relative emphasis on defamiliarization, so
> they will appear—as they in fact are—humanly made, and not
> given in nature. Alien cultures, however, can appear so exotic
> to outsiders that everyday life seems to be floating in a bizarre
> primitive mentality. Social descriptions about cultures distant
> from both the writer and the reader require a relative emphasis
> on familiarization, so they appear—as they also in fact are—
> sharply distinct in their differences, yet recognizably human in
> their resemblances. (Rosaldo 1989, 39–40)

Indeed, the notion of such translation implies an assumption of a passage from one cultural realm to the next that makes such an emphasis on
the rituals and tropics of social description of the translator/analyst so
important; there is the feeling that one is somehow crossing modernity,
passing through some imaginary boundary that leads to worlds alien to
our own. This hint of leaving modernity to look at another society or
cultural world haunts not only our social analysis, but also its reception
within and beyond our ethnographic practice. Let me add an additional
problem: what if—in this world of hypermodernity, as Alan Pred calls
it—we encounter what appear to be, as they also in fact are, alternative
takes on modernity, like unwanted bats flying through the rafters of home
cultures and resting in the attics of our own (Pred 1995, 15). I won't carry
the image of the bats much further, although I must mention that the
problem with bats is that they think they too are at home. In the postcolonial context, this is just the problem: the ideological frame of modernity
acts at times as a point of rupture between that which can be claimed as a
legacy—a "sediment" of the former colonial regime and the local or home
culture living in the shadow of the West, even long after Independence.

We will consider for a moment the peculiar work of "essentialism"
that Frantz Fanon grappled with in *Black Skins, Whites Masks* (1967a), as
it illuminates the problem of both history and the ideological construct
of a place, an elsewhere, beyond its frontier impervious to the passage of
time, to technological and economic advancement, crippled, locked outside modernity. However immune we have become to the idea of progress, a notion of the perpetual advancement of "civilization" economies,
and the washing away of traditions, in the realm of popular culture such
ideas still cloud our horizon and inform popular culture. It is a part of

the folklore of the not-so-distant anthropological past, and is very difficult to dismantle, because in spite of objections, it is still contained in films, music, and the many representations of the world out there.

Fanon relates the incident of riding in a train when a young girl spots him: "Mama, see the Negro! I'm frightened," and the outburst becomes the catalyst for a series of reflections of the part of Fanon about the status and meaning of the system of classification the young girl has invoked. "Now they begin to be afraid of me," he writes:

> I could no longer laugh, because I already knew that there were
> legends, stories, history, and above all historicity, which I had
> learned about from Jaspers. Then, assailed at various points, the
> corporeal schema crumbled, its place taken by a racial epidermal
> schema. In the train it was no longer a question of being aware
> of my body in the third person but in a triple person. In the train
> I was given not one but two, three places. I had already stopped
> being amused. It was not that I was finding febrile coordinates
> in the world. I existed triply: I occupied space. I moved toward
> the other . . . and the evanescent other, hostile but not opaque,
> transparent, not there, disappeared, Nausea . . .
>
> I was responsible at the same time for my body, for my race,
> for my ancestors. I subjected myself to objective examination,
> I discovered my blackness, my ethnic characteristics; and I was
> battered down by tom-toms, cannibalism, intellectual deficiency,
> fetishism, racial defects, slave-ships. (Fanon 1967a, 112)

This is a staggering passage: it challenges every attempt to locate the position from which one might begin a social description by making "the familiar strange and the strange familiar." The very underpinning of normalcy—that is, the norms of the West—are thrown into question. Yet Fanon's discussion comes out of what we might call an "ethnographic moment": an instance in which the classificatory catalog of Western tradition that aides in identification of the man on the train as a "Negro" and as an object of fear and exclusion is thrown into relief through a kind of social analysis that interrogates the nature of this commonplace, common sense of a colonial world. Fanon's work begins to question the historical construction of blackness against the backdrop of the ideological underpinnings of the colonial regime. That blackness is marked at all

is a completely arbitrary social fact, a social fact half-acknowledged in
Fanon's impulse to laugh, a notion that quickly passes as the prison gates
of the language confine him to the designation "Negro" and relegate him
to erasure. I would argue that in part his discussion is aided by his location
in diaspora, from Martinique; a decorated veteran and medical student,
he floats in a liminal netherworld, in neither a home nor alien culture but
in a subject position forced to reconcile the two poles of existence though
a third, perhaps emergent, location in diaspora. The dilemma for those
living in diaspora is that they can never really go home, as home is a location infused with the cultural logic of the "alien culture."[1]

In the colonial era, however, "every ontology is made unattainable" as
the black subject languishes in the prison of social and cultural erasure
(Fanon 1967a, 109). For Fanon, existence in "triple"—divided between
the past, the present, and the weight of black caricature—seems to hold
no final resolution. At once, he turns to subject himself to "an objective
examination," revealing what are at once the arbitrary products of objectification and the legacy of antiblack caricature as a historical construct
(112). Being present as a "Negro" means only momentarily being present
in one's individuality. Identity relinquishes its sovereignty to typification
as the performative act of naming embodies an erasure of the person for
Fanon (Gordon 1995). In the bad faith of antiblack constructions, the
black subject lacks presence; although visible in excess, his presence is
disregarded as equivalent to that of others who in turn occupy space as a
presence. But this absence of a place in the world, this being, out of place
(to borrow Mary Douglas's phrase) has a wider significance; as Fanon
points out, the ideological supports of this invisibility are the "pervad-
ing norms of black inferiority in Western societies," and a denial of her
"humanity" (Gordon 1995, 98). This denial can take many forms, constituting the "primitive/savage" other as living in a different time and
therefore somehow on the margins of humanity, or modernity. The black
subject is an embodiment of this absence, a state that can never "translate
into a human presence" (98). Yet such justifications for white presence
occupying the pinnacle of this regime of truth stand in relation to blacks
or other subjects as merely another folk tradition, a local construct, a discursive embodiment of bad faith. The taken-for-granted posture of whiteness is possible only if "the white body is expected to be seen by others
without seeing itself being seen. . . . Its mode of being, being self-justified,

is never superfluous," while the presence of the black seems to threaten "reality," to invade the normalcy of white subjects with that lack of self-consciousness of this precarious posture (103). The cultural logic of the identity of whiteness with presence, however, reverberates in the historical record, in film, and in various aspects of the iconography of blacks and whites through a host of registers. The process of erasure of the black subject at times reaches such a level of normalcy that we are comfortable with the thought of this absence. We must, as Rosaldo suggests, "challenge the normalcy of such a commonplace practice" (1989, 42). Samira Kawash points out the "visibility of blackness" comes to seem so "commonsensical in the modern world as to need no explanation," only to be woven into the very symbolic fabric of the social order (Kawash 1997, 134). However we envision the present, we cannot step out of modernity as easily as we can create a space of invisibility or denial of copresence within it:

> All human beings are present and, being human, are also beings to whom and in virtue of whom the world is presented. They are also absent. The ontological situation of humanity hasn't changed under the interpretation of blacks as Absence and whites as Presence. What happens here is an affective appeal to an imaginary, "magical" version of the world that suits the desired duality. This magical appeal is anti-black racism. (Gordon 1995, 103)

For Fanon, this antiblack racism created a stumbling block—an impasse across which it was impossible to travel. The colonial subject could make the passage to citizenship only through independence, and could become liberated only once the mythology of "antiblack racism" was confronted in the realm of consciousness and social practice. I am concerned with the aspects of home and alien cultures that came to be recognized as out of place, as sediments of a past or harbingers of a future that one does not wish to travel to, with a break between one kind of subjectivity and those that follow in the wake of postcolonial society.

Diasporic Nostalgia

In the latter half of the seventeenth century, the notion of nostalgia (derived from Greek *nostos*, a return home, and *algos*, a painful condition) was employed "to denote a form of melancholia induced by prolonged absence from one's home or locale, i.e., homesickness: the longing for a familiar space. It was not yet the longing for a familiar time, since the continuity form the past into the present was still a seamless web" (Lowe 1982, 40). Nostaglia, according to historian Donald M. Lowe in his work on Western bourgeois society *History of Bourgeois Perception* (1982), was "temporalized" as the growth of bourgeois society resulted in disruptions of the temporal landscape and the articulation of the many advances of bourgeois society that precipitated what many began to experience as a break with the past. Nostalgia was the response to this temporalization of a longing for a different time: the past. This interest or preoccupation with the increasingly distant past took on institutional form, as antiquarian societies and the preservation and discovery of documents and artifact of this other world began to be collected. Knowledge embraced an attempt to "recapture" the past through the creation of fields of inquiry such as anthropology, archeology, and mythology (Lowe 1982, 40). The stylistic aspects of art and architecture of other periods came to be idealized through such elements of a nineteenth-century nomenclature as neoclassism, romaticism, orientalism, and primitivism, which have their origin in this idealization of the past (40).[2] More recently, the notion of nostalgia has resurfaced, particularly in psychology, where the experiences from the feelings associated with one's youth to those associated with trying to discover the difference between historical and personal nostalgia, or even the perception of nostalgic elements in popular culture, such as music, are understood through a range of individual responses and ranges of feelings of nostalgia (Batcho 2002). In *Culture and Truth*, Rosaldo explored the meaning of Imperialist nostalgia, a longing for the bygone era of colonialism (Rosaldo 1989). I would like to explore what I call here "diasporic nostalgia," which is a longing for a return home, but not just under any conditions.[3] This is a form of nostalgia that not only looks back, but also forward, to a place that might exist a home where there are viable options for young people, where political disruptions and corruption are under control, a place where one might earn a living: a return to one's country. This nostalgia, for only a part of the past and some part of a future, is the theme of the following discussion.

The Empire of the Heart

The connections of diaspora are not those of markets and immigration policies for the people engaged in the practice of diaspora. The lives they

construct in diaspora, among people foreign to them, are often difficult—
yet, in the grand scheme of things, unavoidable. In many cases, they
become the primary channels of support for the failing economies of family and friends left behind. Their precarious positions in the labor markets
of their host counties cannot easily offset the nature of their responsibili-
ties back home. Such obligations orbit in another realm—an empire of
the heart through which the dreams and aspirations of those back home
are passed on to those in diaspora, and in return, a new imaginary is
transported "home" through the communications and visits of those in
diaspora. What emerges is a powerful set of visions of possible futures,
sometimes shared and other times at odds with each other—this empire
of the heart, however distancing it may become, remains a passionate and
integral part of everyday life. The complex of concerns, ideas, and desires
for political and social change all pass through this fulcrum, in which the
connections of family, friends, and others closely associated with life in
diaspora or in the small circle of those at home are linked through religious, political, or ethnic belonging. I call this provisionally an empire
of the heart, as it contains also dreams for change of the society at large,
and for this reason, the discourse on nation, corruption, patronage, and
migrations are also a part of this complex. The nature of belonging in
diaspora is dramatically altered through the experience of negotiating a
life with in and without one's home society. This new sense of belonging is
not merely a matter of a binary set of relations, as "transnationalism" suggests; rather, diaspora creates a synthesis of these possible positions, and
increasingly those in diaspora must face the real possibility of making a
transition to a third country or negotiating such a move for others. Residence in diaspora may continue for some, and may even become a semipermanent state. In the case of the Senegalese in northern Italy, many of
the established migrants now provide the opportunity for younger cousins and siblings to enter more easily into the Italian context, with the real
goal being future migration to the United States or other destinations. The
empire of the heart is also a world in which people struggle to make the
best of things on their own; it is the world of people who for the most part
fall just below the elite; patronage networks do not reach them, nor do the
powerful associations of the rural world. One can write a letter in Turin,
Italy, and through the diaspora links have it hand-carried (along with gifts
and other items) to New York, Paris, or a dozen other locations all over

the world. The letter doesn't need to go through the post office; it travels, like so many other communications, through the empire of the heart.

The importance of the diaspora has had an impact in Senegalese popular culture. During the 1980s, hip-hop music—inspired in part by the listening tastes of the Senegalese diaspora in the United States—began to combine with local styles to produce "le rap Sénégalais," a fusion of Atlantic-crossing African and North American musical expressions. One of the first Senegalese rappers, Mbacké Dioum, was actually based in the Senegalese diaspora in Italy, but it was the group Positive Black Soul (PBS), founded by Dider Awadi and Amadou Barry, that really gave Senegalese hip-hop its distinctive sound (Devey 2000). By 1995, a profusion of groups had explored the Senegalese music scene, some engaging in lyric elaborations that explored pan-African themes in French, but also in a host of local languages. In the diaspora today, cassettes of Senegalese television also provide the music of such artists as Roy Marque, Fatou Gewel, Matty Thiam Dogo, A. Nader, and Dial Mbaye, and, of course, the popular Daara J, whose song "Boomerang" speaks of hip-hop originating in Africa, moving out to the diaspora, and returning like a boomerang back to Africa.

As Catherine Boone has emphasized, the political topography of the postcolonial African state in Senegal has taken shape in the wake of the complex interplay of colonial legacy and postcolonial territorial differences, structuring institutional choice and practices (Boone 2003). In the Peanut Basin of central Senegal, the legacy of indirect rule and the intricate alliances built between the indigenous royals, the Grands Marabouts (religious leaders) and the postcolonial government created a conservative coalition and power-sharing arrangement that sustained Senghor's ruling party from Independence well into the 1980s. In the Wolof Groundnut Basin, the powers of this coalition reached down to the level of the village and all the way back to Dakar, placing virtual control of the demarcation of political and administrative units, and rural development—including land distribution, labor, access to credit, and the final sale and disposition of agricultural products—in the hands of a small group of notables. With the decline in the groundnut economy, many rural dwellers turned to commercial activities often centered on trade in the urban areas. By the 1970s, significant portions of the Mourid order had shifted from groundnut production to commerce, using the political connections of the leading marabouts to work around government restrictions (Boone 2003, 91). The biggest marabout traders became so powerful during this period that all political factions began to court them in their own right, as they control a virtual army of rank-and-file members scattered throughout the diaspora, working in the far-flung commercial networks of the rapidly developing import–export circuits.

Although the Senegalese diaspora encompasses diverse ethnic groups, the powerful Islamic Brotherhood called the Mourid Order has had a dramatic influence on the nature and dimension of the diaspora throughout the world. By the end of the 1960s, the Senegalese economy, based largely on the export of the peanut farming—a colonial legacy—was beginning to feel the impact of the initial phases of what would become a prolonged period draught precipitating a crisis in agriculture. The groundnut or peanut economy of the period was dominated by Mourid farming communities; the young rural former cultivators began to establish religious centers in urban areas, engaging in various forms of economic activities including petty trade, transportation, traditional artwork and woodwork, and distribution networks in articles ranging from electronics to clothing and aimed at supporting those left behind in the rural world. Today the so-called Baol Baol—named for the region of their origins—virtually dominate the popular urban economy.

The Mourid are now heavily invested in transportation and the production of crafts and traditional artworks, along with real estate, and have begun to envision business ventures in tourism and finance (Devey 2000, 193–194). The Mourid have began to construct a vast empire spanning the globe, including such international centers as "New York, Johannesburg, Taiwan, Paris, Milan, Hong Kong and Dubai," connected in part by informal and formal commercial associations (194). The Mourid have created a vast network of commercial activities, seen most clearly in the Mourid virtual takeover of the Sandaga market in Dakar, the country's premier marketplace—not only all but displacing the Lebanese merchants, but changing the very character of the market itself, with an infinite diversity of products from foodstuffs to pharmaceuticals. Transforming a traditional marketplace by integrating it with aspects of the world economy in turn expands the scope and reach of the Senegalese frontier (196).

The mobility of the Mourid—who have now inspired other groups to join their numbers—is one of the critical qualities of the deep and numerous roots of the diaspora worldwide. Yet while the Mourid establish centers in the far corners of the world, the spiritual heart of the organization remains the pilgrimage destination of Touba, in Senegal, a city whose population has grown so dramatically in recent years that it remains second only to Dakar. But the Mourid now comprise merely one node of a complex Senegalese diaspora spanning diverse ethnicities and religions and increasingly populated by young women entering the circuits of displacement. Although less well-organized than the Mourid, these other nodes of the diaspora are at times housed with Mourid or live independently among groups of kin, friends, and other young Senegalese. More urban young people have found their educations interrupted for lack of funds or the throes of some family crisis that prevented them from continuing their schooling. The making of a "vernacular cosmopolitanism," as Mamadou Diouf has called the world that these young people are creating, is also enhanced by the skills this generation learned along the way, including languages such as English and Italian and a more profound encounter with metropolitan French, as well as work cultures that increase their marketability as workers, translators, and intermediaries (Diouf 2000).

One very hot Sunday afternoon in Turin, just inside the historic center of the town, I sat with Senegalese that I had known for over ten years, talking about some of the changes that had taken place over the years and about changes back home. I said that I had been looking at some of the films of Ousmane Sembene, and a man named Babacar said matter of factly that he hadn't seen any of these films. I said that I thought the he might enjoy them and that distribution of the films had been poor in the country anyway; indeed, that they were more well known outside of the country is one of the great travesties of contemporary cultural criticism. I had only begun to be aware of them and the peculiar manner in which the film had been left, as if by the side of the road, for anthropologists and other social scientists; left, that is, in the realm of the "art film" for the command of the film or literary critic. I thought that an anthropological lens on the film might cast a different shadow—the ethnography does not really end with a trip to the field as the recreation of ethnographic or cultural critic is also a frontier of the anthropological palate. I argue that it is not merely the context of the making of the film and its aftermath that may be of interest to the anthropologist or anthropologically inclined; it may also be the content and the manner in which it enters into a kind of catalog of cultural understandings and representations that are no more "real" than the latest soap opera or talk topic, but may still reveal something about a society that we might not otherwise know. This is not to say that the work of Keats is the key to understanding Western culture or that Bernardo Betrolucci's film *Beseiged* (1998) or Enrico Fellini's *La Voce della Luna* (*Voice of the Moon*, 1990) has cornered the market on Italian cultural discourse, but when these filmmakers take up the representation of new migrants in Italian society—as Michelangelo Antonioni (*La Notte*, 1961) had done as early as the 1960s—it is a sign that it might be time for a discussion of the implications of these changes.[4] The images of a Senegalese migrant selling objects of African art in a passing shot of a train station in Italy in Fellini's *La Voce della Luna* cannot be taken as a insignificant event either in film history or in the social and cultural discourse in Italian society. The figure of the Senegalese street seller—ubiquitous by the late 1980s—was a customary feature of the local and national newscasts, but as the figures populated the background the voiceover of the reporters rarely mentioned their presence, because the street sellers had not yet become a part of an open political discourse on immigration. The figures passed in silence as concerns about their presence in Italian society mounted. There was a similar silence in confrontation with the image of migrants in the films of the masterful Italian director Fellini; not helping matters, these images appear in what might arguably be one of his most difficult and inaccessible films. *La Voce della Luna* deals with the quotidian journey of an insane character, Ivo Salvini (Roberto Benigni), who may—in the last analysis—be a bit of a visionary, given the fantastic images he envisions overflowing out of the mundane occurrences of everyday life that populate the film with an alternative and rich world of the imagination. The visual landscape and imagination of this in Fellini's last film is spectacularly set in motion by the character's preoccupation or perhaps obsession with the moon; no doubt, such a character as Salvini is bound to see what others refuse or choose not to see, including the increasing diversity of the social world, although at the time, many people left the theater hardly acknowledging the non-event, even when African women appear again and again in important dream sequences during the film.

I realized, as I walked to the street on a rainy night in Turin with a group of friends, that they really didn't see the people who socially were still invisible, except in as if in a dream, until prompted to do so. I have had this experience before; for some so-called gypsies, blacks, and other social outsiders have to be pointed out in a photograph: "Oh them, those are only the fill-in-the-blank all-but-invisible outsider, or newcomer, standing next to my cousin." I suppose growing up African American in Oakland, California, there is a certain manner in which we lived for pictures—plowing through the family album or swimming into a trunk of photographs was second nature. I was often taken aback when one of my friends from school was taken through this family ceremony, to my great embarrassment, but it was here in the corners of our living rooms, in the poor light and through the yellowing stacks of photographs taken too soon or overexposed just a bit, or in which your cousin looks "too dark," that we came to live (in spite of being largely invisible in official American popular culture).

We searched for images of black people in the newspapers and stared at the television for news of the black community, but here at home, the war was won through the parade of our lives in images, partaking in ceremonies in private black life—not always glamorous, but visible and of our own making. It was a long time before black filmmakers produced a body of work in my lifetime that began to pencil in black popular culture in the United States.

The End of Empire

At the core of the troubles that plague the postcolonial state is the difficulty with which a nationalist ideology—or, as Fanon put it, "national culture"—may come to be forged in the wake of the dying colonial order (Fanon 1963, 212). National narratives—perhaps encumbered by a poorly articulated print culture, and a world segmented by many ethnic divisions, languages, and local cultures—have encountered some difficulty. As Eleni Coundouriotis insists, in the case of African postcolonial states, "We are presented with the repeated and widespread failure of national narratives that do not hold" (1999, 147). The peculiar nature of postcolonial society forces the creation of a narrative at once encompassing and forward-looking that does not recapitulate a generic European score; the postcolonial nation must invent itself as it severs ties with a past beyond its control. Sembene's last novel dealt with such an inability to envision a postcolonial state that might be imagined beyond the artificially created boundaries set in place through the process of colonial history.

During the disappearance of the Senegalese president and the contemporary government crisis that follows, the various ministers and the prime minister set upon one another in the wake of the "Venerable One's" absence. The novel *Le Dernier de L'Empire* (*The Last of the Empire*, 1983) commands the reader's attention to the succession of power in African regimes, castes, corruption of the elite, and the overshadowing influence of the former colonial world. There is a very Fanonian cast to the book, as it explores that nature of leadership compromised by an essentially "hybrid" elite one, caught between the historical fortunes of various position, identities, and political moments. It takes on the warnings of Fanon against "the pitfalls of national consciousness," in which the rulers of newly independent regimes having thrown of colonialism merely act as "intermediary" agents of international economic concerns, a capitalism that does nothing to transform or develop the former colony (Fanon 1963, 148). The mission of these elite go-betweens can do little to transform the postcolonial regime, as its lack of technical and intellectual resources relegate the role of the "national" elite to that of business agent.

For Fanon, the nation, seen through the lens of this emergent elite, contains no vision of the future of the masses of the population; these guardians of the new nation rather occupy a position inhibiting it from performing its historical role to shape and strengthen a national economy and build a new cadre of scholars, technicians, and business leaders:

> Seen through its eyes, its mission has nothing to do with transforming the nation; it consists, prosaically, of being the transmission line between the nation and capitalism, rampant though camouflaged, which today puts on the mask of neo-colonialism. (Fanon 1963, 152)

According to Fanon, this national elite does not avail itself of the "revolutionary capital, which is the people," but hides itself in the capital and shuttles between the halls of government and international business offices and banking concerns (1963, 150). Having lost touch with the masses, this would-be leadership models itself in the image of elites in Paris or New York, authorizing no style all its own. I think this may be a bit harsh. If nothing else, an ethnographic lens might reveal a new spin on positions of power.

In *The Last of the Empire*, Sembene charts the course of post-Independence political culture through the presidency of Léon Mignane, a figure who, not unlike the late former president of Senegal Leopold Sédar Senghor, embraced a vision of the potentials of a complementary relationship between Africa and Europe in a new form of dependency on the former colonial regime. By the end of the colonial period, French capital supplied the major portion of Senegal's public development fund and virtually all of its technical and overall financial aid. The Senegalese economy during the 1950s and 1960s provided exports—principally peanuts—for the French market, and almost all of the remaining foreign trade was with France (Gellar 1995). During the 1970s, attempts to break the dependency cycle in Senegal were checked by increasing oil prices, the impact of drought in 1972–1973, and the first phases of food shortages and inflation. Expansion in such areas as phosphate mining, fisheries, and even tourism by the 1980s promised an incremental shift from the peanut economy inherited as a legacy of colonialism.

The first International Monetary Fund economic recovery program—the five-year plan for 1980–1985—ushered in a new era of dependency. By 1989, Senegal foreign debt was nearly three times that of the average for sub-Saharan Africa (Gellar 1995, 64). During the years after Independence, the government grew to an enormous entity; the state had invested heavily in mining companies (phosphates), water, electric utilities, and the marketing and manufacture the of Senegalese peanut industry, resulting in the creation of massive "parastatal" companies. This sector was one of the areas in which patronage and the political corruption of government insiders became commonplace. Pressure from donor groups to dismantle and privatize many of the government enterprises, consolidated in part through nationalization programs of the 1970s, led to an agreement with the World Bank as part of a Structural Adjustment Loan in the mid-1980s, calling for the government to "privatize twenty-seven enterprises"; by the mid-1990s, only the small-scale operations had actually been sold off, leaving the vast portion of the structure in place. With the devaluation of the CFA franc in 1994, attempts to bring the national debt under control began to directly affect critical political supporters of the state functionaries, urban workers, and businesses.

In the following section, I turn to explore the last novel of Ousmane Sembene, set at the changing of the guard between the Senghor genera- tion and the regime of Abdou Diouf, who was to hold the Senegalese presidency for almost twenty years. Sembene's novel is set in a period in which a major shift is taking place between the structure of Senegalese society left in place after colonialism and a Senegal that would emerge in part in response to external forces like the World Bank's structural adjustment programs. The rural establishment that had been the base of the support of the Senghor government was deteriorating under the pres- sures of the world market, as peanut prices fell steadily and the national economy sought to diversify across other sectors. The contemporary Senegalese economy is still dominated by agriculture, although it makes up only a small portion of the GDP of the country—by some estimates only 10 percent, as almost half of the active population is employed in agricultural positions.

It is this failure of the Senghor era from Independence to the early 1980s to establish a political culture that might serve as a model for future generations that Sembene turns to in *The Last of the Empire*. Cheikh Tidiane Sall, the minster of justice and a longtime friend and supporter of President Léon Mignane, contemplates the nature and sig- nificance of his political career in the wake of his resignation. The life of the former minister parallels the political culture of the country directly, as he has been an integral part of each historical successive historical period, passing from colonialism and a period of assimilation through Independence to the contemporary seat of power under the Venerable One, President Mignane. The striking contrast between this generation, already in their seventies and eighties, and the generation of young tech- nocrats that comprise the hub of the various ministerial posts headed by Prime Minister Daouda, marks the emergence of a governmental crisis when President Mignane suddenly and mysteriously disappears.

The trajectory of the excolonial subject forms a critical node of the manner in which *The Last of the Empire* suggests the need for a critical interrogation of the character of the postcolonial subjectivities at play several generations beyond Independence. Notions of essential identities and ethnic and cultural purity are challenged in the text and explored through the refractions of essentialism, nationalism, and racism in postcolonial society. Former colonial subjects in the novel seem caught between identification with France and what in many cases seems like a weak link to their post-Independence home. But this "home," further fragmented by the divisions of religious affiliation, caste, and political clan, is a kind of minefield through which only the young seem capable of navigating. The youth are a generation that sees colonialism merely as a distant memory.

Reading *The Last of the Empire*, we are reminded of the great Shakespearean drama separating the superpowers of the East and the West that looms in the background, at times articulated through representatives of Western intelligence or their allies in the African nation set adrift in the novel. Belonging in the specter of the fading of the Independence, the generation has come full circle; in the contemporary context, there is an urgency—perhaps a duty—to come to terms with Senegalese identity cast free of its reliance of the precolonial markings of caste or the colonial legacy of the separation of intellectual and religious elites, or the imagined distance between elder and junior members of the society, and in a fascinating challenge Sembene also touches upon the question of gender divisions, as women in the younger generation have had the opportunity to pursue education and must work out their lives in the shadow of a world of men.

In the government opposition, we find young men and women on equal footing for the first time, although Djia Umrel Ba—over fifty and unrestrained by the political affiliations of her husband, Chiekh Tidiane Sall—presents an alternative vision of an intermediate generation. We will return to generational consideration of gender in the discussion of *Faat Kine* (2000), Sembene's most recent film. What Sembene is mapping is a kind of ethnosociology of power in Senegalese society. Much like his critique of the African bourgeoisie in the film *Xala* (1975), *The Last of the Empire* takes on the Senghor-like regime that has come to the end of political and social usefulness, at once leaving a real power vacuum and a kind of nostalgia for the past.

A kind of nostalgia for the former empire comes from the experience of not only those who once experienced the benefits of French citizenship, but also through the countless French advisors and other representatives of the former regime. The notion of Imperialist nostalgia that was explored by Roslado was marked by a pronounced longing for the past (Rosaldo 1989). We might say this form of nostalgia is refreshed through continuous contact, through cables, or through education in the former colony and expatriate business communities. It is then not only a nostalgia stressing the dimensions of the temporal and the longing for the colonial regime and an ideological home for the assimilé, but also entails a spatial dislocation an imaginary occupation of African national territory. In *The Last of the Empire*, Sembene toys with this possibility, suggesting that the very nature of the neocolonialism must rest on the possibility of military support of the African regime in time of crisis. At one point in the text, the author mentions a watchman at the residence of the French ambassador, holding on to a nostalgic view of empire, remembering his life as a colonial soldier, preferring still the life of the colonial:

> The garrulous old native watchman, happy to have company, was recounting his many billets in France and her former colonies.
> He admitted that he preferred the colonial system to this Independence. (Sembene 1981, 76)

The evocation of the "native watchman" frames an atmosphere of nostalgia that permeates the complex and multiple identities that are available to this excolonial subject. But the use of the term "native"—a throwback to the colonial era—reveals in part the harsh critique of Sembene on the nature of "hybrid" identifications with the former colonial regime and passive posture associated with it, a servile mentality, a consciousness shared in subtle ways by members of the governing elite. Sembene was a Tirailleur Sénégalis during the war, before becoming a dockworker during the postwar period in France. The figure of the Tirailleur often exhibits a characteristic struggle between being a part of a colonial order and breaking with all traditional forms of authority, including the colonial society, as the dreams of full citizenship become increasingly impossible within the colonial system. The "native" exists only in relation to the European, represented by the ambassador, who lives in a residence "drowned in a mass of dark greenery" and marked by the "bougainvillea hedge," a sign of the old European quarter of colonial times (Sembene 1981, 76). The presence of the "native" watchman, now supplemented by "armed soldiers," alerts the reader to the minor changes in visible signs of power and foreign influence. Moreover, this passing mention of the "native" and former colonial soldier gives the ominous suggestion that colonial subjectivity is not easily overcome, that the nostalgia masks a process—perhaps incomplete—by which the "native" may become a postcolonial subject not drawn to the light of the former colonial regime. Sembene reminds us that national identity must always be seen through its struggle with alternate points of reference of Frenchness, assimilation through colonial experience or contemporary education, the poles of historical religious, and ethnic and even caste affiliations that can disrupt national consciousness and belonging.

As the book opens, the reader is drawn into a postcolonial political crisis at the initial stages of which the longtime friend and associate of President Léon Mignane, Minister of Justice Doyen Cheikh Tidiane Sall, resigns his post—an action the minister planned to execute long before the current crisis and in fact had discussed with the now-absent head of state. Doyen Cheikh Tidiane Sall splits with this inner circle, hand-picked by the president and seemingly unable to function in his absence. The reflections of Cheikh Tidiane Sall are principally structured around the legacy that his generation has failed to pass on to the nation. Although surrounded by young political technocrats, few can see beyond their own self-interest or political shortcomings and they march headlong into a struggle to fill the political vacuum left by the absent leader. While Cheikh Tidiane Sall, following the suggestion of a close associate, considers writing his memoirs—a record or we might say a genealogy of the present—he mentions, "I have thought of a title for my memoirs . . . *The Last of the Empire*" (Sembene 1981, 238). The former minister of justice is a man molded by the colonial era, yet much reflection has led him to begin to doubt the firm foundations of his training and political education. He is the first generation to benefit from the opening up of education fought for by the colonial subjects of his father's generation; Cheikh Tidiane Sall, "the son of a sergeant in the corps of Tirailleurs," stands on a critical divide between an African society that only began to be mobilized by European colonialism and a group of early students sent to the métropole to be educated (24). As he enters his retirement, we are reminded that "for three-quarters of his life, he had considered himself French . . . a French Citizen," and that the overwhelming experience of his life had shaped his world in the image of France (84). President Léon Mignane perhaps identified even more with France, as the process of reflection of this peculiar state betwixt and between had been truncated by a vision of complementary relations between Europe and Africa. Here Sembene launches the most scathing critique of the Senghor years, as in many ways the regime was unable to extricate itself from a profound dependence on the former colonial power—one that insinuated itself into the very nature of social being. Doyen Cheikh Tidiane Sall, finding his way through his own cultural and political formation, muses:

> I belong to two epochs. For over half of this century I convinced myself that I was French. I had done everything necessary to be acknowledged as such. And in the end I was convinced. You know, that period was the most important of my life. As I grew, like a sunflower I was irresistibly drawn towards France. There was my sun, the light I needed for my spiritual life. Look around you. Nothing here comes from our country. Nothing was handed down by my father or my grandfather. (Sembene 1981, 35)

Cheikh Tidiane Sall points out that all of the books in his study are from Europe and all those written on Africa are authored by Europeans, and then, turning to his son, he declares "My Frenchness affects me here [he passed his hand over his shaven head]. It's choking me" (36). The legacy of this doubleness lies in the very design of the Senghor/Mignane regime and in turn guides the country. At one point, the family of Cheikh Tidiane Sall is referred as *Tubabs bu nulls,* or black Europeans (126).[5] Searching for some element of the many years that he spent in office at the side of the Venerable One, Cheikh Tidiane Sall surveys his past for some form of legacy to pass on to the new generation of potential leaders. Recalling the words of Fanon, writing of the middle strata the will inherit the new nation, he notes that the political class "remembers what it read in European textbooks and imperceptibly it becomes not even the replica of Europe, but its caricature" (Fanon 1963, 175). Recognizing the outline of this caricature, former doyen Cheikh Tidiane Sall is moved to publicly denounce government corruption and the dilemma of national belonging, underscored by the reliance of the political class on external advisors, financial agreements, and reciprocal national security arrangements. In a celebration of the seventieth birthday of the president in absentia, he launches the first and most sustained of a series of critiques of the regime:

> In my youth, the system then prevailing, commonly known by the name of colonialism, assimilated the first cadres it trained; its aim was two-fold, to make us into "Frenchmen" and to take possession of our land. That method has now had its day. However, we must have the honesty to perceive and acknowledge that colonialism no longer consists in occupying land, but in demeaning the minds, crushing the culture and distorting the growth of a society, and imposing an armada of obtuse advisers whose role within our new administration is not to help us, but to curb every daring reform, every enterprising spirit. (Sembene 1981, 39)

Indeed, Cheikh Tidiane Sall—an integral part of the regime every step of the way—unlike his colleagues has not yet benefited financially from his position in the regime. Recognizing his complicity in the system, he places his hope in the next generation, adding in his address: "Our one chance lies in the youth of our people" (39).[6]

For the independent African nations that emerged in the era of decolonization, the threat of that national military seizure of power was an ever-present danger. Many heads of state were educated in colonial military training programs. Cheikh Tidiane Sall discovers through reflection a path to social transformation, but other figures of his generation do not fare so well. *The Last of the Empire* presents a portrait of the dangers many post-Independence regimes faced in their own national military forces. Manthia Diawara recounts a conversation he had with Ousmane Sembene during a film interview in which the Senegalese filmmaker expressed a deeply pessimistic view of African leadership:

> Sembene Ousmane had once told me in a film interview that we had to begin from zero, by cutting off all the branches and rotten fruit from the tree. He had said that the older generation was corrupt beyond redemption and must be destroyed before it contaminated the younger one. Everywhere in Africa today, people are embarrassed by their leaders' irresponsibility, their greed, their inefficiency and decadence, and their lack of love for the continent, which they have sold to foreigners. (Diawara 1998a, 54)

This "afro-pessimism," as Diawara calls it, perhaps must be tempered with the considerable resilience of the young generation in African societies. Diawara however rejects the notion that Africa is a kind of "antipode of modernity," an idea promulgated by the lingering "supremacists'" ideological turn that attempts to explain away African troubles with revamped racialist ideology (54). Modernity cannot be reduced to a victory here or there over "tradition" or comparison of scales of "development" or the "implacable speed of modernity" and its global economic markets as a gauge for comparing the West and the rest (57). Diawara suggests that the problem rests rather in the manner in which we are modern:

> We are modern in the way in which we keep fighting for our
> independence, defying certain traditional taboos judged archaic
> by our new standards, and in our perpetual attempts to redefine
> our nation-states. Afro-pessimists will remain unable to perceive
> the extent of our modernity as long as they persist in comparing
> our styles and material accomplishments with those of the West.
> A true measure of our modernity lies in our desire for freedom
> and better lives. (Diawara 1998a, 57)

Just as the watchman at the French ambassador's residence expressed a nostalgia for the empire, the long training of the military and the political isolation of the national armed forces may in themselves, as Fanon suggested, pose a threat to emergent democracies. Fanon warned that the military lacked a well-established political culture in many African nations and was often led by forms of "indirect government" articulated through "foreign experts"—military advisors of the former colonial government—exacting an influence on national military leaders. These military "experts," as Fanon refers to them, help to create a national army that "pins the people down, immobilizing and terrorizing them" (Fanon 1963, 174). With the military operation of the French in Algeria and elsewhere in the colonial world in mind, Fanon was suspicious of the "autonomy" of the military.

The national army, according to Fanon, had to be brought into the arch of the revolutionary struggles of the people; an autonomous army might "go into politics" on its own terms, untutored by the ideal and aspiration of the masses. Greater care had to be taken to create a cadre of soldiers that understands that the "soldier . . . is not a simple mercenary but a citizen who by means of arms defends the nation" (Fanon 1963, 201). Further, the army must be "the school of civic and political education," a source of national service to the nation (201). It is important the soldier understands the he or she is serving his or her country and not the dictates of a commanding officer:

> Care must be taken to avoid turning the army into an autonomous body which sooner or later, finding itself idle and without a mission, will "go into politics" and threaten the government. Drawing-room generals, by dint of haunting the corridors of government departments, come to dream of manifestoes. The only way to avoid this menace is to educate the army politically, in other words to nationalize it. (Fanon 1963, 202)[7]

As the crisis escalates, Prime Minister Daouda calls on the national armed forces to restore order, as protests have broken out in the streets over government corruption, in part in response to the speech of Cheikh Tidiane Sall and helped along by the intrigues of some of his government officials. The cultural genealogy of the military leaders literally can be read on their uniforms. Brigadier Gerneral Ousmane Mbaye, chief of staff and an aging military figure whose youth was spent in the colonial forces, carried the decorations of the colonial empire on his uniform, along with those of the Independence era—the very contradictions that robbed the general of the capacity to make the transition to a postcolonial future were on display for all to see. The general, who was to report directly to the now-absent president, arrives for his meeting with the prime minister and "was wearing all his medals: those won in Indo-China, Morocco and Algeria, as well as his French military medals and those, more recent, received since Independence"; dependent on his foreign military advisors, the general is an outsider to the world of politics of the ministers (Sembene 1981, 165). General Mbaye, insulted and outmaneuvered by the young Prime Minister Daouda, who threatens to employ a military assistance agreement with the former colonial power if the general does not put down the disturbances, retreats to a glorious past:

> He remembered past moments of pride and satisfaction. He had twice the honor of taking part in the July 14th parade in Paris, marching from the Place de la Concorde to the Arc de

Triomphe with his black troops. He recalled the great moments
experienced during the years he had spent in the Colonial
Army—all his youth. He had risen through the ranks, aided by
his servile mentality.... At the start of African Independence, he
suddenly experienced nationalistic feelings. He returned to his
country to set up the first National Army. (Sembene 1981, 178)

The Last of the Empire presents the reader with a system of politics
(the Senghor/Mignane regime) so dependent on the patriarch and the
influence of the former colonial regime that it implodes. The generation
of the assimilé cannot envision a future beyond the outlines of these
powerful relationships (Tsabedze 1994). The youth take center stage:
the university students, the young journalists, and other professionals
outside of the arch of government kickbacks and favors. It is with this
generation that the possibility of change rests.

Now I would like to turn to contemporary critique of current
Senegalese President Abdoulaye Wade, who came to power just as the
final representative of the Senghor legacy—former president and disciple of the Independence generation Abdou Diouf—left office in 2000
after a nineteen-year reign (1981–2000) that emerged from the Senegalese diaspora. Diouf, who came to power promising a new direction and
an end to the widespread government corruption that had characterized
his predecessors, quickly reorganized the government and promulgated
a new constitution in 2001.

The Senegalese Diaspora in Italy and Diasporic Nostalgia

Perhaps the true empire of the heart is held together today by those
who—finding few opportunities at home—sail off in every direction to
forge a life in diaspora. Increasingly the Senegalese diaspora includes
women and families making this extraordinary sacrifice, extending
through one's life and postponing the possibility of return indefinitely.
One of Sembene's more recent films, *Faat Kine* (2000), charts what he
has called the everyday heroism of African women; he emphasizes the
manner in which African society and economy are in many ways held
together by the contributions of African women. Indeed, women play a
pivotal role in diaspora as the support and well-being of large groups of
extended kin, friends, and at times others who are newly incorporated
in these intricate networks depends upon them.

For over a decade, I have worked with a community of Senegalese in Italy; when I arrived on the scene in 1990 many had been traveling back and forth between Italy, other European destinations, and Senegal and other African and Middle Eastern destinations. It might be hard to find young people today who do not see themselves as at least a potential part of the extensive Senegalese diaspora, hoping with the help of kin and friends to reach the United States or Canada by way of Europe. Babacar is now thinking of returning to Senegal; he and his sister Fatima form the core of a group of family and friends that spend most of their free time together in conversation, sharing meals, memories, and an ever-deepening interest in European politics associated with the fate of immigration. On one afternoon, as I sat in the apartment of Fatima and her husband Matar—the central location of these meetings—we began to discuss the difficulties facing young people today in Senegal. In the course of the governmental changes, with the administration of Abdoulaye Wade—an opposition group that has been on the margins of power for years—coming into power, many former government employees had lost their jobs in the scramble to hand out positions under the new patronage system. Wade, a vocal critic of the old regime under Abdou Diouf (1980–2001), who was a disciple of Senghor (1960–1980), promised a new direction and a cleansing of the old practices associated with the old order. In the register of diasporic nostalgia, her comments at once critiqued the new government and presented a hope for the future.

Living Out the Economic Crisis Back Home

Although I usually walked over the apartment strolling down Via Garibaldi, that night I remember taking the 67 bus down past the movie theater, which was showing something with Billy Bob Thornton and other American actors and actresses that figured prominently on the marquee. Displaying a bit of English in the advertisement was part of the marketing strategy. Typical of Turin, the zone had its share of small parks, setting off the great boulevards at angles—a refuge for old war memorials and pigeons. On a June evening in 2002, the ancient part of the city still exhibited shop names that had long since fallen out of everyday language, and the feel of the old stone walkways signaled the historic city center. If the elevator was on the blink, the walk up the old building was a bit dangerous, as the floor above the flat where I was to meet my Senegalese friend was for all intents and purposes condemned, with crumbling stairwells and relatively hostile neighbors. By then only one family in the building would speak to the Africans. So angered by the city's placement in a Turinese building of the Senegalese, the neighbors ignored their presence.

We talked about number of things: the political dominance of the traditional Socialist Party that had guided the country since Independence had come to an end in Senegal; Abdou Diouf, a longtime disciple of the former president Senghor, had ended a nineteen-year reign when he was voted out of office in 2001. In his wake, a new kind of political order was coming into place, one ostensibly dedicated to a transformation of the country and a clearing away of the many layers of government corruption. During the 1960s, the Senegalese economy had been dominated by the groundnut industry, representing about two-thirds of the exports during that period—an economy in large measure due to a legacy of colonialism; by the 1970s, however, when Abdou Diouf (the future president of Senegal) became prime minister, groundnut production had already declined to around 40 percent and by 1990 represented only about 20 percent of the nation's total exports (Gellar 1995). Diversification had its costs, however: increasing reliance on foreign aid, the expanding dependence of the Senegalese state functionaries on the government, and subjectivity to the shifting fortunes of foreign interests. However, the failure of the government to improve the living conditions for most of the population set in motion a slow process of resentment, political disaffection, and outmigration. Senegal was one of the first African countries to receive a Structural Adjustment Program, forcing the government into a series of austerity measures and leading to salary reductions and layoffs for civil servants. Further reductions in living standards were directed at curbing the dependency of government functionaries. At the same time, living standards for a large part of the population have not improved significantly since Independence (World Bank 2002, 2003). Few families can survive without some members in diaspora.

The recent and monumental changes in the face of the Senegalese political and economic landscape left an already embattled civil service sector significantly disrupted as the new regime of Abdoulaye Wade cleared the decks of former government employees and their allies, installing new cadres of workers in key positions. Those associated with the former political networks found themselves out of work and many began to join their brothers, sisters, cousins, and friends in diaspora. Mariama arrived in June 2002 as one of the victims of the new government streamlining of bureaucratic posts. Fatima viewed her sister as one of the educated semi-elites, who, having received a degree, was entitled to a fairly stable form of employment in Senegal. This was something she and many others could not aspire to, but hoped that the opportunity might pass on to another generation—those remaining in Senegal being educated in large part through the support of the diaspora. Mariama's arrival had sparked a complex reaction. There had been so much hope that things were turning around with the new government, but the fear remained that things might return to the old corrupt ways of the past.

After customary greetings, with the door open because of the heat, Fatima began to tell me that a friend of her sister Mariama's had just called from Senegal before I entered the apartment proper (the social space extended onto the walkway). The friend, who worked in the same office, had told her that things were really bad at home and that she had done the right thing by leaving the country. Many of the government workers—who had had European-style lifestyles, cars, and the most stable forms of employment one might imagine—now found themselves at home with their families, considering joining the diaspora. Many in their mid-thirties, like Mariama, might have little hope of another government job until the regime changed or their expertise was considered indispensable for some branch of government. Fatima began to talk about the new regime and the manner in which the corruption of the old has taken on a new guise, even as the new order was coming into place:

> Is this right . . . Is this just [e justo]? There was a woman who
> lived across the street from us and they were poor; my father
> used to give the boys some money and put it in an envelope and
> my mother didn't know anything about this. But he would give
> them money so they could eat . . . for a lot of people now, if they
> see that you have three meals a day and that you can cook in the
> morning and conserve some part of this for another meal, and
> have a meal at the end of the day, they think that you are rich. So
> many can't eat even the three meals a day. Now my father would
> give them money and I know that they were poor, I'll just say it,

they were poor and everybody knows it; there was one girl of the family who studied really well and she met someone that was in the government and now they are rich, really rich.[8]

There is an area near (our house) where the houses cost a lot just to get the opportunity to build there and then you have to pay so much a month and they have a house there that is one thousand square meters. We have a big house; my father fixed faucets and was a master plumber and he worked for a firm that did a great deal of the building in Senegal, and so our house— people used to think that our house was a street; my father used to sit out in the front and people would drive by and finally they would come to the end of the route and have to turn around. They would think that they could pass through this street and reach a point beyond but they would have to turn around and pass by my father and they would ask and he would say no this is a residence. Our house could fit six cars and when I went to school as a little girl I was taken to school by a driver . . . This woman . . . and there were some others in there who had studied well but they didn't do anything and now they all have houses in this area and the Mother . . .

Is this just; is this right? And the wife of the president—she doesn't smile and she is cold; she comes to an area that doesn't even have a faucet the women have to walk and carry the water on their heads and she comes and opens a fountain for the people and later she goes to another area and does the same thing these people are mean that is just meanness [cativeria].

And the politicians have just eaten the money. And Wade look at him he is ugly, just ugly. He said that he was coming to clean up all the mess and now he is worse than the rest. He learned to eat the money even better than all the rest.

My sister is educated and she will look for documents and say, Well they have done this and that. But I will tell you the truth, what I have seen with my own eyes and that is the reality. I will tell you the way it is there.

What is at play here is a notion that President Wade is actually transformed by these actions, that his efforts at deceiving the people provide evidence of interference suggesting that there is something beyond the ordinary at work. For figures like the Marabout command, such power is a widely accepted social fact, one shared and understood across a wide range of social classes and ethnic and religious groups in the society. It is perhaps the form that this narrative takes that is more important than its basis in fact, as it constitutes an explanation of a social fact that no one doubts: the misappropriation of funds. Moreover, there is a manner in which the president's possible subjection to external influence is the only explanation for the total disregard for the regions of their birth, as if the connection that they have with African soil and history has somehow been severed irrevocably by their actions against the people. The leaders not only act against the interests of the people, they betray their own ancestors and the lands they once walked on as well. While we were talking, a program on Senghor came on the television, with a Senegalese rapper who read some of Senghor's poetry. The scenes alternated images of the rapper with the backdrop of Dakar.[9] Senghor, as Fatima points out, left his natal region in ruins during his presidency:

> Senghor, he comes from a area called Joal and if you go there,
> there is nothing—not even a car on the streets and when he died
> he said he wanted to be buried in Joal, but his wife had his body
> taken to the Catholic cemetery where his son who died in an
> accident is buried, so he could be near his son. And they say that
> some time later he will be buried at Joal.[10]
>
> But the tomb of his father and the tomb of his mother down
> there is completely ruined. He was president some twenty years
> and did nothing for the region he came from. And Diouf was
> the same—when he knew that he had lost and that his time
> as president was coming to an end, he and he wife took off for
> France and they don't care what happens to Senegal. Senghor
> took his money in Normandy and in the south of France. The
> best butter in the world is made there. The cows only eat grass
> and the butter is of an excellent quality and they call it "The
> President," and Senghor is the one who owns this factory that is
> his butter. He died, what was it, five or six months ago, and he
> died in France, but they brought his body back to Senegal to be
> buried.

The corruption of the political leaders is coupled with the working of other forces behind the scenes that turn the world of politics to their own advantage. In this vision, the leaders are mere figureheads in the hands of others, who wield power through traditional means. Fatima continues:

> This fellow who works for the president as his righthand man is said to have very powerful sorcery and to ply the president's food with something which renders him pliable to the point where "he doesn't even know what he is doing any longer, he just does whatever this one tells him to do"; when he [President Wade] signs a bill, they put money for themselves in there and he signs and they take whatever they wish.
>
> There is a box there that has the money of the president and no one can look into this box and that is where the money for all these houses and other things comes from and this one is in control of that box.

This person behind the scenes who controls the actions of the new president has many of the characteristics of the contemporary Marabout, such as their powers to transform a medium like money and the will of the president to their desired ends. It is unclear just who this person is or where he may have come from, but in the networks of the diaspora his presence explains the peculiar behavior of the reformer President Wade, now under the control of this new power. The nature of the box is of interest in the narratives; as in the case of the Marabout, the box is a link to the power of the Jinn or other spiritual forces that operate in a world beyond the control of human agency, as if to manipulate the very source of "money" as though it were a symbolic medium originating beyond the human realm.

The Marx-inspired marker of "neocolonialism" is here cast as a cosmological link to an unseen power; it is unclear what this force is or who controls it, or the manner in which others come to be enriched, but the mechanism forms part of a cosmology in which money is a kind of power that can overturn the present social order. It is not just a stand-in for the West; this power has African origins and defies easy identification. This new order clearly comes into place through a process that Fatima would consider to ring with injustice, as her discussion is punctuated by the phrase "Is this right? Is this just?" Fatima seems to express a sense of diasporic nostalgia for a time that might have come with the regime of President Wade, and that might come sometime in the future, but that is not yet meant to be. But what is the redress of such actions? In what court of authority can one turn to in order to over turn the reign of those who control the box?

Fatima later said that when her sister first arrived, a few months before we spoke in June 2002, she lay on her bed and cried every day. "She studied technology, 'informatica' [computer science]," she added. In the ministry of technology, her position was a part of the previous administration government package; when the government changed, she and other workers inhabited a kind of labor limbo for a while, but after months of working with no salary, her mother arranged for her to join her brother and sister in Italy. Shortly after her arrival two of her coworkers—thinking that she had just gone for a vacation—urged her to remain, as things had, according to them, deteriorated even further and many were being sent home for good. The crisis of the civil servant is acute; in part because they do not have any of the survival skills that many of those in the diaspora possess; their work regime has been fairly protected by their specialized education until now and it is unlikely that they will find anything equivalent in the near future. Their best hope is to reach a site from which they might navigate the diaspora; if not Italy or France, then an even better site for staging diasporic practice: a visa to the United States or Canada. This might provide access to goods and/or job opportunities that could sustain a movement back home for those who wish to engage in trade or who are forced by circumstances to change employment.

CHAPTER 5

Sites of Erasure

Black Prisoners and the Poetry of Léopold Sédar Senghor

> The black man is pure representation for Fanon. The black man is hypervisible yet invisible simultaneously ...
>
> —RADHIKA MOHANRAM, *BLACK BODY: WOMEN, COLONIALISM AND SPACE*

> If I have so often cited Fanon, it is because more dramatically and decisively than anyone, I believe, he expresses the immense cultural shift from the terrain of nationalist independence to the theoretical domain of liberation.
>
> —EDWARD SAID, *CULTURE AND IMPERIALISM*

Dreaming of an Ancient World

In this chapter and chapter 6, I present a meditation on the lives and work of two Senegalese scholars, politicians, filmmakers, and former colonial soldiers: the late Léopold Sédar Senghor, former president of Senegal, and the late filmmaker and cultural critic Ousmane Sembene. The work of these two figures encompasses a period in African history beginning in colonialism, passing through an era in which African colonial subjects attempted to "assimilate" into French society through the few educational opportunities offered them, and ending at Independence and the post-colonial present. I take as a point of departure in the following sections an incident that occurred during the Second World War in a transition camp on the outskirts of Dakar, Camp de Thiaroye, variously described as a mutiny or uprising of returning Tirailleurs Sénégalais, soldiers of the French black forces drawn from all over West Africa and among the first to be repatriated from Europe in 1944. Many of the soldiers had been prisoners of war (POWs) and insisted on their rights guaranteed by the minister of the colonies in a dispute that some suggest is one of the most important labor conflicts of the era. The soldiers' "protest over the failure of the French authorities to provide them with back pay and demobilization premiums" resulted in the most serious confrontation between "alienated" African soldiers and the French state (Echenberg 1991, 101). Still awaiting return to their home villages during the uprising, some thirty-five Africans were killed and others seriously injured when the uprising was crushed by French troops. "Some thirty-four ex-POWs were arrested and tried on charges falling just short of mutiny. All were convicted and sentenced to terms ranging from one to ten years in prison" (101). Another five of the soldiers died in jail before a general amnesty released the Thiaroye victims in June 1947.

I argue that these soldiers experienced a kind of transitional status—a state somewhere between colonial subject and postcolonial subject, as their mobilization marked the most dramatic diasporic encounters with peoples outside of the world of their villages and home regions. These encounters of African Americans and others in the field and of Jewish prisoners in concentration camps and Europeans beyond the shores of Africa helped to nourish a new vision of the future. Toward the end of the war, conditions in French West Africa had declined dramatically; the rising urban population, drawn out of the rural areas during the war efforts, forced labor, the extraction of a portion of harvest (farmers were often forced to give over portions of their crops to the colonial government as lack of food and shortages impacted colonial terrirories), and taxation regiments created a seemingly unending cycle of poorly paid jobs and for many meant unemployment. Urban centers offered few public services, a network of roads primarily designed for transporting materials to the empire, and increasingly inadequate attention to issue of sanitation. Although the colonial regime was careful to discourage the formation of labor organizations in the wake of the war, spontaneous disturbances and protests began to erupt in the towns. The uprising of Camp de Thiaroye in 1944 among the infantry regiment awaiting demobilization was one of the first signs of these changes. For a generation of African colonial subjects, Camp de Thiaroye became a kind of clarion call for the end of the colonial relationship; it was clear that such a disregard for the lives of soldiers that had fought for France was unacceptable.

Representations that legitimate the power of stereotype or that enhance an encyclopedic catalog of caricatures of race, ethnicity, gender, class, or even religious practice depend upon the erasure of context and the denial and negation of the existence of the subordinate group. The sites of this erasure in turn constitute sites of potential invention— the place of an alternative foundation. The resolution of this problem is not merely a matter of replacing one set of representations with another, but rather what I call "awakening the visible," that is, restoring to context what has been taken away through the process of erasure and thereby constituting a new foundation of the visible and of the imagination. Indeed, every intellectual and disciplinary boundary is policed to some extent by "a set of restrictions on thought and imagination" imposed on its practitioners, an insight of Nietzsche (cited in White 1978, 126). The seemingly fixed and unchanging features of a given discourse may be thought of as preliminary or tentative staging areas for the hazardous journeys of identity and recognition.

For Fanon the process of awakening the visible rests on the interplay of context, experience, and power. In *Black Skins, White Masks* he writes, "I am no prisoner of history. I should not seek there for the meaning of my destiny . . . I should constantly remind myself that the real leap consists in introducing invention into existence" (Fanon 1967a, 229). At the moment in which the wretched of the earth shatter the ideological prison or history of the dominant classes, the possibility of "invention" of the emergence of an alternate agency arises. The moment of this authentic "invention" is inaugurated when the context—of the experience supporting a vision of historical process counter to that of an official history—is erased. Indeed, this is the lesson one learns from the settler who "makes history" and whose life appears as an "epoch, an Odyssey," while others form an "inorganic background" and thus fade into invisibility in the infernal imperialist machine (Fanon 1963, 51).

The late Edward Said in *Culture and Imperialism* (1993) points out that the cultural work of anti-imperialism conducted by an entire generation of thinkers developed in the peculiar environment brought on by the diasporic movement of people from the peripheries to the metropolitan capitals of Europe. For Said, whose reading pivots on an "exilic marginality" that he shares across time with Fanon and his generation, displacement accords the "native" a unique space for cultural criticism. A counterpoint to the world of "European geographical centrality" and authority, "buttressed by a cultural discourse relegating and confining the non-European to a secondary racial, cultural, ontological status," this generation of privileged non-European observers would exploit the play of invisibility (Said 1993, 59). In Jane Austen's *Mansfield Park* the mystery and beauty of place rests on the invisible foundations of slave plantations in Antigua. The utility of colonial possessions is sublimated to the rituals of intimacy effacing the connective tissue of the middle passage and the lives and labor of millions of slaves. "To read Austen without also reading Fanon and Cabral," Said warns us, "is to disaffiliate modern culture from its engagements and attachments. That is a process that should be reversed" (60). The sounding of this invisible realm of interconnections, "engagements and attachments," must be accomplished before the terrain of imperialism can be fully grasped. The subordination of the colonies and the people that inhabited them was critical, as Said argues, to a vision of the world crafted even before the European scramble for Africa or the age of empire began:

> Yet this secondariness is, paradoxically, essential to the primariness of the European; this of course is the paradox explored by Césarire, Fanon and Memmi, and it is but among many of the ironies of modern critical theory that it has rarely been explored by investigators of the aporias and impossibilities of reading. Perhaps that is because it places emphasis not so much on how to read, but rather on what is read and where it is written about and represented. (Said 1993, 59)

This intellectual displacement, however, was to become a crucial part of the so-called Western discourse. This slumbering displacement impacts the very conceptualization of the colonized.

It has always fascinated me that in *Fact of Blackness*, which may perhaps be more aptly translated as the experience of blackness (Macey 2000), Fanon presents us with a French child on a train who, like children everywhere, blurts out what was better left unsaid "Look, a Negro": the fact that the observation comes from a child I think is significant, here implying that an adult might know better than to make such a declaration. The clarity of the expression lies in the sighting of a cultural category that one learns to ignore over the course of time. As Nigel Gibson points out in *Fanon: the Postcolonial Imagination* (2003), what Fanon calls the "triple person" emerges, as "blacks are not simply individual actors responsible for themselves, they are responsible for their race (culture) and their ancestors (history) . . . on top of that there is the racist caricature" (Gibson 2003, 27). This extra "existential load" creates an imbalance, since the individual is unable to emerge from the weight of caricature—a weight that renders the person progressively invisible, buried under the culture, history, and caricature of a collective. The system of classification for the adult remains below the level of discourse, while the child frightened by the parade of images of the "black man"—registered not as part of the cultural or historical moment but as racist caricature—is subjected to the most visceral and immediate power of the ideological architecture. For the adult, what is seen engages a mature system of representation and caricature; for the child, a realm of fear sends an immediate alarm. The carefully crafted protocols of avoidance that take time to learn come into play in the long socialization process, until such practices become second nature.

The eye as detective cannot always reanimate the scene of the crime as Benjamin sought to do; social life is not always responsive to such inquiries. At times impervious to the demands of the visible or lacking election to its empire, the facts of ordinary lives slip into relative obscurity. There is nothing strange about seeing the almost constant parade of images of the Second World War in France, Britain, and the United States; the retelling of the war has become a kind of industry, a firmly established part of popular culture. I recall the parade of television shows and film representations that memorialized the war years, leaving ample heroic figures of the generation to insinuate themselves into neighborhood play. Some of the last figures of this era are passing from the public eye in the United States, but in Europe, the founders of the postwar democratic regimes remain in public life. Though they fade into the light of an emergent world, the act of heroism of this generation is inscribed in every act of postwar recovery and in the very foundations of the western European democratic tradition. One of the most powerful public rituals in honor of this generation has been the standard parade of high-ranking national figures and foreign dignitaries past the Tomb of the Unknown Soldier. The Tomb of the Unknown Soldier is a particular point of high ritual significance. The British film *The Whistle Blower* (1987), the first feature-length film from director Simon Langton, is a story about a world of espionage in which a British businessman played by Michael Caine attempts to uncover the mystery surrounding his son's death and is drawn into a world of betrayal and intrigue. The film opens with a military parade past the grave of the Unknown Soldier, who has made the ultimate sacrifice for his or her country. The ceremony surrounding the Tomb of the Unknown Soldier comes into national focus in times of war, when men and women are placed in harm's way and the sacrifice of those under fire is set before a nation mourning and honoring the fallen.

The sacrifice of the soldier almost always rests on the metaphoric grounds of navigation, the dislocation of the soldier from a "home" defended to the distant field of battle—a literal no-person's land—colors the nature and dimension of such sacrifice. Indeed, from the nineteenth century, in the great transformation of society from the industrial age to the present, common workers have been viewed as a kind of "army": a proletarian force engaged in the terrain of world. This view of capitalism as a kind of battlefield is further enriched by the depiction of the market as the leveling ground or site of a type of competition that "takes no prisoners." The imaginary divide between the former colonial regime and the independent new nation has been viewed in a similar fashion. For Fanon, the colonizer–colonized divide constituted a fixed "order of absolute difference and radical irreciprosity"; such a state accords the colonial subject no place, no positive status in the scheme of the colonial regime as a person that might exercise a type of human agency not scripted by the overall structure of domination (Sekyi-Out 1996, 72). As Sekyi-Out notes, it is the colonial subjects' insurrection from the world of "sequestration, exclusion," and "confinement" in short a revolt against restricted space that for Fanon marks the colony's first historical actions (72). It is this existence only as negation that informs Sembene's film *Le Noir de . . . (Black Girl)*, in which a housemaid taken to France finds that any reflection of her experience as an African woman is systematically erased or negated in the context, as she becomes merely a servant. The housekeeper Diouana is caught betwixt and between home, nation, ethnic identity, and language—in her new residence in France, only her mementos (kept carefully in her travel bags) anchor her to her former self. Her sequestered life is overcome in brief flights of memory and the contemplation of objects that evoke her homeland.

The early films of Sembene seem to accomplish a kind of visualization of Fanon's critique of neocolonialism as the relationship between a former colony and the emergent independent Africa is explored. References to the texts of Fanon often can be found in the fiction of Sembene, as in *The Last of the Empire* (1981), which highlights deep political and ideological cleavages between public figures in postcolonial Senegal. More than this, the portrait Fanon paints of the new form of domination that emerges out of the colonial context—enslaving not only the colonized worker but the mind, the complex frontiers of imagination—causes unfathomable damage in the day-to-day experience of the emergent postcolonial subject. Sembene inhabits this world, in which diverse forms of knowledge and cultural practice collide with the life of a simple housemaid, torn between a past she must leave behind and a future she has been destined to live in by the failure of an independent Africa to offer an alternative to a kind of new dependency on the former colonial power.

Sembene's film *Le Noir de . . . (Black Girl)*, The film is an expanded version of the short story "The Promised Land," originally published in 1962 as part of a collection of short stories entitled *Voltaïque*.[1] The film commences as Diouana, a young girl who is to go off to France and take up her new job as a live-in housekeeper, contemplates her good fortune at the Tomb of the Unknown Soldier, which serves as a backdrop for her future life in diaspora, foreshadowing her desperation and eventual suicide. Sembene juxtaposes these images, as both represent a kind of sacrifice that has gone unacknowledged—that of the soldiers of colonial times that made the birth of the postcolonial era possible and that of the new class of workers subordinated to a new kind of wage slavery under a neocolonial regime, represented in the film by the colonizers return to the Metropole with their Senegalese housekeeper in tow. The Tomb of the Unknown Soldier also brings out another contradiction between the visible and that which can no longer remain visible for Sembene: even the Tomb of the Unknown Soldier pays no tribute to the colonial soldier as it drowns the role of the soldiers in a host of other deaths, the nature of their sacrifice for France is obscured. Yet the image recalls the work of Senghor in the *Hosties noires* collection, where the soldiers—like fallen leaves—provide the fertile national soil in which the youth must grow. "Let us form at their feet the humus of dense rotting leaves," an image no doubt familiar to Sembene (Senghor 1998, 52). But the idea of the soldier whose sacrifices were made in the hope of the triumph of a new generation is turned on its head, as it leads only to the undoing of the youth subjected to the same constraints that the soldiers gave their lives to overcome. Diouana's death also evokes the ambiguity of the postcolonial subjects as she inaugurates the first generation to essentially die in diaspora, to become a part of that nameless place that carries no tradition, no manner of return. Taking her life, she not only cuts the relationship to her past, however, but also to an imagined future of subjugation—like many slaves passing out of sight of her native land, she selected to return to it, even if only in death.[2] In the story, her precarious circumstances find her contemplating her voyage to France close enough to the shore while still in Senegal to glimpse Gorea Island, the point of embarkation of countless slaves destined for the new world. The new world that Diouana is promised, however, as she turns in her identity card—the key to her release—is a different kind of enslavement, one that will eventually sever all sense of belonging, as she, like the slaves before her, enters a state of nonpersonhood. Sociologist Judith Rollins not only did fieldwork among domestics in the United States, but worked as a domestic herself as part of the research; on several occasions, she describes the transformation by which the black servant becomes virtually invisible, her employers ignoring her very presence. Rollins notes the employers' "ability to annihilate; the humanness and even, at times, the very existence of me, a servant and black women. Fanon articulates my reaction concisely: 'A feeling of inferiority? No, a feeling of nonexistence'" (Rollins 1985, 210). As Diouana contemplates her voyage, a new form of objectification awaits her in this distant land:

> But Diouana, looking out of the big window with its wide view of
> the sea, was mentally following the birds flying high over the vast
> blue expanse. The offshore island of Gorea was only just visible. She
> turned her identity-card over and over in her hand, looking at it and
> smiling to herself. She was not quite satisfied with the photograph;
> it did not stand our clearly enough. But never mind, she thought,
> I'm going, and that is what matters. (Sembene 1987, 90)

In this world between a postcolonial regime in which one cannot make a living and the core of a former colonial realm in which one cannot realize a life for one's former identity, in a sense Diouana vanishes out of a past that might recognize her humanity, a link to her ancestral legacy. Her suicide leaves her cut off from this past. She travels rather into another world, one in which she can be neither seen nor accorded a proper resting place, a position "demanding human behavior from the other"—what Fanon claims is the singular "right" of an emergent postcolonial subject (Fanon 1967a, 229). The Tomb of the Unknown Soldier somehow elides these figures that exist in the ambiguities of nationalist discourse, suggesting its fragmentary and incomplete capture of contemporary subjectivities. The national is encased in contingency, always the nodal point of imagined histories and perhaps the end point for those cut off from its meanings, who can find in it no resting place, no ceremonies of remembrance.

In the enactment of national memory and the idea of heroism, fallen soldiers of color do not figure prominently; more general colonial soldiers figure hardly at all. Although these images have continued—most recently overtaking the notion of unpopular wars and police actions—the figures accorded the right of agency and historicity do not seem to come from the former colonies, the outposts of empire, and seem to be denied this most prestigious tour of ideological duty. Although the soldiers might lay claim to a kind of postcolonial agency, as they did in early labor disputes and various forms of postwar anticolonialist activities, including trade union organization, the former soldiers eventually vanish from the imaginary landscape. They do however, come to populate African literature, film, and stage as the voice of dissent or even the exemplar of exile and displacement, posing in their uncomfortable reentry into African society the quintessential Senghorian question "Who am I?"[3] The soldiers were, in the well-known words of Lévi-Strauss, "good to think"; they provided the images of colonial injustice for reformed proponents of "assimilation" and neo-Marxist cultural critics and in the end have fallen prey to the texture of a heroism that refuses to admit them to its number (Lévi-Strauss 1963). Neither embarassed fully by the colonial regime nor completely comfortable in the postcolonial world, the soldiers occupy a peculiar in-between world and are curiously suspect for those on opposing sides of the political spectrum. Much of this potential critique is already prefigured in the work of the 1920s inspired by Lamine Senghor with his "proletarian orientation" and "anticolonialism," framed in the first issue of *La Race négre*, the organ of the Ligue de Défense de la

Race Négre, an offshoot of the Comité de Défense de la Race Négre from which it originated.[4] The crystallization of such journals and intellectual encounters in mulling over the problems of black workers, soldiers, and others formed part of the fabric of a generation of scholars and activists living in metropolitan capitals, linked by a "global black radical circuit" at times loosely associated with the orbits of European political organizations (Edwards 2003, 249). This convergence of transnational concerns for people of African descent in Africa, Europe, Asia, and America brought together a diverse group of people to confront cultural and political questions such as labor, education, and the welfare of soldiers. Working alliances with a number of groups falling under the umbrella of French colonial possessions brought Caribbean, West African, North African, and Vietnamese as well as a wide range of militants into the arch of anti-imperial activities. Even with the anticolonial mood of the times, hearing from the voice of a worker or soldier was a powerful and relatively unprecedented event. Yet once the literary and cultural turn is underway, many of the poets and writers and later filmmakers of this period will try to capture the language and tone of the hybrid language of the African worker or soldiers of the time. Senghor's journal, running the testimony of a Tirailleur Sénégalais in the language of the troops (what the French called petit négre), marks a kind of solidarity and authenticity not often achieved by the educated elite displaced in the metropolitan heartland. The soldier complains of the treatment of the "indigénes" by the Europeans, who thought of them "comme sauvasi, comme plus mauvsis chien encore" (like savages or like the worst dogs), confirming that the soldier, lacking French citizenship, had "no rights"; finally, the soldier decried the asymmetry in pay (pensions) between "natives" and the French (cited in Miller 1998, 43–44). The journal finally notes the soldier's desire to ensure that "Africans never fight under such circumstances" again:

> Mais nous . . . indigénes y a pas faire encore la guerre. Nous y a
> pas droit citouin français. [But we natives won't fight another war.
> We don't have the rights of French citizens.] (Miller 1998, 44)

In his book *Nationalists and Nomads: Essays on Francophone African Literature and Culture*, Christopher L. Miller argues that the use of the soldiers' testimony—the petite négre of the soldier, a language derided by the

French for its supposed "inferiority" to the standard of the colonizer—here acts as "a means of resistance" as the soldier's voice and disillusionment eloquently marks a new site from which a critique might be launched of the colonial empire (Miller 1998, 44). The metropolitan heartland located in Paris or London became a kind of crossroads for students and others from India, Senegal, Vietnam, and the Caribbean. During the interwar years, diverse people from the imagined peripheries converged on the administrative centers of empire in the core of European modernism:

> A common anti-imperialist experience was felt, with new
> associations between Europeans, Americans, and non-
> Europeans, and they transformed disciplines and gave voice to
> new ideas that unalterably changed that structure of attitude
> and reference that had endured for generations within European
> culture. The cross-fertilization between African nationalism as
> represented by George Padmore, Nkrumah, C.L.R. James on
> the one hand, and, on the other the emergence of a new literary
> style in the works of Césaire, Senghor, poets of the Harlem
> Renaissance like Claude McKay and Langston Hughes, is a
> central part of the global history of modernism. (Said 1993, 243)

As Said suggests, the infusion of new directions and new kinds of questions provided by this generation of intellectuals from the colonies resulted in "the transformation of the very terrain of disciplines," a reworking of European knowledge constructs.

I suppose I am inspired by the late Edward Said and hoped for a more inclusive version of "our reading," one that might serve as the basis for a confrontation with selected sites of erasure (see Said 1979).

Negritude, and Other Apparently Spontaneous Acts of Creation

"Negritude," Michel de Certeau once wrote, "exists only as of the moment when there is a new subject of history, that is, when people opt for the defiance of existing" (1997, 75). Although this "new subject of history," negritude, will be associated with a host a names—among them the contributions of such women as Suzanne Lacascade, Jane and Paulette Nardal, and Suzanne Roussy-Césaire—one name will always stand out, as it is wedded with political longevity and the cultural innovations of an emergent nation (Sharpley-Whiting, 2002). The name Senghor will no doubt always—as with any founding figure—remain partly clouded in the fantastic, an intimate of the national fable of Senghor and the building of the Senegalese nation, and the life of this fascinating figure also transects an era of colonial relations that has only recently come to an end. The Senghor family apparently maintains that on the birth of Léopold Sédar Senghor, the former president of Senegal, one of the great baobab trees cracked and the great ancestral spirit that the Serer associate with them made the decision to dwell instead in the young child (Vaillant 1990, 7). It is in fact the spirit of Senghor as poet that concerns us here, as this spirit helped to craft notions associated with negritude. The Senghorian literary critique of colonialism is a biting criticism of the constraints placed on the colonial subject by a system that would grant only partial access to the legacy of rights open to any French citizen; there is in his work an exploration of the richness of the lives of those forced to live in expectation of greater freedoms, of the comradeship and longings of such lives. Senghor's own diasporic journey during the Second World War placed him in a concentration camp—an experience that allowed him to interrogate notions of human dignity, freedom, and identity. I argue that the collection of poetry, written in part during this period, provides a vantage point from which to explore the complex nature of the identity of the colonial soldier or subject and the meaning of participation in a war that would deliver these soldiers only to subjecthood and never to citizenship. The colonial soldier presents a kind of enigma of diaspora, as the soldier stands betwixt and between African and Western cultural traditions, languages, histories, and cartographies in new ways. In reaching back to the African past or borrowing from the colonial present, the soldier created the tools with which to confront a new world. Although the Senghorian African world remains idyllic to some degree, the exploration of this new space of subjectivity, neither African nor European, prefigures the dilemmas of the postcolonial subject. It is this dimension, a struggle with what is to come, that imparts a critical element to the ever-changing nature of the Senghorian vision of negritude.

In many ways, negritude sprang up as a more or less spontaneous act of consciousness or a counterbalance to what seems to be an essentially continuous stream of black caricature, in part envisioned by a most peculiar preoccupation with images of blacks in the West (Pieterse 1998). Senghor—one of the cofounders of the negritude movement, an ideology that contains what some might call a mythic vision of Africa and Africans—has, in turn, himself become a mythic figure.[5] In short, if we wish to come to some understanding of the emergence of black consciousness and its dance with pan-African themes drawn from European anthropology and other scientific and semiscientific discourse, we must pass over the words and thoughts of Senghor. The diasporic encounters of African, African American, and Caribbean writers and intellectuals in Paris and other international centers provided the context for the emergence of a discourse on the nature of "blackness." It is important to point out that this discourse arose prior to its articulation with nationalism; rather what came to be called negritude developed in relation to colonialism in its diverse manifestations and to the legacy of a diffuse black caricature that was an integral part of a European cultural map of the world, essentially a "colonizer's model of the world" (Blaut 1993). While Edward Said rejects the negritude impulse out of hand, Fanon's examination of the intellectual movement is deeply searching and troubled; in *Black Skin, White Masks* he attempts to find justification for adherence to the romantic dictates of negritude. "There was a myth of the Negro that had to be destroyed at all costs" (Fanon 1967a, 117). Yet in the final pages of *Black Skin, White Masks*, Fanon turns the preoccupation of the negritude poets back to the present: "I do not have the right to allow myself to be mired in what the past has determined for me" (230). The search for an alternate formulation of origins or the rediscovery of an antecedent "Negro civilization" is doomed to failure, as the structure of the sense of black "exteriority" in European culture cannot be addressed in the play of historicity linked to this or that past. It is rather in the present that Fanon finds the point of liberation: "The body of history does not determine a single one of my actions. I am my own foundation" (231). The logic of a "dehumanizing rationality" operates as a retrogressive movement, a negation of a potential ontology, a kind of enslavement clothed in the rhetoric of the past. Fanon wished to proceed beyond the kingdom of childhood of the "romantic poets" or the pseudoscientific racialist discourses that they countered to a position from which practice was possible, but this freedom required vigilance to the specters of the past. In the spirit of Marxian framing of the past in the *Eighteenth Brumaire*, Fanon sought the crystallization of a future in which unity might be envisioned in common cultural and political actions, rather than in the origins of black cultural traditions (Martin 1999). We will return to Fanon's call for vigilance and his outline of national culture—one carefully scrutinized for every trace of privilege associated with the past. Yet Fanon may underscore the creativity of negritude in its invention of a past, perhaps on its insistence of an analogous past to that of Europe. For Fanon, this game of the past would always be lost to the weight of black caricature and the power of its negation in the shadow of a Eurocentric cultural logic that accorded no space or importance to the history of Africa.

V. Y. Mudimbe notes that "Senghor has become a myth that is endlessly discussed," an inaugural presence in literary, political, and cultural expression of negritude (1988, 94). Although this presence has until recently obscured a vibrant community of participants and fellow travelers, in the creation of negritude, Senghorian contributions to the notion loom large (Sharpley-Whiting 2002), an idea that was given state sanction in a number of countries, and in this manner cascades over the lives of entire generations of young people, introducing them to ideas of modernity mediated through the valorization of the local and at times momentary invention of African culture and traditions. Negritude is articulated at a critical juncture between the decline of colonial rule and the emergence of the process of decolonization. The French colonial world was, in a peculiar way, dependent on its colonized dependencies and the interwoven economies of this empire. Negritude was after all also a claim to being, in a certain manner, European in an African way; as much as it sought to validate an African identity, it made claims to being European, or rather employing the resources of a hyphenated European identity.

Wole Soyinka, in his introduction to *Myth, Literature, and the African World*, describes himself as contesting "the claims of Negritude since my earliest contact with its exegetes" (1976, viii). The aftermath of the ideology was said to produce poetry in search of Africanness, "an artificial angst" sharpened by a simulation of the movement's founders. In its wake, negritude may be characterized as sparking "an abysmal angst of low achievement" (131). According to Soyinka the social vision of negritude proper, on the other hand, sought the "restitution and re-engineering of a racial psyche, the establishment of a distinct human entity and the glorification of its long suppressed attributes," in an attempt to reject the imposition of European views of African society. Thus, a racialist and Manchurian framework was adopted in the heart of negritude, a redemption song of songs (126). Yet in spite of claims and even reflections on the state of "essential" racial imagery and language, there is a lingering sense that the complex cultural conditions and meanings of this vision may remain elusive. Crafting the new self through the tools of the colonial subject may be bound to fail; the terms are set by another code, another cultural logic that in the end must be also shattered.

Having no neutral public face, Senghor comes easily under attack by "the present generation of African intellectuals" who tend to position themselves as signposts to a future free of colonial legacy and arbiters of the past. Although the thought of Senghor is indeed marked by a generation forged as intellectuals in the colonial world, its contradictions are not so easily dissolved in the clear light of postcolonial rhetoric. It is not so simple to walk away from historical narrative style forged through the ambiguity of identity, belongings, and intellectual passions ignited in the shadow of the idea of assimilation. Nor are the implications of the complex impulses that produced negritude so transparent that they may be brushed aside without further exploration. Such figures as Senghor sought redemption, if at all, from a process that lasted well over a century: the decolonization of the mind. Yet he occupied a position within the structure of French culture that cut to the heart of its academic and literary traditions and was elected to the French Academy in 1983—a mark of his importance in the forging of intellectual traditions and the growth of the French language. In the process he introduced from his own local traditions and more generally from his conception of African qualities and voice new dimensions enhancing the French language and its traditions. Through Senghor's admission the Francophone world and its traditions, for the first time and in the most comprehensive manner, came close to the Senghorian notion of "cultural symbiosis": the interplay of an identity formation that is European and African, among other things. Indeed, the writers and scholars of the Francophone world first recognized as students their cultural inheritance in the French language and wealth of local traditions that they brought to this new colonial world.

Such problems of identity haunt many of the characters' lives of the films of Sembene, a theme often cast in the form of the overpowering expectations of others. Anticipating identification with one culture or tradition, often acute conflicts break out when actors find that their cousin or brother or other relation (or protagonist) has been transformed by an encounter with European society, the war, or education, or has selected an alternate option identifying individual or collective goals that definitively break local traditions. The theme of cultural conflict runs throughout much of the work of Sembene—the intellectual who has lost touch with his community, the colonial soldier who has married a European (and the conflicts that take place within family networks as a result), or the young housekeeper who finds that she is increasingly isolated in France, cut off from an African community back home. The soldier in Camp de Thiaroye is one of the ultimate examples of social displacement, as the soldier represents one of the first groups to be mobilized in European war preparations, colonial pacification, and the repression of dissent in the metropole.[6] The dismantling of a discourse that set colonial subjects apart resonates in our own time. We must examine with care these moments of crisis in which what has been submerged, unattainable to discourse, is brought to the fore in novel ways. This tradition of both alienation from a repressive colonial power and the search for identity of the exile that may reestablish a link with the past in order to overcome a sense of estrangement is shared to some degree by Senghor and Sembene and may be found in the work of others, such as Lamine Senghor in *La Violation d'un pays* (1927) and René Maran in *Batouala* (1921) and also in the work of negritude women such as Paulette and Jane Nardal, among others (see Miller 1998; Sharpley-Whiting 2002).

Black Hosts/Black Victims

During the Second World War, Senghor spent eighteen months in a prisoner of war camp; the camp was a crossroads of various European, African, and other communities. The camps provided a curious cultural space in which all previous experiences were suspended in the uncertainty of the war and simplified by the most compelling demands of dignity, camaraderie, and compassion. Some of the early poems written for the first two collections of poetry by Senghor date from this period. The work was smuggled out by a former Polish professor and guard who was able to place it into the hands of Senghor's old friend. The experience of the camps opened up a new world for Senghor; among the young Tirailleurs Sénégalais he was interned with at Poitiers, Front Stalag 230, many were recent recruits from Africa. Talk of home, music, and new friendships and contemplation of this peculiar exile marked the time (Vaillant 1990). From this period, the exile of the poet in France became a counterpoint to the very humbling experience of the camps, as the poetic realm of the childhood kingdom came into play through the memory of "home," animated by the rich tonalities of local culture and the traditions of older generations. Alfred Joseph Guillaume has called this flight to an anterior reality in the visionary vocabulary of the poet a "primitive impulse," since like Baudelaire, this sensibility seeks the world of "innocence, naturalness, and purity," in lieu of the present alienating and harsh reality of the poet. The world of the imagination for Senghor, unlike the Baudelairian vision, rests on the tangible and living memory of an African past, finding there "a fuller human experience through which the potentialities of social justice are realized" (Guillaume 1976, 2).

The haunting lines of *Hosties noires* (*Black Hosts*, 1948)—Senghor's second volume of poetry, a tribute to the colonial soldier—ring in our ears long after debates of the national assembly have faded from memory. The very title of the volume suggests Senghor's complex relationship with the legacy of the war: the title may refer to black victims or black hosts in the "sense of the sacrificial host of the Catholic communion" (Vaillant 1990, 172), a sacrifice of the black forces "stretched out in water as far as/The northern and eastern fields" (Senghor 1998, 47) for France, fighting alongside their French counterparts:

> We offer You our bodies along with those
>   of French
> Peasants,
> Our comrades until death once we first shook
>   hands
> And exchanged words
> Gnarled bodies, torturously scarred by work,
> But solidly grown and fine as pure wheat.
>   (Senghor 1998, 52–53)

As Janet G. Vaillant (Senghor's biographer) notes, this was a sacrifice both "to France, but also with France," as the soldiers joined in common cause for the benefit of European fortunes (Vaillant 1990, 172). But the ambiguity of the status of the black soldier in the aftermath of the conflict—neither citizen (French citizenship a reward promised the soldiers by the French administration) nor hero—left the soldiers in death in a liminal state betwixt and between Europe and Africa (172). In this volume, Senghor paid tribute to the black masses mobilized for the war effort and left with an incomplete sense of the recognition of their efforts and the nature of their sacrifice. The power of these words touches us also in our time and demand that we pause and strain to hear the cries of this distant time. The verses seem to speak to the vulnerability of the soldier at once to time and memory, to the passage of their bodies like a great tide, leaving only the barest trace of their existence. The task of the poet-as-translator then is twofold, hoping to grant an acknowledgment of the soldiers' ultimate sacrifice to France while also calling to the dead to take their place among the honored ancestors of an African tradition: "The poet prays that God will receive the bodies of the black African soldiers" (172). As Senghor developed a discursive tradition counter to the Eurocentric sensibilities that captures blacks in a web of caricature, his poems converted the defeats of the soldiers in death into a kind of triumph over multiple forms of oppression, replacing the color associated with racial degradation and scorn with a new honor and dignity and raising the soldiers to an place of esteem. The poet writes of honor and redemption, as Senghor's biographer notes: "It is on behalf of the Tirailleurs that he writes, on behalf of those killed at Thiaroye, on behalf of the Africans host devoured in sacrifice, which like the suffering of Christ, can yet be redemptive" (175). The subdued soldiers are often seen in the aftermath of their battle or in the utter exhaustion of their efforts in periods of transition. The bodies of the soldiers are transformed into an iconography of virtue, a moral economy anchoring the position of the colonial soldier as counterweight to peacetime images or visions of savagery, violence, and the policing of the colonial regime.

There is a stark contrast between the visage of Senghor's Tirailleurs Sénégalais and the same soldiers discussed in Fanon, who take on the most violent aspects of colonial repression through which the soldiers in part become associated with the policing of empire. For Fanon, the soldiers represent an elsewhere, buried in a distant past, and viewed from his Caribbean homeland; the Tirailleur embodies qualities of blackness associated with the mysterious and exotic world of Africa. Fragments of this world were visible through the films of Johnny Weissmuller, recasting the lord of the jungle in cinema from the Tarzan-complex based Edgar

Rice Burroughs (1875–1950) novel *Tarzan of the Apes* (1914). The blacks that populated these films—"inferior blacks"—were not the heroic figures that children from any background might identify with, but rather the white orphan son of Lord and Lady Greystoke, the enactment of masculine perfection and virtue (Kasson 2001). As a child, such images provided for Fanon and others a view of the world of Africa, helping to "instill in them the idea that they were not négres," according to Fanon's biographer David Macey (2000, 62). "French West Indians did not even think of themselves as black; they were simply West Indians, and everyone knew that blacks lived in Africa" (62). So the Tirailleurs, well known for their First World War exploits, could readily appear to the Francophone world through the lens of colonial campaigns of pacification and the inhuman feats of the First World War. A figure in Fanon's childhood, the Tirailleurs offered a spectacle of this exotic world of violence:

> In either 1938 or 1939, a group of Tirailleurs Sénégalais
> stationed in Guyane briefly visited Martinique. Fanon and his
> friends had heard of these famous colonial troops and their
> colorful uniforms, and went looking for them in the streets,
> He knew what he had been told about them by veterans of the
> First World War: "They attack with the bayonet and, when that
> does not work, they charge through the bursts of machine-
> gun fire, machete in hand. They cut off heads and collect ears."
> The Tirailleurs also had a reputation for looting, brutality and
> especially rape. To Fanon's delight, his father brought two of
> them home, providing concrete confirmation that he and his
> family were no négres, but Martinicans. Ironically, and quite
> spontaneously, the Fanon family behaved in just the way that
> a white family in France might have done: the charitably
> entertained the troops from the black African colonies.
> (Macey 2000, 62–63)

In a kind of praise poem to the simple soldier, in *Hosties noires* Senghor refers to them as "victims of the cruelty of civilized men," as they are indeed victims of the play of stereotypes from all quarters (Senghor 1998, 54). In part to distance the soldiers from such exotic and disturbing imagery, Senghor selects the most vulnerable moments of informality and comradeship in the field through which to introduce a new visage of the black masses in the war. As Sylvia Washington Bâ has suggested, for Senghor the soldiers are removed from the realm of destruction and force to a domain of beauty and virtue. As Bâ notes, "Senghor prefers to place his black multitudes in contexts emphasizing moral virtues more than physical strength. Never do his 'Black Hosts' evoke force and power other than the spiritual efficacy of their sacrifice" (Bâ 1973, 88). In fact, the soldiers evoke the dead of the underworld in the *Aeneid*, the heavy "unredeemed death" of Virgil, who, as Robert Pogue Harrison argues, "dwells on the season of death" rather than the succession of generations introduced in Homer (2003, 130). Senghor plays on the correspondence between the humanity of the soldiers and a successive generation reminiscent of Vigil and Homer through the figure of both the surviving comrade and an unborn generation, in a sense the children of the soldiers. As Aeneas marks the piety and importance of the past and the dead through the discovery of a new homeland, the soldiers are honored by the linking of their sacrifice to the present. The *Hosties noires* elegy "To the Senegalese Soldiers Who Died for France" dates from 1938, a period in which Senghor had recently reread the *Aeneid*, presenting the reader with its call for recognition and honor. Because their passing has gone all but unnoticed, the poet-voice calls out to give meaning to the deaths of his comrades, offering up their names and restoring their proper place in the order of things and linking once again their honor to the great military traditions of the past, while contrasting the meaning of the sacrifice of the black forces to that of the French, the soldier that stands as the exemplary heroic figure and symbol of the nation. The poet notes that the blood of the Tirailleur flows for the benefit of French just as the "blood of the white hosts," the European peasants, stains the earth, marking the site of battle:

> They put flowers on tombs
>   and warm the Unknown Soldier.
> But you, my dark brothers,
>   no one calls your names.

(Senghor 1998, 46)

The praise of the soldiers, however, must go even beyond mere heroism, as they are restored to their place as ancestors and must regain a place in a never-ending African narrative. In effect, the denial of their historicity in the European tradition rests in their restriction to the realm of the commonplace and the secular. The realm of recognition beyond death transcends the injustices of the European theater of war, setting the achievements of the soldier alongside that of the traditional African warrior. Unlike the Unknown Soldier, the Tirailleurs can never represent the common soldier, the everyman of the war; their efforts are forever relegated to that of a residual order of colonial forces. Recalling the Sartrean conviction that the racial hierarchy—one of the most prominent features of colonial ideology—relegated the colonial subject to the status of the subhuman, an insight latter developed by Fanon (Young 2001, xiv), the Tirailleurs then might represent the great achievements of the empire, but never the accomplishments sui generis of the French soldier. Yet this everyman was a part of Senghor's and others' experience: his uncle was an invalid, having been gassed in the First World War, and his fallen comrades, the simple African soldiers that appear in the collection to whom he dedicated the *taga* or praise poem, faced the hardships of war, keeping their comradeship and steadfastness in the face of the "slave's humiliation" (Vaillant 1990, 174–75). The soldier is linked, like Agamben's *homo sacer*, with the sacrificial and oppressive realm of sovereignty—with what I have called invisibility, with a state of exception that cannot memorialize or bear the name of the victim that sustains it. Senghor transposes the stagnant memory of the national fallen soldier with the vital invocation of a link to valued ancestral forces; the soldiers unite an exilic European theater of death with an African heritage, a continuity that restores the diaspora to its proper place in an imagined homeland and foundational cosmology. The memory of the living is a guarantee of the "continuity of life force" that claims from the "triple wall of night—death, grave, oblivion" the Tirailleurs Sénégalais, who through remembrance and the voice of the poet are a living link to the present (Bá 1973). As Bá suggests in *The Concept of Negritude in the Poetry of Léopold Sédar Senghor*, memory establishes the "communion" that reawakens bonds severed in death (58). With these bonds, the living words of the praise-poem become a bridge toward an affirmation of dignity and vitality.

In fact, in the colonial logic of the time, it was Africans who were to be thankful to their European liberators for saving them from the bleak prospects of life without the benefit of European enlightenment and modernity. In this cultural logic, which inspired the civilizing mission of the Europeans, Africans should be responsible for the repayment of this debt of enlightenment. The conversion of this myth, as Gregory Mann points out, came full circle only during the Second World War:

> Even after more than 30,000 West Africans had died in the First
> World War, those who argued in defense of ongoing conscription
> continued to claim that it was only in soldiers or blood that
> the African colonies could reimburse France for the humanist
> enterprise of colonialism.... Only after the Second World War
> and African soldiers' key role in Liberation was the sense of the
> debt reversed. (Mann 2006, 188)

The notion of the blood debt is then charged with this tainted history of obligations, paternalism, and chauvinism.

Seeking "communion," the words of the poet recover the image of the soldiers from an "othering" colonialist gaze; as Fanon puts it "woven . . . out of a thousand details, anecdotes, stories" and encased in a catalog of stereotypes (1967a, 111). The poet, sparing his comrades the "scornful praise" of others who share nothing with them or with the struggles of the rank-and-file in the field, raises up his voice to defend them and tear down the catalog of negative representations, calling attention to the misuse of the image of the soldiers in the propaganda of the empire when it is only the surviving comrades and family that should call the names of the dead. The notion that the dead must occupy the subordinate position of colonial subject denigrates their memory. The meaning of their sacrifice and its implications for the future becomes critical here, as citizenship is a right fought for by the Senegalese soldiers but not enjoyed by most of them. This is the bittersweet nature and meaning of "victory," and the false note that sounds in the praise of the soldiers without extending the benefits of citizenship that they fought to sustain. Rejection of such false or inauthentic praise is mirrored in Sembene's film *Camp de Thiorye* when the troops are addressed as "brave Tirailleurs" shortly after they arrive in the detention center at the opening of the film. In the liminary poem that opens the collection, Senghor declares war on those who refuse to honor the Senegalese soldiers:

> You are not empty-pocket men without honor
> But I will tear off the Banania grins from all the
>   walls of France

>   (Senghor 1998, 39)

The reference to the posters of the Banania images of Senegalese soldiers in Senghor's *Hosties noires* refers to an image that had a long life in French popular culture: the Senegalese rifleman. Following the First World War the Tirailleurs Sénégalais were such popular figures that they frequently appeared in national parades and celebrations. Their regalia was placed on display in local museums, with some collections even touring throughout the country. In French popular culture, the image of the Senegalese soldier occupied a very peculiar place, as figures that children might identify as accessible and worthy of a certain degree of trust. Jan Nederveen Pieterse suggests in his *White on Black: Images of Africa and Blacks in Western Popular Culture* (1998) that the original advertising campaign for Bonhomme Banania was not that of a black caricature, but rather a Tirailleur "portrayed in a realistic style," showing the soldier eating his breakfast in the field. Although a helping type, the soldier consumes the product, as Pieterse points out, rather than serving or preparing the food for others, giving the figure a modicum of autonomy (Pieterse 1998). This relative autonomy is won by the soldiers' exploits in the field, in defense of the empire. Though the original image gives an "overall impression," suggestive, according to Pieterse, of "an identification with the viewer," as the figure evolved it lost its relative autonomy, diminishing in both size and dignity. Over the generations, the soldier was transformed into a "social type" that would join the encyclopedia of black caricature:

> The product remained popular through several generations of
> French children, while the advertising formula was adjusted
> over time. Initially the Senegalese rifleman disappeared (in the
> wake of World War Two he was replaced by Nanette Vitamine),
> to return later in stylized form. Successively Banania lost his
> legs, chest and arms, until in the end only his head remained,
> with a big smile and lively eyes, and his gesticulating hands.
> Then the hands disappeared and since 1980 the head has been
> transformed into the B of BANANIA. Ironically enough, after all
> these re-stylings Banania, who was originally not a caricature,
> has become one. (Pieterse 1998, 162–63)

Commenting on this full-blown caricature, Sylvia Washington Bá points to the moral alienation and the sense of exile that the image of the smiling soldier in Senghor's lines represents. The soldier was "a grinning black man extolling the virtues of a popular French breakfast food in patois was a familiar sight throughout France," a visage that defiled the memory of the Tirailleurs and was counted among a series of injustices, culminating in what Bá has termed the "white denial of black dignity" (Bá 1973, 68).

In the poem entitled "Assassinations," written in the camp Front-Stalag 230, the bodies of the soldiers merge with the after-effects of the war on the landscape. The "black martyrs" reanimate the landscape with their sacrifice preparing the way for a new beginning, the spring of a new era:

> There they lie stretched out by the captive roads
>   along the
> routes of disaster
> Thin poplar trees, statutes of dark gods draped
>   with their
> long, gold coats
> Senegalese prisoners lying gloomily on
>   French soil.
> In vain your laughter cut short, in vain the blacker
> flower
> of your flesh. You are the blossom
> Of original beauty amid the naked absence
>   of flowers,
> Black blossom and its somber smile, diamond
>   of time
> Immemorial.
>
> (Senghor 1998, 57–58)

This image recalls the multitude of the dead of the underworld in *The Aeneid*: innocent victims cut down in their prime, "thick as leaves that with the early frost/of autumn drop and fall within the forest" (Virgil, 401–7; Harrison 2003). *The Aeneid* is one of the books that Senghor read during his internment in the camps. The image of the fallen leaves is used in the collection to signify the bodies of the soldiers, evoking at once the superfluous or excessive loss of innocence and the notion that these sacrifices may fuel the hopes and aspirations of the next African generation. Senghor then turns toward the hope of a coming spring as the fallen soldiers contribute to a cycle of growth and rebirth.

These ancient combatants initially sought rights from the colonial regime and would later lead fledgling nation-states into a postcolonial era, a process marking them doubly complicit in power and its deployment in and out of the context of empire. Constrained by the terms of engagement of the colonial period, at times by its actions and adopting its language, such figures as Senghor defined a conservative edge in the slow and steady attainment of relative autonomy, but also demonstrated its failure to realize the dreams of the fallen for the future.

Mudimbe rejects an off-handed dismissal of Senghor and seeks to restore his image to the full scope of its complexity:

> Senghor the promoter of some famous oppositions which, out of context, could appear to embrace perspectives proper to certain racist theoreticians: Negro emotion confronting Hellenistic reason; intuitive Negro reason in through participation facing European analytical thinking through utilization; or the Negro-African, person of the rhythm and sensitivity, assimilated to the Other through sympathy, who can say "I am the other ... therefore I am." On this basis, Senghor has been accused of seeking to promote a detestable model for a division between Africa and Europe, between African and European. (Mudimbe 1988, 94)

We may think of Senghor as a combatant on several fronts—ideological, political, and cultural—a battle that required not a doubling of consciousness but an interrogation of it. For Mudimbe, it is Senghor's emphasis on creativity and resourcefulness and not an essential reductionism that characterizes his philosophy. Drawing on the most encompassing scale, the Hellenistic tradition, Senghor pushes beyond conventional conceptualizations toward potential common denominators (Diop 2003).

Called to serve France in 1940 after having been rejected a year earlier for poor eyesight, Senghor like so many others was to become a soldier in a regiment of the colonial infantry. The precariousness of the colonial soldier, the strategic balance of soldering in the heart of the crisis of France during these years, is the subject of the humanity of his poems. A whole generation came of age under the guise of terms such as "fatherland" and "empire," the terrain across which the colonial soldier was constituted. Senghor poses the problem of this precarious identity in his poetry, navigating the waters of multiple worlds not easily segmented into colonial and colonized, European, or African. Again and again he returns to the image of the blood joining in the soil of the battlefield and binding at least potentially the lives lost in the conflict. Senghor notes the passage of European peasants and Tirailleurs in the same fields:

> Into the trenches where the blood of an entire
>   generation flows
> Europe is burying the nations' leaven
> And the hope of new races.
>
> (Senghor 1998, 48)

Racial essentialism is not the primary meaning of these references; however, the black African blood bonds are of great significance because of the vital realities bound by these blood ties, invoking at once continuity with the past and a link to undiscovered potentialities, marking the contours of an idealized world of the future.

In the early days of May 1940, German troops moving into Belgium and the Netherlands soon found their way to French soil. As part of a military unit sent to defend a bridge near Vichy, Senghor and his comrades-in-arms were taken prisoner by the Germans and placed in a prisoner-of-war camp:

> As soon as the Germans had taken Senghor's unit prisoner,
> they pulled the blacks out of the ranks and lined them up
> along a wall. Senghor quickly understood that the Germans
> intended to shoot them on the spot. Just as the firing squad
> was at the point of firing, "we called out, 'Vive la France, Vive
> l'Afrique noire.'" At that very moment, Germans put down their
> guns. A French officer had persuaded them that such slaughter
> would be a stain on Aryan honor. Which he cried first, "Vive
> la France" or "Vive l'Afrique noire," Senghor says he cannot
> remember. (Vaillant 1990, 167)

According to biographer Vaillant, this initial encounter with the Germans provided an emblematic experience of the war years for Senghor: "Looking back on this dramatic experience, Senghor realized that it had crystallized his sense that he was a child of Africa and of France" (1990, 167). That fact that a French officer had saved his life and that of his comrades was also something that Senghor kept alive in his memory of the event (167). This was not the fate of other French West

African soldiers, who were summarily executed as their French comrades were taken prisoner; the experience of Senghor runs not only counter to memory but to the mythic contours of some French officers' passivity in the face of the suffering of colonial soldiers (Echenberg 1991).

In the opening poem of *Hosties noires*, Senghor writes "Ah! de dites pas que je n'aime pas la France—je ne suis pas la France, je le sais" ("Ah! Don't tell me that I do not love France—I am not France, I know"). This ambiguous relationship of the colonial subject and soldier to France calls into question the very nature of France and of what "nation" may mean to the colonial subject. Senghor was in fact a French citizen by 1935, as was required of him in order to hold the prestigious title of *agrégé* of the University of Paris in Grammar, a distinction Senghor was the first black African to hold (Vaillant 1990, 107).[7] Even citizenship could not mediate being at once African and French, when the two poles of being were analogous but not equivalent.[8]

There is no way to disambiguate the nation from the empire or the experience of being a part of the cultural world of France while simultaneously inhabiting another cultural universe. Despite the notion of French assimilation, there was always something that could never be incorporated, something that might always remain apart. In some ways, this is the logic of assimilation; it is a process that retains the distance of the "other" intact and at arm's length. Moreover, the strange shifting fortunes of France during the period further complicated matters and resulted in deep internal divisions and a weakened and impoverished colonial power by 1944. As Nancy Ellen Lawler notes, by 1945 "France was in the throes of a grave moral crisis resulting from the circumstances of its capitulation in 1940 and its collaboration with Germany between 1940 and 1943" (1992, 14). Even Charles de Gaulle, the architect of the Free French forces—many of whom were recruited from French West Africa—was "condemned to death as a traitor in 1940" (14).

The naturalization of the assimilation ideal helped to mask the asymmetrical power relations of education and other forms of access to the colonial state/empire. In fact, "I am not France, I know" is uttered in desperation by the main character of this poetic series, the protagonist of a poetic narrative; not by Senghor, who set up a distance between himself and the creation of this intermediary. A thin vein separates the two, no doubt, but it is the action of this alter ego, not Senghor, that is placed in the position of replicating the dilemma of a subject position set between contradictory attitudes toward France.

The entire series, however, calls into question the possibility of allegiance to France, of misplaced loyalties and the sacrifices of the soldiers; his critique at times is very harsh, as in a poem dedicated to his old friends George and Claude Pompidou, "Prayer for Peace," written in Paris in January 1945:

> Yes, Lord, forgive France, who hates occupying
>   forces
> And yet imposes such strict occupation on me
> Who offers a hero's welcome to some, and treats
> The Senegalese like mercenaries, the Empire's
>   black
> watchdogs,
> Who is the Republic, but
> Hands over whole countries to Big Business
> That has turned my Mesopotamia and my Congo
> Into a vast cemetery under the white sun.
>   (Senghor 1998, 71)

These are surprisingly harsh words, employing the language of critique of an allegiance to France that would in turn degrade the status of the soldiers to mere mercenaries—an accusation often launched from both within and without the military camp. This sacrifice in the face of such forgetting is not only disrespectful to the life of the soldiers, but also renders their bodies as articles of commerce, denying them the exalted language of heroism and nationalism of the empire. As mere objects, the commodity of logic denigrates the allegiance of the soldier, even though it has been the order that these combatants have ensured that has enabled the maintenance of wealth in the colonial world. In return, an emergent civilization has become a cemetery. The relation of the living to the dead is one that demands a negation of the ideals associated with the promise of the nation. Senghor is in fact demanding that the "blood debt" of the soldiers, who have given the ultimate sacrifice of their lives, be recognized as such and properly memorialized.

For Senghor, all critique of France is qualified by an abiding passion for French culture and society and, notwithstanding his transcendental retentionist views of African sociocultural worlds, a rich appreciation of local tradition and social practice (Diawara 1998a). Visions of Africa and Europe converge in Senghor in the invention of a utopian space, uninhabitable and unattainable. While a deep sympathy with a local ideal of Africa made Senghor an adept politician and postcolonial leader, the notion of European links to this world imposed perpetual neocolonial relations with France in the name of an almost mystical Afro-Europe.

The complex connections between Europe and Africa were filtered in part by the set of obligations and expectations derived from the military and colonial service of African soldiers, the advantages gained from such service, and the shifting ideas of political belonging forged through this set of relationships. Gregory Mann argued that the social and cultural contemporary terrain of "citizen, subject and immigrant" is infused with the legacy of historical and contested identities (2006, 200). Many young migrants to France claim the right to immigrate to that country based on the contributions to France of the Tirailleurs Sénégalais during the two World Wars. During the 1990s, the specter of the Tirailleurs entered national French discourse on immigration and the so-called *sans-papiers*, when African migrants without residence papers—some having lived for decades in France—began to claim the right to stay. Countering the far-right rhetoric and insisting that French belonging had to be "earned," the *sans-papiers* pointed not only to their own "arduous labor" but that of their ancestors—the colonial soldiers (197). As Mann notes:

> While the tirailleurs may not have been considered
> "immigrants," the memory of their martial contributions
> remains an important component of public discourse over West
> African presence in France. Thus, it is that figure of the tirailleur,
> rather than that of the worker, that animates debates over
> African immigration. (Mann 2006, 200)

Indeed, by the period of African independence, Mann argues, "the military relationship had come to serve as a synecdoche for the African-French relationship," making it part of the core of a set of ideas about mutual obligations, compensation for military service, and the nature of political belonging (205).

By the middle of June 1940, the Germans had moved into Paris; the French government sought an armistice, hoping to end hostilities, keep

France unified, and at the same time maintain the administration of the empire and its heart in the metropole in a radically reconfigured polity (Vaillant 1990, 167–68). The story of this France, divided between the Germans in the north and the Vichy regime in the south, remains to be told, as it is deeply embedded in the forgetting of national trauma and shame. Whole generations of French students have come of age without knowing this story's role in the Holocaust or its precise location in this sad history of local residences, public buildings, and state agencies.

In recent years, the slow process of discovering the role of the French during these years of the war has drawn French society into an effort to understand the nature of French responsibility for actions that were often a prelude to atrocities committed during this period. Such an attempt to recover a hidden past has now inspired investigations into the nature and scope of collaborations. The colonial world, caught between the Vichy regime and the beginning of the liberation efforts, gave birth to an ambiguous transitional period and a divided France. Sembene by contrast is adamant about the equivalence in practice of the Pétain regime and that of De Gaulle—"De Gaulle, Mitterand or Pétain, that makes no difference to us"—blurring the distinction between colonial, fascist, and neocolonial regimes (Sembene 1993, 83).

The poems of *Hosties noires*, Senghor's second collection of poetry, were written between 1938 and 1945 and roughly span the years of recruitment and engagement of African troops during the Second World War. The ambiguity of the title, casting the black soldiers as either victims or sacrifices, is underscored by the peculiar netherworld that the soldiers occupy. In and through the progression of the work, a haunting poetic tribute captures lives between cultures, languages, and the powers of the natural and colonial worlds. *Hosties noires* must be set within the broader framework of the relationship and constitution of a colonial subjectivity and the emergence of a postcolonial figure precipitated in many ways through the liminal spaces of the war. I would argue that *Hosties noires* represents not only a protest against the neglect of the acknowledgment of the role of the black colonial soldier, but also and primarily an assertion of a black subjectivity that is bound up with the process of moving between pre- and postwar worlds and an experience radically altered during this passage. Not only is the emergence of a new form of mass culture being brought into existence through the creation and engagement of colonial troops, but the technology of the war provides a new imaginary, a world that interrupts the flow of life with the din of its machines and the operation of its weapons of war. Such sounds of war often erupt in the lines of the poems, breaking the flow of temporality and providing the opportunity for excursions to the past, searching for the fragments of a noble heritage, as in the poem "Ndisse." The work poses a kind of timeless world of tradition, a prior reality posited in the realm of the agrarian landscape, an almost inchoate domain from which the African past speaks to the present. It is in this domain that the poet seeks the glory of the past in the face of the humiliation of the war.

Nowhere in the collection is this transformation more powerful than in the poem written for the fallen soldiers of Thiaroye, dated "Paris, December 1944":

> Black Prisoners, I should say French Prisoners,
>   is it true
> That France is no longer France?
>
> (Senghor 1998, 68)

Perhaps one of the most significant protests of the period was the incident at Thiaroye (Senegal), which, like the Sharpeville massacre in apartheid South Africa in 1960, marked a generation. Many were on the front lines in May and June 1940, and the survivors of these units were often interned in *Front-Stalags* (German labor camps), located largely in northeastern France, for periods of up to four years. During the process of repatriation to their natal villages throughout West Africa, many of the troops—some a part of the French Free Forces in southern France in the summer of 1944—suffered a number of indignities. They were all but left on their own in the countryside with few, if any, provisions. The difficult conditions the men faced, coupled with poor treatment by the French colonial command, was expressed in many often serious incidents on the way home. Colonial soldiers violently objected to the segregation of troops, confined to quarters while under British command. On December 1, 1944, at the barracks of Thiaroye, near Dakar, an uprising took place among the thousand or so African ex-prisoners-of-war who were part of the first contingent of soldiers to be repatriated from the European campaign. The French command fired on their own soldiers in what was to become the ultimate symbol of colonial violence in that period. Although similar uprisings occurred in other parts of French West Africa, that of Thiaroye was the most significant and is often viewed as once of the inaugural events of the labor movements in the region. In part, the dispute occurred over wages due to the soldiers. The taking of the lives of the black soldiers at Thiaroye by French officers marks a critical moment of a transformation in colonizer/subject relations in French West Africa. Expectations of assimilation within the framework of the French empire were shattered by the comrades-in-arms; it became clear to the members of the rising generation that independence was the only viable option. Senghor, following the spirit of negritude ideology, invoked the world of the past of the noble warrior tradition and monumentalized this tradition:

> You are the witnesses of immortal Africa
> You are the witnesses of the New World to come.
>
> (Senghor 1998, 68)

Standing in death between the two worlds, the soldiers become the monumental subject of a yet-to-be-written African tradition; they are in a sense the victims of a heroism that can only become heroic in a postcolonial future. The great irony of this is that the monumentalization of Thiaroye in this volume disappears altogether in the political life of Senghor after independence. His regime participated in the forgetting of these soldiers and of the impact of Thiaroye, as they became a kind of political liability. They marked inescapable roads of critique leading to the postindependence regime and its dependence on the very same mechanisms of power. The new regime's subsequent dependence on the neocolonial powers replaced the colonial regime with a complex constellation of international players, banking concerns, and economic development schemes.

Although Senghor was a critical figure in the liberation of those imprisoned for the "mutiny" of Thiaroye, he did little as a president of the republic to institutionalize the recognition of these soldiers in the newly independent Senegal. With no monument marking their mass graves during his tenure, they are honored only in the grave of the Unknown Soldier. No other tribute save these poems acknowledges their passage through the colonial world.

Sembene's *Camp de Thiaroye* ridicules the notion of the brave Tirailleurs in the first address of the troops in the camp by Captain Labrosse, "Brave Tirailleurs." This speech appears to be a replication of the discourse of heroism of the colonial troops and part of an argument for the expanded use of these troops outside of Africa. It also, however, signals a mixture of the myth of African loyalty and the paternalism of the French, masking the asymmetry of the practice of command in the language of mutual obligation. A critique of this view, however, seems to be present in the manner of the captain, particularly in the way he quickly dispatches the troops to the care of the lieutenant after a few cursory comments, as if undermining the importance of the Tirailleurs altogether.

The idea of heroism was in fact more essential to the colonial self-image than it was to the soldiers or their descendents, as we might imagine. The strategic location and erection of the twin statues to the colonial troops in Bamako and Reims in 1924 honored the colonial order, not the colonial solider, who would struggle for years to make good on the promises made to them for their service, including back pay and pensions (see chapter 7). Exhibiting the troops in the metropole was a way that the empire might become visible. Parading various portions of the colonial soldiers through the streets of the metropole and placing their uniforms and other artifacts of military vintage on display let the bodies of the dead soldiers speak to the present, the uniforms on display peopling the unit's imaginary ranks. What is consumed at the exhibition is merely the idea of soldiering, a promise of the defense of and loyalty to the citizen and nation. The parade of the black soldier in France merely underscored the ritual and symbolic signification of their absence/presence; their hypervisibility ensured their disappearance.

The Victims of Heroism

For Senghor, the indignities of the war resonate with an indictment of the scars of the past, slavery, and colonization (Kesteloot 1991, 206–7). In the poem "The Enlisted Man's Despair," the agency and freedom of the "Volontaire" is counterposed to forced labor and the extraction of resources from Africa by the colonial power—a continued stream of "nothing but sand, taxes, extra duty," and "whips" (Senghor 1998, 49). The soldier, "given a servant's clothes, which he took to be/The martyr's simple garment," balances on the brink of disappearance. The "sacrifice" of the soldier is affronted by the dehumanizing conditions of the colonial world, the war, and the humiliation of their abandonment in German prison camps (Kesteloot 1991, 207). The final lines of the poem lament the historical silencing of the soldier while acknowledging the passage of a comrade: "O weak, too weak child, such a loyal traitor to your genius!" (Senghor 1998, 49). Being silenced in the discourse of an official record might come to be the fate of any soldier, or for that matter, any platoon of soldiers. We have seen as much in our fictional accounts of the Vietnam War, which in its representational records (particularly in film) for example, minimizes the role of black soldiers and other soldiers of color, preferring instead the heroic white soldier who seems to command at every level from the Pentagon to the jungle. It is however in the domain of the historical narrative of the war that colonial soldiers first succumbed to the humiliation of official forgetting.[9] In the end, their own independent postcolonial governments came to see the soldiers as a kind of political liability, a link to a compromised and colonial past. For postcolonial African governments like Senegal, the soldiers represented a kind of cosmopolitanism due to the nature of their travels and encounters with Europeans, African Americans, and others in the course of the war years. This cosmopolitanism was not of the elite variety, however, but rather served to open new possibilities for a subaltern class that constituted the first African populations to experience a mass mobilization—a kind of diasporic consciousness. The process of mass mobilization created the peculiar publics of Italy and Germany, as it correlates in the forced mobilization of the colonized in African contexts (Echenberg 1991, 47). As Manthia Diawara writes in *In Search of Africa*, both Sembene and Ngugi we Thiong'o "link the rise of national consciousness in Africa to World War II, in which Africans fought alongside white people to resist fascism, xenophobia, and racism" (Diawara 1998a, 142). The politicization of these colonized troops would be an integral part of their partial integration into the French military complex.

In *Camp de Thiaroye*, as we shall see in chapter 6, Sembene highlights the attempts of the officers that remained in colonial Africa—many former functionaries of Vichy France—to humiliate the colonial soldiers who claim new rights as they stand to reenter civilian society. While the soldiers demand the same rights as French soldiers, the officers try to reinscribe their status as "colonial," taking the pay they earned while in work camps and taking the uniforms that the Americans had given them, replacing them with the uniform of the Tirailleurs. The promises of ameliorating their condition and that of their children—including the right to attend adequate schools and training centers—seemed to vanish in this effort to make them once again "subjects" and not citizens of France. Yet the officers who served with the soldiers in the European theater granted them a new respect and consideration as comrades at arms and defenders of France.[10] French officers had commanded black troops since the founding of the Tirailleurs, and the bond they developed with the soldiers was often very close, separating them from those with little first hand knowledge of their contributions to the war effort or their distinguished history.

Perhaps fearing the colonial soldiers' potential for collective organization and contest both within and without an emergent national structure, the new African regimes abandoned their memories to the ritual surroundings of the grave of the Unknown Soldier (Echenberg 1978). Of the countless representations of the Second World War, from the comic to the tragic, few have represented the lives and contributions of colonial soldiers. One of the most critical sites of cultural production during the postwar period was the almost continuous appearance of films, histories, memories, and other cultural acknowledgements of the impact and scope of the war. The colonial soldier, however, has been confined to the shadows of the master narrative: empire, nation, and progress.[11]

CHAPTER 6

Comrade Storyteller

Diasporic Encounters in the Cinema of Ousmane Sembene

> Photographic images often appear to defy time or, at least,
> partially to escape its implacable sequence. The ability to with-
> draw the appearance of the moment and preserve it from time's
> deliquescence looms large in the history of our fascination with
> the camera.
>
> —SCOTT McQUIRE, *VISIONS OF MODERNITY: REPRESENTATION,*
> *MEMORY, TIME, AND SPACE IN THE AGE OF THE CAMERA*

> *White* however has the strange property of directing our atten-
> tion to color while in the very same movement it exnominates
> itself as a color. For evidence of this we need look no further
> than the expression "people of color," for we know very well that
> this means "not White."
>
> —VICTOR BURGIN, *IN/DIFFERENT SPACES:*
> *PLACE AND MEMORY IN VISUAL CULTURE*

Framing Modernity

Ousmane Sembene (1923–2007) in his film *Camp de Thiaroye* brings
together two of the most pressing issues for Africans during the 1940s
(the era in which the film is set): citizenship and labor. The extension of
citizenship to everyone in French West Africa and equal pay and parity
with the European worker were the two political demands that began
to take shape during this time; Sembene, as a former soldier and trade
unionist, was well aware of these discussions. Simple as it may seem at
face value, these two notions would spell the end of the colonial order
as the full realization of either could only come about in a postcolonial

world (Gadjigo 2007, 129–30). Sembene's official biographer and friend, Samba Gadjigo (author of *Ousmane Sembene: Une Conscience Africaine* [2007]), told me recently that for his generation, educated on the French classics, Sembene's work *God's Bits of Wood* (1962) was one of the first books that he and other schoolchildren read that included the names and details of families that were recognizable as African and had African names and concerns. He awakened a world of the imagination for an African audience about African historical and contemporary contexts, for many for the first time. In this discussion, I will continue with the theme of the colonial soldier, who embodied both the desire for citizenship and the struggle for parity, and ultimately, for a postcolonial Africa. I will discuss primarily Sembene's film *Camp de Thiaroye* (1988) (directed by Ousmane Sembene and codirector Faty Sow Thierno) and the context of African liberation treated in this work.

Sembene is considered one of the founding figures of African cinema; many contemporary filmmakers owe a great debt to his craftsmanship and determination. Sembene's first short film, *Borom Sarret* (1966), was a masterful rending of the journey of a *bonhomme charett*, a carter of Dakar, Senegal, who although barely making a living gives his days wages to a Griot singing praises the of his noble lineage. We see Dakar from the perspective of the carter, who loses everything when he crosses over a forbidden imaginary line separating the poor from the city's elite. Oliver Barlet observes that "the film lays down a programme for the cinema: to set and conquer African space in the face of modernity which is presented as a Western intrusion into the land of Africa" (2000, 72–73). Certainly, in each frame Sembene constructs an unparalleled African imaginary.

The trope of navigation is often employed in the many films and fiction of Sembene; in converting the Western narrative structure of the journey to the self-actualization of the individual, Sembene seeks to tell the story of the collective articulation of consciousness, resistance, and political struggle. Largely self-educated, Sembene was influenced by the artistry of the Griot and the vitality of the everyday lives of ordinary people. A storyteller and political activist, he depicted the world that he found himself a part of in his working life. People of ordinary circumstances are drawn into the tapestry of his tale on film and in fiction: a series of letters, the uncle of a migrant to France attempting to

cash a check (*Mandabi*, 1968), or a day in the life of a simple cart driver
(*Borom Sarret*, 1963) or domestic worker (*Le Noire de . . .*, 1966)—these
are the stories that Sembene asks us to attend to a world often hidden
by the overshadowing grand narratives of official histories. He was born
in 1923 in Zigunchor, a small Senegalese fishing community, and at the
outbreak of the Second World War was swept up by the French Army
and then the French Free Forces fighting in Europe. His own experiences in the war from this period aided him in painting the rich cultural
world of *Camp de Thiaroye*, perhaps one of the most complex portraits
of colonial soldiers to date. After the war, he returned to France, working as a dockworker in Marseilles and becoming a trade union leader
and a member of the French Communist Party. His political views were
nourished by both his activism and events, soon to be reflected in his
fiction. In 1956, he published his first novel, *The Black Docker*, based
in part on his experiences. With the publication in 1960 of *God's Bits of
Wood* he was already one of the most highly regarded African writers of
his generation.

After a very successful series of publications, he attended the Moscow
Film School in 1964, working later at the Gorki Film Studios. The shift to
cinema was prompted by a desire to reach a wider audience in a language
they might understand, since—confined to French—his works of fiction
were known primarily in France. He wanted to reach a wider African
audience, but struggled in his early work to film in African languages.
He hoped to film his first feature, *Le Noire de . . .*, in an African language,
but the French backers of the film insisted on the use of French. He was
an innovator and an ardent proponent of a rupture with African dependence on European assistance, cultural models, and styles of life. The
characters in his films and fiction struggle to realize lives honoring the
past without being bound by it, seeking out a future that may ennoble the
common life while remaining attentive to the needs of the collectivity.
He was also a staunch critic of Senghor and the national ideology based
on the notion of "negritude" that was promulgated in Senegal, and the
late president's symbiotic relationship with France, the former colonial
power. Many of his films question the ideas of nobility and caste and
the politics of a corrupt elite out of touch with the masses. Often a lone
voice resonates with people longing for a change, as in *Guelwaar* (1993),
when a Christian activist calls for an end to dependence on foreign aide

and, in one of the most extraordinary scenes of African cinema, young people stomp truckloads of foodstuffs from foreign aid trucks into the ground, as the voice of the departed leader can be heard taking the government to task for its shameful dependence on gifts from external lending agencies.

Picturing Colonial Soldiers

I take as my point of departure for this discussion a photograph of colonial soldiers on their way to France—one of the first candid images of these soldiers I ever encountered.[1] I explore its meanings here, as its novelty speaks to the invisibility of the soldiers. The figure of the colonial soldier is a recurrent character in the literature and film work of Sembene; a former soldier himself, he grants the soldier a privileged vision of the social order—a perspective shaped by close contact with Africans from various parts of the French colonial world, African Americans, and a host of Europeans, all encountered outside of Africa, on the battlefields, in concentration camps, and at various points along the journey. While the colonial soldiers of the First World War were accorded a place in the heroism of the nation, this quickly changed and in time they verged on disappearance. After all, the photograph and its use as a historic document concern us here: proof that the black regiments were poised to disembark on the contested terrain of France, the precarious emergent nation-state in what we might call its moment of awakening. The state system that we have come to identify with the postwar configuration of Europe was in fact not present at the time of the photograph, but lay in its distant future.

I came across this photograph in Anthony Clayton's book *France, Soldiers, and Africa* (1988), a text that documents the world of the colonial soldier. Not unlike countless others, this image was of prisoners of other stories situated at the innermost portion of the book and disclosed meanings supplementary to the rest of the work. The book and its subject matter are poised on the brink of erasure, revealing the representation of the colonial soldier, who plays catchup with the figure of a national counterpart already firmly situated in the narratives of both World Wars. Although I did not come upon the soldiers by chance, I was struck by the way this presence suspended the rest of the narrative for me, and in such an unexpected manner. To my surprise, the rest—the military history and its place in the greater narrative of the European social formation, a foundational contemporary drama and one that had always commanded my attention before—began to fade. The continuous motion of this flickering historical light brought into play a new relationship to the body of the image, giving it a density and transparency it had previously lacked as a part of the dead pages or supporting evidence of a text firmly situated in the Western imaginary.

The silent face of the photograph was peopled with a subaltern situated at the very heart of a historicity that could no longer contain it; in this present, the peculiar tensions between Africa and Europe made their claim to my attention. Undoubtedly, the image had an ancillary role in the text, like so many others; it was placed there as a document associated with the narrative of military engagement of the black forces in France. It is the manner in which this project stands by itself with a handful of others systematically ignored in the heart of a tradition that may justify my hesitance to allow this snapshot to fall back evenly with the other pages of this volume. Only on rare occasions do fugitive images of the colonial or African American soldiers of the Second World War dance into the light of popular and or scholarly attention. Yet the diasporic encounter of these soldiers with the people they fought alongside, liberated, and left behind is a critical mode for re-envisioning the relationship between Africa, Europe, and the Americas.

Of course, the colonial soldier was a global figure, inasmuch as this category of person was consumed by the making and maintenance of empire. In an unfamiliar and hostile terrain of empire and alliance, these soldiers found their way to a racialized vanishing point. Their bodies reveal the contours of visibility, the hypervisible that may not be seen, placing the subaltern view in the center of a historicity that could no longer contain it and jumping out the pages of this book to make a claim in the present, a peopled silence.

This is a haunting photograph drawn from the Centre Militaire d'information et de Documentation sur l'Outre-Mer, nestled among many others at the very heart of the text, a moment in time frozen during the Second World War, capturing a simple line of soldiers en route to a France. This in itself is not remarkable; countless images of the war have graced the darkened rooms of movie theaters, the crumpled personal records of soldiers, and the fantasy world of soak-in-the-sun or read-it-on-the-train fiction. These colonial soldiers, a random sampling of the *force noire* of French West Africa, have somehow escaped global visual culture. This picture is presented as "evidence," corroborating a specific military history and participating in the text as a kind of "window on the world," transporting the reader to the present of another time. In that distant instant of arrival in an impatient French port, such men were poised on the edge of their own disappearance, of vanishing into the obscurity of the war and its aftermath. Of course, the very caption of the image contains an element of the moment's sedimented past, as it reads "Tirailleurs Sénégalais about to land in the south of France, 1944." Properly speaking, the idea of France in this year was an open matter. The soldiers' task was to liberate France, to make France again, to reconstitute the vanishing empire of signs in which they were born as colonial subjects.

Arriving in 1944 to France, a country most had never seen and few would see again, those in the photograph are Tirailleurs Sénégalais, some wearing helmets, others in caps, crowded along the deck and gazing off to shore and the impending conflict. The identity of the photographer is unclear—perhaps a fellow soldier, an officer on board, or even a civilian reporter or member of the crew. Yet the image is captivating. In it, the anticipation of unity in the appearance of the soldier is eclipsed by the singularity and urgency of the moment.

The individuality or personality of the soldier is overwhelmed by the pose of the body, the subtle interruption of the structure of the ship, and the inattention of some while others seem to be drowning in the experience. Bodies leaning over the edge of the ship seem to demand that the observer respect the gravity of their mission. The demeanor of the soldiers lifts the instant with the arbitrary light of their youth, and in the peculiar way that the sighting of the south of France commands their attention along with other strange forms of individuation of this collective ritual that may escape our view. After, all this moment—however significant—will be reduced to a part of the process of soldiering.

Through the eyes of the soldiers we can begin to imagine a subaltern view of France and the origins of potential critiques of colonial enterprise by way of the lived experience of colonial troops. This brings to mind Victor Burgin's cautionary note about the immediacy of visual culture. Burgin contemplates the task of the excavation of what we might call the "present," a moment that "is not a perpetually fleeting point on a line 'through time,' but a collage of disparate times, an imbrication of shifting and contested spaces" (1996, 182). It is true that we may never approximate the sensations of the passenger aboard of the wave-tossed troop ship or fully comprehend the emotional impact of the discontinuous, life-changing allegiance from the most intimate of human aspirations to the most abstract and impersonal experience of the soldier. But it is in this "collage of disparate times" that we seek to approach the reflected life of the black troops (182). In this spirit, we must once again return to our photograph reinforced by our meditations on the fugitive image at large.

War marks the landscape of memory. Social consciousness is weighed down by the strange symbolic resonance contained in the forgotten presence that haunts the living in honor of the dead. Social memory and its operation in the contemporary state has become an integral feature of the art of the state. I have argued that the official document is a critical component in the technology of state practice, numeration, and classification and control (Carter 1997, 101–27). The staging and shaping of memory, memorials, and the most public forms of heroism in service of the state constitutes an important aspect of national discourse and its cosmological order. The parade of colonial soldiers in the heart of the metropolitan community was customary on occasions of national display. The limited "belonging" of the colonial subject/soldier exemplified the greatness of the nation.

The orchestration of memory in service of the very idea of the black troops can be seen in the pages of *Le Monde Colonial Illusté*, a journal that during the 1920s contained a quiet endorsement of the Tirailleurs Sénégalais underscoring the need to secure and maintain defense of a wide-ranging colonial domain. The exploits of the soldiers in the making of the empire were being memorialized and drawn into the image of the loyal subjects of the patria/homeland. A short article appearing in the journal in August 1924 announced the inauguration of two monuments, one erected in January in Bamako, and a second, a replica, which was to be placed in Reims in July in order to honor the "glorious heroes" of the Black Army and their leaders. The monument depicts a French officer holding a standard in the foreground, behind which four uniformed soldiers stand poised for action; two of the soldiers wear helmets, one is without a helmet and another wears the cap of the Tirailleur (Figure 7). Built to honor the people of Africa who have given their lives in defense of France, the memorials stand as metonymic markers of the relationship of the living and the dead. The ceremony in celebration of the monument was to be a great spectacle in which the various uniforms and other paraphernalia of the soldiers units would be placed on display, ranging from the first days of these regiments to the most recent military fashions. Still, social and economic conditions in the region, as critics of the regime pointed out at the time, called more for "hospitals, maternity clinics and dispensaries that could better demonstrate French recognition of the West African contribution to the war" than the erection of memorials (Mann 2006, 96).

Acts of heroism held a place in the life and constitution of the colonial world, as loyal subjects laid down their lives for the patria/homeland or greater France, albeit often under duress. The image of the colonial

Figure 7. Monument dedicated to African colonial soldiers. *Le Monde Colonial Illustré*, Paris, April 1924.

soldier is shrouded in the very fabric of violence and the suppression of spontaneous resistance that characterized and brought into being the colonial process. Looking back, it is easy to succumb to the desire to read in the everyday lives of these men an active anticolonial trace, or rather to seek out the decisive moment of their complicity with the colonial order—being instruments of a repressive regime was a role that these troops were often to play in the distant reaches of an imperialist realm. From "pacification" to garrisoning, they remain symbols of the arbitrary interventions in the rural lives of cultivators from which they were in large part drawn.

Countless protests by local people attempted to circumvent the process of conscription. After the establishment of the 1919 conscription law, young men were called up on a universal basis, forming the foundations of a new mass colonial army drawn from every level of French West African society, including cultivators and elite former slaves and slave holders. As Mann points out, the legacy of slavery among the soldiers was to have a profound impact on family structure, political belonging, and social activism for generations (Mann 2006). The ambiguous status of the slave/subject in many ways helped to fuel the struggle for citizenship and independence.

The interethnic and interregional consolidation of such an unparalleled mass mobilization and militarization of this segment of West African society brought to life a new image and everyday reality in African experience. Contingents of colonial soldiers from the First World War included a large portion of recruits drawn from Senegal, who were destined to suffer heavy casualties. Their departure caused an unprecedented disruption of social life in French West Africa. The slave origins of the military were still evident in 1918, as many of the soldiers ventured for the first time beyond the outer reaches of their natal villages. Successfully orchestrated recruitment efforts in the same year dramatically changed the makeup of the Tiralleur units, encouraging African "notables" as well as former slaves and others to join the "force noire" of the colonies. The relative hostility with which recruitment efforts had been met resulted in uprisings on a number of occasions, as in Dahomey. Uprisings were actually anticipated in the 1919 conscription law, which included provisions mandating imprisonment for those seeking to obstruct the conscription process in any way. This tension between the local villages and the military arm of the empire is dramatized in the film *Emitai* (1971). The soldier became in fact a popular figure in the novels and films of much of postcolonial Africa, as the ambiguities of the status dramatized the neocolonial nature of the new social order and its unresolved ties to the past.

The photograph brings us fairly close to the soldiers, yet the photographer stands at a discreet distance in order to fully illuminate the nonchalant attitude of these young men in the face of their collective and uncertain destiny. Many will never return to their home villages. Some will find their way to German or French prisoner-of-war camps, work details, and summary executions, while others will survive the war, return to their villages, reconstruct their lives, and speak of their experience only with fellow combatants, if at all. Sembene once called them the "first leaven" of the independence movement (1993, 83). The social isolation of these men and their families was never abetted by a massive assault of visual cultural productions that set their lives in the grand narrative of the nation; such consideration and acknowledgement was not accorded them. Popular recognition of the ultimate sacrifice of soldiers is an integral part of their placement in an appropriate sociohistorical context.

If we consider for a moment the massive archive of popular culture and its artifacts that form a part of the solemnization of the Second World War in France, Great Britain, and the United States, it seems at best odd that images of the French West African soldier do not grace a single major production of the international film community. If they appear at all, they remain in the background, as fleeting images and supporting local color. Their images seem fated to fade, like the first pictures in the delicate textures of light, memory, and flights of the imagination slated for other cultural worlds. European film has, according to Sembene, historically trained its sights on other subjects to the exclusion of the black film subject, and this has been especially true in terms of the popular archive of war imagery:

> In the history of the cinema, particularly the European cinema,
> you can see that if there are black people in the films made
> during the war of 1914–1918, they appear as fleeting shadows.
> The same thing is true of the last war. Even American films made
> during these two wars feature black people as shadows. Even in
> films made during the Vietnam War without American approval,

the blacks who appear are still shadows, introduced merely to justify that blacks took part in the war; they are not really central to the movie. So we can say that in the history of cinema, black people were only dancers or fleeting shadows. . . . That time is over now. The history of the world involves everyone, all races. (Sembene 1993, 83)

A prelude to erasure, this form of black caricature is part of a long tradition. In the absence of images that document or even justify the presence of blacks at the scene of master narrative events, a mythic presence has graced the silver screen. The portrayal of Africa and the diaspora in film must not be limited to the ethnographic documentary practice under attack in recent years, but rather extend to the entire archive of films that attempt to envision Africa. There is a history waiting to be written of the documentary and newsreel depictions of the colonial era, which circulated an image of the colonies not only to the metropolitan heart of the empire, but to other colonial countries and to the far corners of the world. In these treatments, the soldier/subject was a credit to the colonial world. Much of the new African cinema was produced initially on old film stock, and through the apparatus of these colonial films, centers were first established to produce news from the periphery. The idea of the ethnographic record has actually far outpaced its actual employment in the analysis of "other" cultures' "vast archives of record footage remain unseen and unused"—perhaps "the visual" that stands beyond the contours of cultural expectation is not easily rendered intelligible (MacDougall 1999, 283). *Camp de Thiaroye* at times gives us a vision of what it might be to look behind the production of these newsreels, into the animated lives and conflicts of actual soldiers. Sembene's objection to the work of anthropologist Jean Rouch and others who treated Africans like "insects" under the gaze of the camera must also be considered in relation to the strange ambiguity of the visual and its cultural relegation to the role of counterpoint to modernity.[2]

Popular movies that claim Africa as a backdrop run the gamut from Uys's *The Gods Must Be Crazy* (1980) to the genre-setting *King Solomon's Mines* (1937 and 1950) to the romance of Houston's *The African Queen* (1951) and the adventure melodrama of the Tarzan series and its many versions, from film to Disney cartoons and television series of the 1990s. The ethnographic work of the Marshall films of the San, and the devastation of the San in South Africa, stands out as a particularly powerful documentary that straddles the divide between scholarly project, personal diary and confessional, and travelogue. The savage and primitive Africa was also effectively prepared for popular consumption in a number of scholarly journals, travel writing, and the world of literature. A central concern of many contemporary producers of literature and film is to somehow counter an entire body of work, an archive of black caricature that rests on "a folkloric and simple minded image of Africa" (Sembene 1993). The infantilizing image of Africans who needed the assistance of others is of particular concern in the work of Sembene. In the final scene of *Guelwaar,* young people dump truckloads of donated food into the street, determined to live on their own terms. Neither the image of a glorious past nor the diminishing and debilitating consequences of foreign aid can save them from the future they must forge on their own.

The aura of modernity is prefigured in popular culture and in film theory and practice, which helped to shape and represent other cultures. Rachel O. Moore argues in *Savage Theory: Cinema as Modern Magic* (2000) that in early film theory and practice, it is the fascination with the image-making technology itself that enchants both image maker and audience. Some of the power of the dreamscapes constructed by filmmakers emerges from an intoxication with the framing of modernity. Nowhere is this power demonstrated as clearly as when is posed in contrast to a world utterly devoid of its symbolic and technical mastery, "the primitive makes technology magic" (Moore 2000, 50). Envisioning experiences of first contact with primitive populations the film as a trope of travel between an empowered present and a primitive past in these early efforts posits a naïve subject to marvel at the wonders of the cinema. The spectator might play the role of the primitive in relation to the machine, the apparatus of image making, in much the same way that the nineteenth-century *camera obscura* created a privileged site of vision through its sophistication and consolidation of the technology of the observer. The camera is in essence a gateway into a terrain scarred by an "argumentation of images." The interplay of images invokes a kind of primitivism, a "complex mangle of imputations to and fascinations with people whose very difference generally turns out to be marked by the stampede of progress over their bodies—their status in the realm of the real always circumvented by metaphor, myth, and misrecognition" (51). Theoretical backdrops and/or the constructs of the theater may converge on the point of disappearance of ways of seeing, whole modes of being that do not reflect the fashion of the day. But the kind of sleight of hand we are considering goes far beyond this, as it leads back to a way of framing modernity, of capturing some notion of the present.

The lasting impression of the image considered here leaves one with a sense of impermanence about the atmosphere onboard the ship; everything about this moment seems poised for disappearance. The instant of their arrival signals an awakening of a New France, yet it is the precariousness of the lives of the soldiers that comes to be the centerpiece of our backward-looking gaze. Perhaps it is the way the men seem to seek out signs of what is to come that permeates this trace of their lives with anticipation. The colonial soldier, without knowing it, is a subject slated for disappearance; the very act of soldiering gives birth to an integral ambiguity for the colonial subject. The potential for a new way of being stems from this ambiguity and implies an acceptance of a set of conditions, holding at once the possibility of a rejection of the colonized state and the slight promise of world beyond it. The possibility of such a rejection was in fact always on the minds of those in command; the selection of theaters of action, the garrisoning assignments, and the composition of the troops were always carefully considered to ensure the integrity of the social order. The colonial soldier represents a kind of transitional figure situated between the empire and the people in a kind of liminal terrain between trust and trustworthiness, between home and the imagined embrace of an abstract regime.

Some appear in the grainy representation to strain to make things out on shore, while others take time out to continue a bit of conversation, and still others in the background seem unimpressed by the meeting of worlds and push through the crowd toward other destinations. The documentary presentation of the photo, placed in the center of the book among others of other periods and indeed among other topics of French military history, gives it a strange quality. The soldiers are not in formation—they are not on display, they have not posed for the camera, but are simply there, as if in its pathway, caught in the flux of historical process. The photograph brings together what Benjamin refers to as a kind of frozen point of becoming: "the Then and the Now. . . . In other

words: an image is dialectics at a standstill" (cited in Cadava 1995, 234).
The legibility of the image at once restores it to our time and irrevocably
dislocates the image from its own; to the viewer the event in the photograph's distant "now-time" is merely a promise of a dislocated presence.
"Photography promises that everything may be kept for history, but the
everything that is kept is the everything that is always already in the process of disappearing," according to Eduardo Cadava (234). The notion
that the photographic image records a kind of death that is restored to
life and to its complete historical significance only through a reading, by
which it is transformed into text, remains contingent, however hopeful.
It may be that the photograph confronts us with what the idea of cultural translation presents for our consideration in other domains, that
is, the limits to our understanding. The chiaroscuro of the image, an old
metaphor for the exploration of knowledge, holds little promise of transparency. The optical unconscious of Benjamin has no privileged depths
from which to return to us with new knowledge, as does the unconscious
of Freud; the optical is a world of surfaces, impenetrable and at times as
irretrievable as the present of the picture itself.

   This image is not a part of an exotic project, in that it does not freeze
the picturesque, despite the importance of the presentation of the colonial
troops in French discourse and national ideology. It is an odd mixture of a
souvenir and a personal cotemporal document, as if the viewer were there
with them, with this collective colonial black force at the dawn of what
was to be a new France, in the making of a new Europe. I linger on events
discovered in the pages of a historical text that attempts to acknowledge a
presence in a time of war that has been otherwise overlooked. These colonial soldiers were not only a critical support to the war effort, but the first
to explore a world created by the need to defend the empire.

   Amitav Ghosh, writing a brief history of the British colonial soldier of
the 1940s, highlights the strategic position of these men and women in
India's past, saying "they were the hinge that held the colonial lid in place
over a subcontinent" (Ghosh 1997). Colonial wars waged in the conquest
of India and other territories from Burma to South Africa made use of the
colonial soldier. The suppression of anticolonial uprisings in India, China,
Malaysia, and Egypt was accomplished only through the collaboration of
Indian combatants. Colonial soldiers were employed in the French empire
in campaigns of pacification to garrison permanent detachments and also
to put down selected disturbances in various parts of the empire.

African Colonial Troops: The Tirailleurs Sénégalais

The black African troops, primarily infantry, became an integral part of French military power (Figure 8). Campaigns of L' Armée d' Afrique (1830–1962) span periods from the initial occupation of empire in Algeria and Morocco to the critical deployment of Tirailleurs during the Second World War in Europe and Africa, and a decade later at Dien Bien Phu (Clayton 1988, 3).[3] The *force noire* was a large army recruited from French West Africa and elsewhere (93). During the First World War, their numbers swelled to 160,000 fighting in the trenches, of whom virtually all were conscripts (Lawler 1992).[4] Annual recruitments of from ten to twelve thousand men from French West Africa during the years between 1919 and 1939 place the troops' numbers (after an acceleration of recruitment efforts in 1939) at around 150,000 serving in the French army by the time of the empire's collapse, according to Lawler (29). Historian Myron Echenberg puts the French recruitment of Africans participating in the Second World War much higher overall, in excess of some two hundred thousand (Echenberg 1991). In the film *Camp de Thiaroye*, the naturalized national space of the contemporary nation-state is challenged by the historical narratives of Senegalese and African American

Figure 8. Tirailleurs Sénégalais with buglers. *Le Monde Colonial Illustré*, Paris, April 1924.

soldiers who fought in the Second World War. The film is a coproduction (Algeria, Tunisia, and Senegal) and received the Special Jury Prize at the Venice Mostra for its technical quality (Barlet 2000, 49).

The colonial soldier had a foot in multiple cultural traditions, having access to European and complex African traditions, as a result of Africans being drawn from a wide geographic area and many different ethnic communities. The complexity of everyday experience and interaction across such cultural worlds becomes an integral part of Sembene's filmic portrait of the soldier. The Tirailleurs are part of a rich military culture that, as Mann has argued in his examination of the soldiers' lives in his recent book *Native Sons: West African Veterans and France in the Twentieth Century* (2006), extends to the lives of many who were drawn into the periphery of the process of soldiering. This military culture encompassed "African and European women, Tirailleurs's children growing up in the military camps, and civilians with a charitable urge"; the soldiers' pay became an important part of the local economy as the soldiers and their families became increasingly dependent on remittances. When the soldiers were deployed abroad, they often "disappeared" for years at a time, rarely getting leave to return home; their affairs were handled by siblings, a spouse or parent, or even the local commander (Mann 2006, 149–50). But the colonial military culture that the soldiers shared with officers "was charged with racism, paternalism, and occasional violence" (150), and while ideals of reciprocity and mutual obligation animated this cultural world, it was often a contested terrain. With the introduction of conscripts during the war and the displacement of seasoned colonial officers to the front, the texture of this world was placed under great strain and began to slowly break down. In time, soldiers began to object to the paternalism of the French officers and others, demanding equal treatment to that of French soldiers and recompense for the blood debt of military service for veterans and widows.

Although as Mann argues, "the idea of recompense for military service even colonial military service—became naturalized, and continued to be so even during the height of anticolonial political movements," in the wake of the defeat of the 1940s, the sense of mutual obligation to the soldiers was all but suspended (Mann 2006, 189). This is the same moment when soldiers, having shouldered the burden of combat, found able-bodied Frenchmen who sat out the fighting, food shortages, and even a challenge to the special legal status that had exempted them from the *indigénat* codes, applicable to those with the legal status of French subjects (as opposed to citizens) and protecting them from arbitrary local courts, "native jurisdiction, in criminal, civil, and commercial cases" and the shifting powers of nonmilitary justice (115). Indeed, the former soldier "came to occupy a liminal position between citizen and subject" as a result of this and other concessions to those who served the colonial order (201). The exemption in place for former soldiers since 1918 and reconfirmed in 1924 was withdrawn by 1941, amid fears that returning soldiers would not submit to the authority of local commandants and the chiefs in their home areas on return. Coupled with the logistical demands of demobilization, the poor economic conditions following defeat, and the anxiety about legal status, the demobilization of the Second World War was "disastrous," culminating in a dramatic series of rebellions, with the uprising at Thiaroye marking the "climax of the period of rebellion" and certainly the momentary decline of a great military cultural tradition (109).

The relationship between a Senegalese solider and African American soldier in the context of the demobilization of a Senegalese regiment at the close of the Second World War throws into relief the powerful forces that have separated and brought together these communities over the course of time. From the complexities of enslavement through European expansion, colonialism, and a world war, the creation of the African diaspora—brought to account as the men face one another—defines a rich pathway to the exploration of relations between Africans and the African diaspora. Sembene brings these figures from the African diaspora as a way of opening up this wider discussion of what it means to be African in the postcolonial context. The African American actor who plays the part of the black American in the film was told by Sembene when he arrived for the shooting, "You arrived on a plane but your ancestors left here on a slave ship" (Sembene 1993, 84). He was taken to Gorée Island, the point from which many slaves were taken to the Americas; the actor wept when he toured the building that offered the last views of Africa for so many. When asked why he wept, he told his host that he wept because this was the place from which the slaves departed. Sembene turned to him, saying, "What matters to us is the future" (84). We create stories, Sembene reminds us, to "be rooted in your own history and culture," not to take revenge for the events of the past (84). This concern with the future is one of the most intriguing aspects of the film, which was made after a ten-year hiatus. Sembene takes up what I consider the second part of a trilogy that begins with *Black Girl*, continues with *Camp de Thiaroye*, and ends with *Guelwaar*, the bitter disappointments of the war years. Many of the soldiers in the camp were former prisoners of war who had not only experienced the worse of the war but also in some ways the most complex social and cultural exchanges that the conditions of these years had to offer. These complex exchanges took place in the field as they encountered African American soldiers in camps where they were interred with members of the Jewish community and in the informal contact they attained with French families during their residence in Europe. When these men returned from the war, they were no longer the same; their vision of the world was transformed by the humbling posture of the soldier, defeated at times by climatic conditions and subjected to the most extreme circumstances.

The soldiers' isolation during the war placed an extra burden on their families and their home communities. Sembene treats both the nature of this hardship and the resistance to forced extraction of crops in *Emitai* (1971), in which the Diola women of the Casamance come into direct conflict with the colonial army as they resist the provision of food to a repressive colonial regime (Murphy 2001). As Sergeant-Major Diatta, the noncommissioned officer of *Camp de Thiaroye*, returns from the war to meet his family at the docks, he learns of a massacre in his village, Diola. Historian Timothy H. Parsons in *The African Rank-and-File: Social Implications of Colonial Military Service in the King's African Rifles, 1902–1964* (1999) documents a complex network of family relations and a comprehensive "military family policy," gradually moving from the informal arrangement of the families themselves to a full-blown policy encouraging the establishment of a stable family life for the soldiers in the King's African Rifles after the Second World War. The incorporation of the family in the military ideology in part ensured the making of future soldiers; as early as 1957, African youth could follow "a four-year program that combined military training with a conventional secondary school education" (Parsons 1999, 156). In the French system, educational opportunities gradually opened up for military training, finally leading to entrance of the children of ex-colonial officers to modified officer training centers in the metropole (Echenberg 1991). While the French organized official army brothels (Bordels Mobiles de Campagne), the British left "military prostitution" and concerns with the health problems associated with them to their "field officers" (Parsons 1999, 163). In *Camp de Thiaroye* we find Diatta, a noncommissioned officer of the Tirailleurs Sénégalais, entering a brothel in Dakar set up for American soldiers, among other clients; when it is discovered that he is a colonial, he is thrown out of the house. He protests, saying that he has only come in to get a drink. As he leaves, he is picked up by a black sergeant of the American military police, who thinks that he is a soldier away from his post without permission. The case of mistaken identity sets into sharp focus not only the privilege entailed in the new form of American imperialism, but also that the "colonial soldier is out of place in his own country" (Young 2001). Old forms of racism and social exclusion remain unchanged; Diatta's attempts to find a place in the new social order fail in part because he is no longer a person of the old empire but a person in transition to a new order, one yet unrecognized by those around him. He is not, as Marcia Landy claims, living on the margins or "the in-between of two cultures, unable to return to the past, fantasizing a future that is impossible under colonialism" (1996, 45). Diatta is also already living in another, distinct reality, prefigured at times by his connection to a diasporic imaginary, as in the encounter with the American soldier. Diatta is already familiar with the music and cultural life of African Americans; he is aware and a part of the diversity of the West African troops; his own cultural background and local language remain in his grasp; he is not a figure alienated from his past, but rather one who seems to possess the attributes of a person able to live in an emergent future. To put it another way, Diatta is learning to live beyond the classificatory structures that have bound him; culture, diversity, difference, and knowledge work as the liberating elements of this new field of vision of being. The colonial frame is ending, and Diatta has already shifted to take in elements of the emergent new frame of political reference: independence and the dominance of the Americans and the world that must emerge after the war. Sembene reminds us of the pantomime of colonialism at the end of the Second World War; as the regimes stood in virtual ruins, the colonial officers and the fragments of the conservative military apparatus that had remained in place as the war raged on were taking their last gasp. Diatta has an episodic vision of this new world, while some are still confined to the dream that was colonialism. It is the scope of the cultural world that Sergeant-Major Diatta envisions that sets him off, relating easily to the collective world of the rank-and-file soldiers and acting as their intermediary at times. He is the classical man apart—the kind of soldier that the French administration feared. Yet Sembene also demonstrates that in the end, Diatta must follow the lead of others and relinquish his claim to becoming French. His friend Captain Raymond has an interest in the world that the soldiers have come from, and though his opportunity to explore these complexities has come too late, he begins to extend the rudiments of reciprocity that signal a glimmer of hope, perhaps for both men, leaving open the possibility of a post-war association. Captain Raymond, however, is a product of the colonial world, and the trace of paternalism haunts his understanding of what is taking place before his eyes; he cannot envision an independent Africa and perhaps only vaguely a world without the *indigène*, or subject.

Although families did not accompany soldiers to the front, the relationship between wives and families in the villages in *Camp de Thiaroye* is represented not only as a kind of African space bordered by the barbed-wire prison camp–like structure of the demobilization center, but as a point of longing for the men of the camp, as if Africa begins in the villages. Working with archival sources and interviews of former colonial soldiers and many of the women who lived the military life of the soldier family, Parsons uncovered a fascinating world of formal and what he calls "unsanctioned" relationships; the latter formed a part of the complex and varied associations with women in the field. Wives and children—often as early as 1899—accompanied men to the field, as there was no "day care," and some soldiers even were found to be moonlighting as day-care providers on duty, in a case of a wife who was ill (Parsons 1999). From the point of view of the army, the family impeded the military's operational capacity: "The early colonial forces made no distinction between peacetime and active service and were often weighed down by the wives and children of African servicemen" (158). In one field report of the period cited by Parsons, a military functionary complained that at times there were more members of the families present in an encampment then there were soldiers. The report continues, "Companies cannot move anywhere without leaving an appreciable proportion of [their] strength to guard women and children"; in the case of active campaigns, the families had to be abandoned while the troops attended to military matters (158). Even after the practice was discouraged and men were cautioned to remain celibate during field activities, soldiers participating in "some support units found ways to continue to meet their wives clandestinely." With the discouraging of this practice, two worlds collided, as the image of an isolated independent male does not reconcile itself with the African system of social relations, which cannot be suspended or separated from an integral social and cultural world quite in the manner that the European system desired (158). During periods of active service, soldiers engaged in a host of arrangements with local women; during the war in Europe, periods of inactivity or early periods in which soldiers might receive education benefits in the colonial capital provided opportunities for contact with potential local partners. The difficulty that soldiers faced returning home with a European wife is a theme that comes up often in the fiction and films of Sembene, such as when Sergeant-Major Diatta, who has a French wife and child, comes into conflict with his own family, who have selected a potential wife for him in his absence.

The returning soldiers represented in *Camp de Thiaroye* would have been given priority for repatriation, as they were former prisoners of war. During 1944, the limited number of troop ships lead to tensions among the troops waiting to be sent home. There were "near mutinies aboard ships taking groups of prisoners home"; military authorities were so desperate to remove "the African troops from French soil" that some troops were sent to Liverpool on British ships to await transport to West Africa (Lawler 1992, 194). Concentrations of the soldiers were surveyed carefully for any sign of disruption as they were quickly dispatched from urban centers to demobilization camps:

> As early as November 1944, Colonial Minister Pleven ordered Governor-General Cournarie to move the returning tirailleurs out of Dakar as rapidly as possible. "The prisoners of war," he warned "may be a factor in stirring up discontent among the people, especially around Dakar where there are so many of them." Thus, in the camps in the AOF [Afrique Occidentale Française] as in those in France, thousands of Tirailleurs

Sénégalais, with little to keep them interested or occupied,
idle and bored, conscious that they had lost their value as
combatants, became increasingly resentful, restless, and prone to
mutiny. That at Thiaroye near Dakar was only the most serious of
many incidents. (Lawler 1992, 194)

Many of the soldiers understood that they were to receive back pay, bonuses, and even a demobilization allowance. When wages were in fact paid, the exchange between French and West African francs considerably reduced the final amount. The information that soldiers received from their officers in Europe, Nancy Ellen Lawler notes, often differed from that given in the camps, where many were told that they would receive additional pay when they returned to their home districts (Lawler 1992). At the end of the war, these soldiers had neither pensions nor citizenship, and they were to find that the forced labor and impoverished conditions of the war years had further threatened the lives of those they left behind in their native villages.

The first generation to see the homeland of the French fighting side by side with soldiers from diverse national origins and finally interned with Jewish and other prisoners of war, the Tirailleurs—transformed by all these experiences—brought home a new spirit and new confidence. Aoussi Eba, one of the former Tirailleurs interviewed by Lawler, notes new sentiments present among the returning soldiers:

People wanted the same rights as the French—towards
assimilation. It was after the Second World War—even then.
There was a slogan everywhere—Africa for Africans. Everywhere
you heard it. We thought then that that was good. . . . I was a
sergeant then. We heard that slogan everywhere—in the bars—
everywhere. After the war, emancipation was simple. There was
a new spirit of emancipation. The tirailleurs returned with that
spirit. After all, it was inappropriate—the kind of life we lived
here—with the whip over us. (Lawler 1992, 15)

The role of the ancient combatants was that of liberator to the old order of the empire. The soldiers were aware of their contribution and began to demand equal treatment.

In one scene in the film, Captain Raymond—who has served at close quarters with the Tirailleurs—and Sergeant-Major Diatta, both men who seem to share a common interest in the welfare of the soldiers, stroll out to the periphery of the camp to talk. They stand before a great baobab: that ancient and majestic tree that would become the symbol of the new nation. This zone, an intermediary space between the camp proper and the village, marked only by the great trees that dwarf the soldiers, seems to constitute a kind of transitional space between empire and the ultimate break with France that looms in the horizon. In many ways, a new Africa begins in this space; it is where notions of the future can be discussed freely, and it leads to the surrounding villages, where a normal life awaits the soldiers awaiting demobilization. The "intimate bond" with the landscape is an intricate part of the manner in which a tree, a plain, or some other feature is transformed through folklore and social practice into a symbol that represents the dreams and aspirations of a community (Benvenisti 2000, 256). In this way, a landscape may be endowed with a kind of national or ethnic identity. In *Camp de Thiaroye*, the landscape takes on this sacred quality, as the very earth is claimed as "native." In one scene shortly after the regiment arrives in the camp, Pays—a soldier deeply affected by his internment in Buchenwald—walks up to the barbed-wire fence and looks longingly at the surrounding terrain. Corporal Diatta, his comrade, approaches, reaches down, takes up a handful of earth, lets it fall bit by bit over Pays's outstretched hands, and assures him, "This is African soil. . . . It's not Buchenwald." Yet the soldier's confinement tells a different tale.

In another scene, Muslim soldiers are seen sacrificing a goat in preparation for their meals, essentially beginning the daily ceremonies entailed in making a kind of sacred space—a place that is both ritually and practically their own. Such boundaries as the barbed wire of the camps, the military uniforms, and the discipline of the soldiers, we are reminded in the film, cannot eradicate the cultural, religious, and ethnic richness of the men or sever their connection to worlds that encompass the mundane temporality of the soldiering life. Neither the past nor the present can be confined any longer by the colonial powers represented in the film or by the rag-tag military command, more concerned with the ceremony of empire than the developments of Senegalese social or political consciousness. Such a disjunction with developing circumstances is readily seen in the manner in which the dissidents and even Captain Raymond are labeled "communist," calling attention to the disarray of French political ideology of the period; no longer "fascist," the conservative military officers cling to the idea of empire with no real conviction or no clear ideals representing the emergent political situation and rely on their discipline as if awaiting orders specifying what form the new France will take. At a loss to explain the new assertiveness of the soldiers, they respond to their lack of control by resorting to violence. They become trapped in their own transition camp.

In a sense, Sembene opens a world in which the nation of France is weak, perhaps too weak to hold on to its empire, even as the powerful outlines of an overarching world power represented by the Americans come into view.[5] It operates in the background. Captain Raymond tells his fellow officers as his regiment files off the ship in the Dakar harbor, that if it were not for the Americans, his men would have come home in rags—indirectly referring to the French economic crisis of this period. The colonial era was in fact drawing to an end, as a new form of power was coming into place. The economic and political structures that would come together to rebuild Europe at the end of the war would in turn facilitate the building of the French zone. Many West African economies would be linked directly to the French national central bank, guaranteeing economies and setting the terms of trade within its sphere of influence. The entrance of multinational funding organizations that in the end would manage the fortunes of emergent African nations long after the colonial world faded is foreshadowed by the presence of the American in the film and the poverty of the French during this period. Neocolonialism, in short, was in a sense already taking form in the period that Sembene presents us with in *Camp de Thiaroye*. The clarity of national narratives and the clear-cut trajectories of the historical record are called into question, as the experience of the soldiers and the contribution that they made to the war effort complicates the French narrative of liberation. The silences of both the colonial regime and the Independence generation and subsequent contemporary Senegalese governments on the status of the soldiers in official histories of the period remains unresolved, and government officials continue to shy away from sending representatives to the grave site of the fallen soldiers at Thiaroye (Murphy 2000). As Marcia Landy notes in her discussion of the film in *Cinematic Uses of the Past*, the film runs against the grain of official histories, drawing on the registers of oral history, official discourse (colonial), "mythic, and literary allusions, cinema history, folklore and common sense," presenting a tale that follows a style that becomes at once "fragmentary and episodic" and creating a new terrain or genealogy for the present (Landy 1996, 53).

The labor dispute of the soldiers in turn casts a shadow on the position of the emergent African nations, which, fearing the political strength of the returning soldiers, would selectively marginalize them in the future. The soldier is subject to a kind of historical erasure on two fronts, disappearing once as a soldier whose individuality may be read from the mass of other soldiers and again as a mass or collective force, unified in the act of rejecting the degradation and humiliation of the camps and demanding the right to a wage earned during internment in the work camps. Sembene carefully crafts both aspects of the soldiers' experience through the noncommissioned officer Diatta and the comrades who take matters into their own hands, at one point taking the commanding officer of the French West African forces into custody.

The film documents conditions in 1944 in a French transit camp in which African veterans struggle to receive the severance pay promised by the French command. The mutiny of the soldiers and the French attack on the camp, marked by the dark and solemn tonality of the film, clouds the historical record of the events with this act of violence, out of step with the changing power relations during this period. As even the opening scene clearly demonstrates, a new neocolonial power has emerged as the allied nations set pace for the new era; the Americans navigate the world, sure of themselves and their ability to command. The French officers cower in their quarters and officers' club, hoping against hope that they can once again establish the proper respect for the colonial order among the black troops, whose loyalty they can no longer be assured of. In the end, the attack on the unarmed men in the middle of the night is an act of cowardice, revealing the moral bankruptcy of the failing colonial order. An American officer says to the French officers in charge, in one scene near the end of the film, in effect "You have lost your empire here" (in Senegal).

Provisioned with American uniforms, one of the African veterans is mistaken for an African American soldier, setting up a subtext of mistaken identities, perhaps through which comparisons of the impact of French imperialism and American racial inequalities during the period may be made. The encounter of the Tirailleur and the American soldier is one of the most fascinating moments of African cinema as the diaspora is in a sense taken account of, and this encounter opens a dialogue about the nature of blackness in the military. The Tirailleur is much more educated and knowledgeable about the life of the American soldier, following jazz and some American authors; the American soldier seems unsure of himself and at a loss about what to say and how to approach this historic encounter. Sembene's challenge may be to understand what these parties have to say to one another; we must begin to explore the terrain that has brought about this meeting in the first place. While the soldiers of the camp held the commanding officer of the French forces in protest of their comrade in arms being kidnapped by the Americans, the French seem doubly weakened, at once threatened by the Americans and held at the mercy of French colonial soldiers. The strike against the camp underscores a momentary loss of judgment in the wake of this humiliation. The reaction is overly severe, as the French—fearing a more widespread uprising—crush the disturbance before it leads to more serious problems. Yet this type of uprising was still to reverberate through the West African community like a shock wave. Such use of violence under the command of De Gaulle merely revealed the continuity of French domination; some insisted that from the world of Pétain to the France of De Gaulle little had changed in the colonial system that helped to determine the relationship between black soldiers and white officers.

Camp life reveals the interplay of fluid identities, as diverse understandings drawn from the different cultural and social backgrounds of the men meet in the camps. There is a parallel historical process unfolding in the camps, or—to put it another way—an alternative historicity follows the soldiers and their superiors in the film. The languages of the camp encompass the diversity of the soldiers selected from the many points of West Africa, each seasoning the life of the camp with its own indigenous language and cultural traditions. Petite French became the common language of the soldiers and the French of the "official culture" hovered in a kind of elite and separate world, with each group bridging the gap through key intermediaries and translators. Then there is the silence of one of the returning soldier, Pays; once an inmate, like many others, of Buchenwald, he is not convinced that he is not still interned in the camps of the Germans. His trauma and that of his colleague never reaches the level of discourse, and is in the film set against the disturbing images of the camps that float in the memories of the men and perhaps are even embodied in a kind of a *habitus* of former prisoners.

The world of the returning soldiers is fluid and at first full of anticipation of returning to their villages. This posture is juxtaposed against the fixed and inflexible regime of the camp commanders. The complex negotiations of diverse cultural and religious traditions are also worked out by the men of the camp, who acknowledge these differences and at times even enjoy interactions with members of different communities. Two colonial regimes come face to face in the camps, as the defenders of an occupied France encounter the French officers who have fought alongside the black troops in Europe, while their counterparts uphold a now-outdated vision of the nation. The colonial world is now incorporated into the structures of power of the New France and not abandoned by it. The officers sympathetic to the Vichy regime enjoy their domain of authority and refuse to relinquish it to the outsider Captain Raymond, who accompanies the colonial troops home to Senegal. In the end, Raymond must succumb to the pressure from the right to defend the empire; in a curious way, the good captain is trapped in a part of a frame that can no longer contain his attachment to the Tirailleurs and reconcile it with the battle between an emergent and independent African and the colonial order. Out of place in Africa and losing ground at "home," Captain Raymond relies on his duty, abandoning the rest.

Early in the film, Sergeant-Major Diatta's aunt and cousin Bintum bring him palm wine from their village of Effok that he passes on to the men when they complain of the food in the camp. The men are sustained once again by African food; refusing to eat the rations they are given, they go to the village and bring back a sheep that is ritually killed by the Marabout. The link to the village and to the Africa they have left behind is critical to their own process of demobilization, which step by step they take into their own hands. Over the course of the film, we see Sembene's focus on the collective emerge as a dominant theme. The lives of the Tirailleurs as a collective, making decisions and acting in concert, define the day-to-day lives of the men of the camp. In the final scenes, the men have finally overthrown all forms of external authority, placing the camp under their own control and even overthrowing the dominance of the French language with their own common dialect.

They elect representatives other than Sergeant-Major Diatta, who speaks
"French like the whites," as a representative of their the group. In the end,
it is Sergeant-Major Diatta who must join the collective. "We are all just
infantrymen [Tirailleurs]," one of the soldiers declares as they prepare
to take control of the camp. In the final scenes of the film, Sergeant-Major Diatta speaks to Captain Raymond, who comes to attempt a recon-
ciliation with the command of the camp and the soldiers only when he
is given permission by the other men. A conversation early in the film
between the two men, when Sergeant-Major Diatta asks Captain Raymond to take a bag of coffee home to his wife in France on his return,
begins in a much more cordial tone but quickly turns to the issues that
will separate the two soldiers. Though Captain Raymond is convinced
that the new emergent army will correct many of the errors of the past,
Sergeant-Major Diatta has already begun to suspect a greater continuity
between the colonial orders, past and present:

> *Captain Raymond*: Do you know about the conference of
> Brazzaville?[6]
> *Sergeant-Major Diatta*: It would be difficult to forget; you see,
> I draw a parallel between Effok and Oradour-sur-Glanes.
> *Captain Raymond*: You can't make such a comparison. You can't
> compare Nazi barbarism with the excesses of our army. No, it's
> not possible.
> *Sergeant-Major Diatta*: It's a colonial army with the same
> mentality. The officers who in 1940 refused the rallying of
> African forces to the Free French Forces and who shot the
> Senegalese who joined are today there beside the leaders of Free
> France and control the colonies.
> *Captain Raymond*: Don't get carried away. You know the French
> people. You know it's not the same.

The massacre at Effok—the natal village of Sergeant-Major Diatta—in 1942 is here compared with that of Oradour-sur-Glanes, what
became in France emblematic of the murder of the innocent at the
hands of the German S.S. Das Reich division. In Oradour-sur-Glanes, a
small French town, on June 10, 1944, men, women, and children were
drawn into the circle of the war by the German division, augmented
by replacement soldiers forcibly conscripted into their number; when

the day was done over six hundred people of the town lost their lives and the sleepy community was burned to the ground. The rationale for such brutality was that the town might harbor or support fighters of the Resistance, and although Oradour-sur-Glanes became in turn a kind of symbol of French Resistance, it is unclear if the townspeople were actively engaged in the Resistance movement. Clearly, the German troops hoped by means of terror and intimidation, through the showering of violence and brutality on such local communities, to warn those who sought to join the Resistance.

It is the role of Oradour-sur-Glanes as a symbol of the French Resistance, and therefore a part of the symbolic texture of the emergent New France rising from the ashes of the war, that makes the reference of Sergeant-Major Diatta so powerful. As historian Donald M. Reid observes, "Oradour took on a unique status as the embodiment of innocence destroyed by military force" (2003, 4).[7] In turn, Effok plays this same role; for African soldiers and others, it represents a betrayal of the trust of the soldiers and others in France and thus shatters any hope of assimilation. From the moment that Sergeant-Major Diatta learns of this tragedy at the dockside when his relatives greet him, a rupture is created for him between the goals of rejoining his family in France and concluding his studies there and a commitment to a struggle for Africa—a fight not only for the sacrifice of the Tirailleurs lost in Europe, but for the innocents who have fallen at home in Africa. With his own parents killed in 1942 in the Effok massacre while he was away in Europe, he is now a child of the massacre; his village razed, he has no choice but to embrace the idea of an emergent and independent Africa. This interchange between Captain Raymond and Sergeant-Major Diatta is one of the most important in the film, as this emergent world of Africa comes most into evidence as the men follow diametrically opposed trajectories. Captain Raymond returns to France with a new regiment of Tirailleurs and Sergeant-Major Diatta represents the initial contours of an independent Africa. In one of the great ironies of these years, however, the so-called communist faction critical to the liberation of France is represented in part by Captain Raymond. His progressive ideas and overly friendly attitude toward the black troops mark him as an outsider and present the viewer with another dimension of betrayal. As British historian Richard D. E. Burton suggests in his book *Blood in the City: Violence and Revelation in Paris 1789–1945*, communist sections were systematically crushed by the surgical seizure of power of the forces of De Gaulle moving in to secure Paris ahead of the Allied forces (Burton 2001). Captain Raymond is complicit to some measure with the very forces that will wipe away the very vision of France that he struggles to uphold. Later, when the men stage a protest over their back wages and other benefits promised to them, Captain Raymond offers to mediate the crisis, hoping to calm the men by appealing to his superiors in France:

> *Sergeant-Major Diatta*: Since Morlaix the officers have been lying. Are there two rules in the army, one for blacks and one for whites?
> *Captain Raymond*: I don't like the way you speak.
> *Sergeant-Major Diatta*: And how should I speak? Or rather I must not speak. I must shut up and condone injustice.
> *Captain Raymond*: You can call the Governor. I will tell him your grievances. I will see the Colonial Minister in Paris.
> *Sergeant-Major Diatta*: Have you become the Good Samaritan or the Saint-Bernard of the Vichyists? A right is neither discussed nor negotiated. We're back from Europe, where we fought your enemies. Now we fight for Africa.

Indeed, the officials of the Vichy regime (1940–1942), its representatives in the colonies, and later the Gaullists, failed to fulfill their commitment to the Tirailleurs, and the repressive measures of free France held little promise of an amelioration of conditions. Sergeant-Major Diatta turns to the assembled officers, representing the collaborationist left behind when the Tirailleurs had been called into the war:

> *Sergeant-Major Diatta*: Major, you insult the soldiers who fought all the battles. . . . They belonged to the first army of Free France, which went from Fort Lamy, across the Tibesti, and chased Mussolini's soldiers at Kuffarin Southern Libya. They were the first to enter Tripoli and they were the first to enter Paris in August 1944. . . . Where were you in 1940, in 1939 to 1940?

The French West African forces formed the basis of General Leclerc's raids against the Italians in North Africa in 1940–1941; with the Free French Army, they were a part of the Allied invasion of Italy in 1943,

reached Tripoli in 1943, and engaged in campaigns in Provence in August
1944. This "battle-hardened" force was then relieved of their duties and
sent back to Africa (Echenberg 1991, 98–99). De Gaulle ordered the
black African troops home to "whiten" the French forces replacing them
with fresh young Frenchmen, "that young Frenchmen be given a taste
of victory, a share in the Allied success in riding France of its shame
and humiliation" (99). The so-called whitening (*blanchissement*) of the
forces was so successful that the Allies to some degree underestimated
the French reliance on black African troops in the liberation of France
(Echenberg 1991). Some soldiers, Echenberg suggests, were almost taken
by surprise with the abrupt transition:

> Literally without warning, serving black African soldiers were
> relieved of their front-line positions, of their arms, and even of
> the uniforms they were wearing, and were sent back to the south
> to spend the winter waiting for ships to take them back to Africa.
> (Echenberg 1991, 99)

Not only were the "battle-hardened" soldiers taken out of their front-
line positions, but they then waited in camps for return passage home.
The early scenes of *Camp de Thiaroye* shadow this process and emphasize the unbridgeable gap between colonial subject and French citizens:

> Unlike the French soldiers, who were quickly issued back pay
> and were discharged, the Africans languished in camps because
> shipping space proved difficult to obtain. . . . African soldiers,
> numbering in the thousands, had quite rational grounds for
> resenting the shabby and discriminatory treatment they received
> in the fall of 1944. (Echenberg 1991, 98)

Camp de Thiaroye was merely one of the many protests and labor conflicts that initiated a period of the disillusion of empire.

Through a politics of representation, the film challenges the European
and American histories that have obscured the linkages between American racial segregation and exclusion during the war years and the colonial incorporation of the Senegalese into France, marking the beginnings
of contemporary African migrations to Europe. This meeting of soldiers questions the meanings of African diaspora and its history in the
making of the West. The film also poses the problem of reading one

history against another: that of Africans and African Americans and that of a West differentiated by individuated national histories. But the soldiers also for the first time meet members of the Jewish diaspora, ordinary French people, and comrades in battle and in the camps. The film presents the crossroads of navigation and challenges us to disambiguate the many strains of the narrative through space and time.

CHAPTER 7

Travel Warnings
Observations of Voyages Real and Imagined

> Voyagers, navigators, and travelers of all sorts were enjoined to
> record the movement of the compass needle from true north
> along with the longitude and latitude of the observation; to
> observe the inclination of the dipping needle; to note the ebbs
> and flows of the tides with their times and heights; to sketch
> plans of coasts, recording promontories, rocks, and shoals, with
> bearings and soundings. The observant mariner should also note
> the character of the ocean's bottom; changes of wind and weather
> at all hours (especially trade hurricanes, waterspouts, and the
> latitudes and longitudes where the trade winds begin change,
> and cease); unusual meteors; lightning and thunders; and the
> salinity of the sea at various depths, temperatures, and places.
>
> —ERIC J. LEED, *THE MIND OF THE TRAVELER:*
> *FROM GILGAMESH TO GLOBAL TOURISM*

The early lists of the traveler developed into guidebooks and finally
travel reports, a record of the detailed observations of the traveler. All
of this was organized into the form of a journal from the Renaissance
on, crafting what was to become a highly ritualized form of knowledge
through which the world was appropriated as information about an elsewhere (Leed 1991, 188). A new focus on factual accounting left fantastical tales in the past as a new, scientific genre came into vogue. These
reports were in a sense a bridge from the self to the observable world—
a link to the myth of objectivity through which the self was cleansed
in the light of reason and experience-based knowledge, thought to be √
universal. The report was shaped by the scientific rationale of the times,

sketching out a kind of narrative order, a set of conventions guiding the discursive meandering of the traveler. According to Eric J. Leed, writers following the recommendations of Baconian style sought to produce a believable report, free of the clutter of scholarly work, in the simplified style and plain spoken cadence of sailor's language. This unaffected prose was to rest on the supports of simplicity in all things, quantification, and the distance of cold fact and experience. Above all, as these recommendations became part of eighteenth-century narrative convention, the author must never become the subject of the text, as a strict distance must be maintained between the world of the observer and the observed. As this document took shape, it facilitated the objectification of other worlds through the development of its particular style:

> The travel report was a peculiar form of literature in which all
> subjectivities were projected outward, into the world, as objects
> to be described, recorded, classified, named, and catalogued.
> The travel report was classically an objectification of a self; that
> is, the materialization of emotions, and the transformation
> into "objectivity" of the stranger's limitations, partialities, and
> ignorance. (Leed 1991, 189)

In the popular register, however, as Mary Louise Pratt points out in *Imperial Eyes: Travel Writing and Transculturation* (1992), survival literature—a more romantic and sensational rendering of the traveler's tale— challenged the authority of "bourgeois" forms. Literature of "first-person stories of shipwrecks, castaways, mutinies, abandonments," and other experiences of displacement was circulated as inexpensive pamphlets and collections (Pratt 1992, 86). Such literature provided an imagined space that brought diverse societies within the contact zone into relationships in the safety of a distant realm—an order removed from the constraints and the normalcy of home. This popular register, embraced for its representation of an exotic elsewhere and as entertainment, no doubt also helped to formulate a vision of this distant and other world:

> Throughout the history of early Eurocolonialism and the slave
> trade, survival literature furnished a "safe" context for staging
> alternate, relativizing, and taboo configurations of intercultural
> contact: Europeans enslaved by non-Europeans, Europeans
> assimilating to non-European societies, and Europeans

confounding new transracial social orders. The context of
survival literature was "safe" for transgressive plots, since the
very existence of a text presupposed the imperially correct
outcome: the survivor survived, and sought reintegration into
the home society. (Pratt 1992, 87)

Ethnographic writing is, in a sense, a kind of inheritance of both
of these literary traditions, embracing an idea of humanity writ large:
humanity's "cultural accounts" have, willingly or not, painted a portrait
of the preoccupations of ordinary people striving to satisfy the demands
of an erstwhile scientific conceit through the curiosity of diverse times.
Challenges to anthropological reportage along the way have called into
question the practice itself: the pretense of setting up a Western cultural
reference point as the universal arbiter of any sort of information (Clifford
1997). As an anthropologist, I have often wondered, in the corridors of
hotels hosting Anthropological Association meetings, at receptions after
held for an invited speaker in Macaulay Hall at Johns Hopkins, or in the
privacy of my home talking to friends collected on the rare occasions
that we find ourselves in the same city: what about the things anthropologists refuse to write about? The surplus value of all those "field trips"
is that information is often ritualized, as in stories of Victor Turner performing Ndembu dances at parties or E. Evans-Pritchard at the pub, but
what about the things that just could not be written about because the
friend, the investigator, could find no legitimate role to play in the telling of such knowledge? The most telling part of the aftermath of various
kinds of reflexivity in anthropology may in fact be, as Michael Herzfeld
suggests, not those that look deep into the self but rather "the kind that
places the cultural assumptions of the ethnographer in question, that
clarifies the ethnographic encounter and its limitations as predicated
upon the imperfect meshing of two different codes, with its multiplicity
of divergent identities and presuppositions" (2001, 45-46). This examination would be according to Herzfeld truly "empirical," as it would lead
to the intensification of the analysis and not to a kind of "empiricism." I
would like to suggest that anthropologists walk a fine line between the
complexity of the way they come to know and their attempts to disable
conventions of presentation or to reinvent them in order to express what
they feel they must say, can say, or must not talk about until they understand the manner in which to tell the tale.

What follows is not the end of a tale, but rather a new beginning. I wish to explore, however briefly, the nature of the new cultural complexity in Europe and elsewhere and some of the fantastical models of theorists, novelists, and filmmakers that address the problem of arriving at a new kind of more inclusive social pluralism.

The Historic Center

Strolling the arcades of Turin not long ago, crossing the heart of the historic city and winding my way through the crowded streets where I too am a foreigner, I was struck by the hostility I was at times greeted with, even— and this surprised me—by grade-school children. The presence of what Jacques Derrida has called "the foreigner in general" has long succumbed to the commonplace such that a well-defined attitude toward the presence of this other may be articulated with great facility and pronounced deliberateness (Derrida and Dufourmantelle 2000). As often as not, I encounter those who—recognizing this new climate of rejection— make it a point to invoke the ancient art of hospitality. There is little middle ground, as the presence of the migrant community has come in the last decade to define the contours of a renewed sense of what it means to be a part of a national community. The xenophobic dimensions of this "integralism," Douglas Holmes notes, play against the manner in which it acts as a kind of encompassing "consciousness of belonging" (Holmes 2000). As Holmes points out, it is not merely a matter of the expression of xenophobic or racist ideology, but rather an intricate cultural vision, preserving a trace of the past with a militant project for the present. The resistance of this tendency for cultural closure presents, I would argue, the best hope for a social formation in which the new centers of diversity and heterogeneity may be embraced.

Just off the Via Garibaldi in Turin, on my way out to the local Porto Palazzo market, I saw the first graffiti of the then Lega Nord, a right-wing anti-immigrant precursor with contemporary elements of national right-wing political groups. I remember very distinctly the way in which many on the Italian left brushed off the importance of such groups at the time, relying on the time-honored and somewhat peculiar balance of traditional party politics then in force. Few young people can remember with any clarity the political figures of a decade ago, which have since been almost completely replaced by a generation of politicians relatively new to the realm of national leadership, and, for that matter, the political struggles that marked the emergence of Italy into a new corridor of select western European countries with bright economic futures in the emergent global marketplace. Yet the political deployment of such issues as immigration and increasing European cultural diversity in the national discourse provokes lively debates on the local airways, cafés and bars, and corner meeting places. Lamine Sow, a young representative of the Italian General Confederation of Labour (CGIL) trade union organization, notes that the greatest problem faced by migrants is that of social integration. On the job, the culture of work regulates relationships; in the realm of the public migrant workers are subjected to relatively open forms of social exclusion and cultural isolation. Across from the trade union office where Lamine works, scribbled on a wall was an anti-immigrant slogan: "Work to the Italians." Lamine approached one of his superiors and suggested that he intervene; perhaps he could speak with the owners of the business and ask them to at least paint over the sign. Instead, Lamine was asked to speak with the workers of this firm, whose ultimate decision it would be to remove the slogan, implying not only that the graffiti was the property of the workers, but also that somehow it was their right to offend others. The philosophical and ethical rationale for asylum and the hospitality of "open cities" are lost in a present in which impassioned exhortations against the newcomers must no longer be confined to the ragged slogans scribbled on the roadside. Immigration has become more than a mere social crisis in the European imaginary and now vies for the status of the spectacle of an era.

On either side of Via Garibaldi, one moves progressively toward the periphery at one end—the expansive working-class housing projects and the industrial sector—and on the other, the remains of working-class residences dating back to the 1840s; beyond this lies the road to Milan. It is in this center, in the winding *vicoli*, (small streets or paths) that the street is shadowed with a church or a judicial center and perhaps a chic restaurant or an ancient local store. As we walk past the neon-lit storefronts of Via Garibaldi or the damp side streets, navigating the hazards of mopeds and delivery trucks, the taunts of youth give way to the glares of older residents. Any "foreigner" of color knows to keep a sharp eye out for groups of young people, passing cars, and even other groups of newcomers that might make claims to this parcel of urban terrain. I turn over in my mind what anthropological significance that glare might have and then turn to my friend, who pushes me to one side, out of the way of a passing car, and tells me about his cousin coming up from Senegal to work in the same factory that he does, if he can find him a job. His apartment is already full of relatives whom his parents and others back home felt would be better off in Europe under the supervision of their uncle, cousin, or friend's son, who seems to be doing so well there.

The sun pours over the tops of the buildings, but so far below we only feel the summer heat, as the light in these densely packed streets is rendered almost inconsequential. I know these streets—they are familiar to me—but my guide makes them reveal new secrets, as in walking them together we inhabit a stereotype as we pass: blacks in the heart of the historic center of the town. It is here that our presence is most contested, cutting against the grain of historical tradition. "Overdetermined from without" in Fanon's words; we wear our exclusion on our skin (Fanon 1967a, 116). As we pass the glistening storefronts, he again turns to me and says that he is tired of all this and wants to go back home to Senegal. I look up and catch a glance that he has thrown down the street; it falls on the passing Italians, on the scene of trash in the streets, and over the sound of the cars, and, further off, over the loading and unloading of the shops, as activity picks up to resume the afternoon workday. We have spoken of this for more than ten years now—the coming and going, and the difficulty for family, friends, and relatives dying away from home— but in this moment, the weight of this experience somehow reveals its sadness and its disappointment, as if the nature of this struggle just now becomes to hard to hold. He and I both know that it might not be possible for some time to return. I know what he means, though, and fumble for a response, but I end up repeating his words: "You're ready to go back now?" We've come to this point again, and again it's clear that living in diaspora is a state from which there is little escape.[1]

In the contemporary migration of Senegalese and others in Italy, small groups of migrants collect around a core of family, religious affiliates, and friends. The initial communities that formed groups across wide regional, ethnic, and religious affiliations in the early period of the diaspora have given way to smaller groups, organized most often on ties of extended kin and friendship. The hoped-for return of many migrants may come only at the end of a long working life in diaspora, as most would acknowledge that there is little to return to back home.[2] Back home, even some of the extended family members once established in comfortable middle class jobs found themsevles laid off from government and other high-level jobs during the recent Senegalese economic crisis, joining the Senegalese diaspora in Italy through the help of their relatives. Babacar and others were tired of turning on the news and seeing local political activists decry the decline of the city due to the presence of immigrants and calling for the expulsion of the lot. One afternoon in Turin, a small group of Senegalese and I were talking as the local news was playing on a TV in the background; when the story of a local right-wing political figure came on, someone joked that they (Senegalese and other migrants) had in essence made the career of this man, who has benefited from decrying the negative aspects of the migrant presence in the city. "He gets up in Porto Palazzo and gives speeches against the *extra-communitari* (migrants) and the market is filled with nothing but extra-communitari," they note. The point is well taken; it is tragicomic, as the new governmental measures close in on the migrant communities and their families back home, who—not understanding the situation—send cousins, brothers, and sisters into the Italian context, hoping for the best and entrusting the fate of their loved ones to relatives who seem from such a distance to have landed on their feet.

The real state of emergency with regard to immigration may be the one back home, not the national one declared on immigration by three-time Prime Minister Silvio Berlusconi.[3] Porto Palazzo is the hub of buying and selling in the local market, and along the streets that lead up to and away from the market, shops of migrants have sprouted up—at first in a trickle and now lining the intricate patchwork of the streets. It is one of the hubs of the city that has been cast in the local minds and increasingly in national newspapers as one of the northern Italian cities that are exemplary sites of *spaciatori di strada* (drug sellers); indeed, on the side streets, one must be cautious when taking a photograph, lest the Russians, Tunisians, Moroccans, or others think you are working for the police. People have more to fear from the Italians who control that market of drugs—the street drug sellers, say—than from the poor *spaciatori* just trying to make a living. To one side of the piazza, many Senegalese have makeshift shops on the street in front of the warehouse, now run by Chinese merchants. You can buy anything from fine cloth from Africa or

Holland, to Senegalese peanuts, fresh Moroccan bread, to the traditional fruits, vegetables, clothing, handbags, and undergarments from the Italian sellers. The market has a new feeling now, as the streets that lead from it are now lined with shops run by migrants and are filled with the sounds of Arabic, Chinese, and Wolof, to name only a few. It is a kind of cultural ground zero, in an Italian city where this coming together of diverse traditions marks a new currency in what is being learned and taught in these streets among the people assembled; it is the stuff of a new world. This world of the future may leave its imprint in a host of linguistic innovations, or memories of a multicultural hub of businesses, or in the lyric line of some future poet recounting its contours for an audience of her peers in a foreign country years from now, but its presence—hardly acknowledged in official circles—will live on.

When I first learned about the Senegalese community in Turin, I met them in this very market—I was buying towels for my apartment, as my family was coming in the next week, and one of the leaders of the Senegalese and his closest friend were examining the same towels hanging down the sides of the sides of the stall. I accompanied Babacar to the market one day, and while we walked down some winding side streets looking for a mirror for the house of the Senegalese, we talked about family and living in the city and the lack of work back home. When I asked Babacar why he had not held out back home—perhaps letting his wife do some trading—he turned on me quickly, and in a very sharp and angry tone said, "It would be shame for me to stay back home! I have five children . . . what could I do there, sell this African stuff?" He got so upset that he finally began to laugh, realizing that he had given me enough of a jolt to cause me to step back a pace or two. By this time we had found the mirror that was to be installed over the sink in a common room. Now Babacar lives not a stone's throw from the market, in public housing and not a half mile from the bus stop that once took him to work each day—one of the few migrants to have received housing through the local government. Slightly over a decade ago, Senegalese were afraid to cross the ribbon of roads that separates the market and its environs from the rest of the city. But in the market and the area surrounding it, as Mamur (a resident of the Corso Vercelli house of Senegalese) said one night as I was being taken back home after a ceremony, or rather yelled to local police: "We are not afraid of you here!" The officers merely turned and went on their way, to my satisfaction. Mamur liked to joke around, and stood well over six feet, five inches tall. That night he pointed out to me how much of a home this quarter had become.

Now there is no question of it. I spoke to the police detail assigned to the market area in 2002; the unit barracks is actually in Moncalieri. Patrolling suited up in a full complement of flak jackets and other gear, they see the quarter as "one of the most dangerous" areas in the city. Indeed, they must confront newly formed international extortion rings and drug selling, along with the problem of illegal migrants. There is also a new attitude that the streets belong also to the migrant communities that live and work there; there is a kind of comfort here that one does not feel in other parts of the city. Of course, my friends warn me to watch out—that there are flexible territories spanning the realm that might be called "drug corners," much more out in the open than in some American cities. Yet safety is relative; for some migrants, the place seems more accommodating than the city a decade ago, which many feared to cross outside of the safety of numbers, fearing violent attacks by local Turinese Italians.

While Italians are thinking about their new role in the expansive European Union, newcomers like the Senegalese are contemplating what we might call a global theater of operations. Living in diaspora requires an awareness of not only the best ways to live in a given place, but also the presence of mind to contemplate all the possible escape routes to other potential residences, lives, and livelihoods—not only for oneself, but also for the many relatives and friends that find themselves forced to join the diaspora. Indeed, some young people see themselves pursuing their dream of someday traveling to Paris or New York; as one recent migrant to Italy told me, "Since I was a little boy, I have always wanted to go to the United States, but I am the only child of my mother and she didn't want me to go, I was too young . . . and so now I have come here first, and hope that one day I will, in a year or two, go to the Untied States." Italy is seen by many as a way station to other destinations; if not for the migrants themselves, for their children or relatives or even friends, who may find the right set of circumstances to move on to Canada or the United States. Diaspora links sites through familial, ethnic, and religious networks, connecting not only past population movements but those of the future as well.

As the European Union grows larger, seeking perhaps to expand its membership even further, the emergent shape of the new Europe appears to the person on the street somewhat mysterious. There are new security measures and debates over such issues as immigration, labor, and education that have filtered into the national attention in various member nations, igniting cause for concern over the status of such issues in the new constellation. Such anxiety over the uncertain nature of the emergent European Union easily translates into an uneasiness about the prospects of children competing in the new world, where local recommendations and perhaps even educational achievements may be subject to new standards. Reorganization of the university structure in many countries threatens to destabilize the relative autonomy of these institutions. The thought of internal competition for jobs in the new Europe—where, in the absence of borders, qualified applicants can seek employment in any member nation—is another source of anxiety for parents who scramble to enroll their children in English classes and labor under the imponderables of uncertain expectations for their children. Always a kind of "limited good," educational opportunities in the post-Fordist world are clearly one of the only channels to success in the rapidly globalizing world, one in which the command of multiple languages, familiarity with diverse business etiquettes, and the ability to relocate at a moment's notice are adaptive attributes. Living and working in Germany or Sweden, say, and vacationing in Italy in the summer has never been a problem for the many working-class transnational families that have shuttled between work and school, and children have grown up with only a "vacationer's knowledge" of the parents' country of origin. For that matter, it has never been a problem for the globe-trotting elite, whose children have attended schools in the United States or northern Europe, returning home (if at all) with advanced degrees from foreign universities and/or careers abroad. But for those in the middle classes, the present crisis poses the specter of movement within Europe and away from the relative comfort of life in one's own country. It is hard to envision a life for most untouched by the global economy—the speed of business fortunes, the preoccupation of border controls and identification regimes—and for young people without the strong possibility of living elsewhere somewhere down the line. For others, the potential of a harsh working life with few of the benefits of generations past is an increasing reality.

In this setting, the newcomer comes to be seen as just another social encumbrance. A figure associated with the possibility of future displacement, the newcomer carries the kernel of a dialectical relationship that might change everything for the worse. Through the person of the newcomer, an elsewhere comes cascading down on local reality like a meteorite. For the newcomer, this strange new land offers an opportunity to recuperate, even if a generation lost ground back home. One of the great advantages of living in Europe for many migrants is the ability to receive on-the-job training and attend special technical schools where they might learn a trade; more restrictive immigration legislation in Italy now makes this kind of enrichment very difficult, if not impossible, as migrants are essentially granted entrance to the country to perform a specific type of work for a given employer. As Jean-Marie Tshotsha, the late longtime Rwandan activist for migrant groups in Italy, said, "All the migrant is to this country is man power . . . that's all we have become" (2001). The ideological shift to viewing migrants as merely "guest workers" marks an eclipse of the idea of a natural evolution (incorporation) of migrants into European society. In the early nineties, before immigration discourse had fully taken hold of national politics in Italy, it was common for Italians who were migrants from the south of Italy in Turin to identify with the experience of the newcomers. This notion went along with an idea that the newcomers would in time learn to live in Italy and accommodate their lives to the local traditions, pastimes, and Italian way of life.

Many Italians live in quarters that reinforce local solidarity through years of municipal and national neglect, and for a time there was hope that the newcomer who worked in the factory or tended a market stand might become a familiar part of the landscape, a novelty, and a contributor to local gossip—the real glue of community. In the local communities I am most familiar with, residents were keen to point out that the criminal networks were associated with known Italian organized crime and initially saw the newcomer as merely a pawn of these systems. The social representation of the immigrant as criminal has taken many forms, becoming particularly prominent in media representations since the 1990s and complicating many juridical procedures, in which a taken-for-granted ideal type of migrant stands in for information that is difficult to verify (Quassoli 2001). Now, in the same quarters once associated with southern Italian internal migrants, newcomers run shops, restaurants, and market stalls, many frequented by Italians. In the world of labor, migrants have made significant gains in union membership and even local representation through neighborhood associations and other organizations. Yet the representation of detention centers and the myriad boats of would-be migrants cloud the presence of the newcomer.

As Žižek suggests, ideological constructions or prejudices are not often overturned in the preideological level of the everyday. Rather, resistance to the anti-immigrant constructions of the national political discourse and local media at times succumbs to the rising pressure of such negative representations. An ideology really takes hold of us when it has the power to contradict our everyday experience in favor of its stereotype and discursive formation. The friendly encounter with the Senegalese welder or the Tunisian trade union representative in the quarter, the good neighbor, may not be able to contravene the notion that the country is being "overrun" by newcomers. As Žižek notes:

> An ideology is really "holding us" only when we do not feel any
> opposition between it and reality—that is, when the ideology
> succeeds in determining the mode of our everyday experience of
> reality itself.... An ideology really succeeds when even the facts,
> which at first contradict it, start to function as arguments in its
> favor. (Žižek 2002, 49)

The triumph of the center-right in Italy has meant (among other things) that the basic logic informing issues of immigration is increasingly focused on limiting the benefits that newcomers receive from their stay in the national territory. Posed in the neoliberal cultural logic of the day, restrictive measures increasingly circumscribe the stay of the newcomer. Although the state may see migrant workers as the providers of labor power, they are much more than this, as they represent social relations—like living satellites communicating with home compounds, families, and friends across Europe and the world, providing essential knowledge for those forced into navigating a new global economy.

Much of the treatment of strangers falls under what anthropologists have referred to as the cultural practice of hospitality. Hospitality ideology can be seen as the underlying cultural logic informing the creation of such governmental practices as asylum, the passport system, and various humanitarian practices. Moreover, a kind of resentment against violations of hospitality aimed at the newcomers without documents culminated in designs for legislation to prosecute those who assisted them in any way. Equating such acts of hospitality that were accorded to undocumented newcomers with acts of terrorism, a proposed French measure exposed the raw power of the anti-immigrant social movements of the late 1990s. As Jacques Derrida notes, the so-called Pasqua proposal laid bare the policing of the national community:

> Under examination in the parliamentary assemblies, in the
> National Assembly and in the Senate, is a proposal to treat as
> acts of terrorism, or as "participation in a criminal conspiracy,"
> all hospitality accorded to "foreigners" whose "papers are not in
> order," or those simply "without papers." This project, in effect,
> makes even more draconian article 21 of the famous edict of
> 2 November 1945, which had already cited as a "criminal act"
> all help given to foreigners whose papers were not in order.
> Hence, what was a criminal act is now in danger of becoming
> an act of terrorism. (Derrida and Dufourmantelle 2000, 16)

The post-9/11 linkage between control of the borders and the threat of terrorism in the United States has brought the issues of immigration and freedom from the threat of terror together in new ways. A seemingly zero tolerance of illegal immigration and an increasing concern for the efficiency of border patrols along with greater scrutiny of potential residents and tourists has ushered into place a new awareness of security. The U.S. government since 9/11 has pressed the European Union on the implementation of biometric technology in future passports to ensure that tourists and others may be tracked with greater accuracy if necessary, and greater confidence that they are who they claim to be. This shift to "body surveillance" marks an alarming preference for techniques that bypass the narration of identity of human subjects for retinal scans, fingerprints, video imaging, and other ways of reading the subject's body.

More flexible forms of population control seem to be taking shape in restricted regions, as systems of identification for means of public safety become increasingly important to the state's intent of guarding against terrorism. Concerns in the post-9/11 era over the nature of security and the status of the strange has resulted in some cases in a preference for systems of identification over various readings of the undocumented as "illegals." It has become clear to some in the United States that improving identification of resident migrant populations is preferable to having numerous unknown residents adrift among the population. Minimal recognition of the residents employing the Mexican government–issued consular identity card or Matrícula Consular (an identity card used by Mexican officials since the 1870s to identify and keep track of its citizens in the United States) allows a number of previously blocked services to be offered to the card holders. All over the United States, cities, financial institutions, and police departments now accept the matrícula as a means of identification. With the card, migrants can open bank accounts and conduct other business regardless of their immigration status, although some fear (as with any identification system) that the cards are subject to fraud; those who support the relaxation of controls point out that increasing the ability of authorities to identify and serve the migrant community actually may enhance public safety (Swarns 2003). Acceptance of the cards has meant an increase in banking and business activities of the cardholders, who now have access to debit cards. Although estimates of the number of undocumented migrants from Mexico hovers around four million, making this population more identifiable in a security-conscious era may be more important than more rigid and difficult-to-enforce measures such as deportation.

In *Seeing Like a State*, James C. Scott notes that one of the key projects of the modern state was the complete legibility of its population, cities, and state structures. Legibility always implies a position of authority from which the society is read, "a viewer whose place is central and whose view is synoptic," as in the surveillance of cities (Scott 1998, 79). Legibility "amplifies the capacity of the state for discriminating interventions" that may concentrate on the command and control of the internal population or on the policing of borders and the deportation of strangers (79). The strange thing is that in the development of the contemporary state and its keeping of people within certain limits—peasants out of cities and certain categories of worker away from glutted job markets, or a temporary peace orchestrated between ethnic communities in conflict—has been the primary concern. Such systems of internal control of populations include the South African passbook and the strict guidelines for internal movement of the former Soviet Union with its work-book program, and also occur in the United States, where the right of the citizen to free domestic travel actually had to be reaffirmed by the Supreme Court following the deportation of so-called Dust Bowl undesirables during the 1930s (Torpey 2001, 130–31). Following Foucault, one could easily look at the rates of incarceration as another index of population command and control a process through which individuals in effect lose full rights to citizenship. Migrants—sometimes women accused of drug trafficking—often occupy a kind of limbo existence; taken into custody at the border, they wait in prison, serving sentences before their eventual deportation (Angel-Ajani 1999). Surveillance provides the information required for a number of possible interventions; the system of documentation implemented for keeping track of the German Jewish population during the Nazi era was also used to register other Germans so that they might be easily conscripted for the war effort. The obsessive documentation of the presence of Jewish populations in the shadow of the Nazi domination of Europe made prisoners of European Jews, who overnight came under the gaze of a government apparatus that sought to eliminate their very existence. The extent to which Jewish identity had to be "made legible" by the state marks the frailty of such techniques, which can never be seen as neutral. As Scott points out:

A thoroughly legible society eliminates local monopolies of information and creates a kind of national transparency through the uniformity of codes, identities, statistics, regulations, and measures. At the same time it is likely to create new positional advantages for those at the apex who have the knowledge and access to easily decipher the new state-created format. (Scott 1998, 78)

To the newcomer, the state often appears through mysterious agents (state police, health officials, or local government functionaries) and by means of what seems at times a baroque assemblage of documents: documents that enable access, validate identity, and acknowledge the presence of the newcomer among the local population (residence, work, health, identity). The acquisition of this paper profile requires a substantial investment of time, patience, and understanding of the way things work in this symbolic order of the state. Many migrants expressed to me the fear that the texts of the new immigration laws in Europe wished to document their presence only so that it would be easier to deport them.

Indeed, many quiet deportations have followed the form of traditional expulsion procedures, making recourse to representation difficult at best. In Italy, the story, interestingly enough, takes the same form among newcomers and Italians, only its meaning changes—police coming in the night as migrants merely seem to disappear the next day, proof of the practice can be verified in the everyday lives of the migrant community. For some Italians the notion of migrants disappearing in the night is reassuring; for the newcomer it is a matter of fear accompanied by a sense of having no control over ones future. To the newcomer, some arbitrary power hovers in the shadows, confirmed only by such things as the new immigration law (the Bossi-Fini legislation) that doesn't seem to favor migrants. For Italians, there are at least two distinct reactions to the story: some may acknowledge the working of the state to eliminate the worst elements of the immigration crisis, while others entertain fears that things may have at time gone too far, that the image of Italy in the world community may be harmed by harsh treatment of potential migrants. And so it is with so many other nation-states facing global population movements in the post-9/11 universe(s).

In the not-so-distant past, before the first comprehensive legislation dealing with immigration (the Martelli Bill), matters were handled on an *ad hoc* basis; ministries managed migrancy related to labor and aspects of public safety. Some Italian medical doctors even complained of being threatened with censure for treating undocumented workers during the late 1980s, just prior to immigration becoming a seemingly permanent feature of national discourse. For anthropologists, the idea of hospitality not only rests in the realm of ritual practice but is also bounded by the constraints of local cultural traditions. The use of the ritual of hospitality at the national and supranational level has in effect ushered in the symbolic architecture of a new order of the European Union. The curtailment of hospitality, asylum claims, and the granting of official permission of residence to newcomer workers and their families mark the contours of a new world. It is not surprising that new measures may result in the use of biometric smart cards in passports, ensuring that the imaginary body of Europe definitively configures its new imaginary citizens.

The idea of hospitality and the manner in which it is challenged in European political discourse leads one to question the very foundation of contemporary democratic notions of pluralism. In the end, some of the diversity at the gates will become a permanent part of the European social formation; some of what Derrida has called "Europeans, among other things" will live out the rest of their lives in diaspora with all of its entailments (1992, 83). To this extent, perhaps some notion of pluralism and democratic practice at the level of what Deleuze calls "micropolitics"—a constellation of tactics unleashed as collective engagement with politics linked to transformation in the art of the self—must insinuate itself into a new European imaginary (Connolly 2002, 107-11). Micropolitics of this sort involves the kind of shifts in mood and attitude that enable dramatic changes at the level of the macropolitical; such a shift might occur with a shift in political climate, in the wake of a governmental campaign to stem corruption, or in the wake of a particularly devastating brush with ethical or national crisis, as in the post-9/11 transformation of domestic and foreign policy in the United States. Small groups forming alliances with others may also initiate change at the level of micropolitics; such a change took place in Europe at the close of the 1990s as center-left coalitions felt the pressure of a slight right-wing shift in the mood of the population, as issues like immigration, economic austerity measures, and a disaffection with the constellation of ruling parties resulted in the sweeping into power of center-right coalitions that—as in the case of Italy—had little governmental experience and thus were untainted by charges of corruption. In Italy, this changing mood provided the grounds on which to seize upon inquiries of the judiciary into charges of corruption and payoffs in Milan and elsewhere to establish a national accounting in the full-scale breakup of the grip of parties that had been in power since the close of the Second World War. Immigration has been one of the central issues of the political world since the early 1990s and has been amplified by the concern for the control of borders in the European Union.

Perhaps, as William A. Connolly contends, we must look beyond the "pluralism" historically associated with one "democratic" regime or another and interrogate the ethical realm of a deep pluralism irreducible to the national or local spheres (2002, 149-50). The fast pace of the contemporary world and the movement of populations into new and previously unknown contexts presents a crisis of political and ethical engagement with the new global and highly interconnected world. Exploring Kant's notion of cosmopolitanism, Connolly argues that the Kantian understanding of the development of cosmopolitanism is based on an appeal to an idea of the workings of a providential force in history, placing moral action in part beyond the reach of human agency. For Kant, "the fundamental character of morality is not known by conceptual reasoning, it is recognized apodictically," leaving the model of Kantian morality firmly encased in a singular Western cultural logic, unable to "tolerate plural sources of morality" (Connolly 2002, 181). Although Kantian cosmopolitanism might provide one aspect of what might be a "plural matrix" of cosmopolitanism, it cannot set the standard of a universal imperative of ethical conduct (184). The very nature of global changes, Connolly argues, has set into motion a basic interplay of alternative systems of knowledge and sources of morality that demand an opening of an imperial intellectual Western model (183). The late-modern subjectivity to the transformations of pace, capital, and the movement of people and ideas have disintegrated discrete bounded units, so that people live in a newly defined normalcy in which multiple paths to morality present themselves, presenting the potential for a new kind of ethical practice through the formation of alliances across borders, class divisions, and the complications of race and gender. The condition of the era is relative—every position being equal—but provides the grounds for a negotiated common ground through dialogue:

> The late-modern compression of global distance, the tightening
> of global interdependencies and inequalities, the accentuation
> of diversity on politically organized territories and the
> multiplication of global danger through the acceleration of
> speed in military delivery systems, communication networks,
> production processes, commercial activity, cross-territorial
> migrations, refugee movements, tourism, disease transmission,
> criminal networks, ecological effects, drug trade, interstate
> social movements, nuclear danger, and climatic change.
> (Connolly 2002, 183)

In such a world, we must be cognizant not only of the concentric imaginary circles that connect one polity to another, however we imagine them to be, but also of what Connolly calls the "eccentric connection" sites of potential engagement between diverse groups and perspectives, utilizing the "speed" of global connection to attain unique alliances and ignite emergent political fields (2002, 185).

In search of a "deep pluralism nourished by a generous ethos of engagement," a kind of achieved state of belonging, persons and groups with divergent points of view might find a potential common ground (Connolly 2002, 129). For Connolly, deep pluralism "forms the lifeblood of democratic politics by folding creativity and generosity into intracultural negotiations over issues unsusceptible to settlement through preexisting procedure, principle, or interest aggregation alone"; such frontiers reveal the contemporary terrain of the practice of democratic tradition (137). Such a "deep, ethos of multidimensional pluralism" would pivot on the notion of acceptable dimensions of the process of "comparative contestability," through which different points of view supported by alternative "final sources of morality" would be open to discussion, while accepted as the limits of identity and "community" integrity (184). In the spirit of deep pluralism, "dialogue and debate across cultures, theories, perspectives" would be encouraged (199, 214–15), culminating in "a plural matrix grounded in respect for diverse responses to persisting mysteries of being" as a preferred outcome (200–1). The cultivation of a "deep pluralism" is perhaps our best hope as we face not only the most orchestrated closure of social formations in Europe and elsewhere, but also the peculiar opening to what we imagine to be societies that share common traditions and a more or less integrated historical trajectory.

The limits of utopian visions of social harmony are balanced by the William Blake-like (1757–1827) immensity of thoughts of the underside of modernity. Modernity gone mad is depicted not only in the world of literature, but also in the philosophizing of social theorists, which contain depictions of a world ruled by the logic of efficiency and surveillance and by an obsessive preoccupation with the health of the population or the integrity and nostalgia of "community." Taking a step back, we must note that we are perhaps—as Giambattista Vico warned—captured by the view of our own times, of a present that succumbs so effortlessly to our own conceptions of it that the principles underlying their construction are lost to us. In some manner, as I have suggested, social theory is always searching for this present, the present of "our times," in order to awaken us from our social, cultural, and historical distancing and perhaps to alert us to the dangers of our course. Indeed, the operative metaphor of the journey of navigation is highlighted in our search for this present.

The Currency of Identity

Modernity cast in the light of many social theorist has contained a host of warnings concerning the unfolding logic of capital, bureaucracy, ideological constructions, and the perversions of emergent forms of power, such as in the works of Marx, Weber, Althusser, and Foucault, respectively. The echo of these preoccupations can be found in Andrew Niccol's haunting film *Gattaca* (1997), deeply colored by the sharp, other-worldly photographic economy of cinematographer Slawomir Idziak. Pushing the logic of inclusion and exclusion forward through the practice of a genetic engineering reminiscent of scientific racism, the film reveals a world dominated by the planned architecture of human society. Employment opportunities are distributed according to the proper genetic profile. Those unsuited to higher pursuits are selected and marked at birth as "invalids." Others are in essence designed from birth, weeding out every genetic imperfection so that future genes will conform to an ideal genetically orchestrated world. In the futuristic world of *Gattaca*, an invalid that aspires to join the aerospace program, Vincent Freeman (Ethan Hawke), must impersonate a genetic superior. He essentially must purchase the genetic profile of Jerome Morrow (Jude Law), who—paralyzed in an accident—agrees to provide all the aspects that an advanced biometrics regime might use to validate identity, including hair samples, fingerprints, blood, and urine specimens, along with particles of skin that will help Vincent appear to be a fit applicant to the program.

This is a chilling portrait of the manner in which intolerance can become a routine medical procedure, relegating those who have not been designated genetically acceptable to the lower reaches of society, inaugurating and naturalizing discrimination. In the genre of science fiction, biometrics marks the body as a site of surveillance and control that has perhaps gone beyond a reasonable quest for the validation of identity and the safety of a given social community. Our contemporary methods of policing national territories have given way to once again locating the preferred technical practice of identification in the body through biometrics. Admittance to the space labs of the Gattaca Corporation in the film was controlled by the sampling of a speck of blood of each entrant; now, through biometrics fingerprinting, retinal scans, and other methods incorporated into passports by means of smart cards, we may see the merging of fiction and reality (Lyon 2000; Fuller 2003). The peculiar feature of this process is that in a penchant for surveillance of the human subject, what has made the individual recognizable—a brush with a particular history, the lingering attributes of place, the sonic identification accorded to a natal region, that is, things that until now have carried the assurance of identity—will be completely effaced in lieu of markings that—like the brands of North American slave—make no room for recourse to the person for verification.

David Lyon says of this reliance on body surveillance, "Autobiography and social webs of identities are diminished if not discounted in such body surveillance identification regimes" (2000, 307). The incorporation of biometric devices into the emergent European passport may delineate a new kind of crime, increasingly important to the legibility of states and the protection of international frontiers but dangerously preoccupied with what Foucault has called a "permanent lexicon of crime and punishment" (1977, 111). The greater care taken with the verification of identity relegates those without legitimate access to valid signifiers of identity to the margins not only of the state, but of the global currency in which such identity markers circulate. Identity becomes then a kind of currency that—given the possibility of fraud—may be bought and sold. The currency of identity is a form of symbolic capital differentiated by one's position in the play of values and rates of exchange, so that identities may vary in terms of their value in a given market.

Contemporary relations with Europe are clouded by the legacy of a kind of what Frederick Cooper has called a "refusal of responsibility" at the very dawn of the end of the run of the great European colonial empires, and acutely articulated in policy and colonial practice by the middle of the 1950s (Cooper 2002, 80). The French colonial world began to devolve power to the semiautonomous individual territories (Dahomey, Senegal, Niger, Gabon) in French West and equatorial Africa units previously linked only through imperialism, French tradition, and legislature, thus attenuating not only the overarching links between these territories but also every manner of cost for the metropole (80). Failing to mold a productive, well-ordered empire in its own image, France and other colonial powers were faced with reworking an empire. Colonial workers sought parity with metropolitan workers, and trade union groups dreamed of the long-term benefits of the work world; in addition to citizenship, it became clear that such a world might exhaust some of the resources of the colonial order:

> Colonialism on the cheap was no longer possible; the investments of the development years were not rapidly paying off, and the social costs were escalating. The Africa that colonial officials had fantasized creating was not to be. They faced the difficulties of ruling Africa as it was. (Cooper 2002, 77)

The logic of incorporation was faltering as it became clear that the journey to full citizenship could never be completed for the vast majority of Africans. As Frederick Cooper notes:

> The French government was not only devolving power, but also disavowing the central tenets of its post-war policy and imperial ideology. It was pulling back from the implicit offer that incorporation into the French Union would mean that all imperial citizens could aspire to French standards of living, French levels of social services, and French education. It was conceding something to claims—as much those of Senghor as Sékou Touré—for forms of cultural expression distinct from those of France, but most important it was abdicating responsibility for the material welfare of Africans. This move was softened by the continued provision of aid, but this was now foreign aid, gifts rather than an imperial obligations; and it would be hardened by French political intrigue and military support for Africans it deemed friendly against those it believed acting contrary to its interests. But sovereignty would have its consequences. (Cooper 2002, 80–81)

It is unclear just what the nature of "sovereignty" might mean in the postcolonial context, a circumstance shadowed by the emergent cultural, economic, and political imperialism of such powers as the United States, strategic instruments of global influence like the World Bank and the IMF, and, more recently, confederations of power, markets, and investment opportunities like the European Union.[4]

Europe and European cultures have always occupied a privileged position in anthropological theorizing and in the Western philosophical, historical, and humanistic traditions employed to distinguish the West from the rest of the world (Yengoyan 1997). It is in this terrain and through it that issues of blood, bone, and culture have become the subjects of science, politics, and power. We often recall the armchair anthropologist who was committed to the understanding of distant cultures, not only, as Aram Yengoyan has recently pointed out, from the anthropological perspective, but from a broad range of inquiry—philosophical, theological, and humanistic—in an attempt to capture the breadth of human experience. The breadth of human experience was always exacted with a price, however, leaving immutable divisions and territories of classification across which travel was impossible for vast portions of the world. Such work was often involved in keeping the unique as such, with the distancing of customs and the collection and documentation of the world out there. Once this process turned upon itself—that is, investigated the world of the European—it sought to capture in a totalizing framework the traces of its own past. The complementary nature of these preoccupations with the cultural alien, unique and distant, and with the historical self, culturally near yet mildly exotic, have given us a host of notions that have become a part of our taken-for-granted ways of thinking. The idea of evolution (the application of racial taxonomies based on phenotypical features to the local population and then to others) and the art of measurements (the analysis of the body and skull and now the search for the mystery of genetic traits and material—the final elaboration of the myth of the fingerprint, we might say) find their origins in these strange lands. Such concepts have led us to give a special place in our thinking to ideas like underdevelopment, backwardness, primitiveness, and also to capitalism, community, boundary, and nation. Throughout this cycle runs a preoccupation with identities, with the nature of the world over there, and an at-times-unstated conviction about the way the world is or ought to be here.

Fanon wrote in the *Fact of Blackness* "I am overdetermined from without"; the great weight of the historical construction of race imprisons the "other" in its unfolding logic (Fanon 1968). The "infernal circle," as Fanon calls it, of misrecognition of the "being" of the other must be confronted with an articulation of the self, not mediated by dominant discourse as body, ancestry, or race; given this circumstance, Fanon continued, "there remained only one solution: to make myself known" (115). There is a necessity to provide other forms of representation—to attempt to place knowing on a common ground. As David Harvey has recently noted, "defining the other in an exclusionary and stereotypical way is the first step in self-definition"; perhaps this flurry of meditations on exclusions and definitions marks a new European reflexivity (Harvey 1993, 27).[5]

Now it seems that Europeans can think of nothing else but clearing their towns' walkways and main streets of the troublesome foreigner. To this end, a vast apparatus both formal and informal has been constructed to oversee the dismantling of internal borders, the control of external frontiers, the improvement of cross-border policing, and the establishment of harmonious rules, policies, and procedures of exclusion. The selection of *ad hoc* groups given original briefs on terrorism and drug running to come up with recommendations for dealing with criminal surveillance, asylum seekers, and illegal immigrants gives some indication of the border anxiety that has infected this so-called new Europe.

There is little talk today about the European colonial legacy, despite that fact that entire quarters of many major European cities are now inhabited by former colonial peoples and postcolonial relations are marked by a new isolation and attenuation of the responsibility for the past. France has all but abandoned its classic colonies like Senegal and the former French zone of West and Central Africa, joining with the United States, the IMF, and others to share the burden of the depressed economies of this region. The historical memory is a fragile thing, and time has washed away the notion of the empire once so crucial to the notion of the European, so that the meanings of the European divorced from this particular twist of the nation-state are now not difficult to imagine. The new anxiety has more to do with the integrity of the European, facing the other on its doorstep. It has even been difficult to remember that Senegalese and others have been crucial to the making of European societies. As Derrida has recently noted, it is crucial to the future of European societies to allow for the possibility of being "European, among other things"; such a recognition of the diversity integral to the European may accommodate the drafting of a new European "birth certificate," one more inclusive and forged in the traditions of tolerance, rather than the intolerance that now commands the day (Derrida 1992, 83).

What I have said so far rests on the assurance that we in fact know what we mean when we say "European," that we referred to the same entity in the past of European-ness as we do in the present; the European referent is somehow continuous and unproblematic through time and space. Some years ago, I had a conversation with a researcher from Denmark who was engaged in a project crafted to study the relationship between national health care recipients and health care providers from newcomer backgrounds. It was apparently not difficult to identify the newcomers, but it soon became readily apparent that no one was so sure who the Danes were. How many generations does it take to be considered Danish? In the words of Simmel, "by virtue of the fact that we have boundaries everywhere and always . . . so accordingly we are boundaries." The anxiety surrounding European identity may reveal one of the most commonplace features of any identity—that is, as a process it constitutes not only a provisional boundary, but one that is perpetually under construction. The making of the identity as an integral part of national self-identity and the representational side of the nation is always in process. The appearance of the stranger then not only ignites a crisis of hospitality, but also engages a basic instability of being and belonging. When the markers between the inside and the outside are seen to be arbitrary in spirit and practice, a new ethical ground may be reached concerning people who for one reason or another come to be displaced. As Etienne Balibar points out, once newcomers accustom themselves to the taken-for-granted "national sociability," people of "extra-community origin risk appear[ing] as quintessential Europeans" (1999, 202).

The confusion about the nature of European identity registers on another front, as in recent years European passports have been "counterfeited in significant numbers," leading officials of the European Union to consider the use of biometric data in future passport designs. Computer chips placed in each of the new European passports might be "embedded with digital fingerprints or eye scans," assuring the identity and other particulars of the bearer. The cards are no science fiction fantasy, as biometric "crossing cards" have been in use in the United States and Mexico since 1998; the United States embassies and consulates in Mexico have already issued some six million such cards containing a digital photograph and fingerprints (Fuller 2003). The United States requires adherence to the U.S. Enhanced Border Security and Visa Entry Reform Act of 2002; beginning in October 2004 countries wishing to engage in "visa-free travel to the United States" must include biometric identifiers in passports (Fuller 2003). The European Union has committed millions

of euros to this plan and deployed thousands of fingerprint and retinal scan records in a curious effort to find the fraud-proof symbol of
European belonging, a passport.[6]

Fingerprinting identification, face-recognition technology, retinal
scanning devices, and other biometric and surveillance techniques of
course go along with the need to establish a massive automated archival
capacity so that records may not only be accessed, but in the serpen-
tine logic of surveillance can be crosschecked and counterbalanced with
bits of information on data storage systems elsewhere—perhaps multiple hits in diverse locations might assure the accuracy and reliability of
sources.[7] This is very close to the identification regimes with "foolproof"
surveillance systems that operate in the fantasy worlds of the future, as in
Gattaca. Firms specializing in the maintenance of the accuracy of information shuttled to their third-party data sources and then made available to certify the inquiries of others have already come into being. Such
second-guessing of information or "dataveillance" regimes have been
established for some time now (Lyon 2000, 296). That all of this identification technology misses the point of belonging almost goes without
saying. John Torpey locates the "proliferation of identification documents in the period from the late nineteenth century to the first World
War" (2001, 93). During the nineteenth century, a more liberal ideal held
sway, nurturing the idea of freedom of movement and markets over the
intervention of state authority. It is in the transitional period beginning
in the late nineteenth century that a sharpening of the lines between
"national and alien" would come into play as bureaucratic regimes concerned with controls on population movement take shape (93).

Diasporas and European Futures

Population transfers today are truly transnational, involving the movement of capital, goods, and people on a previously unprecedented
scale. Diasporas are bound up in the historical processes of global
capitalism, the changing fortunes of nation-states, and the complex
interplay of power relations within and between nations of origin and
settlement.

Unlike the experience of Europe throughout the nineteenth and much
of the twentieth centuries (during which it found outlets for demographic pressures in what demographers call relatively "empty" areas,

where countless "neo-Europes" were created overseas), migrants coming from many regions of the world today find national immigration policies that severely limit their freedom of movement (Livi-Bacci 1997, 142). The inability to see the analogue of European economic development in places like West Africa, where the so-called modern sectors of the economy have not come to dominate the great expansive agricultural worlds of many countries of origin of the new migrants, has sent nongovernmental agencies and national European banks and *ad hoc* committees off to understand the nature of such economic asymmetries in efforts to stop the inward flow of migrants. There is an inverse flow of aid—as migrants flow into Europe, capital often flows in the other direction. This relationship is being attenuated now, as former colonial regimes scramble to set their economic houses in order as part of the European Union by cutting off dependent states linked to their colonial pasts.

We are led to understand from a host of sources that the creation of the postwar "neo-Europes" have given way to the creation of today's "neo-Africas" and "neo-Asias" in Britain, France, Italy, and other countries. This vision of Europe and its formation in the present is infused with the murmur of vital statistics that resonate across an imagined global order, with declines in birth rates and demographic aging here contrasted against high rates of population increase and youthful age structures over there (Livi-Bacci 1997). The scheme of definition often used in such discussions is "rich and poor"; Keith Hart has referred to this opposition between rich and poor countries as the main class opposition in the contemporary world. While rich countries are completing a phase of population expansion, the so-called poor countries embarked on an "extraordinary and non-repeatable" expansion of their own; the transfer of this population during their productive years in the form of labor is to some degree what is at issue (Livi-Bacci 1997, 159). The control of formal and informal labor markets is often mediated through the creation of legal and illegal worker categories.

From the vantage point of different nation-states, the results of attempts to control, delimit, and affix meanings to migratory flows look very different "on the ground" (Gupta and Ferguson 1997, 170). For some countries, such as France, Germany, and Britain, postwar migration prior to the 1970s and colonial encounters have formed particular patterns of population movements in the 1980s and 1990s. Countries like Italy, Spain, and

Portugal came into the immigration game as former countries of emigration that provided much of the labor to the powerful economies of the north and now form the core sites of arrival for undocumented men (and increasingly, women) who labor as construction workers, agricultural hands, and domestics. There is often a conflict between the democratic ideals and the new restrictive regimes being put into place across Europe, requiring a sometimes troubling modification of civil and social rights in order to fight immigration, as the state attempts to accomplish the mapping of the unwanted.[8] Migrants are engaged in "pre-cartographic operations"; enacting the itineraries of the traveler, they find themselves in the unfortunate position of being one of the very flows often seen to be antithetical to the logic of such dominant codings.

Evans-Pritchard once quipped that the Nuer, one of the most well-known peoples in the anthropological cannon, were expert at sabotaging ethnological inquiry and that he was the subject of a kind of Nuerosis resulting from their opposition to his studies. May we speak then of a kind of contemporary "Eurosis," an inclination of Europeans to evade the investigation of the unmarked part of the self/other divide that has been employed as part of a cultural imperialism throughout the world?[9] We must recall that in spite of the specter of multiculturalism, ethnic relativity, and a new pluralism of politics and race, no real transformation of Europe and the rest will occur without a profound restructuring and reconceptualization of the power relations upon which the representations of such communities rest. The nation is imagined as a community, and the idea of Europe from its very beginnings is bound up in this manifestation of the imaginary. The idea of community presented in the rhetoric of the northern leagues in Italy is one of a hermetically sealed and ethnically pure enclave, one safeguarded from newcomers and the democratic ideals of the past. In this vision, "regional nationalisms" have become "more exclusive than the nationalism of the state" (Balibar 1999, 213). Under the Berlusconi regime, much of the local cultural logic of exclusion has been drawn into the state; the national state of emergency to combat illegal immigration is a good example of this passion for control and purity. Liisa Malkki has stressed the nature of the contemporary nation-state system that operates through multiple registers at once "politico-economic, historical, cultural, aesthetic, and cosmological" (1995, 5). It is a great irony that, included in the notion of community of the right, drawn along the lines of the medieval commune, we find the socially exclusionary contours of a ghetto, the moral imperative implied in all racialist thinking.[10] As a result of the success of right-wing thinking becoming part of the taken-for-granted backdrop of the present, those who hold the idea of Europe like a talisman against some feared calamity are, in short, plagued by what it may have come to represent, by a lingering sense of superiority toward the so-called non-Westerner and by a deeply rooted conviction that the dissolution of the myth of Europe may occur before the dawn of its very realization in the everyday world of its territories.

A brief glance at some of the recent writings of generalists on Europe reveals the outlines of a preoccupation with European identity and the ambiguities of possible European futures. During the 1990s, a number of expressions of the idea of Europe have been proposed in order to assure us of the cohesion of the entity we refer to by this name: a Europe seeking to redefine itself. Such titles as *The Rise of Regional Europe* (Harvie 1994), *A Grand Illusion?: An Essay on Europe* (Judt 1996), *Trouble in Paradise? Europe in the 21st Century* (Kramer and Kyriakopoulos 1996), *Europe in the Balance* (Bertram 1995), and *One World, Ready or Not* (Greider 1997) give some indication of the unsettling nature of the emergent Europe.

In his book *Europe Adrift* John Newhouse spirits in the issue of immigration cloaked in an old Orientalist framework of African realities:

> The area extending from North Africa's Maghreb in the west through the Levant and Turkey is a jumble of disconnected issues and problems.... Some of these have deep and tangled roots. A few, as in Algeria, are of recent origin. Most have a pathology that mixes political, economic and social ills. All harbor violent tendencies that are potentially explosive. Together they form a rather porous frontier that separates the less troubled societies farther north from multiple threats to continental stability. (Newhouse 1997, 252)

> Streams of unwanted refugees have provoked a backlash and political extremism in various regions. The influx of darker-skinned people is putting pressures on France, Italy and Spain. (298)

This vision of a kind of cultural desert in the so-called south of the world is the connective myth through which the world beyond the boundaries of the West is apprehended. In defense of "Western civilization," the "troubled" regions must be separated from the West, while zones of ethnic purity, democratic ideology, and cultural compatibility must stand together (Herzfeld 2001, 148).

In this light, migrants are seen as cultural nomads who link hostile social worlds. The "laws of the frontier" are invoked: countless images of the so-called boat people confirming an imagined universal right of "cultural defense"; Cubans appearing to border patrol airplanes reported on the nightly news of July 24, 2003, as a human interest piece; would-be migrants in a Chevrolet truck rigged with pontoons and a driveshaft-propelled rudder; and the many boats and other means of transportation crossing the water to Spain and Italy, as we have discussed elsewhere. Cemeteries at the frontier's edge, where landfall is most frequent, now act as the final resting place of nameless young people who failed in their attempts to enter Europe and bypass the waiting security forces. Not unlike an accusation of witchcraft, the suggestion that those who originate in these troubled regions are the bearers of a kind of difference symbolized by their dark skin (a natural symbol of another social order) or the divergent traditions of civilization that arch in untold ways outside of the ways of the West, marks the newcomers as an embodiment of "impurity and danger" and destines them for expulsion (Douglas 1973).

Newcomers simply do not share what Ernest Renan has called "the common possession of a rich legacy of memories from the past and consent in the present, the leisure to live together and the will to continue to develop one's heritage" (1882). Heritage here—a culture surrogate—recalls a restricted view of culture (not an anthropological understanding), highlighting the "shared" legacy of societies imprisoned in an unchanging past; a tradition that moreover is not acknowledged but rather is appropriated to a vision of the integral qualities of cultural logic. They stand outside of this heritage; their foreignness consists of their imagined inability to assimilate this common legacy. This unpredictable source of myth and failed border crossings lays the foundation of our notions of population, nation, and migration and the shape our future may take.

Notes

Introduction

The epigraph is drawn from the famous essay by Bernard S. Cohn, "History and Anthropology: The State of Play" (1990, 21). Cohn was fond of saying that in anthropology we needed to "create a new sociology," to in a sense upend our routine ways of doing things and start all over again, considering what in anthropology was useful and what needed a serious rethinking or reconceptualization. I hope this book reflects and captures some of the spirit of his great vision and his dedication to scholarship, filtered through my experiences in the field.

1. Many anthropologists have considered the legacy of race, nationalism, and gender in postslavery and postcolonial societies and the contested terrain in these societies that results from this legacy. In this book I follow these insights for Europe (see Carnegie 2002; Williams 1991a; Malkki 1995).

2. Relatives of the young men now comb the coast trying to discourage other Senegalese from making the dangerous journey. They are joined by political officials, local women's organizations, and others who join in the fight to save a generation. On the waterways of the Mediterranean, on the islands of its interior, and in the territories of nation-states that jut out into its heart, small cemeteries have been erected under the modest solemnity of everyday practice. Many are tended by shipmates who survived the crossing, the undocumented, and even the local residents of such areas who have been drawn into the misfortune of strangers.

3. Eastern European migrants tend to return to their countries of origin when economic conditions improve and therefore present only a temporary solution to labor shortages. Their presence in the labor market, however, helps to degrade labor conditions for non-European migrants, because non-European's informal employment impacts their right to stay but effects no change in European workers' residence status. Other European Union residents can work in the informal sector and legally stay in the country once the job comes to an

end, while migrants from outside the European Union face deportation once their job disappears.

4. Today, work is often subcontracted out to firms that hire migrant workers and others on limited or indeterminate term contracts. In the past, many contract jobs, which are increasingly rare today, afforded workers relative job security and benefits.

5. In medium and large firms today it is common for benefits to be held up in litigation between trade unions and employers over the details of agreements made in the past. Both Italian and migrant workers are held in limbo while they await final determinations. In the case of Babacar's back wages the union won, but the final allocation of the settlement has yet to take place.

6. Immigration legislation tied to worker status in a number of countries, such as Spain and Italy, confuses the distinction between, for example, legal and undocumented workers. As Kitty Calavita and Liliana Suárez-Navaz have pointed out, "few real distinctions exist between the two" since "legal status is always a fragile state and almost inevitably gives way to periods of illegality" (2003, 116). In periods of economic decline, for instance, many of the Senegalese I work with in Italy fall from official to unofficial work, making them vulnerable to a denial of permission to stay in the country because they cannot claim their off-the-books income.

7. *The L Word*, a television series produced and written by Ilene Chaiken for the cable television network Showtime, is a good example of treatment of a population previously subjected to a kind of invisibility. The title of the show invokes this social invisibility and entreats the viewer to discover the world of Los Angeles women in the hip, young center of the world of cinema pursuing their lives and loves and exploring the dimensions of gay and straight experiences. This well-written drama first aired on January 18, 2004 and received one of the fastest green lights for its second season of any show in the network's history. In some measure, the drama has an aura of "newness" due in part to the invisibility of the individuals' lives in the community it explores.

8. The late cultural critic and philosopher Madan Sarup (1930–1993) once wrote of the classical boundary-maintaining social mechanism in the work of Emile Durkheim: the deviant suggesting that we might replace him with the contemporary migrant (Sarup 1996, 12). In Durkheim "each time the deviant act is punished, that authority of the norm is sharpened," allowing a deviant presence to act as a way of manifesting an invisible social boundary (12).

9. Paul Gilroy correctly identifies the colonial legacy as an integral element of the contemporary global context: "Contemporary discussions of immigration, asylum, nationalism, and other areas of government where race is strongly resonant have been enriched not only by the capacity to reflect clearly on the

history of decolonization but also by consideration of the conceptions of political power that resulted from detours through the bloody history of colonial societies and the planetary ambitions of race-driven imperialism" (2005, 17).

10. See Abdou Maliq Simone's discussion of invisibility contrasted with the hypervisibility of an African city in which everything is known about others' actions. He writes: "Invisibility can act as a political construction—that is, a means of both configuring and managing particular resources and the medium through which specific instantiations of the political are deployed" (2004, 66). His use of the notion of the spectral is similar to my historical discussion of the use of invisibility throughout the book.

11. Indeed Trica Danielle Keaton has noted a similar discourse in French urban social life by which "youths and immigrants are identified" and associated in the French imagination with "dead-end vocational tracks, prisons," and the urban centers that they inhabit (2006a, 7).

12. I was actually authorized by local officials to make visits confirming the residency of a number of Senegalese and Moroccan migrants, allowing them to receive the documentation required for obtaining residence in the city and actually to be entered into the official count of residents (see Carter 1997).

13. René Maran's *Batouala*, an early example of such literature, was first published in 1921 and suggested both a black modernity and a complex black identity that included aspects of an assimilated European-ness and an identification with blacks internationally. Perhaps the most controversial part of the work was the introduction, in which Maran offered a critique of colonial policy. He himself was a veteran colonial officer of the French colonial service; he was born in Martinique but since his childhood spent many years in different parts of Africa. The reception of the book on its own terms was drowned out; the public preferred a discursive French folk ideology constructing blacks as permanent strangers in the Francophone world. As Brent Hayes Edwards wrote, the reception of the book at the time was overcome by dominant stereotypes, racial tonalities, and the strict subordination of the colonial subject. It was simply overwhelmed by the force of a discursive context that insisted on reading any expression of the black modern as a threat—for as I have pointed out, the modern self-construction of France relied on an array of representational strategies to distance the nègre as the silent "other," as well as political strategies to mitigate against any black internationalist alliance undermining the smooth borders of the nation (Edwards 2003, 97).

14. Ellison in *Shadow and Act* notes the ritual disappearance of blacks from the national discourse, in part to avoid direct confrontation of the "problem" (social, economic, and cultural) of the black presence. Ellison argues that color prejudice and the stereotyping of blacks in the United States is felt as a deep need on a personal level to believe in the constellations of justifications of black

subordination. In this manner Ellison writes: "Whatever else the Negro stereo-type might be as a social instrumentality, it is also a key figure in a magic rite by which the white American seeks to resolve the dilemma arising between his democratic beliefs and certain antidemocratic practices, between his acceptance of the sacred democratic belief that all men are created equal and his treatment of every tenth man as though he were not" (1972, 28). In the wake of such a need to believe, blacks and others placed in this kind of categorical limitation fail to attain the universality of human presence, a state in which all human beings might be subject to the same rules. This common ground (in what Alfred Schutz calls anonymity) is broken when we begin to consider individual unique qualities. Equivalence in human representative qualities is not quite the same as representing an individual life, which will change from person to person. Lewis R. Gordon notes that, in the context of the anti-black world (as blacks are over-determined), it is at this point that "to see that black is to see every black." In this case the black individual fails to attain the kind of interchangeable human weight that anonymity might accord them under normal circumstances. "The black's individual life ceases to function as an object of epistemological, aesthetic, or moral concern . . . One is led to believe, for instance, that one can 'have blacks' by virtue of having that black, that anonymous black. The black representative emerges." The black representative provides the "magic rite" by which blackness is both present and invisible: "We can stand a society without responsibility for the blackness we exclude by way of the blackness we include, which we identify as blackness *in toto*" (Gordon 1997, 75).

15. I have worked with Senegalese and other migrants in Italy and the United States since 1990, when I conducted research in Turin, Italy, and the United States.

16. Problems of representation are often linked not only to worlds of the present but also to the protean realms of an unacknowledged past. Over the years, as I watched Italian news programs or read Italian newspapers or talked with friends and with people from the mayor's office, the trade unions, or the local corner store, I found that the presence of my friends from Senegal was noted, if at all, as a problem to be solved at the political level. Throughout the 1990s as anti-immigrant ideology began to take hold, popular culture was flooded with images of the undeserving migrant. Images of the many Senega-lese "others" working regular jobs alongside Italians were largely absent. After an interview I conducted with a local journalist from *La Stampa*, Turin's premier newspaper, was published, I had migrant and local activists thanking me, point-ing out that a proper image of the working life of migrants was rarely covered in the press. If migrants were not employed as part of a highly volatile political debate, they labored in the shadows.

17. Living in the shadows can also be coupled with an increasing reality of surveillance and social scrutiny, prompting Togolese author Kossi Komla-Ebri to emphasize in his semi-autobiographical novel *Neyla* (2002) a relief at returning to Africa from Italy, where he had the feeling of being a kind of *bestia rara* (exotic beast) under the gaze of Europeans. Komla-Ebri, a surgeon in a hospital near Milan, began to write at the urging of his children, who insisted he share with others the rich cultural heritage they had experienced through his stories and childhood experiences. He is one of a handful of writers in the Italian language who expresses a new cultural vision in what has been called migrant or immigration literature, which shares a complex perspective. Right-wing political organizations have framed a notion of European identity that may provide a buffer to the potential emergent social worlds made possible by global migrations and resulting in an unprecedented cultural diversity.

18. In Italy in 1991, tens of thousands of Albanians sought refuge in the country but were summarily expelled because they no longer could claim to be fleeing a "communist" country. The threat of an "Islamic danger" at the close of the Gulf War in 1990–1991 was beginning to manifest itself in government immigration practice. Once seen as bearers of European culture, Albanians were shuttled off overcrowded boats into makeshift detention centers in soccer stadiums or local schools and deported, Albanian "immigrants no longer represented as heroes" of anticommunism (see Albahari 2006). The classic refugee from the Cold War era has disappeared and no preferred subject navigating the diaspora has taken the place of this ideological and cultural figure. Today refugees from genocidal war in the Sudan, civil conflict in Liberia, or carpet bombing in Lebanon seem to have little privilege in the world community as hospitality has withered and the spirit of asylum has all but died.

19. The manner in which gender discourse and literary authority functions to render invisibility is explored by Belinda Edmonson in *Making Men* (1999). The restoration of the vitality of the working-class experience is obscured by class bias and racial prejudice in Tiffany Ruby Patterson's *Zora Neal Hurston and a History of Southern Life* (2005), in anthropologist Paul Stoller's *Money Has No Smell: The Africanization of New York City* (2002), in the exquisite meditation on diaspora by Jacquline Nasssy Brown, *Dropping Anchor, Setting Sail: Geographies of Race in Black Liverpool* (2005), and in the work of Heather Merrill in *An Alliance of Women: Immigration and the Politics of Race* (2006). See also Abdou Maliq Simone's *For the City Yet to Come: Changing African Life in Four Cities* (2004). Each of these works explores an aspect of invisibility that obscures the lives of populations struggling to be made known.

20. Indeed after meeting anthropologist Trica Danielle Keaton during the 105th American Anthropological Association meetings in San Jose, California, I found

that we were independently drawn to the work of Dr. Clark in relation to the uprisings. For an insightful counterpoint to my brief comments see Keaton 2006a.

21. Regarding the background and context of the French uprising, see Tricia Danielle Keaton (2006b) and the emerging discussion of blackness and race in France (E. Fassin 2006; Silverstein 2006; D. Fassin 2006).

22. See the wonderful work of anthropologist Asale Angel-Ajani (1999) on the nature of incarceration of migrant women in Italy.

23. In his rereading of the work of Fanon in his book *Fanon's Dialectic of Experience* (1997) Ato Sekyi-Out acknowledges Fanon's critique of the exaltation of time over space, prefiguring Foucault's examination of Marxism's "devaluation of space." For Fanon, spatiality seen through the lens of the existentialist becomes a realm focused on the dimension of openness, left to the human subject in a domain constrained by colonial domination. The nature of coercion then becomes critical to the understanding of the notion of freedom, with liberation underlying the subject's ability to overturn this particular form of domination. An analysis of the structuring of the various social roles and positions constituting the colonial order is then crucial in this lived space, as it is for Antonio Gramsci essentially political. In the end there is a very Gramscian moment in Fanon as the struggle to forge a common ground is always a struggle over competing versions of not only particular histories but the most expansive dimensions of human liberation emerging out of experience.

24. If we contrast the generation of Mustapha Abu Ali with contemporary Palestinian filmmakers, who are largely in diaspora, we come upon a complex examination of the Palestinian condition, which deeply influenced the circumstances of wide-scale involvement in the day-to-day conflicts of the Palestinian–Israeli conflict among a generation for which the conflict has become a way of life. Palestinian filmmakers have taken up such topics at times with humor, as in director Ahmad Habash's animated *Coming Back* (2003), a story of a little bird returning to its homeland. In *Chronicles of Disappearance* (1996), director Elia Suleiman explores the impact of the rapidly changing political and social situation on Palestinian identity and personhood, as political, economic, and personal instability is reflected in everyday life. Attitudes toward women and the practice of veiling (*hijab*) and unveiling are explored in the work of Osama Al-Zain among Muslim women of the United States in his film *Transparency* (2002). The film works through the very personal reasons and experiences of a number of women. Israeli filmmakers are also exploring the everyday experiences of the conflict, for example Ram Levi's *Close, Closed, Closure* (2002). Levi examines the politics of closure and the thin veil of tolerance so easily destroyed between Palestinian and Jewish families. These films were all part of a Palestinian film festival in Israel in 2004 called *Dreams of a Nation* (Rapfogel 2003; McCarthy 2004).

25. As Trica Danielle Keaton points out in her examination of French textbooks, this invisibility continues to haunt the "official" story of the war, as apart from a few period photographs of the Tirailleurs, they are largely absent from historical discussions of the war. As Keaton notes, "These men, many . . . Muslim, who died in service of France and the war effort, remain for the most part erased from the textbooks" (2006a, 125).

26. I would like to thank Pamela Reynolds for introducing me to the work of Richard D. E. Burton and encouraging me to think about the legacy of violence in both state practice and experience.

27. Frederick Cooper has argued that increasing activism across West Africa, particularly that concerned with areas of labor, health care, and citizenship, was in a sense the first sign of the decolonization process (Cooper 2002).

28. The first Africans to be so mobilized, the soldiers' experiences of a complex cultural and historical moment were unique. They were the first to see Europeans in their "natural" environment undergoing the strains of occupation, and they met African Americans on the field of battle and in the camps along with other huddled remains of the conflict peopled by the Jewish, French, American, and African soldiers interned there as fellow prisoners. They saw, we might say, before they may have been aware of what they were seeing, the end of empire. Their families responded to the rhythm of troop movements and life in the camps, and their children grew up encouraged by their experience to pursue military careers, linking service and home life across the generations.

29. As Samira Kawash notes, "the very visibility of blackness, a visibility that seems so commonsensical in the modern world as to need no explanation, is itself a part of the epistemology of racial difference" (1997, 134).

30. As bell hooks has recently pointed out poverty in the United States is relegated to invisibility, conflating race with class in the peculiar politics of race and class. While blacks are often central to media images of the poor, "most officially poor people are white." Yet in the mass media, hooks argues there is an "almost invisibility of the white poor" (2000, 116). As the "hidden face of poverty in the United States" masks the "untold stories of millions of poor white people," the notion of poverty in the country is deeply contested in what hooks calls "the politics of invisibility" (117).

31. Here I borrow heavily from Lewis R. Gordon's discussion of the mechanisms of invisibility in his treatment of race and autochthonous or indigenous groups in *Existentia Africana: Understanding Africana Existential Thought* (2000).

32. Novelist Chinua Achebe recounts the story of the late prominent Nigerian educator, humanist, and social critic Dr. Tai Solarin (1922–1994). Dr. Solarin was in a post office in the United Kingdom during the 1950s (a period

of colonialism in the country) attempting to send a package home. The postal clerk, lost in calculations and somewhat bewildered by the foreign destination, scans the address and finally asks Solarin in exasperation, "Nigeria—Nigeria—is Nigeria ours or French?" Solarin replies, composed as ever, "Nigeria is yours, madam." Achebe takes the matter directly to the issue of the social presence of countless colonials, people represented in unknown geographical coordinates and appearing through the parcel and indeed through an entire postal system to connect an elsewhere to its imperial complement. Distance and the imbalance between systems of knowledge and classification by which some narratives, lives, and geographies have more symbolic weight than others prompts Achebe to note: "To even inconsequential minions of imperial rule, subject peoples were all 'invisible,' along with their sometimes unpronounceable homelands" (2000, 98–99). Though Senegal is no longer a matter of colonial geography, the postcolonial world and its hometowns, Ikenne, Nigerian, or Touba, Senegal disappears nonetheless for the postal worker in Turin, Paris, or Oslo through the monotony of "global" narratives that differentially weight localities. Unfortunately such places often break through the fog when associated with traumatic events: genocide in Darfur, civil strife in Congo, sectarian violence in Iraq. Viewed from the other side the West is intimately linked to developments in these distant places, appearing on the conceptual map as a visible and powerful presence.

33. Samira Kawash writes, "The modern conception of racial identity maintains an uneasy relationship to the visual; the visible marks of the racialized body are only the signs of deeper, interior difference, and yet those visible marks are the only difference that can be observed. The body is a sign of a difference that exceeds the body" (1997, 130).

34. It is important to keep in mind, as Deborah Poole has cautioned, that we must not only look at the visual in terms of meanings but must also attend to the manner in which "images accrue value" (1997, 10).

35. I must thank my colleague Jane Guyer for pointing out the great weight of the work of Hegal in Western thought and the importance of this legacy concerning questions of social distinctions.

36. In fact, following the First World War the so-called minority treaties facilitated the disposition of groups placed under the protection of an emergent international order under the League of Nations because they could claim no certain place in the newly formed nation-states. The treaties, guaranteed by an international body in the guise of the League of Nations, assured minorities a kind of protection because they stood outside the normal legal protection of the nation-state. For perhaps the first time in European experience, it became clear that they lived in a state of exception as "only nationals could be citizens, only people of the same national origin could enjoy the full protection of legal

institutions" so that persons of different "nationality" needed a "law of exception" until they could be fully "assimilated" or effectively purified of their "origin" (Arendt 1976, 275). For these stateless people the right to residence and to work was never resolved, and mass relocation was not a regular feature of the lives of people in diaspora until the period following the Second World War. The contemporary status of persons subject to the law of exception has since taken on the more ominous tonalities of ethnic cleansing and even genocide.

37. Indifference is the ideological support of invisibility, as its sanction places those relegated to invisible status beyond the bounds of the relevant social and cultural community. Like stigma, it signals the limits of empathy.

38. This state-imposed invisibility has no clear boundaries or temporal limitation. The United States argued for an "indefinite detention" for the "detainees" held at Guantanamo Bay under the authority of the Department of Defense, setting up special military tribunals rather than allowing those held to have access to the court system. While the lawfulness of the detentions following the Supreme Court ruling might be reviewed in the Federal Courts and might have to be supported by the legislature in the end (and indeed the court has overturned many of the Bush administration's claims), the government's insistence on the control of a special territory in which the rule of law is essentially suspended is troubling.

39. The United States Supreme Court ruled in June 2005 that the base at Guantanamo Bay, Cuba, is not beyond the reach of the American legal system as the Bush administration had maintained. United States Federal Courts have jurisdiction over the detainees and must examine whether they have been lawfully detained. The camp creates a number of challenges for the American court system and the executive branch of the government, which continues to maintain it has "sole discretion" over the detainees due to their value as sources on information and status as "enemy combatants." The military commissions reviewing the status of the detainees thus far are operating under military order, under the ultimate authority of the executive. The passage of information and investigative access between the judiciary and the executive branches may reside in the troubled waters of "national security" for some time before the matter is resolved and the detainees have unfettered access to an impartial review process (Lewis 2003; Amnesty International Annual Report 2005).

40. Agamben warns us that "the camp is the space that is opened when the state of exception begins to become the rule." It is this space then that "inaugurates a new juridico-political paradigm in which the norm becomes indistinguishable from the exception" (1998, 170). Indeed Agamben points out that the camps define a "zone of indistinction" such that questions of subjective rights and juridical protections no longer make any sense. The inhabitant of the camp is essentially

stripped of every political status and reduced to the very rudiments of a life to such an extent that the very humanity of the subject may be called into question.

41. As Judith Butler has demonstrated, the detainees of Guantanamo Bay have been entirely removed from judicial oversight and contact with the outside world and have therefore lost the effective support of citizenship and legal and political subjectivity, and have also faced the "social death" of the prisoner. The doubling of the detainees taken as hostages in Iraq is a chilling play on the spectral presence of the prisoners, mirrored in the uniforms they are forced to wear as they are filmed by captors who will use the images for their own ends. In part buffeted by the state, national identities, and local and regional histories, these "zones of indistinction," spatial or categorical, mark the availability of invisibility and its inauguration, delimiting the world we know and care about.

42. However as Ewa Plonowska Ziarek points out, Agamben's work concerning the biopolitics of race and gender could stand some revisions of the concept of bare life. Further, his focus on the sovereign decision obscures the "contested terrain in which new forms of domination, dependence, and emancipatory struggles can emerge" (Ziarek 2008, 103).

43. William A. Shack has written excellent works, for example on the "Harlem-style" culture associated with jazz music and the nightlife in Paris, both fine examples of the "lost worlds" of the contemporary African diaspora (Shack 2001).

44. Some of the preoccupation with "other cultures" lies in an "exoticist project to recuperate in a distant elsewhere values that modernity 'here' stands to obliterate" (Bongie 1991, 5). There is a double work of violence here: a kind of symbolic violence to the subject, who in being for others serves only to be silenced and who in being something other than imagined is relegated to invisibility; and the second work of violence that can result in a social and cultural death as well as the actual and gruesome deaths in the shipwrecks of migrant boats at sea or the accidental transit deaths of those attempting to enter countries hidden in trailer trucks or the holes of cargo ships. The presence of an Other beyond the confines of this global sweep of homogenizing influences generates a kind of nostalgia for what may have been lost in the race to the present. The navigation of such a space can be treacherous.

45. For a discussion of the state's role and responsibility for the management of violence and indifference see Brackette F. Williams's *On the Normally Evil* (1991b).

46. See for example Charles W. Mills's discussion of herrenvolk Kantianism, based on a notion of differential personhood accorded on the basis of cultural distinctions, race, and philosophical principles (Mills 1998).

47. Kristen Hastrup points out that "reflexivity and relativity are not means of analysis but part of ethnography" (1995, 49), as these features enable the very conduct of ethnographic practice.

1. A Nonracial Education

1. As Michael D. Harris explains, "Walker is noted for the creation of tableaux, installations of a sort made of silhouettes cut from black paper. The works are arranged on blank canvas or on walls, often turning corners, and the white background highlights the silhouettes and metaphorically points up the reductionist character of racial discourse into black and white terms and ideas. The work has the haunting spectacle of a fatal three-car accident with its routine depiction of the unspeakable, the perverse, and the supposedly dark secrets of racial histories in the United States" (2003, 210).

2. Maroons were communities of escaped slaves; they form one of the most romantic symbolic points of struggle against the slave regime "so heavily romanticized during the heyday of the negritude movement" (Price and Price 1997, 8). In some cases, as in parts of Brazil, descendents of these communities still occupy the sites of the historic communities today. Maroon communities are one of the favorite figures in many Afrocentric schemes. It was here, tucked away from the world, that African communities lived in an alternative space, freely practicing aspects of their experience forbidden elsewhere.

In a discussion of maroon communities in *Africans in Colonial Louisiana: The Development of Afro-Creole Culture in the Eighteenth Century*, Gwendolyn Midlo Hall describes an extensive network of settlement and "passages" that linked plantation slaves with the maroon networks of "intelligence and support" (1992, 212). The plantation system of lower Louisiana was essentially woven into the arch of these "passages"—the maroon families did not distance themselves from the plantations; they surrounded them. This vision of an autonomous world where "Creole slaves openly asserted their control over their lives, their families, their property, and their territory" (212) is one that Hall in effect restores to history. This story resonates with the preoccupation of those who trace the distant continent of diaspora, seeking clarity, and the authenticity of an identity untouched by the coursing of time. And yet, if such practices are entirely products of the New World, will this creative response satisfy those who seek a point beyond Western influences? Perhaps in the end, such a creativity through which the clarity of new locations might emerge is the evidence of cultural resistance so often sought elsewhere.

Iain Chambers suggests in his book *Migrancy, Culture, Identity* that what is sought in the passage from slave to personhood "is to establish a sense of identity, to find a voice and to claim a political and cultural place," and yet this struggle for identity must take its own route independent of that we may wish for; it is, after all, an object *for* our consciousness, as Hegel might say, not always *of* it (Chambers 1994, 38).

3. The play of language and its importance is captured in the work of Primo Levi in his treatment of "larger jargon"—a language that was, as Sander Gilman puts it, "a language of the murderers, combined with bits and pieces of the language of the victims and some words that were created only in the camps" (1991, 294). Italian comes to represent for Levi a distant land before the Holocaust and the integrity of the identity of the narrator. In addition, there was the Yiddish of the camps, second only to "larger jargon," and a language Levi did not understand before entering the camps. Language was one of the ways of placing Jews beyond yet within the West; the so-called internal other of Western discourse has long been the cultural corollary of blood and soil. "The image of the language of the Jews and the idea of a "Jewish" language and discourse is central to any self-definition of the Jew." Against the anti-Semitism that claimed that Jews could not master the language of the host nation, Levi poses "the memory of language and the language of memory" as key defining markers of Jewish experience (Gilman 1991, 298).

4. Stereotypes are fictions that live through masquerading as naturalized and seemingly indispensable parts of our worlds. The historical creatures called stereotypes may be crystallized as portions of common sense, the taken-for-granted bedrock of popular ideologies and or fashions (Carter 1997, 159). Not all stereotypes gain dominance in the world of common sense.

5. The recent call for a census of the Roma or so-called gypsies in Italy has resulted in a mass exodus. Authorities hope to photograph and fingerprint young people in order to better control their movements and school attendance in the future. Some now warn of the criminalization of the Roma in an emergent "police state," worsening an already marginal Roma status in Italian society.

6. The resurgence of ethnic violence and the struggle in many countries for the control of internal homelands has brought about an unprecedented proliferation of internally displaced persons. Internally displaced persons are people displaced within their own national territory number some fifty million in the world today, of which thirteen to fifteen million are refugees, or persons that have actually crossed an international border. This constitutes a growing humanitarian crisis that the international community has only begun to address. The vulnerability of the displaced is exacerbated by the fact that in many cases, their status is foreseen by no international agreement, so they fall victim often to the very state or its allies that had a hand in their dispersal. While the refugee that crosses an international border has a right not to be returned to the country in which she might fear for her life, the internally displaced person at present has effectively no possibility of claiming intervention by the international community.

7. As Gilroy notes, "The culture and politics of black America and the Caribbean have become the raw materials for creative processes which redefine what it means to be black, adapting it to distinctively British experiences and meanings. Black culture is actively made and remade" (1987, 154).

8. Of course, these same potential points of solidarity were effectively dismissed as the Irish working class fought for its privilege in the racially segmented labor force to the disadvantage of an aspirant black working class (see Roediger 1991). It is on this very point of the nature and meaning of slavery and indenture that people of African descent and others construct divergent histories of the nation in the Caribbean and the Indian Ocean.

9. One of the difficulties with the travel trope and therefore with the image of the ship is its relationship to European self-creation through what Bernard S. Cohn in *Colonialism and Its Forms of Knowledge* (1996) has called the Observational/Travel modality. This modality is related to a "repertoire of images and typifications that determined what was significant to the European eye" so that the world is seen from the perspective of the European viewer (6–7). It is not only that the voyage of the slave ship is conceived as part of a European narrative of capital in various historical formulations, but also that the subject cannot be substituted in any simple way to produce an alternative vision for the subaltern. The subaltern, does not, strictly speaking, travel. Travel as a construct or a modality of a kind of imperial moment is saturated with notions of a privileged relationship to the world. The position of the traveler was as unquestioned as the structure of the ordered world within which the travel might take place. Travel structures the world for an imaginary male and dominant figure connecting the corners of a largely subjugated world. We must conceive of an entirely new form of movement through space and time in order to capture the voyage of the slave. Although the voyage of the European through time and space constitutes the creation, classification, and establishment of certain kinds of knowledge and social practices, the slave represents a negation, the presentation of a cosmological dilemma.

10. Slave status served not only an important economic role—as in North America, where slaves (not land) became one of the prime sites of investment—but also as a crucial component of the Western cultural logic concerning the nature of the human world. As Fanon cries out, "I am fixed" (in which I take the meaning of "fixed" in this "double" way—not outside of modernity but rather enmeshed in it), and here I understand the Derridian notion of "supplement" as conveying this almost necessary addition, a term without which the whole cannot be comprehended, that may in fact change the meaning of its partner. Yet this imprisonment in Western modernity allows for a restricted repertoire of representations, cast only in negation of the potential of difference, denying

its ontological value. This is the work of the stereotype. Homi Bhabha notes that the simplification of the stereotype lies in its dependence on the notion of "fixity." A product of racial taxonomic ideology, "it is an arrested, fixated form of representation that, in denying the play of difference (which the negation of the Other permits), constitutes a problem for the *representation* of the subject in significations of psychic and social relations" (Bhabha 1994, 75).

11. The right to the exemplary is the privilege of a dominant position under-scored by power, social class, and the control of resources, and essentially entails the right to be unmarked or the model for others to follow in a social order. This position is always dependent on context, position, and power. Although white-ness is a kind of model of the unmarked category of the United States, only some forms of whiteness can be said to be exemplary and must be authorized by some form of power. These two roads to the exemplary follow different registers. See Michael B. Naas's introduction in *The Other Heading* (Derrida 1992, xliv–xlv) and Bonnie Urciuoli's *Exposing Prejudice* (1996).

12. St. Clair Drake 1982, *Diaspora Studies and Pan-Africanism*, cited in Harris (1982, 360).

13. As Stuart Hall has recently cautioned, "It is to the diversity, not the homogeneity, of black popular culture that we must now give our creative atten-tion. This is not simply to appreciate the historical and experiential differences within and between communities, regions, country and city, across national cul-tures, between diasporas, but also to recognize the other kinds of difference that place, position, and locate black people. The point is not simply that, since our racial differences do not constitute all of us, we are always different, negotiat-ing different kinds of differences—of gender, of sexuality, of class. It is also that these antagonisms refuse to be neatly aligned; they are simply not reducible to one another; they refuse to coalesce around a single axis of differentiation. We are always in negotiation, not with a single set of oppositions that place us always in the same relations to others, but with a series of different positionalities. Each has its point of profound subjective identification. And that is the most difficult thing about this proliferation of the field of identities and antagonisms: they are often dislocating in relation to one another" (1992, 30).

14. In this we must look to the emergent realties of collectivity in process (Turner 1969). Although it is part of the tradition of the social sciences to look for clear social groups, classes, and other containers, some aspects of social life do not fit in our boxes, as they are in the process of becoming—blurring the very marking devices we use to frame them. The collective experience of journey, arrival, and at times, the hoped-for return, are in this view the environing social and cultural marking processes that denote the process and products of passage, to borrow the language of Victor Turner (1974, 167).

15. The "black" in black cultures for Stuart Hall is a kind of "shifting signi-fier"; that envisioned through Gilroy's gloss seems to narrow through the work of the trope of the ship. Hegemony for Hall is not the destruction of difference but rather its celebration, the "articulation of differences which do not disap-pear." When it is the space between diasporas and within them that may be left to explore, positions in process and the consideration of "different kinds of dif-ference" may allow other diasporas to speak to us (Hall 1994, 58).

16. I thank Sara Berry for this insight. A periodization of the notion of the diaspora may be useful here; I would arbitrarily split the discussion into three phases, the first dealing with the creation and articulation of the world of the New World Negro; a second dealing with the wake of colonialism and the politi-cal resonance of the notion of difference—"diaspora as holocaust," as Sara Berry has called it; and the final element defying definition—the diaspora of the peo-ple I have identified in this discussion, New African diaspora.

17. European travelers remain fairly well-documented historical figures and reached such destinations as "Canada and the United States, or Argentina and Chile, or New Zealand and Australia," but the "other" half of the fifty million non-Europeans hailing from Africa, India, and China or from the Indonesian archipelago and elsewhere rarely set foot on any of these lands (Mintz 1995, 5). This movement, moderated by "European racism" and under "European super-vision and control," may caution our enthusiasm for the new upturn in global passage, notwithstanding an accounting of a more historical perspective that, if anything, has shown us that we cannot stop what Mintz has called the "hippity-hop of globalization" (20). Part of this enthusiasm stems from a desire to undo old mythologies like that of the immigrant America.

18. As Panivong Norindr notes, one of the founding myths of the United States is that of an immigrant nation: immigrants from Europe, we are told, "discovered" and settled the "New World," establishing an empire out of "noth-ing." What this myth masks and forgets is the violence done to the peoples who already lived here. It is this history of violence and forgetting that the new immi-grant, especially those from Asia, is supplementing (Norindr 1994, 234).

19. This situation is the subject of a thought-provoking parody in Gianni Amelio's film L'America (1994), set in Albania in 1991. After the fall of the regime, a young Italian con artist attempts to gain a government contract for a joint Albanian–Italian shoe company, and as the deal unravels finds himself stranded in Albania. Finding an anticommunist hero to front the company is a sure way to gain state support, so Gino (Enrico Lo Verso) and his partners select at random a homeless man who has been pining away in a socialist prison for fifty years. As it turns out, the man is an Italian deserter from the forces of Mussolini, who invaded and occupied Albania in 1939. While caring for this

man, who was selected as the "chairman" of the would-be company, Gino loses his passport and everything connecting him to an Italian identity, and finds himself taken to be an Albanian citizen, like the thousands who attempted to enter Italy after the fall of the government. Gino comes full circle to understand how Albanians fleeing the abject poverty of their country in 1991 might see Italy in the way that Italian migrants to the United States viewed *L'America* in another era.

20. Indeed, this realm is the most untenable position; United Nations conventions that attempt to outline the fundamental rights of the uprooted are unenforceable humanitarian guidelines, because the site for the "rights" and the use of force remains the nation-state system. Poor states become virtual holding areas for the internationally displaced.

21. The Victoria, Texas, deaths sparked many activists to intervene in attempts to ensure that fewer people lost their lives crossing or fell prey to criminal networks or human smugglers on route on either side of the border. While conservative groups call for greater "controls" on international migration, the reality on the ground constitutes a kind of humanitarian crisis—a boon for smugglers and a wedge issue in politics that never seems courageous enough to seek long-term solutions.

22. Once the vision of a singular world, an uncontested "community of the pure" is no longer fashionable without accounting for other worlds, other cultures; we will have come full circle, but today this does not seem to be the case (Hall 1994).

2. Remembering Khartoum and Other Tales of Displacement

1. Naming a child Khartoum is, it seems to me, the acknowledgment of a process rather than the recognition of an event.

2. Within the very same week that my family and I arrived in Turin, Italy, in the summer of 2001, the mother of a longtime friend sent a present to us from Dakar through a young women who was returning to Italy after her holiday.

3. The Nuer and Dinka represent for anthropological literature inaugural "others." They fit into a kind of classical tradition of the "exotic" other. For a discussion of the "savage slot" in anthropological thinking and the construction of the self-definition of the so-called West, see Trouillot (1995). Some suggest that the Nuer have diverged from the Dinka in recent centuries; others, looking at the classical sources on the Nuer (see Evans-Pritchard 1940), seem to think that the line between Nuer and Dinka may have been more fluid in the past, allowing one group to attach itself to the settlements of the other and in time becoming dependents of the neighboring group (see Holtzman 2000).

4. In this chapter I draw on the work of E. Evans-Pritchard and Godfrey Lienhardt, partly following the logic of the incident in the Roman shelter, and

also to represent anthropological traditions often associated with the work of these authors. Lienhardt is often associated with work in the phenomenological realm and the world of the Dinka; his investigation of their notion of selfhood, time and space, and the idea of divinity is unparalleled. I wish to emphasize here the innovative manner in which Evans-Pritchard's work employs a notion of ecological and cultural dynamic that inform the lives of people. In his famous ecological chapter in *The Nuer*, they emerge as people for whom the landscape is living tissue. The Nuer vision of landscape is integral to their self-definition. When we look through the lens of migration, we often displace people from the cultural, ecological, and social centers of their lives. Abstract notions like "flows" and "dynamics" entail the detachment of a group of people from a world of meanings. What we might call "experience" and "form" are often lost in our discussions of diaspora.

5. The Sudanese government finally signed a peace agreement ending a civil war in the South that had raged for twenty-one years in May 2004. At the same time, a campaign of ethnic cleansing was underway in the western region of Darfur. In Darfur, militas—known as Janjaweed-recruited nomadic peoples often historically in conflict with the region's settled populations, dominated by the Fur, Masalit, and Zaghawa, who have been systematically driven from their homes. Over one million people have been displaced by the conflict many in refugee camps in Chad. Some two million have been affected by the crisis and the death toll may rise as high as one million during the next year if there is not an immediate halt to the violence. The international community was slow to respond to the crisis; even with an immediate response, UN Emergency Relief Coordinator Jan Egeland estimated that "about 350,000 people could die this year of disease or malnutrition" (Reuters 2004b). Although the Khartoum government has denied its involvement in the conflict, the administration organized and armed the Janjaweed militias, and for over two months blocked the access of humanitarian aid workers to the region. Once the rainy season begins, roads will become impassable, increasing the threat of malaria and the spread of disease in the camps. Although the United States is one of the largest contributors to relief efforts—some $116 million since spring 2003 and another $164 million pledged by the end of 2004—State Department officials fall short of designating the crisis a "genocide." Secretary of State Colin Powell said just before his trip to the area in July 2004, "We see indications and elements that would start to move you to a genocidal conclusion" (Marquis 2004).

6. In his report to the United Nations Security Council on June 3, 2004, Secretary General Kofi Annan wrote of Sudan, "For all but 11 of 48 years since independence in 1956, the Sudan has been engulfed in civil conflict. Generations of Sudanese people have known nothing but the terrible consequences

that perennial war has wrought upon the country, including large-scale death and destruction, mass internal displacement, refugee crises, and famine" (UN Security Council 2004a).

7. According to the United Nations High Commissioner for Refugees, Sudan has one of the world's highest levels of internally displaced persons— 2.6 million, with 1.7 million in the state of Khartoum near the capital region (http://www.unhcr.org/pages/49e483b76.html).

8. See Sharon E. Hutchinson's discussion of the contemporary struggle of the Nuer, who at times must go for long periods to "far-off Khartoum" to study or to work as labor migrants in the construction industry. Hutchinson notes a labor history that compels many migrants to be away for years at a time; taking pride in their work, migrants "assert . . . that they have built Khartoum" (1996, 70).

9. Levi's writings on the Holocaust have recently been collected in *The Black Hole of Auschwitz* (2005), translated by Sharon Wood. The urgency of keeping alive the memory of these atrocities so that they might act as a cautionary tale for subsequent generations is a central feature of this work.

10. Following the death of President Juvénal Habyarimana, who was killed in a plane crash (now thought to have been caused by members of his own political party), the presidential guard initiated a wave of violence targeting known government opposition. The violence escalated, and within one hundred days, about one-tenth of the population—more than eight hundred thousand people—had been murdered.

11. The Report of the International Commission of Inquiry on Darfur to the United Nations Secretary General failed to find "genocidal intent" on the part of the government of Sudan and therefore did not find a policy of genocide in Sudan; the commission found the events in Darfur no less troubling. Although a functionary or individual may entertain a "genocidal intent" in attacking victims with the specific intent of annihilating a part or group thought to be a "hostile ethnic" community, such actions must be determined on a case-by-case basis according to the commission. But international offenses, like those in Darfur, that constitute "crimes against humanity or large-scale war crimes may be no less serious and heinous than genocide" (UNICOD, 2005, 132).

12. As noted in the International Court ICTR (United Nations International Criminal Tribunal for Rwanda) appeals chamber, genocide "is a crime which has been committed by the low-level executioner and the high-level planner or instigator alike" (cited in UNICOD 2005, 132). There may need to be more consideration of aspects of "effective control" of attacks and the nature of "instigation" on the part of government authorities to really get at the nature of widespread atrocities in the contemporary world. Confirmation of such links and the smoking guns of governmental policy machines are hard to come by, and the lack of efforts to stop such actions may it self be a form of complicity.

13. In Sudan, the groups of educated Southern local civil servants that acted as intermediaries with traditional groups in the South were not well integrated in the leadership of Southern groups and were somewhat hesitant speaking for the communities they were called on to represent. During the change to a newly independent Sudan, the serious problems of power sharing, resource allocation, and a less centralized form of government were never fully addressed. These issues have been at the heart of civil conflict in the country since independence (see Deng 1995; D. Johnson 2003).

14. The forging of internal borders often follows the polarization of ethnic, racial, regional, and or religious groups. "This proliferation of internal borders— whether imaginary, symbolic, or a cover for economic or power struggles—and its corollary, the exacerbation of identification with particular localities, give rise to exclusionary practices, 'identity closure,' and persecution, which, as seen, can easily lead to pogroms, even genocide" (Mbembe 2001, 87).

15. UNICOD 2005, 43–44.

16. Darfur means "the homeland of the Fur people"; "dars" or "homelands" may be thought of as districts. Darfur has a diverse population representing more than thirty different ethnic communities, including cattle and camel herders and agriculturalists.

17. The Secretary General of the United Nations, in June 2004, included the Darfur crisis in a document to the Security Council otherwise devoted to the resolution and monitoring of the crisis in southern Sudan. Warning that the resolution of the southern conflict could proceed only with an ending of marauding and violence in Darfur, it stated that "The catastrophic situation in Darfur is a problem that will make a Sudanese peace agreement much harder to implement. A meaningful agreement in Darfur will be fundamental to the success of a future United Nations role in the Sudan; to conduct a consent-based monitoring and verification operation in one part of the country while there is ongoing conflict in another part would prove politically unsustainable inside the Sudan and internationally" (UN Security Council, Report of the Secretary General on the Sudan, no. 0436965, June 3, 2004). See also Security Council Resolution 1547, no. 0438626 (June 11, 2004), which refers in paragraph 6 to the Secretary General's report and the ongoing crisis in Darfur.

18. The spill over of the North–South conflict brought the war to a number of other regions as well, including eastern Sudan, the Southern Blue Nile region, the Nuba Mountains, and Darfur. "Fighting has spread into theatres outside the southern Sudan and beyond the Sudans' borders. Not only are Muslims fighting Muslims, but Africans are fighting Africans. A war once described as being fought over scarce resources is now being waged for the total control of abundant oil reserves" (D. Johnson 2003, i).

19. See the press article written by Secretary General of the United Nations Kofi A. Annon "Darfur: A Peaceful Option," *The Washington Times*, May 26, 2005.

20. Members of the so-called African tribes speak their own dialect in addition to Arabic; members of Arabic tribes speak only Arabic. With a high measure of intermarriage, shared cultural traditions, and no significant differences in "outward physical appearance" from one another, distinctions between the groups must be underscored ideologically. The media and some political circles have increasingly insisted on promoting the idea of an Arab–African divide since the 1980s; the "sedentary and nomadic character of the groups constitutes one of the main distinctions between them" in fact (UNICOD 2005).

21. While the SLA/M's support comes largely, although not completely, from the Fur, Masalit, and Zaghawa, the JEM is composed mostly of Zaghawa supporters. The Zaghawa have strong ties to Chad and are both camel herders and agriculturalists.

22. As Flint and de Waal have noted, "The Kalashnikov rifle changed the moral order of Darfur" (2008, 46). See Flint and de Waal (2008) on the militarization of Darfur and the role of leaders such as Musa Hilal of the Mahamid of Darfur's nomadic Zizeigat Arab group. Musa Hilal, after his father Sheihh Hilal was incapacitated in 1986, became, according to Flint and de Waal, "the most powerful leader of the government-supported militias that have come to be known as 'Janjawiid.'" With government support and the prestige of his father he became a singular force in Darfur (35).

23. The notion of counterinsurgency can turn a peaceful village into what may be considered a "legitimate" military target for the government; activities of the Janjaweed are often clouded by the need to engage in counterinsurgency. The Janjaweed are often referred to as "armed bandits or uncontrolled elements" by government authorities, while "giving them authorization or encouragement to attack their long-term enemies" in the name of counterinsurgency (UNICOD 2005, 37).

24. The idea of Nuer and Dinka people, as Douglas H. Johnson suggests, may capture the reality of contemporary Sudan more accurately, as "tribes" shift and change all the time (D. Johnson 2003).

25. See also Lacey (2004).

26. Though the militias are loosely affiliated with the government and have no legal basis under Sudanese law, the Popular Defense Forces (PDF) has a legal basis in Sudanese law and is considered a paramilitary group parallel to the regular army. Some militias may have a command structure that includes tribal leaders and officers from the regular army, but these groups have no legislative basis under Sudanese law, and all of these groups have been referred

to by victims as Janjaweed. The PDF fights alongside government forces, often wearing the same uniforms of the units they are fighting with, and supply lines run from the PDF to the Arab tribal militias, including uniforms, ammunition, and payments. Weapons, ammunition, and regular supplies are distributed to the militias by "the army, senior civilian authorities" at the local level, as noted by the PDF (UNICOD 2005, 33–34).

27. Although the Anglo-Egyptian Sudan was administered as a condominium in which both the United Kingdom and Egypt were to share equal dominium, in practice the United Kingdom remained in control of the relationship.

28. Human Rights Watch researcher Julie Flint notes, "The first, and most striking, thing I found in Darfur was a completely empty land—mile after mile of burned and abandoned villages that constitute irrefutable evidence of a scorched-earth policy the government says doesn't exit. Hundreds of thousands of Masalit farmers, Sudanese of African descent, were living in the rural areas I visited little more than six months ago. Today there is, quite literally, no-one" (2004).

29. Most attacks began in the early morning hours, lasting for several hours or, in some cases, several days. Attack accounts contain evidence of "aircraft used for reconnaissance purposes," or air support used to supply ground troops with additional weapons and ammunition. A host of weapons were employed during attacks, from Kalashikov G3s and rocket-propelled grenades (RPGs) to Toyota pickup trucks fitted with Dushka (12.7 mm) machine guns and Hound rocket launcher systems, which were used to fire into and across villages during attacks. Many of the same trucks, mounted with machine guns and other weapons, were used after the attacks to carry looted property from the village, and most of the heavy weaponry was the property of the Sudanese armed forces.

30. The government of Sudan may increasingly face resistance from its own soldiers. Some soldiers are said to avoid orders in order to stay out of the conflict. *The Economist* reported: "Some servicemen are so repelled by what they have been made to do in Darfur that they are finding ways to avoid obeying orders. One air force officer complains that he was told he would be bombing rebels, but instead saw women running out of the huts he had attacked with their robes ablaze. 'I couldn't do it any more,' he says" (*Economist* 2004).

31. U.S. Senator Sam Brownback and Representative Frank Wolf, in a report on their visit to Sudan, noted that "it was clear that only villages in habited by black African Muslims were being targeted. Arab villages sitting just next to African ones, miles from the nearest towns, have been left unscathed" (Brownback and Wolf 2004, 4).

32. Sudan agreed to send about three hundred African Union troops, deployed to protect the unarmed truce monitors on July 6, 2004, on the eve

of the United Nations Security Council resolution on Darfur. Speaking before the African Union meeting in Addis Ababa, UN Secretary General Kofi Annan told the group, following his recent visit to Darfur, "The ruined villages, the camps overflowing with sick and hungry women and children, the fear in the eyes of the people, should be a clear warning to us all. Without action, the brutalities already inflicted on the civilian population of Darfur could be a prelude to even greater humanitarian catastrophe—a catastrophe that could destabilize the region" (Maclean 2004).

33. The government is in possession of the only helicopters and airplanes capable of bombing the civilian population; although Khartoum denies any involvement in the crisis, its complicity and collaboration with the Janjaweed seems clear.

34. The hybrid United Nations–African Union force accepted by the government of Sudan in 2007 is no guarantee of a lasting peace.

35. Secretary General SG/SM/10628, SC/8824, AFR/11431, September 11, 2006.

36. That is when the resolution of such a crisis requires, as in the case of Sudan, ground troops. President Omar Hassan al-Bashir insisted for some time that United Nations troops would not be allowed to return to Sudan as peacekeepers. Secretary General Ban Ki-moon stressed that fact that in order to bring about peace, all agreements must be respected, long before the international court issued a warrant for al-Bashir for war crimes.

37. Crimes against humanity are distinguished from war crimes by the fact that they may occur in peacetime or periods of armed conflict as "part of a widespread or systematic practice of atrocities (or attacks)" directed against the civilian population (UNICOD 2005, 52). Such offences against human dignity as "murder, extermination, enslavement, deportation, forcible transfer of population, torture, rape, and other forms of sexual violence" are among the incidents that define this category of international crime (52).

38. The interplay of the political ecology of the region turns up in Darfur with a vengeance, with the delicate balance of nature tipping to push the pastoralist from the North much further south and much earlier than in years past, while drought and the expanding desert and Khartoum presses nomads into the Janjaweed. However, both political factionalism from Khartoum and the progressive ideology of "Arabism" in the post–Cold War period has contributed to a polarization and fixing of cultural markers of identity.

3. The Inexhaustible Sense of Exile

1. The photograph, like a shipwreck, confines the photographed to a time and space forever alienated from a present. This becomes particularly compelling

when the photograph is used as a vehicle for representing our own and or other culture(s)—a compass employed for the navigation of cultural distance. The desire to see images of immigrants in Italy in recent years has been fueled by a search for proof of the migrants' possession of a wholly alien life, evidence that might justify the exclusion of newcomers. This may sound strange, but it is the manner of representation and urgency with which the images are sought that gives way to more than a curiosity about the "significant details" such photographs may reveal.

2. Like social reformer Jacob August Riis (1849–1914), author of the famous *How the Other Half Lives* (1890), some of the journalists hoped to expose the poor conditions of the migrants, though other images were destined to end up in the employ of anti-immigrant positions in local and national media outlets.

3. Of the best of the images, we say that it is finely crafted, in possession of a kind of beauty, when we are suspicious of its manufacture, that it is a fake or a counterfeit. Somehow, an uneasy sensibility plagues our relationship with the form and yet it accompanies us like an old friend—an eye in the world that sees while remaining unseen. Like a meteorite the world (out there), "comes to be 'inside' photographs" (Sontag 1990, 80). The selection process of the shot, or the magic in the eye of the photographer, comes to the forefront only when we are asked to reflect on the art or when we have become its victims. Frozen in a photographic imaginary more interpretive than visual, a spatial marker of memory more than temporality, we sense—however subtly—the photograph's inscription of the presence of its subject. The record—a document of the integrity and fluidity of this dance, or the viewing, describing, and interpretation of the image—shuttles between the world (out there) and the meanings (for us) employed to account for it (Price 1994, 6). Yet in an instant, this ambiguity—integral to image making—may vanish, confining the subject to an undeniable classificatory register: the criminal, the immigrant, the refugee, the black, and so on. The photograph marks the primary contours of official legibility for the state in documents of identity, along with the surname (Scott 1998, 71). As Roland Barthes mused in *Camera Lucida*, whatever the photograph "grants to vision" or lends to the organization of sight, we can be certain that "a photograph is always invisible: it is not it that we see" (1981, 6). Rather, it is what is working through a photograph that at times we see. There is something funereal about the mugshot and how each migrant that passes through the regular arm of the state is first given the honor of the identity card, the permission of stay, a kind of forced photographic public garment. Copies of this picture are filed away as if lying dormant for the day that they may serve some use, no doubt for the state. The identity card and the photograph that it contains also hold a promise of equitable and fair treatment, of the opportunity to work and enjoy the fruits of labor, of some form of

social participation in the host society and perhaps representation in local affair of government (municipal). The card is, in short, a kind of passport to social visibility. Yet today in the European Union the card indicates an odd status shared by some ten million legal long-term residents who are noncitizens and are therefore excluded from certain basic rights (Dunkerley 2002). European Union citizenship remains determined by national citizenship, in effect limiting the free movement and residence of millions of legal residents.

4. Immigration in the early nineties achieved the status of a "crisis" in Italy. At the national level, many focused on the new political developments issuing from the provisions of the Martelli Bill and its subsequent revisions, while on the local scene, preoccupation with the impact of the newcomers on the life of the quarter seemed most important. In many cases, the immigrant is entangled in a complex web of assumptions and stereotypes and is confined to representation in the most abstract form: a numeric link in a chain leading to an unwanted population. Freedom from this world of the imagination is difficult, as it is made with the same fabric as the most taken-for-granted aspects of the commonsense world, that is to say, it is naturalized and naturalizing. The shift to the right in the government has brought about a renewed thirst for images of the migrants, as the new government has designed a program of law that will make the very presence of migrants without documents a crime. Efforts to control further migrations and to present a contrast between the needy worker and the trouble-making clandestine migrant have begun to surface.

5. It is at times difficult to imagine that a certain contemporary modality of looking and the conviction that "seeing is believing" actually has a history. We seldom stop to question the visual, so our "ways of seeing" achieve a kind of naturalized comfort in our world. In this strange zone beyond the level of the discursive, the photographic representation situates its images in a moment of disappearance and forgetting. A marker and an "instantaneous flash of death," the photograph announces its own precariousness as a form of representation (Cadava 1995, 226). It is odd to think that we might wish to see something as it were, only to forget it, yet this is the way of ritual, part of the ritual process that anthropologist Victor Turner explored long ago. It is also an integral element in the availability of invisibility—the tendency to acknowledge things that may be lost to us on other occasions, only to awaken and discover this unacknowledged universe in some distant future, coming to know again that which has been hidden from us—if only a moment ago. It is as though we animate the image with our very being, in order to set in motion what has been stilled by the rising and falling of the shutter. In this phenomenon is the photographic time that may even immobilize the hint of an atmosphere only dimly illuminated in the lives of those caught in the monocular gaze of the camera (Shore

1998). This is as close to dreams as we may come, and dreamscapes have always fascinated photographers, blurring in an instant the aesthetic and the documentary or truth claims of the process.

6. I thank Dr. Anna Botta of the Smith College Department of Comparative Literature and Italian Language and Literature, for introducing me to the work of Roberto M. Dainotto.

7. An early interest in the "gray and bureaucratic" life of the city lead scholars to explore the documentary and philosophical elements in local and regional economic development; the *Rivista Storica Itailana* (an Italian historical journal) was established as early as 1884, growing out of interdisciplinary discussions (Bongiovanni 2001, 234–41). Turin became not only the center of a rich intellectual life, but also one of the core cityscapes of a rising industrial world, the political community that struggled over it, and the intellectual groups studying the process of a changing nation.

8. The chapel of Turin Cathedral, just to the north of Palazzo Reale, links the Savoyard capital and residence, with the realm of the divine becoming deeply implicated in the display and ceremony of power. John Beldon Scott explores the connection between the otherworldly chapel that Guarini constructed, the shroud, and the power of the Savoyard in his book *Architecture for the Shroud: Relic and Ritual in Turin* (2003). Moving toward the distant Alpine gateway to the North, the Dora Grossa—another Roman city artery—is now the present-day Via Garibaldi, a pedestrian street that runs a full kilometer and spills into Piazza Statuto, the site of the last great labor protests, which leads off toward the Susa Valley.

9. The storage areas of the Vercelli house were always filled with mementos, photographs, posters, and newspaper articles that lead the memory back home or to the myriad places in the diaspora that marked a place where loved ones could be found. The discovery of a local print shop's images of Chiekh Amadou Bamba (c. 1853–1927), followed a short while later by pendants and buttons of Chiekh Ibra Fall (c. 1858–1930), affectionately known as the "light" of the Mourid Movement signaled the significant presence of the Baye Fall in the Corso Vercelli house (Roberts and Roberts 2003, 109). Each was a potential sign of a journey that would lead back home, an imaginary compass held aloft for just such navigations.

10. Few had ever entered any of these residences and the thought of ever having to see migrants up close and not through the sanitized lens of a camera would no doubt fill many with horror. One city official told me quite frankly that even the police were afraid to enter these houses, something I found hard to believe, although it lent another dimension to the idea of the unpredictable migrant as a danger to the community if provoked. Inside this house and many

house just like it, however, a world unfolded that Italians may have found not unlike their own experience in foreign places and perhaps even comforting; it might have gone a long way to dispelling stereotypes and misunderstandings that have unchecked found their way to the present.

11. In one room, the ceiling had fallen in on one side and Senegalese masons were repairing the damage; in a residence that at times held more than a hundred people in six rooms there was a small sink in one of the rooms on the top floor and no shower. People took sponge baths at the top of the stairs. The winters were cold in the sub-Alpine city, and the summers almost unbearable. The plaster of the wall, cracked and caked with traces of the industrial city, often took on the dampness of the external world, but proved a cooling balm in the summers. The Vercelli house was known throughout the city as a symbol of the problem with foreign workers. "You rent to one or two and soon you have fifty" summed up the local folk justifications against renting to migrants and an indication of what might happen if one did.

12. Comparing the craft of painting to the photographer's art, Benjamin turns to a photo taken by Dauthendy of a woman in Moscow: "Immerse yourself in such a picture long enough and you will recognize how alive the contradictions are here, too: the most precise technology can give its products a magical value such as a painted picture can never again have for us. No matter how artful the photographer, no matter how carefully posed his subject, the beholder feels an irresistible urge to search such a picture for the tiny spark of contingency, of the Here and Now, with which reality has so to speak seared the subject, to find the inconspicuous spot where in the immediacy of that long-forgotten moment the future subsists so eloquently that we, looking back, may rediscover it" (Benjamin 1979, 243). The "spark of contingency" that has "seared the subject" remains a channel through the frozen moment of the image to the narrative space of the forgotten context of the image making.

13. Elizabeth Edwards accorded photography the role of "demystification of the physical world"; like the many technical inventions of the nineteenth-century, photography helped to dramatically change the manner in which the world was seen (1990, 237).

14. Patricia A. Morton, in her examination of the Paris Exposition of 1931, found a convergence between ideas and justifications for colonial rule and the very architectural forms and organization of the public display at the fair: "Krzysztof Pomian theorizes the collection as a go-between between the visible world of objects and the invisible world of meanings. The pavilions represented the invisible order of French colonialism made visible and concrete by the architectural expression of the colonies. . . . Architecture played a central role in the description and classification of cultures of the colonized races into hierarchies based on stages of evolution" (2000, 89).

15. In the Stockholm exhibition of 1897, a "world of consumption," along with its dazzling promise of point of detachment—a bird's-eye view from which the city beyond could be taken in as a new form of spectacle—was solemnized by a postcard. In his book *Recognizing European Modernities: A Montage of the Present* (1995), Allan Pred set the 1897 Stockholm exhibition in the context of new patterns of consumption and class division taking shape at the turn of the century in Sweden. The exhibition was a site not only of what Pred calls "wishful Bourgeois mythologizing," by which the proper behavior in public and private spaces was promoted for the ordering of the everyday lives of the city's working population, but also of the inaugural ground of a world of desire, nationalism, and a consumer culture: "Stare at what is immediately beneath: the halls and pavilions containing all the goods you can imagine. The entire world of consumption literally at your feet. A haven on earth where everything is possible. An earthly paradise where there is no end to material happiness, to a now and future happiness made possible by national progress. Grow dizzy from the surrounding sights of bliss and harmony, grow giddy with visions of consuming desire, grow light-headed with fantastic images of the future, rush across a flying bridge to the central cupola in order to confirm that you have entered heaven, to inform others that you are sitting on top of the world, to write a 'wish-you-were-here' postcard. Articulate modernity. Buying and writing postcards that could be mailed on the spot—postmarked Kupolen—became a 'real mania.' By the end of the exhibition, over 100,000 cards had been purchased and sent from the cupola location, thus, in all probability, defining the initial popular breakthrough of the postcard in Sweden." The exotic world of the other in the Stockholm exhibition was, according to Pred, primarily employed as "an advertising ploy" (1995, 60). The articles of exotica given away for free were largely meant to link a restricted set of commercial meanings to a kind of nostalgia for the exposition and the commodities on display there. The exhibitionary rhetoric of other expositions served to produce a kind of mobilization of diverse forms of power and feelings of empowerment in the participants: modernity consumed, spectators drinking in the momentary "imaginary transcendence" of the constraints of the mundane world in this itinerant landscape.

16. Native peoples succumbed to the European passion for the collection of curiosities and the preoccupation with the now-peopled imaginary evolutionary landscapes. The triumphs of capitalism and industry were exhibited side by side in the great World's Fairs with human collections, curios of exotic lands who on occasion performed local dances and demonstrated "primitive" technologies. The living exhibit was complimented by the fascination with photography as an anthropological tool. Such expositions of "human exotica" were featured in the World's Fairs of Paris in 1889 and 1900, Chicago in 1893, Buffalo in 1901, and St. Louis in 1904 (Morton 2000; Hinsley 1996, 121). The desire to see the

daily routines of local life soon gave way to certain penchant for entertainment, as millions of spectators turned out in the late nineteenth century to consume an enactment of the global. The range of "peoples of the world," assembled to this end, is revealing in its attempt at encompassing the previously unknown frontiers of the globe (Street 1992, 122). The public interest was accompanied the enthusiasm of commercial impresarios and the professional curiosity of scientific amateurs: "'Natives' were brought over to perform at London theatres, as in the case of some Batwa pygmies seen at the Hippodrome in 1905. Eskimos. So-called 'Aztecs,' members of Bantu races, Australian aboriginals, and Sioux Indians, as well as the Ainu from Japan and Batwa Pygmies from the Congo were all variously brought to Europe to be exhibited to the general public, also incidentally providing anthropologists with a source of study that saved them the difficulty of procuring specimens themselves" (122).

17. The photograph was at once a record of the fair and a link to the greater world represented through its exhibits. Containing an implicit promise of an exotic imaginary such a copy allowed people to "take home personalized, visual souvenirs, extending the fair's influence far beyond the millions of visitors who passed through . . . its gates" (Breitbart 1997, 45). The desire for this other world was an integral part of the very process of fair making. The ability of the expositions to provide entertainment, a vision of the exotic, and a reenactment of "authentic" native experience and ways of life was fully endorsed by the commercial logic of the enterprise. As culture became ossified along the lines of its materiality, this process was articulated through concerns with the primacy of scientific representation, classification, and documentation. While some of the images of the events of the fairs document events as they unfold, others are staged for effect and compliance with cultural expectations: "If authenticity conflicted with the desired image, it was ignored . . . it is often impossible to tell the 'real' image from the re-creation. Both have become representations" (31).

18. For those who peopled the fairs, participation became a significant feature of their lives, some having traveled great distances from homes to which many would never return; by 1904, some of the "native" workers in the fair cycles had appeared in as many as three World's Fairs (Breitbart 1997, 40). The social and cultural dislocation the fairs exacted on the lives of those who populated the historical tableaux and anthropological villages was seldom calculated as part of the cost of the display. The theatrical quality of some of the exhibitions was a feature of the fair itself and not limited to the portions reserved for "indigenous" peoples; rather, the whole complex was a new kind of organization of visual culture—a privileging of spectacle and industry (40).

19. Each exhibition was meticulously documented, recovered in a popular and official archive: any act of photographic recovery must return to the context

from which it has been drawn. For John Berger, this means telling the story of this frozen instant by placing the image in "narrated time," accomplishing its recontextualization in the flow of a narrative, not in its own time which is irretrievable (McQuire 1998, 60).

20. If we think for a moment about the many uses and meanings of the images we circulate—a postcard, a greeting, an image of a newborn relative shuttled over the Internet, or the framed family photo in the corner of an office—we can see that the ceremony of our interchange with these pictures has changed, is changing, and will no doubt continue to provide surprising combinations.

21. One of the favorite videos from Senegal to watch during leisure time is that of the Griot, a kind of traditional African historian and story teller who celebrates the accomplishments and good standing of noble families in Senegal. The audience is a veritable who's who of Senegal; the singing of the Griot is punctuated by the gift of money in recognition of the gift that the Griot mentions. The Griot now travels all over the world performing for Senegalese audiences throughout the diaspora. No matter where migrants find themselves, they may hear news from home and enjoy the competition of Griot who wish to rise to leading positions in national and diasporic popularity. Griot may amass great wealth and influence through their association with important families and political leaders; beyond this, contact with the diaspora provides an untapped resource, as the visit of the Griot becomes a celebration of Senegalese culture and oral tradition abroad. The travels of Griot and religious leaders of the many Muslim brotherhoods place members of diaspora communities in relationships to centers of power that would be impossible to access in Senegal. Diaspora allows new arrangements of power to emerge for those willing to innovate the old order, while the diaspora is included on the circuit of ritual activities that extend from Senegal. Perhaps in some small way, these activities move beyond class and caste boundaries, but of course this does not mean freedom from the new forms of exclusion imposed by many host societies as migrants encounter the structure of marginal or at least limited urban racial spaces that they must call home.

4. Crossing Modernity

1. This delicate balance of subject positions takes on the tonalities of humor in Ousmane Sembene's *Guelwaar*, when Barthélémy, who arrives with the air of a metropolitan, demands that the local police chief, Gora, assist him in finding the body of his father, who through some mix-up has gone missing in the hospital. At one point, Barthélémy even produces his French passport, insisting on the superiority of French governmental procedures. As the film progresses Barthélémy begins to understand the complexity of Senegalese

cultural practices and to see Police Chief Gora as a master of negotiation among the diverse ethnic and religious constituencies, an astute translator and cultural intermediary and an able diplomat, remarking at one point "J'ai toujours ete sénégalais" ("I have always been Senegalese"), finally returning home perhaps to continue the legacy of his activist father, Guelwaar (Murphy 2001, 207). Barthélémy, the eldest son of Guelwaar—a Christian leader and open critic of the government's dependence on foreign aid—represents not only the myriad members of the Senegalese community in diaspora, but also the closest link to the generation of his father, the assimilated Independence generation largely educated in France, living embodiments of a Franco-African tradition that continued after Independence through French aid, special advisors, and a governing elite that divided its time between the French capital and Senegal. However, this younger generation is capable of making a transition to a new world, one in which Senegalese political culture might attain an autonomy from the former colonial power.

2. This section is based in large part on Donald M. Lowe's *History of Bourgeois Perception* (1982).

3. Diasporic nostalgia then seeks a kind of *eurchronia* (a better society in the future) rather than a utopia (a concept implying spatial rather than temporal distance from the present; Lowe 1982, 46).

4. See Antonioni's film *La Notte* (1961).

5. A distinction that emphasizes differences of both class and caste.

6. In both the films *Guelwaar* (1993) and *Faat Kine* (2000) Sembene presents a progressive youth culture unafraid to challenge the errors of their parents' generation in government and social life. In *Guelwaar* the youth respond to a figure not unlike Cheikh Tidiane Sall, save that he is a member of the Catholic community; he takes the government to task for its dependency on foreign aid, the principle theme of the film.

7. In Algeria this lesson was learned with a vengeance. Although Fanon warns of the need to educate the army politically, in Algeria it was indeed the "crystallization of the caste spirit" among the officers that provided a ready-made political class for the post-Independence state, making the transition to a nonrevolutionary generation difficult (Fanon 1963, 202–3). Just as for a cadre of officers experience in the anticolonial campaigns becomes the price of entrance to the world of politics, in the world of *The Last of the Empire,* the price of entrance is military knowledge derived from a former colonial source.

8. In the period between 1995 and 2001 there was a slight growth in the Senegalese economy austerity measures, but wage reductions and food shortages were deeply felt by much of the population. The World Bank working group expressed concerns over the bifurcation in the population, between

those who have found ways of managing the economic crisis and those who have increasingly fallen into poverty (World Bank 2002).

9. As we talked on, the video with excerpts from Senegalese television was on in the background.

10. Léopold Sédar Senghor was born October, 9, 1906, in Joal, a coastal town in Senegal.

5. Sites of Erasure

1. "The Promised Land" is a short story contained in the volume by Ousmane Sembene *Tribal Scars and Other Stories*.

2. See Michael A. Gomez (1998) for a discussion of African slaves who "fly" back to Africa.

3. T. Denean Sharpley-Whiting in *Negritude Women* delineated the erasure of women from the "genealogy of Negritude," the complex contribution of women writers like Suzanne Lacascade, introducing an Africanist/Creole literary voice during the 1920s and claiming a unique black Francophone position. The complexity of such a voice of Creole and African heritage came when such a discourse would have been considered nothing short of scandalous. As Sharpley-Whiting notes "her identification with Africa, her writing in French imbued with Creole expressions, her rich descriptions of Martinican cultural practices, and her denunciations of French racism and anti-Semitism combined to relegate her to the dustbin of black Francophone letters of the era and in years to come" (Sharpley-Whiting 2002, 14–15).

4. Miller notes that the radicalism of such figures as Lamaine Senghor would reappear toward the end of the Second World War; the work of Fanon may inherit the critique of language and the insistence on independence.

5. Here I must qualify the notion of "founding" of the negritude movement, as it becomes increasingly clear that many notions of this idea, once thought to be essential to this movement, were at play in the work of others long before negritude took shape in the hands of Senghor or others. On this point Brent Hayes Edwards's excellent treatment of early literary work of the African diaspora sets the stage for the development of negritude in the work of a number of figures such as Lamine Senghor and others working in 1920s Paris. See Brent Hayses Edwards, *The Practice of Diaspora: Literature, Translation, and the Rise of Black Internationalism* (2003), and also Miller (1998) and Sharpley-Whiting (2002).

6. The Tirailleurs Sénégalais, recruited from all over French West Africa, were founded by decree by Napoleon III in 1857. The formation of the first battalion is attributed to General Faidherbe; the troops were first employed in the conquest of the Western Sudan and the maintenance and expansion of the colonial empire and in the two World Wars (Lawler 1992, 21).

7. The title of *agrégé* of the university, according to Vaillant, was one that "professors and ambitious French parents considered synonymous with intellectual superiority" (1990, 107).

8. Senghor became in fact the grammarian of the French Constitution.

9. This process began in the informality of communications between partners in the war efforts and trusted allies and was initiated by the Supreme Commander of the Free French Forces, General De Gaulle. De Gaulle was to become a larger-than-life figure; the marshalling of his French Free Forces began in Africa with the careful orchestration of African and other would-be soldiers to fight for France, yet it was De Gaulle who would find it opportune to diminish the importance of the colonial soldiers in the liberation of France by essentially ensuring that they played a minor part in any representations of the liberation forces through the so-called whitening of the troops. Their role in the liberation of France and much of the conflict that was to follow was in effect obscured from both the French people and their allies.

10. It is curious that despite the extraordinary popularity of the First World War, images of the colonial soldier in France graced a number of advertising campaigns. The soldiers rarely enter the domain of fictional realism and remain all but absent from representations celebrating the liberation of France or struggles against the German occupation of France. For that matter, they do not appear in the films of American reenactments of the Second World War. African Americans have also for the most part been absent from the American film industry's historical films on the war.

11. Few have recorded the lives of soldiers caught between social and cultural worlds in transition. In African literature and somewhat in film, the colonial soldier is caught between the world of metropolitan France and a homeland that can no longer understand the strange demands he makes to take part in local politics or toy with relationships with the neocolonial powers, claiming back pay and other benefits that recall and complicate the nature and meaning of colonialism.

6. Comrade Storyteller

1. The photo is found in Anthony Clayton's book *France, Soldiers, and Africa* (1988).

2. Radhika Mohanram suggests that gender and race combine to encapsulate the "other" in a world set off from modernity; filmic images in this discursive climate can, then, render people only as kinds of "problems"—exceptions to be viewed with scientific interest. Mohanram writes: "This construction of identity allows gendered (white) male subjects to enter temporality, modernity, progression and development. It also functions to create a hierarchy wherein the

bodies of women, perverts and blacks occupy a more ambiguous space, marked as primitive, undeveloped, forever aspiring to play 'catch-up' with their straight white male counterparts, who are already situated in modernity" (1999, 53).

3. In Senegal, "men of color," often from the French West Indies, had been called into the service of the military as noncommissioned officers and regular troops in the Napoleonic era. Former slaves whose freedom was purchased by France were required to serve in gratitude for fourteen years in one of the French battalions, formed as early as 1819 (Lawler 1992, 19).

4. Again, Myron Echenberg puts the figure at closer to 175,000 African forces participating in the First World War (Echenberg 1991, 88).

5. American intelligence had considered landing sites, one of them potentially Dakar, just after Pearl Harbor (see Lawler 1992).

6. A new African army with greater access to citizenship modeled along assimilationist principles was articulated at Brazzaville. As Echenberg writes, "De Gaulle's grudging promise at Brazzaville in 1944 to work out a new deal for Africans and for colonial peoples generally was partly a response to the military efforts of France's colonial subjects, partly an admission of the failures of earlier colonial policies, and partly a recognition of the new international climate ushered in by the Atlantic charter" (Echenberg 1991, 104, 117).

7. See also Farmer (1999).

7. Travel Warnings

1. In her treatment of the diaspora experience of Italians in *Italy's Many Diasporas*, Donna R. Gabaccia notes the use of military metaphors to refer to mass migrations across the globe. Entering the global economy as the "new workers of the world," Italians from Buenes Aires, New York, and Marseilles spoke of their experience as "campaigns," and returning migrants were called "reduci" (veterans) as they returned either in victory or defeat from their sojourn abroad (Gabaccia 2000, 82–83). Women left behind were called "white widows," in contradistinction to the widows draped in the black of mourning garments; the hardships and workload greatly increased for such women, who took on the substantive management of the everyday toil of the family (87). Grouped in communities called "colonies," Italians set up lives based on the village communities from which they originated in diaspora.

2. With savings from earnings in Europe, some may return home to start a business venture on a very small scale, but for most, it is clear that someone will have to replace them in diaspora, becoming the link to the global economy without which many families simply would not survive. After more than a decade in Italy, my friend is tired of working on a foundry cleaning team—a good job—returning home only a few times in many years and for the most part

living outside of the Italian social world. Back home, the equivalent of the "white widows" of the present are the sole caretakers of children, family compounds, and aging relatives, and only occasionally travel to Europe.

3. The declaration of a national state of emergency on immigration has brought in sweeping police state powers and will extend holding units devoted to the "identification and classification" of the so-called illegal immigrants who are now, under the new measures, criminals in Italy.

4. As Paul Gilroy points out, race-driven ideologies helped to insulate the colonized from parity with their European counterparts: "Disturbing views of government in action can be derived from close historical studies of colonial domination, to which the idea of 'race' and the machinations of racial hierarchy were always integral" (2005, 17).

5. In his discussion of the South Asian diaspora in Britain, Peter van der Veer says that the "negative valuation of the 'established' of the unsettling movement of 'strangers'" (1995, 7) may at once fortify the sense of belonging among the "established" and among those who are otherwise marginalized, so that exclusionary practices aimed at the migrant may feed more or less directly into nationalist discourse (7). Van der Veer continues, "Whereas the diaspora of others fortifies the sense of belonging among the established, one's own diaspora tends to strengthen the longing to be elsewhere" (7).

6. One of the most recent glitches in the identification process occurred in the now-infamous Brandon Mayfield case, when a lawyer from Portland, Oregon, was detained as a material witness in the Madrid train bombing. The FBI mistakenly matched him with partial latent fingerprints "found on a plastic bag found near the scene of the attacks" in March 2004 (Kershaw and Lichtblau 2004). The digital image of the original was sent to the FBI for analysis from Spain; in a peculiar turn of events, the "poor quality of the digital image" was blamed for the error. The FBI database was searched against the partial latent print, comparing it to millions of known prints, which led to a "match" with fingerprints on file from Mr. Mayfield's military service. The incident calls into question the aggressive measures of the Justice Department in a post-9/11 climate to-under the cover of a "federal material witness statute"—detain persons suspected of having information about a crime. The director of the American Civil Liberties Union of Oregon argued that "The Justice Department is using the material witness statute in a way that it was never meant to be used, and this is just the most dramatic example of that trend" (Kershaw and Lichtblau 2004).

7. In fact, the proposed cost of the contract system that would employ an interlinked network of computers to track visitors to the United States even before they set foot on American soil is set at an estimated $15 billion and counting. Keeping track of over three hundred border crossings on land, air,

and sea and checking information against persons that might pose a terrorist threat is a daunting task, to say the least. In the proposed systems, a visitor will in essence be "screened by a global web of databases" long before they come face to face with a border guard (Lichtblau and Markoff 2004). Thought to be a "virtual border," the system set up by the Department of Homeland Security will monitor some three hundred million foreign visitors a year, selecting techniques from facial recognition to biometric sensors hidden in passports to control the frontier.

8. The struggle to keep people out is ongoing, as in Italy (with its new state of emergency for immigration), a country that is still trying to be seen as a leader in the new European constellation by aligning its immigration policies with the climate of closure. The Martelli Bill of 1990 in effect provided Italy with the first comprehensive legislation on immigration in its history, and amnesties for undocumented workers in 1987, 1990, and 1995 were conducted in hopes of coming to terms with growing numbers of unemployed migrants and the ever-present problem of their insertion into the informal economy. Now the measures turn on policing, fingerprinting, and the posting of soldiers on street patrols and in so-called sensitive public areas with expanded arrest powers, in a growing concern with the continued influx of "refugees" by boat, initially from the south of the country and now with renewed focus on the entire country.

9. It is certain that we need a new group portrait of Europe, and if we are to accomplish this, we must place the European at the back of the line like everyone else and arrange a portrait that does not necessarily privilege their European-ness as a kind of free-floating element that cannot be mixed with anything else (a purity of form).

10. In The *Origins of Totalitarianism* (1976) Hannah Arendt not only warned us against race thinking, but viewed processes of exclusion and inclusion from a broad perspective in which the contours of European state formation could be understood to some degree also in relation to colonial histories.

Bibliography

Abbas, Ackbar. 1997. *Hong Kong: Culture and the Politics of Disappearance.* Minneapolis: University of Minnesota Press.

Achebe, Chinua. 2000. *Home and Exile.* Oxford: Oxford University Press.

Agamben, Giorgio. 1998. *Homo Sacer: Sovereign Power and Bare Life.* Stanford, Calif.: Stanford University Press.

————. 2005. *State of Exception.* Chicago: University of Chicago Press.

Albahari, Maurizio. 1996. "Between Mediterraean Centrality and European Periphery: Migration and Heritage in Southern Italy," *International Journal of Euro-Mediterranean Studies* 1, no. 2: 141–62.

Amnesty International Annual Report. 2005. Pol 10/001/2005. May 24.

Angel-Ajani, Asale. 1999. "Diasporic Conditions: African Women and the Cultural Politics of Crime, Race, and Gender in Rome, Italy." PhD thesis, Stanford University.

————. 2006. "Expert Witness: Notes Toward Revisiting the Politics of Listening." In Victoria Sanford and Asale Angel-Ajani, eds., *Engaged Observer: Anthropology, Advocacy, and Activism*, 76–92. New Brunswick, N.J.: Rutgers University Press.

Annan, Kofi A. 2005. "Darfur: A Peaceful Option," *Washington Times,* May 26.

Appadurai, Arjun. 1996. *Modernity at Large: Cultural Dimensions of Globalization.* Minneapolis: University of Minnesota Press.

Arendt, Hannah. 1976. *The Origins of Totalitarianism.* New York: Harcourt Brace.

Austen, Jane. 2003. *Mansfield Park.* New York: Penguin Classics.

Bâ, Sylvia Washington. 1973. *The Concept of Negritude in the Poetry of Léopold Sédar Senghor.* Princeton, N.J.: Princeton University Press.

Baldwin, James. 1985. "Stranger in the Village." In *The Price of the Ticket: Collected Nonfiction 1948–1985*, 79–90. New York: St. Martin's/Marek.

Balibar, Etienne. 1999. *Race, Nation, and Class: Ambiguous Identities*. New York: Verso.

Baptiste, Espelencia. 2002. "A Nation Deferred: Language, Ethnicity, and the Reproduction of Social Inequalities in Mauritian Primary Schools." PhD dissertation, Johns Hopkins University.

Barlet, Olivier. 2000. *African Cinemas: Decolonizing the Gaze*. London: Zed Books.

Barthes, Roland. 1981. *Camera Lucida: Reflections on Photography*. New York: Hill and Wang.

Basch, Linda, Nina Glick Schiller, and Cristina Szanton Blanc. 1994. *Nations Unbound: Transnational Projects, Postcolonial Predicaments, and Deterritorialized Nation-States*. London: Gordon and Breach Science Publishers.

Batcho, Krystine I. 2002. "Nostalgia and Reminiscence." Paper presented at the 2002 Hawaii International Conference on Social Sciences, Honolulu, HI.

Bellu, Giovanni Maria. 2004. *I fantasmi di Portopalo: Natale 1996: La morte di 300 clandesini e il silenzio dell'italia*. Milano: Mondadori.

Benhabib, Seyla. 2002. *The Claims of Culture: Equality and Diversity in the Global Era*. Princeton, N.J.: Princeton University Press.

Benjamin, Walter. 1968. *Illuminations: Essays and Reflections*. New York: Schocken.

————. 1979. *One-Way Street and Other Essays*. Edmund Jephcott and Kingsley Shorter, trans. London: NLB.

Ben Jelloun, Tahar. 1998. *Il razzismo spiegato a mia figlia*. Milan: Bompiani.

Bennett, Tony. 1994. "The Exhibitionary Complex." In Nicholas B. Dirks, Goff Eley, and Sherry B. Ortner eds., *Culture, Power, History: A Reader in Contemporary Social Theory*. Princeton, N.J.: Princeton University Press.

Benvenisti, Meron. 2000. *Sacred Landscape: The Buried History of the Holy Land Since 1948*. Berkeley: University of California Press.

Bertram, Christoph. 1995. *Europe in the Balance: Securing the Peace Won in the Cold War*. Washington, D.C.: Carneige Endowment.

Bhabha, Homi K. 1994. *The Location of Culture*. London/New York: Routledge.

Blackmore, Josiah. 2001. "Foreword: A Shipwrecks Legacy." In C. R. Boxer, ed. and trans., *The Tragic History of the Sea*. Minneapolis: University of Minnesota Press.

Blaut, J. M. 1993. *The Colonizer's Model of the World: Geographical Diffusionism and Eurocentric History*. New York: The Guilford Press.

Bongie, Chris. 1991. *Exotic Memories: Literature, Colonialism, and the Fin de Siècle*. Stanford, Calif.: Stanford University Press.

Bongiovanni, Bruno. 2001. "La Mondernistica." In Angelo d'Orsi, ed., *La Città, la storia, il secolo: Cento anni di storiografia a Torino*. Bologna: Il Mulino.

Boone, Catherine. 2003. *Political Topographies of the African State: Territorial Authority and Institutional Choice.* Cambridge, U.K.: Cambridge University Press.

Bourdieu, Pierre. 1998. *Practical Reason.* Stanford, Calif.: Stanford University Press.

Bourdieu, Pierre, Luc Boltanski, Robert Castel, Jean-Claude Chamboredon, and Dominique Schnapper. 1990. *Photography: A Middlebrow Art.* Shaun Whiteside, trans. Stanford, Calif.: Stanford University Press.

Breitbart, Eric. 1997. *A World On Display: Photographs from the St. Louis World's Fair 1904.* Albuquerque: University of New Mexico Press.

Brown, Jacqueline Nassy. 2005. *Dropping Anchor, Setting Sail: Geographies of Race in Black Liverpool.* Princeton, N.J.: Princeton University Press.

Brownback, Sam, and Frank Wolf. 2004. "Trip Report: Darfur, Western Sudan, June 27–29, 2004." http://www.house.gov/wolf/.

Burgin, Victor. 1982. *Thinking Photography.* London: Macmillan.

———— 1988. *The End of Art Theory: Criticism and Postmodernity.* London: Macmillan.

———— 1996. *In/Different Spaces: Place and Memory in Visual Culture.* Berkeley: University of California Press.

Burroughs, Edgar Rice. 1914. *Tarzan of the Apes.* Chicago: A. C. McClurg.

Burton, Richard D. E. 2001. *Blood in The City: Violence and Revelation in Paris 1789–1945.* Ithaca, N.Y.: Cornell University Press.

Butler, Judith. 2004. *Precarious Life: The Powers of Mourning and Violence.* New York: Verso.

Cadava, Eduardo. 1995. "Words of Light: Theses on the Photography of History." In Patrice Petro, ed., *Fugitive Images: From Photography to Video,* 221–44. Bloomington: Indiana University Press.

————. 1997. *Words of Light: Theses on the Photography of History.* Princeton, N.J.: Princeton University Press.

Calavita, Kitty, and Liliana Suárez-Navaz. 2003. "Spanish Immigration Law and the Construction of Difference: Citizens and 'Illegals' on Europe's Southern Border." In Richard Warren Perry and Bill Maurer, eds., *Globalization Under Construction: Governmentality, Law, and Identity,* 99–128. Minneapolis: University of Minnesota.

Calvino, Italo. 1974. *Invisible Cities.* New York: Harcourt Brace.

Campbell, James T. 2006. *Middle Passages: African American Journeys to Africa, 1787–2005.* New York: Penguin.

Carby, Haxel V. 1998. *Race Men.* Cambridge, Mass.: Harvard University Press.

Carnegie, Charles V. 2002. *Postnationalism Prefigured.* New Brunswick, N.J.: Rutgers University Press.

Carter, Donald. 1997. *States of Grace: Senegalese in Italy and the New European Immigration.* Minneapolis: University of Minnesota Press.

Césaire, Aimé. 1955. *Discourse on Colonialism.* Reprint, New York: Monthly Review Press, 2000.

Chambers, Iain. 1994. *Migrancy, Culture, Identity.* London: Routledge.

Chandra, Viola. 2001. *Media Chiara E Nociioline.* Rome: Derive Approdi.

Chavez, Leo R. 2001. *Covering Immigration: Popular Images and the Politics of the Nation.* Berkeley: University of California Press.

Chow, Rey. 1993. *Writing Diaspora: Tactics of Intervention in Contemporary Cultural Studies.* Bloomington: Indiana University Press.

Clark, Kenneth B. 1965. *Dark Ghetto: Dilemmas of Social Power.* New York: Harper and Row.

Clayton, Anthony. 1988. *France, Soldiers, and Africa.* London: Pergamon Group.

Clifford, James. 1994. "Diasporas," *Cultural Anthropology* 9, no. 3: 302–38.

————. 1997. *Routes: Travel and Translation in the Late Twentieth Century.* Cambridge, Mass.: Harvard University Press.

Cohen, Anthony P. 2000. "Introduction: Discriminating Relations—Identity, Boundary, and Authenticity." In Anthony P. Cohen, ed., *Signifying Identities: Anthropological Perspectives on Boundaries and Contested Values,* 1–14. New York: Routledge.

Cohen, Robin. 1997. *Global Diasporas: An Introduction.* Seattle: University of Washington Press.

Cohn, Bernard S. 1996. *Colonialism and Its Forms of Knowledge.* Princeton, N.J.: Princeton University Press.

————. 1990. *An Anthropologist among the Historians and Other Essays.* Delhi: Oxford University Press.

Connolly, William E. 1996. "Tocqueville, Territory, and Violence." In Michael J. Shapiro and Hayward R. Alker, eds., *Challenging Boundaries: Global Flows, Territorial Identities.* Minneapolis: University of Minnesota Press.

————. 2002. *Neuropolitics: Thinking, Culture, Speed.* Minneapolis: University of Minnesota Press.

Cooper, Frederick. 2002. *Africa Since 1940: The Past of the Present.* Cambridge, U.K.: Cambridge University Press.

Coundouriotis, Eleni. 1999. *Claiming History: Colonialism, Ethnography, and the Novel.* New York: Columbia University Press.

Coutin, Susan Bibler. 1993. *The Culture of Protest: Religious Activism and the U.S. Sanctuary Movement.* Boulder, Colo.: Westview Press.

————. 2003. "Illegality, Borderlands, and the Space of Nonexistence." In *Globalization Under Construction: Governmentality, Law, and Identity.* Minneapolis: University of Minnesota Press.

Creech, Morri. 2006. *Field Knowledge*. London: WayWiser Press.

Cross, Malcolm. 1994. "Economic Change, Ethnic Minority Formation, and New Identities in Europe." Paper prepared for the Wenner-Gren Foundation for Anthropological Research, symposium no. 117, "Transnationalism, Nation-State Building, and Culture," June 14–22, 1994, Mijas, Spain.

Cruise O'Brien, Donal B. 1971. *The Mourid of Senegal: The Political and Economic Organization of an Islamic Brotherhood*. Oxford: Clarendon Press.

Dainotto, Roberto M. 2000. "A South with a View: Europe and Its Other." *Nepantla: Views from South* 1, no. 2: 375–90

Davis, Christopher. 1999. "Exchanging the African: Meeting at a Crossroads of the Diaspora," Diaspora and Immigration Special Edition, *South Atlantic Quarterly* 98, no. 2: 59–83.

de Certeau, Michel. 1984. *The Practice of Everyday Life*. Berkeley: University of California Press.

_____. 1997. *Culture in the Plural*. Minneapolis: University of Minnesota Press.

Deng, Francis M. 1995. *War of Visions: Conflict of Identities in the Sudan*. Washington, D.C.: The Brookings Institution.

Derrida, Jacques. 1992. *The Other Heading: Reflections on Today's Europe*. Pascale-Anne Brault and Michael B. Naas, trans. Bloomington: Indiana University Press.

Derrida, Jacques, and Anne Dufourmantelle. 2000. *Of Hospitality*. Stanford, Calif.: Stanford University Press.

Devey, Muriel. 2000. *Le Sénégal*. Paris: Karthala.

Diawara, Manthia. 1991. "Camp de Thiaroye," *Black Film Review* 6, no. 3: 14–15.

_____. 1998a. *In Search of Africa*. Cambridge, Mass.: Harvard University Press.

_____. 1998b. "Talk of the Town," *Artforum,* February: 64–71.

Diop, Mamadou. 2003. Personal communication.

Diouf, Mamadou. 1999. "Urban Youth and Senegalese Politics: Dakar 1988–1994." In James Holston, ed., *Cities and Citizenship*. Durham, N.C.: Duke University Press.

_____. 2000. "The Senegalese Mourid Trade Diaspora and the Making of a Vernacular Cosmopolitanism," *Public Culture* 12, no. 3: 679–702.

_____. 2001. *Historire Du Sénégal: Le modele islamo-wolof et ses peripheries*. Paris: Maisonneuve & Larose.

Douglas, Mary. 1973. *Natural Symbols: Explorations in Cosmology*. New York: Pantheon.

Drake, St. Clair. 1964. "The Meaning of Negritude: The Negro's Stake in Africa," *Negro Digest* 13, no. 8: 33–48.

Dunkerley, David. 2002. *Changing Europe: Identities, Nation, and Citizens*. London: Routledge.

Echenberg, Myron J. 1990. "Race, Ethnicity, and Social Class in the French Colonial Army: The Black African Tirailleurs, 1857–1958." In N. F. Dreisziger, ed., *Ethnic Armies: Polyethnic Armed Forces From the Time of the Hapsburgs to the Age of the Superpowers*, 50–68. Ontario: Wilfrid Laurier University Press.

————. 1991. *Colonial Conscripts: The Tirailleurs Sénégalais in French West Africa, 1857–1960.* Oxford: James Currey.

Eco, Umberto. 1990. "Quando l'Europa diventerà afro-europa." *L'Espresso.*

Edmonson, Belinda. 1999. *Making Men: Gender, Literary Authority, and Women's Writing in Caribbean Narrative.* Durham, N.C.: Duke University Press.

Edwards, Brent Hayes. 2003. *The Practice of Diaspora: Literature, Translation, and the Rise of Black Internationalism.* Cambridge, Mass.: Harvard University Press.

Edwards, Elizabeth. 1990. "The Image as Anthropological Document: Photographic 'Types': The Pursuit of Method," *Visual Anthropology* 3: 235–58.

Ellison, Ralph. 1972. *Shadow and Act.* New York: Vintage.

Enwezor, Okwui, and Octavio Zaya. 1996. "Colonial Imaginary, Tropes of Disruption: History, Culture, and Representation in the Works of African Photographers." In Okwui Enwezor, Olu Oguibe, and Octavio Zaya, eds., *In/Sight: African Photographers, 1940 to the Present.* New York: Solomon R. Guggenheim Museum.

Eshun, Ekow. 2005. *Black Gold of the Sun: Searching for Home in Africa and Beyond.* New York: Pantheon.

Evans-Pritchard, Edward. 1940. *The Nuer.* Oxford: Oxford University Press.

Fanon, Frantz. 1963. *The Wretched of the Earth: The Handbook for the Black Revolution That Is Changing the Shape of the World.* New York: Grove Press.

————. 1967a. *Black Skin, White Masks.* New York: Grove.

————. 1967b. *Towards The African Revolution: Political Essays*, Haakon Chevalier, trans. New York: Grove Press.

Farmer, Sarah. 1999. *Martyred Village: Commemorating the 1944 Massacre at Oradour-sur-Glane.* Berkeley: University of California Press.

Fassin, Didier. 2006. "Racial Policing." Paper presented for a panel entitled "Race After the Riots in France," at the American Anthropological Association 105th Annual Meeting, November 17, San Jose, California.

Fassin, Eric. 2006. "The Black Minority in France, Visible and Invisible." Paper presented for a panel entitled "Race After the Riots in France," at the American Anthropological Association 105th Annual Meeting, November 17, San Jose, California.

Fellini, Federico. 1990. *La Voce della Luna.* Torino: Einaudi.

Fernandez, James W. 1986. *Persuasions and Performances: The Play of Tropes in Culture*. Bloomington: Indiana University Press.

Fischer, Michael M. J. 2003. *Emergent Forms of Life and the Anthropological Voice*. Durham, N.C.: Duke University Press.

Flint, Julie. 2004. "Sudan: Peace, but at What Price?" Testimony before the U.S. Senate Foreign Relations Committee (June 15). http://hrw.org/english/docs/2004/06/15/darfur8850_txt.htm

Flint, Julie, Jemera Rone, and Leslie Lefkow. 2004. "Darfur Destroyed: Ethnic Cleansing by Government and Militia Forces in Western Sudan," *Human Rights Watch* 16, no. 6A: 1–75.

Flint, Julie, and Alex de Waal. 2005. *Darfur: A Short History of a Long War*. London: Zed Books.

_____ 2008. *Darfur: A Short History of a Long War, Revised and Updated*. London: Zed Books.

Foucault, Michel. 1977. *Discipline and Punish: The Birth of the Prison*. New York: Vintage.

Freund, Giséle. 1980. *Photography and Society*. Boston: David R. Godine.

Fristenberg, Lauri. 2001. "Postcoloniality, Performance, and Photographic Portraiture." In Okwui Enwezor, Chinua Achebe, and Museum Villa Stuck, eds., *The Short Century*. Munich: Prestel.

Fuller, Thomas. 2003. "Europe Moves Toward Issuing Passports with Data Chips," *New York Times*, June 20.

Gabaccia, Donna R. 2000. *Italy's Many Diasporas*. New York: Routledge.

Gadjigo, Samba. 2007. *Ousmane Sembene: Une Conscience Africaine*. Paris: Homnisphéres.

Ganbo, Jadelin Maibal. 2001. *Rometta e Giulieo*. Milan: Feltrinelli.

Gardner, Mary. 1995. *Boat People: A Novel*. New York: W. W. Norton.

Gellar, Sheldon. 1995. *Senegal: An African Nation between Islam and the West*. Boulder, Colo.: Westview Press.

Ghosh, Amitav. 1997. "India's Untold War of Independence," *The New Yorker*, June 23–30.

Gibson, Nigel. 2003. *Fanon: The Postcolonial Imagination*. Malden, Mass.: Polity.

Gilman, Sander L. 1991. *Inscribing the Other*. Lincoln: University of Nebraska Press.

Gilroy, Paul. 1987. *There Ain't No Black in the Union Jack: The Cultural Politics of Race and Nation*. Chicago: University of Chicago Press.

_____. 1993. *The Black Atlantic: Modernity and Double Consciousness*. Cambridge, Mass.: Harvard University Press.

_____. 2000. *Against Race: Imagining Political Culture beyond the Color Line*. Cambridge, Mass.: Harvard University Press.

_____. 2005. *Postcolonial Melancholia*. New York: Columbia University Press.

Giordano, Ralph. 1995. "Auschwitz—and Life! Why I Have Remained in Germany." In Susan Stern, ed., *Speaking Out: Jewish Voices from United Germany*, 39–49. Chicago: Edition Q.

Goldberg, David Theo. 2000. "In/Visibility and Super Vision: Fanon on Race, Veils, and Discources of Resistence." In Lewis R. Gordon, T. Denean Sharpley-Whiting, and Renée T. White, eds., *Fanon: A Critical Reader*, 179–202. Oxford: Blackwell.

Gomez, Michael A. 1998. *Exchanging Our Country Marks: The Transformation of African Identities in the Colonial and Antebellum South*. Chapel Hill, N.C.: University of North Carolina Press.

Gordon, Lewis R. 1995. *Bad Faith and Anti-Black Racism*. N.J.: Humanities Press.

_____. 1997. "Existential Dynamics of Theorizing Black Invisibility." In *Existence in Black: An Anthology of Black Existential Philosophy*, 69–80. New York: Routledge.

_____. 2000. *Existentia Africana: Understanding Africana Existential Thought*. New York: Routledge.

Greider, William. 1997. *One World, Ready or Not*. New York: Simon & Schuster.

Guillaume, Alfred Joseph. 1976. "The Primitivist Impulse in the Poetic Vision of Baudelaire and Senghor." PhD dissertation, Brown University.

Guiraudon, Virginie, and Christain Joppke. 2001. *Controlling a New Migration World*. London: Routledge.

Gupta, Akhil, and James Ferguson, eds. 1997. *Anthropological Locations: Boundaries and Grounds of a Field Science*. Berkeley: University of California Press.

Hall, Gwendolyn Midlo. 1992. *Africans in Colonial Louisiana: The Development of Afro-Creole Culture in the Eighteenth Century*. Baton Rouge: Louisiana State University Press.

_____. 2005. *Slavery and African Ethnicities in the Americas: Restoring the Links*. Chapel Hill, N.C.: University of North Carolina Press.

Hall, Stuart. 1992. "What Is the Black in Black Popular Culture?" In Michele Wallace and Gina Dent, eds., *Black Popular Culture*. Seattle: Bay Press.

_____. 1994. "Transnationalism, Nation-State Building, and Culture." Paper prepared for Wenner-Gren Symposium no. 117, June 14–22, Mijas, Spain.

Harris, Joseph. 1982. *Global Dimensions of the African Diaspora*. Washington, D.C.: Howard University Press.

Harris, Michael D. 2003. *Colored Pictures: Race and Visual Representation*. Chapel Hill, N.C.: University of North Carolina Press.

Harrison, Faye V. 1992. "The Du Boisian Legacy in Anthropology," *Critique of Anthropology* 12, no. 3: 239–260.

Harrison, Ira E., and Faye V. Harrison, eds. 1999. *African American Pioneers in Anthropology*. Urbana/Chicago: University of Illinois Press.

Harrison, Robert Pogue. 2003. *The Dominion of the Dead*. Chicago: Chicago University Press.

Harvey, David. 1990. "Between Space and Time: Reflections on the Geographical Imagination," *Annals of the Association of American Geographers* 80, no. 3: 418–34.

————. 1993. "From Space to Place and Back Again: Reflections on the Condition of Postmodernity." In Jon Bird et al., eds., *Mapping the Futures: Local Cultures, Global Change*, 2–29. London: Routledge.

Harvie, Christopher. 1994. *The Rise of Regional Europe*. London: Routledge.

Hastrup, Kristen. 1995. *A Passage to Anthropology: Between Experience and Theory*. London: Routledge.

Helbling, Mark. 1973. "Claude McKay: Art and Politics," *Negro American Literature Forum* 7, no. 2: 49–52.

Herzfeld, Michael. 1993. *The Social Production of Indifference: Exploring the Symbolic Roots of Western Bureaucracy*. Chicago: University of Chicago Press.

————. 2001. *Theoretical Practice in Culture and Society*. Oxford: Wiley-Blackwell.

Higginbotham, Elizabeth. 2001. *Too Much to Ask: Black Women in the Era of Integration*. Chapel Hill, N.C.: University of North Carolina Press.

Hinsley, Curtis M. 1996. "Strolling through the Colonies." In Michael P. Steinberg, ed., *Walter Benjamin and the Demands of History*, 119–40. Ithaca, N.Y.: Cornell University Press.

Hirsch, Eric, and Michael O'Hanlon. 1995. *The Anthropology of the Landscape: Perspectives on Place and Space*. Oxford: Clarendon Press.

Holmes, Douglas R. 2000. *Integral Europe: Fast-Capitalism, Multiculturalism, Neofascism*. Princeton, N.J.: Princeton University Press.

Holston, James. 1999. "Spaces of Insurgent Citizenship." In James Holston, ed., *Cities and Citizenship*, 155–76. Durham, N.C.: Duke University Press.

Holtzman, Jon D. 2000. *Nuer Journeys, Nuer Lives: Sudanese Refugees in Minnesota*. Boston: Allyn and Bacon.

hooks, bell. 1992. *Black Looks: Race and Representation*. Boston: South End Press.

————. 2000. *Where We Stand: Class Matters*. New York: Routledge.

————. 2004. *We Real Cool: Black Men and Masculinity*. New York: Routledge.

Hutchinson, Sharon E. 1996. *Nuer Dilemmas: Coping with Money, War, and the State*. Berkeley: University of California Press.

Ifekwunigwe, Jayne O. 1999. *Scattered Belongings: Cultural Paradoxes of "Race," Nation and Gender*. New York: Routledge.

_____. 2003. "Scattered Belongings: Reconfiguring the 'African' in the English–African Diaspora." In Khalid Koser, ed., *New African Diasporas*, 56–70. London: Routledge.

Ignatiev, Noel. 1995. *How the Irish Became White*. New York: Routledge.

Jackson, Michael. 1998. *Minima Ethnographica: Intersubjectivity and the Anthropological Project*. Chicago: University of Chicago Press.

James, Winston. 2000. *A Fierce Hatred of Injustice: Claude McKay's Jamaica and His Poetry of Rebellion*. New York: Verso.

Jameson, Fredric. 1971. *Marxism and Form*. Princeton: Princeton University Press.

Johnson, Douglas H. 2003. *The Root Causes of Sudan's Civil Wars*. Oxford: James Currey.

Johnson, E. Patrick. 2003. *Appropriating Blackness: Performance and the Politics of Authenticity*. Durham, N.C.: Duke University Press.

Jordan, June. 1992. *Technical Difficulties: African-American Notes on the State of the Union*. New York: Pantheon.

Judt, Tony. 1996. *A Grand Illusion? An Essay on Europe*. New York: Hill and Wang.

Kasson, John F. 2001. *Houdini, Tarzan, and the Perfect Man: The White Male Body and the Challenge of Modernity in America*. New York: Hill and Wang.

Kawash, Samira. 1997. *Dislocating The Color Line: Identity, Hybridity, and Singularity in African American Literature*. Stanford, Calif.: Stanford University Press.

Keaton, Trica Danielle. 2006a. *Muslim Girls and the Other France: Race, Identity Politics, and Social Exclusion*. Bloomington: Indiana University Press.

_____. 2006b. "The Lived and Social Reality of Race in the French Outer-Cities: The Case of Clichy-sous-Bois." Paper presented for a panel entitled "Race After the Riots in France," at the American Anthropological Association 105th Annual Meeting, November 17, San Jose, California.

Kelley, Robin D. G. 2002. *Freedom Dreams: The Black Radical Imagination*. Boston: Beacon Press.

Kershaw, Sarah, and Eric Lichtblau. 2004. "Judge Rejects Bomb Case Against Oregon Lawyer," *New York Times*, May 25.

Kesteloot, Lilyan. 1991. *Black Writers in French: A Literary History of Negritude*. Washington, D. C.: Howard University Press.

Komla-Ebri, Kossi. 2002. *Neyla: un incontro, due mondi*. Milan: Edizoni Dell'Arco-Marna.

Koser, Khalid. 2003. "Mobilizing New African Diasporas: An Eritrean Case Study." In Khalid Koser, ed., *New African Diasporas*. London: Routledge.

Kramer, Reed. 2004. "Act Now to Stop Dying on a Massive Scale in Darfur, U.S. Lawmakers Urge," AllAfrica.com. http://allAfrica.com/stories/printable/20040780001.html.

Kramer, Steven Philip, and Irene Kyriakopoulos. 1996. *Trouble in Paradise? Europe in the 21st Century*. Washington, D. C.: National Defense University Press.

Lacey, Marc. 2004. "Sudan Frustrated as Militias Hide in Plain Sight," *New York Times*, August 6.

Lamri, Tahar. 2006. *I sessanta nomi dell'amore*. Rimini: FaraEditore.

Landy, Marcia. 1986. *Fascism in Film: The Italian Commercial Cinema, 1931–1943*. Minneapolis: University of Minnesota Press.

_____. 1996. *Cinematic Uses of the Past*. Minneapolis: University of Minnesota Press.

Lawler, Nancy Ellen. 1992. *Soldiers of Misfortune: Ivoirien Tirailleurs of World War II*. Athens: Ohio University Press.

Leed, Eric J. 1991. *The Mind of the Traveler: From Gilgamesh to Global Tourism*. New York: Basic Books.

Leonard, Karen. 2003. "South Asian Workers in the Gulf: Jockeying for Places." In Richard Warren Perry and Bill Maurer, eds., *Globalization under Construction: Governmentality, Law, and Identity*, 129–70. Minneapolis: University of Minnesota.

Levi, Primo. 1996. *Survival in Auschwitz: The Nazi Assault on Humanity*. Reprint, Stuart Woolf, trans. New York: Touchstone. (Orig. pub. 1958.)

_____. 2005. *The Black Hole of Auschwitz*. Sharon Wood, trans. Cambridge, U.K.: Polity Press.

Lévi-Strauss, Claude. 1963. *Totemism*. Boston: Beacon Press.

Lewis, David Levering. 2003. "A Small Nation of People: W. E. B. Du Bois and Black Americans at the Turn of the Twentieth Century." In *A Small Nation of People: W. E. B. Du Bois and African American Portraits of Progress*, 23–50. New York: HarperCollins.

Lichtblau, Eric, and John Markoff. 2004. "U.S. Nearing Deal on Way to Track Foreign Visitors," *New York Times*, May 24.

Lienhardt, G. 1961. *Divinity and Experience: The Religion of the Dinka*. Oxford: Clarendon Press.

Livi-Bacci, Massimo. 1997. *A Concise History of World Population*. Malden, Mass.: Blackwell.

Löfgren, Orvar. 1999. *On Holiday: A History of Vacationing*. Berkeley: University of California Press.

Longman, Timothy. 2001. "Identity Cards, Ethnic Self-Perception, and Genocide in Rwanda." In Jane Caplan and John Torpey, eds., *Documenting Individual Identity: The Development of State Practices in the Modern World*,
345–58. Princeton, N.J.: Princeton University Press.

Lowe, Donald M. 1982. *History of Bourgeois Perception*. Chicago: University of
Chicago Press.

Lyon, David. 2000. "Under My Skin: From Identification Papers to Body
Surveillance." In Jane Caplan and John Torpey eds., *Documenting
Individual Identity: The Development of State Practices in the Modern
World*, 291–310. Princeton, N.J.: Princeton University Press.

MacDougall, David. 1999. "The Visusal in Anthropology." In Marcus Banks
and Howard Morphy, eds., *Rethinking Visual Anthropology*, 276–95.
New Haven, Conn.: Yale University Press.

Macey, David. 2000. *Frantz Fanon: A Biography*. New York: Picador.

MacGaffey, Janet, and Rémy Bazenguissa-Ganga. 2000. *Congo-Paris: Transnational Traders on the Margins of the Law*. Bloomington: Indiana University
Press.

Maclean, William. 2004. "Annan Warns AU Over Darfur, Sudan Agrees to
Troops," Reuters, July 6.

Maher, Vanessa. 1996. "Immigration and Social Identities." In David Fogacs
and Robert Lumley, eds., *Italian Cultural Studies: An Introduction*, 160–77.
Oxford: Oxford University Press.

Malkki, Liisa. 1995. *Purity and Exile: Violence, Memory, and National Cosmology
Among Hutu Refugees in Tanzania*. Chicago: University of Chicago Press.

Manalansan, Martin F., IV. 2005. "Migrancy, Modernity, Mobility: Quotidian
Struggles and Queer Diasporic Intimacy." In Ethine Luibhéid and Lional
Cantú Jr., eds., *Queer Migrations: Sexuality, U.S. Citizenship, and Border
Crossings*, 146–60. Minneapolis: University of Minnesota Press.

Mann, Gregory. 2006. *Native Sons: West African Veterans and France in the
Twentieth Century*. Durham, N.C.: Duke University Press.

Maran, René. 1921. *Batouala*. Paris: Editions Albin-Michel. Reprint,
Portsmouth, NH: Heinemann, 1987.

Marquis, Christopher. 2004. "Powell to Press Sudan to Ease the Way for Aid in
Darfur," *New York Times*, June 30.

Martin, Tony. 1999. "Rescuing Fanon from the Critics." In Nigel C. Gibson, ed.,
Rethinking Fanon: The Continuing Dialogue, 83–102. New York:
Humanity Press.

Marx, Karl. 1987. *The Eighteenth Brumaire of Louis Bonaparte*. New York:
International Publishers.

Mbembe, Achille. 2001. *On the Postcolony*. Berkeley: University of California
Press.

McCarthy, Julie. 2004. "Julie McCarthy Reports on Dreams of a Nation," National Public Radio, *Morning Edition*, March 16.

McGrane, Bernard. 1989. *Beyond Anthropology: Society and the Other*. New York: Columbia University Press.

McKay, Claude. 2008. *Complete Poems: Claude McKay*. Urbana: University of Illinois Press.

McQuire, Scott. 1998. *Visions of Modernity: Representation, Memory, Time, and Space in the Age of the Camera*. London: Sage.

Merleau-Ponty, Maurice. 1968. *The Visible and the Invisible*. Claude Lefort, ed., Alphonse Lingis, trans. Evanston, Ill.: Northwestern University Press.

Merrill, Heather. 2004. "Space Agents: Anti-Racist Feminism and the Politics of Scale in Turin, Italy," *Gender, Place and Culture* 11, no. 2: 189–204.

_____. 2006. *An Alliance of Women: Immigration and the Politics of Race*. Minneapolis: University of Minnesota Press.

Merrill, Heather, and Donald Carter. 2002. "Inside and Outside Italian Political Culture: Immigrants and Diasporic Politics in Turin," *GeoJournal* 58: 167–75.

Michelet, Jules. 1875. *The Sea*. London: T. Nelson & Sons.

Miller, Christopher. 1998. *Nationalists and Nomads: Essays on Francophone African Literature and Culture*. Chicago: Chicago University Press.

Mills, Charles W. 1998. *Blackness Visible: Essays on Philosophy and Race*. Ithaca, N.Y.: Cornell University Press.

Mintz, Sidney W., 1995. "The Localization of Anthropological Practice: From Area Studies to Transnationalism." Paper presented for Intergenerational Conversations: Anthropology Postwar/Millennial, November 6, University of Chicago.

Mintz, Sidney W., and Richard Price. 1992. *The Birth of African American Culture: An Anthropological Perspective*. Boston: Beacon Press.

Mohanram, Radhika. 1999. *Black Body: Women, Colonialism, and Space*. Minneapolis: University of Minnesota Press.

Moore, Rachel O. 2000. *Savage Theory: Cinema as Modern Magic*. Durham, N.C.: Duke University Press.

Morton, Patricia. 2000. *Hybrid Modernities: Architecture and Representation at the 1931 Colonial Exposition, Paris*. Cambridge, Mass.: MIT Press.

Moses, Wilson Jeremiah. 1998. *Afrotopia: The Roots of African American Popular History*. Cambridge, Mass.: Harvard University Press.

Mudimbe, V. Y. 1988. *The Invention of Africa: Gnosis, Philosophy, and the Order of Knowledge*. London: James Currey.

Murphy, David. 2000. *Sembene: Imagining Alternatives in Film and Fiction*. Oxford: James Currey.

Newhouse, John. 1997. *Europe Adrift*. New York: Pantheon.

Norindr, Panivong. 1994. "Coming Home on the Fourth of July: Constructing Immigrant Identities." In Angelika Bammer, ed., *Displacements: Cultural Identities in Question*, 233–50. Bloomington: Indiana University Press.

Okri, Ben. 1992. *The Famished Road*. New York: Doubleday.

Palmer, Colin. 1998. "Defining and Studying the Modern African Diaspora," *Perspectives, The American Historical Association Newsletter* 36, no. 6. Available online at http://www.historians.org/perspectives/issues/1998/9809/9809vie2.cfm.

Parsons, Timothy H. 1999. *The African Rank-and-File: Social Implications of Colonial Military Service in the King's African Rifles, 1902–1964*. Portsmouth, N.H.: Heinemann.

Patterson, Tiffany Ruby. 2005. *Zora Neale Hurston and a History of Southern Life*. Philadephia: Temple University Press.

Paz, Octavio. 1961. *The Labyrinth of Solitude*. New York: Grove Press.

Peña, Susana. 2005. "Visibility and Silence: Madrid and Cuban American Gay Male Experience and Representation." In Ethine Luibhéid and Lional Cantú Jr., eds., *Queer Migrations: Sexuality, U.S. Citizenship, and Border Crossings*, 125–45. Minneapolis: University of Minnesota Press.

Pieterse, Jan Nederveen. 1998. *White on Black: Images of Africa and Blacks in Western Popular Culture*. New Haven, Conn.: Yale University Press.

Polgreen, Lydia. 2006. "A Doctor's Struggle in Darfur," *New York Times*, May 30.

Poole, Deborah. 1997. *Vision, Race, and Modernity: A Visual Economy of the Andean Image World*. Princeton, N.J.: Princeton University Press.

Pratt, Mary Louise. 1992. *Imperial Eyes: Travel Writing and Transculturation*. New York: Routledge.

Pred, Allan. 1995. *Recognizing European Modernities: A Montage of the Present*. New York: Routledge.

————. 2000. *Even in Sweden: Racisms, Racialized Spaces, and the Popular Geographical Imagination*. Berkeley: University of California Press.

Pred, Allan, and Michael John Watts. 1993. *Reworking Modernity: Capitalisms and Symbolic Discontent*. New Brunswick, N.J.: Rutgers University Press.

Price, Mary. 1994. *The Photograph: A Strange, Confined Space*. Stanford, Calif.: Stanford University Press.

Price, Richard, and Sally Price. 1997. "Shadowboxing in the Mangrove," *Cultural Anthropology* 12, no. 1: 3–36.

Prunier, Gérard. 2005. *Darfur: The Ambiguous Genocide*. London: London University Press.

Puri, Shalini. 2004. *The Caribbean Postcolonial: Social Equality, Post-Nationalism, and Cultural Hybridity*. New York: Palgrave Macmillan.

Quassoli, Fabio. 2001. "Migrant as Criminal: The Juridical Treatment of Migrant Criminality." In Virginie Guiraudon and Christian Joppke, eds., *Controlling a New Migration World*, 150–70. London: Routledge.

Radhakrishnan, Rajagopalan. 1996. *Diasporic Meditations: Between Home and Location*. Minneapolis: University of Minnesota Press.

————. 2003. *Theory in an Uneven World*. Oxford: Blackwell.

Ramirez, Horatio N. Roque. 2005. "Claiming Queer Cultural Citizenship: Gay Latino (Im)Migrant Acts in San Francisco." In Ethine Luibhéid and Lional Cantú Jr., eds., *Queer Migrations: Sexuality, U.S. Citizenship, and Border Crossings*, 161–88. Minneapolis: University of Minnesota Press.

Ramos, Jorge. 2005. *Dying to Cross: The Worst Immigrant Tragedy in American History*. New York: Harper.

Rapfogel, Jared. 2003. "A Report of Dreams of a Nation: A Palestinian Film Festival," Senses of Cinema, January 24–27. http://www.dreamsofanation.org.

Reid, Donald M. 2003. "Teaching in Tragedy by Teaching the History of Its Remembrance: Oradour-sur-Glane and American Students in September 2001," *The History Teacher*, August 2002. http://www.historycooperative. org/journals/ht/35.4/reid.html.

Renan, Ernest. 1882. *Qu'est-ce qu'une nation?* Paris: Calmann Lévy.

Report of the International Commission of Inquiry on Darfur to the United Nations Secretary-General, Pursuant to Security Council Resolution 1564 of 18 September 2004 [UNICOD]. 2005. Geneva, January 25.

Reuters. 2004a. "Annan Calls on Sudan to Protect Darfur Villagers: Both U.N. Leader and Powell Have Sought to End Ethnic Crisis," July 1. http//www. msnbc.com/id/5326406 (accessed July 2004).

————. 2004b. "Alerting Humanitarians to Emergencies: Crisis Profile—What's Going On in Sudan's Darfur," June 15. http://www.alertnet.org/printable. htm?URL=/thefacts/reliefresources/11198858462.htm (accessed June 2005).

————. 2005. "Sudan Not Trying Darfur War Crimes: UN Official," October 23.

Riccio, Bruno. 2003. "More Than a Trade Diaspora: Senegalese Transnational Experiences in Emilia-Romagna (Italy)." In Khalid Koser, ed., *New African Diasporas*, 95–110. London: Routledge.

————. 2007. *"Toubab" E "Vu Cumprâ": Transnzionalitâ e reppresentazioni nelle migrazioni Senegalese in Italia*. Padova: Coop. Libraria Editrice Universitaria di Padova.

Rich, Paul B. 1990. *Race and Empire in British Politics*. Cambridge, U.K.: Cambridge University Press.

Riis, Jacob August. 1890. *How the Other Half Lives: Studies Among the Tenements of New York*. Reprint as part of Bedford Series in History, New York: Palgrave Macmillan, 1996.

Roberts, Allan F., and Mary N. Roberts. 2003. *A Saint in the City: Sufi Arts of Urban Senegal*. Los Angeles: UCLA Fowler Museum Press.

Roediger, David R. 1991. *The Wages of Whiteness: Race and the Making of the American Working Class*. New York: Verso.

Rollins, Judith. 1985. *Between Women: Domestics and Their Employers*. Philadelphia: Temple University Press.

Rosaldo, Renato. 1989. *Culture and Truth: The Remaking of Social Analysis*. Boston: Beacon Press.

Ross, Kristin. 1995. *Fast Cars, Clean Bodies: Decolonization and the Reordering of French Culture*. Cambridge, Mass.: MIT Press.

Rulfo, Juan. 1971. *The Burning Plain and Other Stories*. George D. Schade, trans. Austin: University of Texas Press.

Rydell, Robert W., 1993. *World of Fairs: The Century of Progress Expositions*. Chicago: University of Chicago Press.

_____. 1999. *All the World's A Fair: Visions of Empire at American International Expositions, 1876–1916*. Chicago: University of Chicago Press.

Rydell, Robert W., and Robert Kroes. 2005. *Buffalo Bill in Bologna: The Americanization of the World 1869–1922*. Chicago: University of Chicago Press.

Said, Edward. 1979. *Orientalism*. New York: Vintage.

_____. 1993. *Culture and Imperialism*. New York: Vintage.

_____. 1995. *The Politics of Dispossession*. London: Vintage.

_____. 1999. *Out of Place: A Memoir*. New York: Vintage.

Sarup, Madan. 1994. "Home and Identity." In George Robertson et al., eds., *Traveller's Tales: Narratives of Home and Displacement*, 93–104. New York: Routledge.

_____. 1996. *Identity, Culture, and the Postmodern World*. Athens, Ga.: The University of Georgia Press.

Scott, James C. 1998. *Seeing Like a State: How Certain Schemes to Improve the Human Condition Have Failed*. New Haven, Conn.: Yale University Press.

Scott, John Beldon. 2003. *Architecture for the Shroud: Relic and Ritual in Turin*. Chicago: Chicago University Press.

Sekyi-Out, Ato. 1997. *Fanon's Dialectic of Experience*. Cambridge, Mass.: Harvard University Press.

Sembene, Ousmane. 1962. *God's Bits of Wood*. Portsmouth, N.H.: Heinemann.

_____. 1981. *The Last of the Empire: A Senegalese Novel*. Portsmouth, N.H.: Heinemann.

_____. 1987. *Tribal Scars and Other Stories*. Portmouth, N.H.: Heinemann.

_____. 1993. "Ousmane Sembène's Remarks after the Showing of His Film 'Camp de Thiaroye.'" In Samba Gadjigo, Ralph Faulkingham, Thomas Cassiserer, and Reinhard Sander, eds., *Ousmane Senbène: Dialogues with Critics and Writers*, 81–6. Amherst: University of Massachusetts Press.

Senghor, Lamine. 1927. *La Violation d'un pays*. Paris: Bureau dd'études de diffusion.

Senghor, Léopold Sédar. 1948. *Hosties Noires*. Paris: Editions du Seuil.

————. 1998. *The Collected Poetry*. Melvin Dixon, trans. Charlottesville: University of Virginia Press.

Shack, William A. 2001. *Harlem in Montmartre: A Paris Jazz Story between the Great Wars*. Berkeley: University of California Press.

Sharpley-Whiting, T. Denean. 2002. *Negritude Women*. Minneapolis: University of Minnesota Press.

Shore, Stephen. 1998. *The Nature of Photogaphs*. Baltimore: The Johns Hopkins University Press.

Silverstein, Paul. 2006. "New Martial Races: The Racialization of French Suburban Violence." Paper presented for the panel entitled "Race After the Riots in France," at the American Anthropological Association 105th Annual Meeting, November 17, San Jose, California.

Simone, Abdou Maliq. 2004. *For the City Yet to Come: Changing African Life in Four Cities*. Durham, N.C.: Duke University Press.

Slater, Don. 1995. "Photography and Modern Vision: The Spectacle of 'Natural Magic.'" In Chris Jenks, ed., *Visual Culture*, 218–37. London: Routledge.

Smith, Shawn Michelle. 2004. *Photography on the Color Line: W. E. B. Du Bois, Race, and Visual Culture*. Durham, N.C.: Duke University Press.

Sontag, Susan. 1990. *On Photography*. New York: Doubleday.

————. 2003. *Regarding the Pain of Others*. New York: Farrar, Straus, and Giroux.

Soyinka, Wole. 1976. *Myth, Literature, and the African World*. Cambridge, U.K.: Cambridge University Press.

Stern, Susan. 1995. *Speaking Out: Jewish Voices From United Germany*. Chicago: Edition Q.

Stewart, Jacqueline Najuma. 2005. *Migrating to the Movies: Cinema and Black Urban Modernity*. Berkeley: University of California Press.

Stoller, Paul. 2002. *Money Has No Smell: The Africanization of New York City*. Chicago: University of Chicago Press.

Street, Brian. 1992. "British Popular Anthropology: Exhibiting and Photographing the Other." In Elizabeth Edwards, ed., *Anthropology and Photography 1860–1920*. New Haven, Conn.: Yale University Press.

Styan, David. 2003. "La Nouvelle Vague? Recent Francophone African Settlement in London." In Khalid Koser, ed., *New African Diasporas*, 17–36. London: Routledge.

Swarns, Rachel L. 2003. "Old ID Card Gives New Status to Mexicans in the U.S.," *New York Times*, August 25.

Tagg, John. 1993. *The Burden of Representation: Essays on Photographies and Histories*. Minneapolis: University of Minnesota Press.

Taylor, Mark C. 2003. *The Moment of Complexity: Emerging Network Culture*. Chicago: University of Chicago Press.

Thompson, Ian. 2002. *Primo Levi: A Life*. London: Metropolitan Books.

Torpey, John. 2001. *The Invention of the Passport: Surveillance, Citizenship, and the State*. Cambridge, U.K.: Cambridge University Press.

Trouillot, Michel-Rolph. 1991. "Anthropology and the Savage Slot: The Poetics and Politics of Otherness." In Richard G. Fox, ed., *Recapturing Anthropology*, 17–44. Santa Fe, N.M.: School of American Research Press.

_____. 1995. *Silencing the Past: Power and the Production of History*. Boston: Beacon Press.

_____. 2003. *Global Transformations: Anthropology and the Modern World*. New York: Palgrave Macmillan.

Tsabedze, Clara. 1994. *African Independence from Francophone and Anglophone Voices: A Comparative Study of Post-Independence Novels by Ngugi and Sembéne*. New York: Peter Lang.

Tshotsha, Jean-Marie. 2001. Personal communication.

Turner, Victor. 1969. *The Ritual Process*. Ithaca, N.Y.: Cornell University Press.

_____. 1974. *Dramas, Fields, and Metaphors: Symbolic Action in Human Society*. Ithaca, N.Y: Cornell University Press.

Twine, France Winddance. 2000. "Racial Ideologies and Racial Methodologies." In France Winddance Twine and Jonathan Warren, eds., *Racing Research, Researching Race: Methodological Dilemmas in Critical Race Studies*, 1–34. New York: New York University Press.

UNICOD. 2005. United Nations International Commission of Inquiry on Darfur to the United Nations Secretary-General. Pursuant to Security Council Resolution 1564 of 18 September 2004. Geneva, January.

United Nations. 2005. Monthly Report of the Secretary-General on Darfur. Security Council, 14 October 2005 (S/2005/650. 0554385).

United Nations High Commissioner for Refugees. 2010 UNHCR country operations profile, Sudan. http://www.unhcr.org/pages/49e483b76.html (accessed February 18, 2010).

UN Security Council. 2004a. Report of the Secretary-General on the Sudan, no. 0436965, June 3.

UN Security Council. 2004b. Resolution 1547, no. 0438626, June 11.

Urciuoli, Bonnie. 1996. *Exposing Prejudice: Puerto Rican Experiences of Language, Race, and Class*. Boulder, Colo.: Westview Press.

Vaillant, Janet G. 1990. *Black, French, and African: A Life of Léopold Sédar Senghor*. Cambridge, Mass.: Harvard University Press.

Van de Walle, Nicolas. 1991. "The Decline of the Franc Zone: Monetary Politics in Francophone Africa," *African Affairs* 90: 383–405.

van der Veer, Peter, ed. 1995. *Nation and Migration: The Politics of Space in the South Asian Diaspora*. Philadelphia: University of Philadelphia Press.

Van Hear, Nicholas. 1998. *New Diasporas: The Mass Exodus, Dispersal, and Regrouping of Migrant Communities*. Seattle: University of Washington Press.

Viarek, Ewa Plonoswka. 2008. "Bare Life on Strike: Notes on the Biopolitics of Race and Gender," *The South Atlantic Quarterly* 107, no. 1: 89–103.

Viarengo, Maria. 1999. "Scirscir N'Demna? (Let's Go for A Stroll)." In Graziella Parati, ed., *Mediterranean Crossroads: Migration Literature in Italy*. Madison, Wis.: Fairleigh Dickinson Press.

Virgil. 1990. *The Aeneid*. Robert Fitzgerald, trans. New York: Vintage.

Wa Kabwe, Désiré, and Aurelia Segatti. 2003. "Paradoxical Expressions of a Return to the Homeland: Music and Literature among the Congolese (Zairean) Diaspora." In Khalid Koser, ed., *New African Diasporas*, 124–39. London: Routledge.

Watney, Simon. 1999. "On the Institutions of Photography." In Jessica Evans and Stuart Hall, eds., *Visual Culture: The Reader*, 141–60. London: Sage.

Weiss, Brad. 2002. "Thug Realism: Inhabiting Fantasy in Urban Tanzania," *Cultural Anthropology* 17, no. 1: 93–124.

Wells-Barnett, Ida B., and Frederick Douglass. 1893. "The Reason Why the Colored American Is Not in the World's Columbian Exposition." Reprint, Robert W. Rydell, ed., Urbana: University of Illinois Press, 1999.

White, Hayden. 1978. *Tropics of Discourse: Essays in Cultural Criticism*. Baltimore: Johns Hopkins University Press.

Williams, Brackette F. 1991a. *Stains on My Name, War in My Veins: Guyana and the Politics of Cultural Struggle*. Durham, N.C.: Duke University Press.

————. 1991b. "On the Normally Evil." Unpublished manuscript.

Williams, Raymond. 1978. *Marxism and Literature*. Oxford: Oxford University Press.

Willis, Deborah. 1994. *Picturing Us: African American Identity in Photography*. New York: The New Press.

————. 2003. "The Sociologist's Eye: W. E. B. Du Bois and the Paris Exposition." In *A Small Nation of People: W. E. B. Du Bois and African American Portraits of Progress*, 51–78. New York: HarperCollins.

Winant, Howard. 2001. *The World is a Ghetto: Race and Democracy Since World War II*. New York: Basic Books.

World Bank. 2002. "Poverty Reduction Strategy Paper," World Bank Group. Dakar, Senegal.

_____. 2003. "Memorandum of the President of the International Development Association to the Executive Directors on a Country Assistance Strategy for The Republic of Senegal," Report No. 25498-SE, Senegal Country Office, March 5, Dakar, Senegal.

Yengoyan, Aram A. 1997. "Yengoyan on Handler's 'Schneider on Schneider,'" *American Ethnologist* 24, no. 1: 208–10.

Young, Robert. 2001. *Postcolonialism: A Historical Introduction.* London: Wiley-Blackwell.

Ziarek, Ewa Plonowska. 2008. "Bare Life on Strike: Notes on the Biopolitics of Race and Gender," The Agamben Effect Special Issue, Alison Ross, ed., *South Atlantic Quarterly* Winter 2008: 89–105.

Žižek, Slavoj. 2002. *The Sublime Object of Ideology.* London: Verso.

Index

Donald Martin Carter is a professor of Africana studies at Hamilton College. He is the author of *States of Grace: Senegalese in Italy and the New European Immigration* (Minnesota, 1997).